The British Nuclear Experience

The British Nuclear Experience

The Role of Beliefs, Culture, and Identity

John Baylis and Kristan Stoddart

UNIVERSITY PRESS

Great Clarendon Street, Oxford, OX2 6DP,
United Kingdom

Oxford University Press is a department of the University of Oxford.
It furthers the University's objective of excellence in research, scholarship,
and education by publishing worldwide. Oxford is a registered trade mark of
Oxford University Press in the UK and in certain other countries

© John Baylis and Kristan Stoddart 2015

The moral rights of the authors have been asserted

First Edition published in 2015

Impression: 1

All rights reserved. No part of this publication may be reproduced, stored in
a retrieval system, or transmitted, in any form or by any means, without the
prior permission in writing of Oxford University Press, or as expressly permitted
by law, by licence or under terms agreed with the appropriate reprographics
rights organization. Enquiries concerning reproduction outside the scope of the
above should be sent to the Rights Department, Oxford University Press, at the
address above

You must not circulate this work in any other form
and you must impose this same condition on any acquirer

Published in the United States of America by Oxford University Press
198 Madison Avenue, New York, NY 10016, United States of America

British Library Cataloguing in Publication Data

Data available

Library of Congress Control Number: 2014936659

ISBN 978–0–19–870202–3

Printed and bound by
CPI Group (UK) Ltd, Croydon, CR0 4YY

Links to third party websites are provided by Oxford in good faith and
for information only. Oxford disclaims any responsibility for the materials
contained in any third party website referenced in this work.

This book is dedicated to the memory of Lorna Arnold, who had a great impact on the thinking of both authors.

Acknowledgements

The authors are very grateful to the following individuals for interviews and correspondence relating to issues raised in this book: Sir John Major, Sir Michael Quinlan, Sir Frank Cooper, Lord Owen, Sir John Nott, Sir Rodric Braithwaite, Sir Brian Cartledge, Lord Powell, Lord Heseltine, Dr Frank Panton, Mr P.G.E.F. Jones, Mr Dennis Fakley, Mr Peter Hudson, Rear Admiral J.S. Grove, Major General Eric Younson, Lorna Arnold, Professor John Simpson, Professor Marc Trachtenberg, Dr Richard Hewlett, Dr Arnold Kramish, Dr Jan Melissen, Katherine Pyne, Bryan Taylor, Ken Allen, and Dr Robert S. Norris. The authors would also like to thank the Eisenhower Library, the US National Archives, and the National Archives (Kew, UK) for their helpful assistance.

John Baylis is grateful to the Taylor and Francis Group for permission to reproduce material from the following articles: John Baylis and Alan Macmillan, 'The British Global Strategy Paper of 1952', in *The Journal of Strategic Studies*, Vol. 16, No. 2, June 1993; John Baylis, 'The 1958 Anglo-American Mutual Defence Agreement: The Search for Nuclear Interdependence', in *The Journal of Strategic Studies*, Vol. 31, No. 3, 2008; and John Baylis, 'The Development of Britain's Thermonuclear Capability 1954–61: Myth or Reality?', *Contemporary Record: The Journal of Contemporary British History*, Vol. 8, No. 1, 1994. He is also grateful to his daughter, Katie Baylis, for help with the manuscript of the book.

Kristan Stoddart is grateful to the Taylor and Francis Group for permission to reproduce material from the following articles: (with John Baylis) 'The British Nuclear Experience: The Role of Ideas, Beliefs and Culture (Part One)', *Diplomacy and Statecraft*, Issue 23, No. 2 (June 2012); (with John Baylis) 'The British Nuclear Experience: The Role of Ideas, Beliefs and Culture (Part Two)'; *Diplomacy and Statecraft*, Issue 23, No. 3 (September 2012); 'The Labour Government and the Development of Chevaline, 1974–1979', *Journal of Cold War History*, Vol. 10, No. 3 (August 2010); 'The Wilson Government and British Responses to ABMs, 1964–1970', *Journal of Contemporary British History*, Vol. 23, No. 1 (March 2009); 'Maintaining the Moscow Criterion: British Strategic Nuclear Targeting, 1974–1979', *Journal of Strategic Studies*, Vol. 31, No. 6 (December 2008); 'Nuclear Weapons in Britain's Policy Towards France, 1960–1974', *Diplomacy and Statecraft*, Vol. 18, No. 4 (December 2007); (with John Baylis) 'Britain and the Chevaline Project: The Hidden Nuclear

Acknowledgements

Programme, 1967–82', *Journal of Strategic Studies*, Vol. 26, No. 4, (December 2003), reprinted in Andrew Lambert (ed.), *Naval History: 1850–present* (London: Ashgate, 2007). He is also grateful to Palgrave Macmillan for permission to reproduce material from *Losing an Empire and Finding a Role: Britain, the USA, NATO and Nuclear Weapons 1964–70* (Palgrave Macmillan, 2012); *The Sword and the Shield: Britain, the United States, NATO and Nuclear Weapons 1970–1976* (Palgrave Macmillan, 2014); and *Facing Down the Soviet Union: Britain, the USA, NATO and Nuclear Weapons 1976–1983* (Palgrave Macmillan, 2014).

We also want to thank the following organisations and people for permissions granted for the epigraphs: the National Press Club, Oxford University Press, Professor Brian Cathcart, Palgrave Macmillan for permission to quote from the Macmillan diaries, Phil Tinline for permission to quote from the BBC Radio 4 documentary 'The Bomb, the Chancellor and Britain's Nuclear Secrets', Dr Sokov of the Monterey Institute for International Affairs and Jonathan Schilling and the Schilling Estate.

Contents

List of Abbreviations	x
Introduction	1
1. The Emergence of a Deterrence 'Habit of Mind'	16
2. The Chiefs of Staff, Nuclear Weapons, and Global Strategy	42
3. From Atomic Weapons to Thermonuclear Weapons	60
4. Forging the 'Special' Anglo-American Nuclear Relationship	74
5. Polaris, Independence, and Interdependence	97
6. The Polaris Improvement Programme and Chevaline	119
7. The Polaris Replacement Debate under Labour	133
8. The Adoption of Trident	151
9. NATO Modernization Plans, SDI, and the End of the Cold War	170
10. Trident Replacement/Renewal: From 'New Labour' to the Coalition Government	185
Conclusion	206
Appendices	
1. British Nuclear Weapons, 1945–present	219
2. US Nuclear Weapons supplied to the UK, 1945–present	220
3. Strategic Strike Planning by Bomber Command, 1962	221
4. Nuclear Targetting (1972)	223
5. United States/United Kingdom Agreements in the Military Nuclear Field	224
6. Brief for the Chief of the Air Staff, 1981	226
7. Anglo-American Understandings on Nuclear Release Procedures: President–Prime Minister Correspondence	228
8. Main Committees Dealing with Nuclear Weapons Issues in the 1940s and 1950s	230
Endnotes	233
Bibliography	285
Index	291

List of Abbreviations

ABM	Anti-ballistic Missile
AEA	Atomic Energy Authority
AEC	Atomic Energy Commission
ALBM	Air Launched Ballistic Missile
ASW	Anti-Submarine Warfare
AWRE/AWE	Atomic Weapons Research Establishment
CAS	Chief of the Air Staff
CASD	Continuous-at-Sea-Deterrence
CDS	Chief of the Defence Staff
CFE	Conventional Forces in Europe
CIGS	Chief of the Imperial General Staff
CND	Campaign for Nuclear Disarmament
COS	Chiefs of Staff
DOD	Department of Defense
DPS	Defence Policy Staff
DRPC	Defence Research Policy Committee
EU	European Union
FCO	Foreign and Commonwealth Office
GLCM	Ground Launched Cruise Missile
ICBM	Intercontinental Ballistic Missile
INF	Intermediate Range Nuclear Forces
IRBM	Intermediate Range Ballistic Missile
JCAE	Joint Committee on Atomic Energy
JIC	Joint Intelligence Committee
JPS	Joint Planning Staff
JSSC	Joint Strategic Survey Committee
JTWC	Joint Technical Warfare Committee
MDA	Mutual Defence Agreement

List of Abbreviations

MIRV	Multiple Independently Targetable Re-entry Vehicle
MLF	Multilateral Nuclear Force
MOD	Ministry of Defence
MRBM	Medium Range Ballistic Missile
NATO	North Atlantic Treaty Organization
NIC	National Identity Conception
NPG	Nuclear Planning Group
NPT	Non-Proliferation Treaty
NSC	National Security Council
OR	Operational Requirement
PPGs	Provisional Political Guidelines for the Initial Defensive Tactical Use of Nuclear Weapons
PSA	Polaris Sales Agreement
PTBT	Partial Test Ban Treaty
R & D	Research and Development
SAC	Strategic Air Command
SACEUR	Supreme Allied Commander Europe
SACLANT	Supreme Allied Commander Atlantic
SALT	Strategic Arms Limitation Talks
SDI	Strategic Defence Initiative
SDR	Strategic Defence Review
SDSR	Strategic Defence and Security Review
SHAPE	Supreme Headquarters Allied Powers Europe
SLBM	Submarine Launched Ballistic Missiles
SNF	Short Range Nuclear Forces
SORT	Strategic Offensive Reduction Treaty
START	Strategic Arms Reduction Talks
TNA	Theatre Nuclear Forces
UNSC	United Nations Security Council
USAF	United States Air Force
VCAS	Vice-Chief of the Air Staff
VSTOL	Vertical/Short Take Off and Landing
WMD	Weapons of Mass Destruction

Introduction

> *What must now be better understood are the root causes, the mindsets and belief systems that brought them (nuclear weapons) into existence.*
>
> General George Lee Butler[1]

This book is not designed to make a case either for or against the British nuclear deterrent. It will be for the reader to make up his or her mind on that question. Instead, the book has two major objectives. First, it sets out to chart the British experience with nuclear weapons from the Second World War down to the present day. There are numerous excellent studies that provide a history of British nuclear policy within specific periods since 1945, but none that cover the development of nuclear policy and strategic doctrine over the period as a whole.[2] The second objective is to analyse this experience by moving away from traditional interpretations of why states develop and maintain nuclear weapons and adopting a more contemporary approach to political theory. Traditional mainstream 'realist' explanations tend to stress the importance of factors such as 'the maximization of power', the pursuit of 'national security interests', and (in its neo-realist variant) the role of 'structure' in a largely anarchic international system. While not dismissing these approaches, this book argues that British experience suggests that focusing on 'ideational factors' such as 'beliefs', 'culture', and 'identity' provides a more helpful insight into the process of nuclear decision-making than the more 'materialist' realist approach.[3] The perspective adopted in this study derives from a number of related literatures which come under the heading of 'constructivism'. What follows is a brief outline of these studies.

Belief Systems

According to Holsti, *belief systems* may be thought of:

> as a set of lenses through which information concerning the physical and social environment is received. It orients the individual to his environment, defining it for him and identifying for him its salient characteristics... [It also] has the function of the establishment of goals and the ordering of preferences. Thus it actually has a dual connection with decision-making. The direct relationship is found in that aspect of the belief system which tells us 'what ought to be', acting as a direct guide to the establishment of goals. The indirect link... arises from the tendency of the individual to assimilate new perceptions to familiar ones, and to distort what is seen in such a way as to minimise the clash with previous expectations.[4]

According to another writer, Robert Lane, belief systems can be defined as 'a set of values, beliefs and attitudes regarding one's place in a human scheme of things marked by politics and government action'. They embody 'the most primitive, unexamined ideas', which are often taken for granted partly because they are never challenged. These 'primitive, unexplained ideas' represent core beliefs about human nature; about whether man is inherently evil or redeemable.[5] Such assumptions of human nature clearly play a crucial role in determining the political goals and values of decision-makers. Belief system theorists argue that such cognitive factors are often ignored because they cannot be tested empirically. In their view, however, such theoretical difficulties must not be allowed to obscure the insights which can be gained from studying the causal links between belief systems and policy formulation.[6]

Belief system theorists tend to emphasize the link between beliefs and policy. Smith and Hollis have argued that 'personality has a legitimate part in shaping the collective decision':

> This insight has given rise to a new focus in the study of decision-making on the role of individual and group 'belief systems'. According to this approach, policy cannot be understood only in structural terms (as a result of bureaucratic competition) or 'in standard behavioural terms' (as a result of rational calculations). Policy can also be understood as an attempt by individuals or groups to implement different 'beliefs'. This rests on the notion that, in part at least, ideas generate policies. Faced with the complexity of the world in which he lives the policy-maker, like all individuals, has to simplify events to make sense of them. This means that individual 'belief systems', which represent a very selective view of the world, play an important part in conditioning policy choice.[7]

Alexander George has argued that belief systems should be seen as a set of general guidelines or 'heuristic aids to decisions', rather than as 'a set of mathematical algorithms that are applied by the actor in a mechanical way in his decision making'.[8] For George, a person's beliefs help to structure and channel the way in which 'he copes and deals with the cognitive limits on rationality'. In certain areas of policy, he suggests, beliefs are likely to be of particular importance. These include situations with 'highly ambiguous components' which are open to a variety of interpretations; decisions which are of major significance or which are made at the top of the government hierarchy; and long-term planning which inevitably involves considerable uncertainty. Such hypotheses are particularly relevant to a study of this kind, which deals with nuclear weapons and strategic issues. Nuclear deterrence is a highly ambiguous and contested concept which involves requirements which are open to a variety of interpretations. It also involves major decisions taken at a high level which reflect long-term planning.

The link between beliefs and nuclear deterrence is discussed by Robert Jervis in his study *The Illogic of American Nuclear Strategy*. Jervis argues that 'our knowledge of nuclear deterrence...is largely deductive. We have a number of plausible theories, but only very limited knowledge.' This means that beliefs play an important part in the development of deterrent doctrines. According to Jervis:

> The paucity of evidence about the effect of alternative nuclear strategies feeds the enlarged role of doctrines and beliefs. To a greater extent than in the past, they now shape, rather than describe, reality. Of course beliefs are always at least a proximate cause of behavior...On such matters as whether nuclear war can be kept limited, whether a threat is credible, and how many weapons are enough to enable a state to stand firm, there is no reality to be described that is independent of people's beliefs about it.[9]

Jervis also highlights what he describes as the tension between the argument 'that the nuclear revolution is an objective fact and the claim that doctrines and beliefs play a large part in shaping not only perceptions of reality, *but reality itself*'. This reflects a view which we will return to later.

This stress on beliefs and the speculative thinking about nuclear deterrence is also noted by one of the key officials responsible for British nuclear weapons policy from the 1970s to the 1990s. In his study *Thinking About Nuclear Weapons*, written after his retirement, Michael Quinlan accepted that:

> We have no empirical data beyond 1945 about how events may run if nuclear weapons are used, and none at all about nuclear weapons powers coming seriously to war with one another. Even propositions about the achievement of nuclear weapons in deterrence cannot look for rigorous evidentiary proof, since such propositions are essentially about alternative history—about how the world would or might have happened had matters been other than they actually were.[10]

And so, Quinlan argues, in the absence of empirical data 'we have to rely upon concepts, hypotheses, and inferences not directly or fully tested'. 'Certainty', he says, 'is not available, especially across the huge range of possible situations'.[11]

The relationship between personality, values, and strategic choice has also been discussed by Nicholas Wheeler in a study of the roles played by the British Chiefs of Staff in the evolution of Britain's nuclear weapons planning and policy-making between 1945 and 1955. On the basis of his research, Wheeler argued that the role of beliefs and values is crucial in understanding the development of British nuclear strategy. Although inter-service rivalries between the Army, Royal Navy, and Royal Air Force played an important part in strategy-making, his conclusion is that:

> shared assumptions and values...shaped Britain's strategy, and...created the framework within which the inter-service rivalries of the period were played out. However, if inter-service rivalry did not touch the fundamentals of nuclear strategy, conflicts over the character of nuclear war had their roots in the clash of strategic values.[12]

Wheeler's contention, therefore, was that both the fundamentals of nuclear strategy, and the clashes between the services over specific strategic issues are a reflection of the particular beliefs and assumptions of the key strategy-makers of the day.

The importance of shared values, as identified by Wheeler, is taken a stage further in Paul Sabatier's study of 'advocacy coalitions'. Building on the work of writers like Richardson and Jordan, Sabatier has used the belief systems approach to show how individuals with shared beliefs join together across institutional boundaries to work for particular policy outcomes. 'Advocacy coalitions' are formed by individuals with a common world-view and similar deep core beliefs, which, according to Sabatier, are highly resistant to change. 'Deep core beliefs' represent 'fundamental normative and ontological axioms which define a person's underlying personal philosophy'. Such beliefs are regarded as the principal 'glue of politics' that helps to produce ideological coalitions which in turn compete to translate their values into policy. Sabatier views the policy-making process largely as a clash between 'advocacy coalitions' which is mediated by 'power brokers'. These are individuals in key political positions whose central concern is to find a workable compromise between the contending ideological positions.[13] What Sabatier does not say, however, is that sometimes the 'power brokers' support, and perhaps lead, a particular advocacy coalition.

This notion of 'advocacy coalitions' is valuable for the study of British strategy-making. One of the characteristics of the British defence establishment in the period from 1945 onwards was that certain views about the international system were held in common. Martin Ceadel uses what he classifies as a 'defencist school of thought' to argue that the defence establishment as a whole in Britain had a shared belief system. He sums up their collective view in the following way:

> They believed that war could be prevented and that diplomacy as well as military force played a part in achieving this. They believed that war could never be abolished, since states were always in conflict. The best to be hoped for was a diplomatic compromise among states which reflected the prevailing distribution of power—an anarchical society or an armed truce.[14]

Such 'realist' views, it is argued, straddled institutional boundaries and helped to form a powerful 'advocacy coalition' which 'fixed' policy over a long period of time. In his study *The Nuclear Menace: Nuclear Weapons in International Order*, William Walker talks about the *entrenchment* of nuclear policy.[15] There were alternative views of the world both inside and outside government, but it was these 'defencist' beliefs which underpinned the formulation of strategy at all levels during the early Cold War years and beyond.

The idea of 'advocacy coalitions' is also potentially useful in understanding how individual groups in different countries lobby for common objectives. With similar interests and strategic perspectives, particular services in Britain and the United States worked together to help each other out in their domestic struggles over resources. This will be an issue which the present study will pursue to show the role that not only a domestic 'nuclear advocacy coalition', but also a transatlantic 'advocacy coalition' played in the formulation of British nuclear strategy.

Strategic Culture

Closely linked with the 'belief systems' framework is a perspective which focuses on the cultural roots of policy. According to Geiger and Hansen, 'it is from the cultural system of their society that decision-makers acquire the basic categories of thought by which they perceive and attach significance to external social reality'.[16] This stress on the importance of culture in shaping attitudes has been taken up by a number of writers in the strategic studies field to explain the distinctiveness of various national approaches to strategic matters. This has led to the development of the notion of 'strategic culture'. What is meant by 'strategic culture' and what utility, if any, does the concept have?

The term 'strategic culture' was coined by Jack Snyder in the late 1970s in response to a major problem he perceived in the contemporary strategic studies literature. This centred on the tendency of western strategic theorists to assume that there was 'a single, universal strategic rationality'. Snyder noted that 'realist' and 'neo-realist' strategic analysis assumed a uniform logic in security. States were assumed to behave in much the same kind of way because of the universal requirement of maximizing power and security in an anarchical international system. Snyder questioned the appropriateness of this approach, especially when it came to trying to understand Soviet strategic policies. In his view there were vast differences between Soviet and American strategic theory and practice due to the different cultural roots of the policies in both countries. He argued that it was useful to think about the distinctiveness of the Soviet approach deriving from a unique strategic culture. Snyder explained this in the following terms:

> Individuals are socialised into a distinctively Soviet mode of strategic thinking. As a result of this socialisation process, a set of general beliefs, attitudes and behavioural norms with regard to nuclear strategy has achieved a state of semi-permanence that places them on the level of 'culture' rather than mere 'policy'. Of course, attitudes may change as a result of changes in technology and the international environment. However, new problems are not assessed objectively. Rather they are seen through the peripheral law provided by strategic culture.[17]

One of Snyder's main concerns was to prevent the problem of 'mirror imaging', which he regarded as a major weakness of Western strategic thought. The Soviet Union's approach to strategy, he believed, was significantly different from that of the United States. It was not inferior (as some American strategists believed it to be) or superior, but different, due to the unique experiences of the Soviet state.

Since Snyder first advanced the idea of 'strategic culture', there has been considerable discussion in the field of strategic studies about the value of the concept. In the ensuing debate Snyder himself became one of the most sceptical critics, questioning the 'helpfulness of the notion' and expressing his 'uncertainty about the behavioural differences' that could be ascribed to strategic culture. Writing in 1990, he described the concept as 'an explanation of the last resort' and warned against 'bogus cultural explanations' of strategic behaviour which reduced all explanations to cultural variables.[18]

Other writers, however, have been more enthusiastic about the notion. Ken Booth has argued that it is a key concept 'whose time has come' and he suggests that it is a far more useful notion than Snyder gives it credit for because it alerts analysts to the cultural roots of strategy, which have long been neglected. Building on Snyder's earlier work, Booth defines 'strategic culture' as 'a nation's traditions, values, attitudes, patterns of behaviour, habits, symbols, achievements and particular ways of adapting to the environment and solving problems with respect to the threat or use of force'.[19] Defined in these terms, 'strategic culture' derives from a state's history, geography, and political culture, which provide reference points and contexts for contemporary thinking about peace and war. According to this view it does not provide an all-embracing determinant of policy, but rather it helps to shape the direction of strategy. In this respect 'strategic culture' is similar to (and closely related to) the notion of 'belief systems'. It provides a set of lenses through which information concerning the physical and social environment is received. It embodies attitudes and beliefs, often at an unconscious level, which influence perceptions of threat and suggests the way forward in developing security policies in terms of traditional, time-honoured responses adapted to contemporary circumstances.

The link between strategic culture and weapons of mass destruction is the main theme of a book edited by Jeannie L. Johnson, Kerry M. Kartchner, and Jeffrey A. Larsen. They define strategic culture as 'that set of shared beliefs, assumptions, and modes of behaviour, derived from common experiences and accepted narratives (both oral and written), that shape collective identity and relationships to other groups, and which determine appropriate ends and means of achieving security objectives'.[20] This is the definition we adopt in this study. Johnson, Kartchner, and Larsen accept that culture is rarely a direct determinant of policy or that it operates alone. They also see it as supplementing realism, rather than replacing it. While accepting that there are some flaws in the concept, nevertheless they view it as an important variable in explaining why states acquire and maintain weapons of mass destruction. Various contributors to the book focus on important questions and issues such as: the role of strategic culture in determining a state's strategic doctrine and plans to use such weapons; the role of the keepers of strategic culture; subcultures within the state's main strategic culture; and whether changes are possible within long-term strategic culture. These are themes dealt with in this study.

One of the central arguments about the concept of 'strategic culture' is whether it is possible to provide evidence of 'cause' and 'effect'—or, to put it another way, whether it is possible to *prove* that strategic culture does in practice shape policy in a significant way. Colin Gray has argued that, while it is wrong to assume that it is possible to provide evidence of reliable causality, it is useful, nevertheless, to see strategic culture as 'context', a category 'transcending both cause and effect'.[21] Gray sees strategic culture as 'the world of the mind, feeling, and habit in behaviour'. This is an approach discussed by David G. Haglund in an article entitled 'What Good is Strategic Culture?'[22] Haglund takes Gray's idea further by distinguishing between strategic culture as *context* and strategic culture as *cognition*.[23] He argues that strategic culture as *context* is 'divisible into (a) national historical behaviour, and (b) national character and identity'. Strategic culture as *cognition*, he suggests, 'is descended from the cognate concept of political culture, and as such has its most salient quality in the dimension of symbolism'.[24] As an approach, we share Gray's scepticism of providing 'reliable causality'. And, although there are some differences between the substrata of the concept of strategic culture identified by Haglund, there are also some important links between them. 'Symbolism' can be an important part of 'national historical behaviour' and 'identity'. We hope to show these links in what follows.

In his study *A Cultural Theory of International Relations*, Richard Ned Lebow argues that the impact of culture is largely ignored in most mainstream approaches to the subject.[25] The role of self-esteem and prestige, or what he calls 'spirit', are more important than Realist, Liberal or Marxists theorists suggest. His version of 'psychological constructivism' argues that 'spirit' is an important and often dominant motivation in the behaviour of individuals and states. Prestige and standing are not simply a smokescreen for the pursuit of power, survival, and material interests, he argues, but are important in their own right. This, he suggests, is a significant reason why states seek to own the most powerful weapons available. In his words, 'states have historically sought prestige by acquiring certain kinds of weapon systems, most recently nuclear weapons'.[26] He links this to the question of 'identity'.

Identity

'Beliefs' and 'culture' are part of the broader concept of 'identity'. Although there appears to be no consensus about the meaning of 'identity', Richard Ned Lebow argues that 'most definitions start from the premise that it embodies some sense of who we are that connects us to, and differentiates us from, others. Identity can be constructed around membership in a community and a set of roles it expects us to fulfil.'[27] For constructivist theorists such as Alexander Wendt, ideas of collective identity are of crucial importance in the kinds of roles that states play in international relations.[28] This is also a view taken by Jacques Hymans. In *The Psychology of Nuclear Proliferation* he argues that when faced with uncertainty and danger, political leaders are forced to 'look deep inside themselves for guidance'.[29] As a result, their decisions, particularly in relation to nuclear weapons, reflect what he calls their 'national identity conception (NIC)'. He defines this as 'an individual's understanding of the nation's identity—his or her sense of what the nation naturally stands for and how high it naturally stands, in comparison to others in the international arena'. He goes on to argue that the leader's 'national identity conception' is a 'set of deep-seated, essentially unfalsifiable *beliefs* about the "true" nature of the nation which are developed through comparison and contrast with the "true" nature ascribed to certain external others'. Leaders with particular kinds of NICs are more prone to develop nuclear weapons. Hymans argues that leaders who have 'a deeply held conception of their nation's identity', which he calls 'opposition nationalist', tend to see their country 'at odds with an external enemy, and as naturally its equal if not its superior'. This tends to generate emotions of fear and pride, which drive them to desire nuclear weapons 'that goes beyond calculation, to self-expression'. The main thesis of Hyman's study is that 'decisions to go or not go nuclear result not from international structure, but from individual hearts. Simply put, some political leaders hold a conception of their nation's identity that leads them to desire the bomb; and such leaders can be expected to turn that desire into state policy.'[30] For such leaders, who he believes are uniquely important in such vital decisions, the desire for nuclear weapons goes 'beyond calculation, to self-expression'.

According to writers who focus on the importance of identity, beliefs play a large role 'in shaping not only perceptions of reality, but reality itself'. Viewed in this way, 'national interests' cannot be objectively determined, but are the result of social construction. According to Michael MccGwire, 'the role a state chooses (or settles for) [i.e. the dominant collective identity within the policy elite] ultimately defines both the national interests that need protecting or promoting (the basis of foreign policy) and the parameters of its security concerns (the basis of defence policy)'.[31] Similarly, Nick Ritchie argues that: 'Collective identities... crucially play a large role in determining what constitutes "national interests" and rational policy choices'.[32] Because collective identities provide 'a framework for understanding the world' and 'a roadmap for government policy' that motivates governments to behave in particular ways, they inevitably have a major influence how 'interests' are determined and how leaders believe they should respond to perceived threats.

Ritchie goes on to argue that it is this sense of having a particular identity that accounts for Britain's attitude to nuclear weapons. In his view, the possession of nuclear weapons has been an important part of Britain's identity in international politics since the 1940s. Throughout the Cold War, he argues, Britain thought of itself as 'a major power, America's primary political and military ally and as a vital part of the Western bulwark against the Soviet ideological and conventional and nuclear threat'. Nuclear weapons are seen as part of a broader self-identity of Britain playing a vital role in maintaining international peace and protecting universal values. He argues that:

> This... is what Britain does, this is what Britain is, this is the political-defence establishment's powerful collective identity: Britain is a 'force for good'; a responsible 'pivotal' power that has a duty to tackle international security threats in defence of shared values in the name of 'international community' using extraordinary military forces of Global reach for the... purpose of creating space for the political settlement of conflicts around the world. This is presented as a morally legitimate, just, rational and enlightened pursuit of national self-interest.[33]

Nuclear weapons are seen as necessary to underpin this interventionist foreign and defence policy.

A similar view is put forward by the American writer Andrew Pierre in a major study of British nuclear policy up to 1970. Pierre argues that key early decisions about nuclear weapons were taken by political leaders who had a traditional conception of Britain's world role. This 'habit of mind', he suggests, continued until the Suez Crisis in 1956. From then on nuclear weapons were viewed as an important way of disguising its reduced status:

> Nuclear weapons are more than modern military arms; they become part of complex political and social phenomena. In the case of Britain, the creation and continuation of an independent nuclear force can best be understood in the context of a once Great Power in decline, attempting to adjust to reduced circumstances. At the time the nuclear force was originally developed, Britain's self-image was that of an imperial, self-sufficient Great Power with a world-wide role. Although she did not possess the same economic and military resources as the two principal superpowers, Britain was thought to be more than just a European power because of her global interests and responsibilities... Britain had no serious rival for third place among the nations of the world... After [Suez] recognition slowly grew that she was no longer a world power and the 'independent deterrent' became at once both a symbol of Britain's Great Power claim and a disguise for her diminished status. It was perceived as helping to maintain the nation's international influence while her power in relation to other states was decreasing.[34]

Sagan's Three Models

The American scholar Scott Sagan has argued that there are three main approaches in the proliferation literature to explain why states develop nuclear weapons.[35] These are 'the security model', the 'domestic politics model', and the 'norms model'. The 'security model' reflects the realist perspective in arguing that states acquire nuclear weapons to increase their national security against foreign threats, especially nuclear threats. The 'domestic politics model' argues that this traditional view neglects the way that nuclear weapons are often political tools used to advance the particular parochial interests of domestic and bureaucratic actors. The 'norms model', in contrast to the other two, focuses on the way that nuclear weapons are often regarded by decision-makers as an important normative symbol of a state's modernity and identity. Sagan's view is that while the 'security model' can tell us something about why states developed and maintained a nuclear capability, the other two models provide important insights. He argues that nuclear decisions are taken for more than one reason and are best explained by different causal models.

We share this view of multicausality. We use the domestic politics perspective to highlight the importance of the nuclear advocacy coalition, which we

Introduction

argue has played a critical role in determining nuclear policy in Britain. This coalition, as Sagan notes, consists of individuals in the nuclear energy establishment, important groups within the professional military hierarchy, as well as politicians and government officials who have beliefs and interests associated with the development and maintenance of a nuclear capability. We try to show how these beliefs and interests come together and become powerful enough to produce their preferred outcomes. We also try to show that the 'norms model' equally provides insights into understanding the British nuclear experience. Following Robert Jervis, in his study of 'The Symbolic Nature of Nuclear Politics', we argue that policy-makers in Britain have tended to see nuclear weapons as something they have to possess and maintain as a symbol of their status as a legitimate technological modern state.[36] In this sense we share the views of Ritchie and Pierre that nuclear weapons can be regarded as an important part of Britain's post-war self-identity.

By considering this wide range of literature and trying to apply it to the British nuclear experience, this study is theory-driven. Insights from different theoretical approaches provide a different—and, we hope, improved—understanding of why Britain developed nuclear weapons and why it continues to retain this capability some seventy years later. Before charting that experience, we now turn to a brief discussion of the background to British nuclear policy during the Second World War.

The Wartime Origins

Britain was the first state that decided it was necessary to develop an atomic weapons capability. Following on from the work of Rudolf Peierls and Otto Frisch at Birmingham University in 1940, the British wartime government set up the Maud Committee, consisting of six eminent scientists, to study the possibility of developing a nuclear weapon.[37] In July 1940 the Committee completed its report with three main recommendations. First, it argued that it was possible to construct a uranium super bomb which was 'likely to lead to decisive results in the war'.[38] Second, it recommended that the work on such a bomb should be continued as the 'highest priority and on the increasing scale necessary to obtain the weapon in the shortest possible time'. And third, that 'the present collaboration with America should be continued and extended especially in the region of experimental work'. The highest priority that needed to be given to the project, the report argued, was due to the fact that Germany was also working on uranium research and 'the lines on which we are now working are such as would be likely to suggest themselves to any capable physicist'.[39]

The Maud Committee accepted that it was possible that the bomb might not be produced by the time the war ended, but the members believed that the prodigious explosive power of such weapons was likely to be of such military significance in the future that every effort should be made to develop them as soon as possible. The report argued that:

> Even if the war should end before the bombs are ready, the effort would not be wasted, except in the unlikely event of complete disarmament, since no nation would care to risk being caught without a weapon of such decisive possibilities.[40]

A copy of the report was taken to the United States in the summer of 1941, with the US still neutral, and groups of scientists were, in a rather unfocused manner, working on the possibilities of the bomb. It was only after receiving the Maud Report that the US took the project more seriously, and even before Pearl Harbour, the Manhattan Project was established largely to pursue the objectives set out in the Maud Report.[41] By this time Britain had set up an organization with the code name 'Tube Alloys', with the aim of establishing the research and industrial programme necessary to develop atomic weapons.[42]

By the end of 1941 Britain was still ahead of the US, and when the Americans suggested a joint programme this was treated with what Lorna Arnold has described as 'cool condescension'. 'Britain', she argues, 'wanted exchanges of information, no more'.[43] By the summer of 1942, however, the US had forged ahead very quickly with the huge Manhattan Project and Britain was struggling to build a few pilot units for a uranium separation plant. As Graham Farmelo has argued, Churchill 'had missed a great opportunity' and it was now the prime minister's turn to seek a partnership with the United States.[44] In a reversal of roles, the US rejected his offers of a joint programme and the exchange of information effectively ceased for a time. Believing that atomic power would be the 'key to national power in the post-war world', Churchill made repeated attempts to persuade Roosevelt to involve Britain in the US programme.[45] In August 1943, these efforts finally paid off, and the Quebec Agreement between the two countries allowed British scientists to play an important (but subsidiary) role in the Manhattan Project, which led to the first atomic test in Alamagordo in July 1945 and the two bombs dropped on Hiroshima and Nagasaki in August 1945. The Quebec Agreement, and a further agreement at Hyde Park in September 1944, also committed both governments to agree to continue nuclear cooperation after the war ended. In these wartime agreements, the roles of the two national leaders and their perceptions of their national security interests was of crucial importance, as Hymans has argued.

In many ways the Second World War reflected traditional shared 'beliefs, assumptions and modes of behaviour' which emphasized the importance of

Introduction

such things as the 'balance of power', military and political alliances, the utility of military force in an anarchical world system, as well as Britain's global role and her perceived contribution to international stability. As Jeremy Paxman has argued: 'Britain came out of two world wars on the winning side and so never had the need to re-imagine themselves as anything other than what they had once been.' After all, the empire had been 'Britain's international preoccupation for a very long time'.[46] At the same time, however, the experience of the Blitz, together with the V1 and V2 attacks on Britain, and her involvement in the strategic bombing campaign, meant that the Second World War ended traditional ideas of relative invulnerability which had resulted from the combination of the UK's island geography and dominant maritime capabilities. This meant, as Michael Quinlan has argued, that the British people and their leaders entered the nuclear age with an awareness and indeed an acceptance of the inescapable vulnerability more vivid—yet at the same time less shocking because less unfamiliar—than did the United States.[47] This produced a different 'security mindset' to the United States, where the concept of homeland sanctuary remained intact at least until the late 1950s and the first test of a Soviet intercontinental ballistic missile carrying the Sputnik satellite. It was this 'mindset' that was to lead to the early acceptance of ideas about deterrence and the search for a 'dominant weapon', like the Dreadnought battleship of an earlier era, but this time designed, it was believed, to overcome Britain's critical vulnerability after the devastation of Hiroshima and Nagasaki.

Pursuing this theme, Chapter 1 highlights the impact that the atomic bombs dropped on Hiroshima and Nagasaki had on Britain's post-war leaders, giving rise to a 'deterrence habit of mind'. The beliefs of Prime Minister Clement Attlee and his Foreign Secretary, Ernest Bevin, were particularly important in the acceptance of the view that a revolution in military affairs had taken place, involving a change in both the character and nature of warfare. The operationalization of these ideas, however, was the work of a number of influential individuals and committees who, over time, developed Britain's nuclear strategy. Chapter 2 takes this argument further by looking at the role of the Chiefs of Staff (COS) as a significant and influential part of the 'nuclear advocacy coalition'. Despite some differences between them, the COS formulated the Global Strategy Papers of the early 1950s which attempted to set nuclear weapons, and the concept of deterrence, into Britain's overall world strategy. It is argued that the 1952 Global Strategy Paper in particular had a significant influence over American ideas of nuclear strategy which were being developed at this time. The ideas and beliefs about the utility of nuclear weapons as the best way to avoid war were evolving at the same time that Britain was undertaking the complex task of setting up the infrastructure for developing atomic weapons. Chapter 3 looks at these developments, which culminated in Britain's first atomic test in October 1952, and the subsequent events which led to the Grapple Trials in 1957/8, which produced a thermonuclear capability. The focus here is on the political as well as the security dimensions of these developments—deterrence, Great Power status, and influencing the United States. Chapter 4 takes the latter theme further by looking at the way the Anglo-American 'special nuclear relationship' was forged in the mid and late 1950s, after the close wartime atomic partnership had been ended as a result of the 1946 McMahon Act. This theme is continued in Chapter 5 with a discussion of the Polaris Sales Agreement of 1963 and the dilemma this created for British policy-makers in terms of trying to balance the continuing strategic desire for independence with the growing necessity (economically) and benefits (technologically) of interdependence with the United States.

Chapter 6 focuses on the start of the debates in Britain, just as *Polaris* was being deployed, about the need to improve the credibility of the British deterrent force in the light of technological advances in Soviet missile defences. This led, through various stages, to the secret Chevaline programme, designed to provide advanced manoeuvrable warheads and penetration aids for Polaris which would allow Britain to continue to threaten to destroy Moscow as the basis of its national deterrent policy. The chapter also considers the ideas about Anglo-French nuclear cooperation that were discussed during the Heath administration. The debates about the requirements of deterrence and the 'Moscow Criterion' are continued in Chapter 7, which looks at the various disagreements which took place within the Labour governments of the 1970s. The focus here is on the continuing influential role of key political leaders, but also the important contribution of two groups under Sir Anthony Duff and Sir Ronald Mason, who were tasked with looking at possible replacements for the Polaris system. Chapter 8 considers the discussions during the early years of the Thatcher administration, based on the Duff-Mason Report, and the eventual decision to purchase *Trident* C-4 and later D-5 missiles from the United States. Chapter 9 then deals with the parallel developments relating to the modernization of theatre and short range nuclear missiles, together with British views regarding American ideas about a Strategic Defence Initiative (SDI), which it was believed had the potential to undermine the credibility of the newly purchased Trident force as soon as it was deployed. The chapter ends with a discussion of the policies of the Major administration and the impact of the end of the Cold War on thinking about British nuclear capabilities.

Chapter 10 brings the story up to date by looking at the evolution of British nuclear policy during the Blair, Brown, and Cameron governments. During this period the tensions between contributing to the nuclear non-proliferation agenda in the post–Cold-War era and maintaining a nuclear deterrent was reflected in reductions to British nuclear forces, as well as the initial decision to go ahead with Trident renewal/replacement, with a final decision postponed until after the 2015 election. The chapter also looks at the debates about Trident renewal/replacement, especially over the opportunity costs of spending scarce resources on nuclear forces on Britain's conventional capabilities. The Conclusion then brings the main arguments of the book together by focusing on the key characteristics of the British experience with nuclear weapons from the Second World War until the present day. It stresses the important roles of beliefs, culture, and identity, which have contributed to the *entrenchment* of support for nuclear weapons amongst the British political elite, but also amongst the majority of the British electorate. It is argued that for Britain to give up its nuclear weapons, significant changes in the predominant beliefs, culture, and self-identity will need to take place. Such changes, it is suggested, are not impossible, but are likely to be very difficult to achieve.

1

The Emergence of a Deterrence 'Habit of Mind'

> [T]he only deterrent is the possibility of the victim of such an attack being able to retort on another great city.
>
> Clement Attlee*

> We've got to have a bloody Union Jack flying on top of it.
>
> Ernest Bevin**

In the first two years after the Second World War ended, an 'atomic climate' was created in Britain as the new Labour government under Clement Attlee laid the foundations of a nuclear weapons programme which was to remain a central feature of British defence policy to the present day.[1] A number of momentous decisions were taken to establish research, development, and production facilities, as well as to develop atomic weapons and a long-range bomber force. It was these decisions which led to the first British atomic test in 1952 and to the deployment of a nuclear deterrent capability by 1955. However, these developments obscured a major debate in British military and political circles over whether the release of atomic energy constituted a new force too revolutionary to consider in the framework of old ideas, or whether the new weapons were merely a more efficient means of destruction which nation states could use to defend or promote their interests in much the same way that they had done for hundreds of years. This was reflected in the new government's question to the Chiefs of Staff shortly after the defeat of Japan. They were asked whether 'The introduction of atomic explosives open[s] up an era of destruction on a scale never before considered feasible, or is it merely an intensive development of the existing concept of war, which science may render controllable by local defence and counter-action?'[2] In turn, answers to this central question reflected a wide range of opinions about the direction that British strategy should take in the nuclear era.

The Nuclear Revolution

In the immediate post-war period attitudes towards atomic weapons were sharply divided. For some contemporary observers, despite the enormous destructive power of atomic weapons that had been demonstrated by the attacks on Hiroshima and Nagasaki, they did not, in any quantitative sense, appear to have altered the nature of war. Neither bomb did as much damage as the air raids conducted with conventional weapons against Tokyo, Yokohama, and Dresden. In a response to the government's request for an assessment of 'The Influence of the Atomic Bomb on War', one Admiralty paper written on 15 August 1945 argued that 'the atomic bomb on its own will not be decisive'.[3] Describing it as no more than a 'bigger and better bomb', the editor of the 1946 issue of *Brassey's Annual* also dismissed the argument that the atomic bomb had revolutionized warfare.[4] The Nobel Prize winning physicist P. M. S. Blackett was another who believed that atomic weapons alone were unlikely to be decisive in a war fought between the Great Powers.[5] Andrew Pierre has speculated that this was probably the generally accepted judgement of the majority of the British military establishment at the time.[6] British military planners in the post-war period were men hardened to the massive destruction of the wartime experiences. As such, many of them tended to take a sanguine view of the advent of the atomic bomb and assigned relatively little importance to it. There were others, however, including many military officers, who took a different view. Sir John Slessor, who, as Chief of the Air Staff, was to become the chief architect of British nuclear strategy in the early 1950s, was not convinced by the 'bigger and better bomb' argument. Although in 1945 he remained uncertain about the precise long-term impact of atomic weapons, he felt that the effects on future warfare might well be profound:

> Whether this will render warfare itself as obsolete as the duel without first destroying civilization is clearly the most vital question in the world which we must solve satisfactorily or perish. If our cities could be attacked by this weapon without any defence or risk of sufficiently immediate retaliation, we would be wasting our breath discussing other means of warfare.[7]

It was the prime minister, Clement Attlee, however, who was one of the earliest proponents of the view that atomic weapons had brought about a revolutionary change in the nature of warfare. In August 1945 he set up an Advisory Committee on Atomic Energy to provide continuity of knowledge from the wartime project and advise on future policy. At the second meeting of this committee (29 August 1945) Attlee seems to have been thinking initially in largely traditional terms when he argued:

> We recognised, or some of us did before this war, that bombing would only be answered by counter-bombing. We were right. Berlin and Magdeburg were the answer to London and Coventry. Both derive from Guernica. The answer to an atomic bomb on London is an atomic bomb on another great city.[8]

This reflected the continuing influence of the strategic bombing ideas from the inter-war period. In a long letter to President Truman in September 1945, however, Attlee emphasized his view that the planning which had been done towards the end of the war for the post-war period was now largely out of date. Traditional ideas were now obsolete. The problem, he wrote, was that few people realized the significance of what had happened. Never before had there been a weapon which could 'suddenly and without warning be employed to destroy utterly the nerve centre of a great nation'.[9] The prime minister argued that despite the destruction of the Second World War, the damage was not different in kind from that which had been done in conflicts in Europe in the past. The new weapons, however, represented not simply a quantitative but, in his view, 'a qualitative change in the nature of warfare'.[10]

Attlee also believed that the worse was still to come. The bombs on Hiroshima and Nagasaki were not the end of a process, but rather the beginning of a scientific development that would bring weapons of even greater destructive power. He foresaw that in the future they would be delivered by rockets and would be available to an increasing number of states. This meant that the modern conception of war to which the existing generation had become accustomed was now 'completely out of date'.[11] He told Truman that, in his view, the most sensible policy would now be one of deterrence. As there was no effective defence available against the atomic bomb, he argued, the only deterrent was the possibility of the victim being able to retaliate against the attacker.

The Search for International Control

Despite this emphasis on the importance of deterrence, Attlee was conscious that in the inter-war period strategic bombing had been hailed as the great deterrent to war and had failed. He had no great faith that things would be different in the nuclear age—and if deterrence did break down, he had no doubt that nuclear weapons would be used. In a speech on 22 November 1945 he warned the House of Commons:

> I think it is as well that we should make up our minds that if the world again lapses into war on a scale comparable to that from which we have just emerged, every weapon will be used, and we may confidently expect that full-scale atomic warfare will result in the destruction of great cities, in the deaths of millions.[12]

These deep anxieties about whether deterrence would work led the prime minister to argue that some form of international control of atomic weapons was urgently needed. In attempting to come to terms with the problems posed by atomic weapons, however, his thinking oscillated between 'idealist' solutions based on the need for a fundamental transformation of international politics and more 'realist' policies which reflected traditional concerns with power and *realpolitik*.[13]

Between August and November 1945 Attlee wrestled with the question of whether Britain and the United States should share information with the Soviet Union in order to create the right environment of trust on which the foundations of an international control system could be built. In August he wrote:

> The most we may have is a few years' start... The only course which seems to me to be feasible and to offer a reasonable hope of staving off imminent disaster for the world is joint action by the USA, UK and Russia based upon stark reality. We should declare that this invention has made it essential to end wars.[14]

In similar vein, he told the Cabinet that 'time is short... only a bold course can save civilization'. He therefore proposed to take the initiative, and wrote to Truman urging a meeting to discuss the question of international control. Attlee's letter to Truman on 23 September is a remarkable testimony to the prime minister's belief that 'new thinking' about the whole basis of international politics was necessary in the nuclear age. He told the American president that 'the world was now facing entirely new conditions'. This meant that if the world was 'to rid itself of this menace', far-reaching changes in the relationship between states would be necessary. This meant that:

> We have, in fact, in the light of this revolutionary development to make a fresh review of world policy and a new evaluation of what are called national interests... We have to secure that these new developments are turned to the benefit rather than to the destruction of mankind. We must bend our utmost energies to secure that better ordering of human affairs which so great a revolution at once renders necessary and should make possible.[15]

Attlee asked to meet Truman to discuss 'this momentous problem' before 'the fears and suspicions which might be developing elsewhere' took hold and prevented any solution from being arrived at. He appreciated that there would be risks associated with involving the Soviet Union in this process, but, in the new circumstances, 'acts of faith' were called for.

Despite Truman's initial reluctance to hold talks with Attlee so as not to offend Stalin, he finally agreed to meet the British and Canadian prime ministers on 9 November. Between Attlee's letter in September and the talks in November a major debate took place at the highest levels within the government about how to deal with the question of international control. Reflecting the views of the prime minister, on 11 October Ernest Bevin told an ad hoc meeting of Cabinet colleagues (Gen 75) that Britain had 'everything to gain and little to lose by making Russia party to knowledge of the atomic bomb process'.[16] It would be worth 'trusting to their good faith', he argued, by negotiating an international control agreement. Looking back with hindsight at the difficulties experienced by Britain and the United States at the Council of Foreign Ministers meeting in September, the Foreign Secretary felt that a major cause might have been Russian annoyance at being left in the dark about the Manhattan Project. It was conceivable, he believed, that taking the Russians into the West's confidence now might have a disproportionate effect on the atmosphere of international relations. Bevin told his colleagues that 'We should take the risk of giving this information to the Russians in the interests of our foreign policy.'[17]

This view was not confined to the prime minister and the Foreign Secretary. The British ambassadors in Washington and in Moscow, together with a number of members of the Cabinet, held similar views at this time. The advice from Lord Halifax, the ambassador in Washington, was that it was unlikely that Russia could be trusted. However, he believed that eventually the Russians would develop nuclear weapons themselves and therefore there was no point 'incurring political resentment by refusing to consider disclosure when disclosure promised to be either superfluous or innocuous'. Sir Archibald Clark-Kerr came to similar conclusions. In a series of telegrams to the Foreign Office from Moscow, the ambassador emphasized that the Russians had expected the West to share the secrets of the bomb with them. 'But as time went on', he argued, 'and no move came from the west disappointment turned into irritation and, when the bomb seemed to them to become an instrument of policy, into spleen'. It was clear that the West did not trust them. Given the conspiratorial lives the Russian leaders had experienced it was perhaps not surprising, he suggested, that 'such western policies seemed to justify and quicken all the old suspicions'. It was seen as a humiliation to Russian pride which 'stirred up memories of the past'.[18]

Similar sentiments were shared by some members of the Cabinet. They agreed with the view that difficulties in relations with the Soviet Union were largely the product of the suspicions of the West. They felt that it would be sensible, therefore, to make an immediate offer of practical know-how and scientific knowledge to the Russians to create the kind of trust and mutual confidence so essential to building a lasting peace. Echoing the prime minister and Foreign Secretary, they argued that risks had to be taken. Traditional approaches to international politics had to be rejected. 'If it was our policy', one Cabinet minister said 'to build world peace on moral foundations rather than on the balance of power we should be prepared to apply that principle at once to the atomic bomb'.[19]

By the time these ministers were expressing such views in Cabinet, however, the attitudes of both the Foreign Secretary and the prime minister had hardened due to increasing difficulties with the Soviet leadership. Within a week of Bevin's comment to Gen 75 on trusting in Russian 'good faith' he was telling the same committee that Britain and the United States should not let them in on the secret of atomic energy without getting something in return. Having given the matter more thought, he had come to the conclusion that 'Russian policy had shown no variation'. This was a view which was very much in line with the advice the Foreign Secretary was getting from his officials and intelligence agencies at the time. In their view the offer of information about atomic energy to the Soviet leaders would have no effect on their behaviour. 'Russian policy', they said, 'was strictly realist in outlook and not influenced by motives of gratitude; they would regard such an offer with suspicion'.[20]

In October 1945 the prime minister also seemed to have modified his own view regarding 'acts of faith' to encourage good behaviour on the part of the Soviet Union. Reflecting the advice from the Foreign Office, he was prepared to offer some basic scientific knowledge to the Soviet leaders, but any practical technical information about how to construct nuclear weapons, he now accepted, had to wait until relations improved a great deal. Although some ministers remained unconvinced, this was the position adopted by the Cabinet as a whole. At the same time, however, despite the distrust of Russian policies which this tougher line indicated, Attlee was not prepared to go along completely with the views of Foreign Office officials. He personally changed official papers prepared for his visit to meet Truman so as to exclude any references 'to the Russian threat'.[21]

Although the prime minister had stiffened his views towards the Soviet Union by the time of his meeting with Truman in November, the paradoxes and ambiguities in his thinking about nuclear weapons and their impact on international politics nevertheless remained. He continued to wrestle with the competing pulls of 'realist' and 'utopian' ideas. He accepted that the chances of controlling the use of nuclear weapons were negligible if the traditional pursuit of national interest remained the predominant theme in the relations between states. What was needed was a change of thinking by states and an agreement to coordinate their policies on atomic energy more effectively and renounce war. Realistically, however, he accepted that states would go on developing nuclear weapons for themselves until some system of effective control was agreed. In his talks with Truman the prime minister argued that within a few years it was highly likely that the Soviet Union would acquire nuclear weapons and the United States' monopoly would be lost. It was therefore of vital importance that every effort was made to strengthen the power of the United Nations and encourage broader internationalist thinking. The time had to be used profitably. 'A real attempt', he argued, 'must be made to build a world organisation upon the abandonment of power politics'. Here we see the prime minister's belief that the Great Powers could make a difference. International politics based on anarchy and self-interest could be changed, Attlee seems to have believed, provided that more emphasis was placed on the United Nations. He argued that 'the New World Order must start now'.[22]

There was, however, a major contradiction in the prime minister's thinking. While every effort had to be made to abandon power politics and build up the United Nations, he accepted that Britain had to deal with the world as it was, with all its imperfections. The international control of nuclear weapons was a goal to pursue, but until that time came it was important to make sure that Britain acquired the most effective weapons available to protect the nation's vital national interests. The difficulty with this position was that the two strands of policy quite clearly contradicted each other. Margaret Gowing lays bare the logic at the heart of Attlee's thinking in the following terms: 'While waiting for mutual trust to be established and Utopia to arrive, each such power must look to its own interests and make itself as strong as possible in nuclear weapons, even if thereby mutual mistrust was engendered and the chances of ultimate international control diminished.'[23] In other words, there was a grave danger that by pursuing national goals the chances of achieving the internationalist vision would be severely undermined.

The prime minister, however, was not alone in wrestling with this dilemma. President Truman faced the same question of whether, despite the growing problems, to let the Russians in on the nuclear secret. In early September 1945, like Attlee and Bevin, he was arguing that 'we must take Russia into our confidence'. However, less than a month later he had gone through the same conversion as the British leaders and was only prepared to share basic scientific knowledge with the Russians, rather than engineering secrets. Within the United States Truman faced pressure from two distinct groups. One group saw nuclear weapons as an American 'sacred trust' which must not be given up, even to the British. The other group had more international objectives and urged the president to seek an agreement with the Russians on the international control of atomic energy for the good of mankind as a whole.[24]

When Attlee and Truman met in Washington on 9 November, therefore, there were contradictions in the positions adopted by both leaders. The British prime minister sought American backing for United Nations action on international control, while his officials (Sir John Anderson and Roger Makins) negotiated a memorandum on the continuation of bilateral cooperation in atomic energy between Britain and the United States. The American president was happy to support the search for international control, but remained apparently unaware of the implications of the bilateral negotiations for the retention of the American monopoly or indeed the objective of international control. The result was that at the end of the Washington conference two agreements were reached which were essentially contradictory.

The Washington Declaration signed by Truman, Attlee, and Mackenzie King (prime minister of Canada) on 15 November emphasized the importance of international control, 'given the terrible realities of the application of science to destruction'.[25] The three leaders agreed to the sharing of basic scientific knowledge, but not technical secrets, and urged the United Nations to set up a commission which would make specific proposals not only for sharing knowledge on atomic energy for peaceful purposes, but also for 'the elimination from national armaments of atomic weapons and of all other major weapons adaptable to mass destruction'.[26] The next day, however, Sir John Anderson for Britain and General Groves for the United States signed a memorandum which agreed to 'the full and effective co-operation' in the field of basic scientific research 'between the three countries especially in the exchange of the raw materials for nuclear production'.[27] While one agreement emphasized international control for the benefit of the human race, the other stressed bilateral relations to restrict knowledge to those that already had it. As Gowing has argued:

> it is strange that no one pointed to the contradiction in the Washington proceedings—between the lofty protestations that the only hope for the world was to lay aside nationalist ideas, and a close three-power agreement based on the hopes of a virtual monopoly of the raw materials of atomic energy. Indeed, the profound consequences of atomic energy made logic almost unattainable. They inspired idealism but also fear, and so the noble thoughts were accompanied by the most sober calculations of Realpolitik.[28]

This contradiction at the heart of the Washington agreements continued to create uncertainties in British policy in the months that followed. In January 1946 an Atomic Energy Commission was set up by the General Assembly of the United Nations to consider the question of international control. Although the negotiations dragged on until May 1948, by the summer of 1946 the discussions with the Russians were effectively deadlocked, reflecting the deteriorating relations between the victorious powers. The American proposal for an international authority, which would gradually take over responsibility for American nuclear weapons while denying such weapons to the Soviet Union, was quickly dismissed by the Russian leaders. Similarly, a Soviet plan that involved the destruction of American nuclear weapons within three months, before an authority with effective safeguards was in place, was unacceptable to the United States.

During the negotiations in 1946 and 1947 Britain's position remained ambivalent. The government continued to give support to the United States' proposals, but in practice there were severe reservations about the restrictions that these would place on Britain's security interests and the development of atomic energy for industrial purposes. The Chiefs of Staff agreed that an attempt should be made to achieve international control because it was 'probably the only alternative to mutual destruction'. It was vital, however, that any agreement should include 'the most unequivocal and comprehensive rights of inspection' possible. Demonstrating their lack of trust in the Soviet Union, they argued that:

> Russia is a country which appears to have both the natural resources and the remote areas for the secret development of atomic weapons. There is the obvious danger that we and the Americans might be led to agree not to produce atomic weapons while the Russians secretly carried out their research and production in the remote areas of the Soviet Union. The right of inspection will provide no security unless it is completely comprehensive. How this is to be achieved under the present Soviet system is the crux of the problem.[29]

This placed the lack of trust (and the need for verification) at the heart of the question.

The Chiefs of Staff were in no doubt that, until this problem was resolved, Britain should get on with the task of developing a national nuclear deterrent capability. In effect, what the COS were saying was that international control was unlikely, but without it there was a great chance of mutual destruction. They were, therefore, advocating the development of a national deterrent even though they had no real faith that such forces would be able to prevent such destruction.

Nuclear Advocacy and the Origins of Nuclear Deterrence Ideas

Ideas about nuclear deterrence were not a product of the post-war period. In mid-1944 concern about the possibility of Soviet atomic blackmail following the end of the war had led to a debate about whether Britain would need atomic weapons under her own control. The consensus at the time was that 'if the possibility of retaliation is to work as a deterrent', then Britain would have to have the means for immediate retaliation. It was essential, it was argued, that Britain had such weapons 'under her own control to use without a moment's delay'.[30] In November 1944 the Chiefs of Staff asked their Joint Technical Warfare Committee (JTWC) to produce a report on the future potential of weapons of war. The terms of reference laid down by the Chiefs of Staff asked the JTWC to look ten years into the future:

The Joint Technical Warfare Committee, availing themselves of the best scientific advice available, are required to review the position and to forecast to the best of their ability developments in weapons and methods in each important field of warfare during the next ten years, having regard both to theoretical possibilities and also to the practical limitations at present foreseeable.[31]

To meet this requirement the JTWC set up an ad hoc scientific committee under the chairmanship of Sir Henry Tizard.[32] Remarkably, such were the demands for secrecy that the committee was denied access to any information on atomic bomb developments, despite the fact that such developments were likely to be of the greatest importance in future weapons development. Nevertheless, the committee contained some of the most distinguished scientists of the day (J. D. Bernal, P. M. S. Blackett, C. D. Ellis, and G. P. Thompson) and was able to build into its report some prescient comments about how atomic energy developments were likely to affect the future of warfare.

The Tizard Report, as it became known, was completed on 3 July 1945. In the section on atomic energy, Tizard and his colleagues argued that, if atomic weapons were perfected and could be developed without prohibitive costs, it would be possible, as a result of the likely development of high-flying jet bombers, to make sudden attacks without warning. In such circumstances, the report argued, 'the only answer that we can see to the atomic bomb is to be prepared to use it ourselves in retaliation. A knowledge that we were prepared, in the last resort, to do this might well deter an aggressive nation.'[33] The conclusion of the report was that Britain should undertake large-scale research into atomic energy; design and manufacture fast, high-flying jet-powered bomber aircraft; and be prepared to use atomic bombs against a potential aggressor. According to Humphrey Wynn, these conclusions provided the framework for the nuclear deterrent philosophy which was 'subsequently enunciated by the Chiefs of Staff'.[34]

In August 1945, shortly after the bombing of Hiroshima and Nagasaki, the newly elected Labour government initiated an investigation into the 'effect of the introduction of the atomic bomb on the science of war'. In a contribution to this assessment one Admiralty paper expressed the view that:

> The net effect of the Atomic Bomb is that the price worth paying for peace is now very much higher, and that the main function of our armed forces should be the prevention of a major war, rather than the ability to fight it on purely military grounds after the war has already been decided either by the collapse of civilian morale, or the destruction of ports and industrial installations.[35]

The general consensus in the Admiralty at the time was that the most effective countermeasure against another state that had atomic bombs was 'the threat of retaliation'. For such a threat to be effective, it was argued that 'no-one should be able to destroy another country's store of Atomic Bombs or its apparatus for launching them in a sudden attack'. Perhaps the most interesting and far-reaching comment contained in the papers produced by the Royal Navy in September 1945 was the view that the best deterrent to war would eventually be a submarine force with a missile capability. It was argued that, in the light of Britain's vulnerability to destruction in the atomic age:

> the delivery of atomic weapons against an enemy beyond the range of rocket attack from our own territory may devolve on the Navy and it is necessary to consider the means by which we should carry it out... The conclusion is drawn that the most effective method for the Navy to deliver atomic missiles against enemy territory (and it is against enemy territory that the attack must be delivered) is by rockets launched from specialized vessels, either surface, or even better, submersible.[36]

This suggests that the royal Naval interest in providing a submarine-based nuclear deterrent, which was to come to fruition in the late 1960s with the *Polaris* force, had its roots in Naval thinking as early as 1945, rather than the mid-1950s as has often been suggested.

The ideas expressed in the Admiralty paper, on the need to develop atomic weapons for the purposes of deterrence, were widely accepted within the defence establishment. In October the Chiefs of Staff expressed their doubts about the chances of being able to rely on the United Nations alone to bring peace and security. In their view, 'the possession of atomic weapons of our own would be vital to our security. The best method of defence against the new weapons is likely to be the deterrent effect that the possession of the means of retaliation would have on a potential aggressor.'[37] They urged the government to press ahead in the field of research and development in order to start the production of atomic weapons 'as soon as possible'. In the same month the government made the decision to set up a research and experimental establishment at Harwell to undertake research on all aspects of atomic energy.

In its first assessment of the impact of nuclear weapons in December 1945, the Royal Air Force also emphasized the vulnerability of Britain and echoed the arguments by the Chiefs of Staff for a policy of deterrence. Reflecting the continuity of wartime thinking, the Air Chiefs argued that deterrence was best achieved by threatening Russian cities. They accepted that experience showed that this was not an easy task, but that for the moment no other targets were available that would bring about swift and decisive results. Should war break out, they argued that:

> Attack must be directed against objectives whose destruction will lower enemy morale, reduce their industrial capacity, and dislocate a large part of the centralised administrative machinery of the country. The only objectives that fulfil these requirements are large cities, and it is our opinion that our only chance of securing a quick decision is by launching a devastating attack upon them with absolute weapons.[38]

This was also the view of the Chiefs of Staff's Atomic Weapons subcommittee in a report produced in early 1946. In this report it was argued that as nuclear weapons would be scarce for the foreseeable future, they would have to be used sparingly against the most important targets. These were likely to be urban centres. The committee argued that 'the bombing of towns and industry now gives a far greater return for war effort expended and may, therefore, become the most profitable type of war'.[39]

The question of whether attacking cities would break civilian morale was an issue taken up by the JTWC in a revised report completed in July 1946. In a follow-up to their report of July 1945, the JTWC argued that the probable destruction of many cities within a few weeks or days introduced a new psychological problem into war. In their view a relatively small number of atomic weapons might be sufficient to bring about a swift victory:

> Given sufficient accumulation in peace and adequate means of delivery, atomic and biological weapons might achieve decisive results with relatively small effort against the civil population of a nation without a clash between the major forces and too rapidly to permit either the building-up of military forces or the exercise of sea power.[40]

However, the outcome of a war, they believed, would depend on how decisive the shock to morale turned out to be. On this 'there was real uncertainty'. If a country was suitably organized, in both physical and psychological terms, it was possible, the report concluded, that 'some hundreds of bombs might fail to cause the collapse of a country'.

Although cities were the most favoured targets for atomic weapons, there were some in the defence establishment who dissented from this view. At a meeting of the Vice-Chiefs of Staff Committee in April 1947, Major-General Ward expressed the opinion that 'it was only by using immediately weapons of mass destruction that we could effectively stand up against an enemy and relieve this country of a considerable weight of air attack by such weapons'. In his view 'mass destruction weapons must be directed against the means to make war, and not the will to make war, although by attacking the former the latter will be affected'.[41] At the same meeting, the Vice Chief of the Air Staff (VCAS), Sir William Dickson, went as far as to express reservations about whether it was wise to rely on weapons of mass destruction at all. In his view:

> in the event of a potential enemy not employing weapons of mass destruction at the outset of a war, the political objections against our initiating their use might be so great that we should be prevented from taking the initiative by being the first to use them. Plans for the use of normal weapons must therefore be prepared as well. Further, he was not convinced that our only hope of survival was to employ weapons of mass destruction.[42]

Dickson's comments reflected an ambiguity at the heart of the debate about deterrence which was to remain for many years to come. Were atomic weapons so revolutionary that their only use was deterrence? This was the view that Bernard Brodie was promoting in the United States at the time. In his book *The Absolute Weapon*, published in 1946, he argued that 'thus far the chief purpose of a military establishment has been to win wars. From now on its chief purpose must be to avert them. *It can have no other useful purpose.*'[43] In contrast, in certain military circles in both Britain and the United States there was a view that atomic weapons should be thought of in conventional terms. According to this view, they could be used just like 'normal' weapons to fight and win wars. Both ideas coexisted uneasily in the debates about deterrence in the immediate post-war period, with little apparent recognition of the incompatibility between them.

Despite his own uncertainty, the CAS and the other Chiefs of Staff were firmly committed to the need for atomic weapons. On 1 January 1946 they sent a report to the prime minister recommending that Britain should develop a stock of atomic weapons. What they were not able to say at this stage was how many weapons would be required. 'It is not possible', they argued, 'to assess the precise number which we might require but we are convinced we should aim to have as soon as possible a stock in the order of hundreds rather than scores'.[44] This vagueness in the COS assessment was characteristic of the failure of military planners at this time to sit down and provide a detailed analysis of the impact of atomic weapons on military strategy. The only attempt at a rough guess at the number which might be required was made by the JTWC in its July 1946 report. Echoing the comment in the COS memorandum to the prime minister in January, it was argued that there was no firm basis on which to assess the quantities of either atomic or biological weapons which might be required to bring about the collapse of a potential aggressor. Such calculations were based on many factors, most of which were imponderable. Nevertheless, they were prepared to hazard a guess:

> our estimate, based on such information as is at present available, leads us to believe that some 120 atomic bombs accurately delivered by the USSR might cause the collapse of the United Kingdom without invasion, whereas several hundred bombs might be required by the United States or the United Kingdom to bring about the collapse of the USSR.[45]

This number, however, seems to have been arrived at without any rigorous scientific study being undertaken. Therefore, although the Air Staff Operational Requirement (OR 1001) for an atomic bomb was issued on 8 August 1946, planning on how such weapons might be used remained highly tentative.

This approach contrasted with a systematic analysis of the utility of nuclear weapons carried out in November 1945 by P. M. S. Blackett, who was a member of the Anderson Advisory Committee set up by Attlee to provide advice to the government. Blackett worked his way through a number of different assumptions about potential conflicts between Britain, the United States, and the Soviet Union and analysed various alternative technical assumptions about the development of atomic weapons. He then considered Britain's vulnerable geographical location, the military potential of the Great Powers, and the realities of the political relationship between them. Blackett's conclusion was that Britain's long-term security would be undermined rather than increased by the acquisition of nuclear weapons. The threat to use such weapons as part of a deterrent policy, he argued, would be counterproductive. It would be bound to lead to an aggressive military reaction from the Soviet leadership. Britain should therefore concentrate on the peaceful uses of atomic energy to bolster its industrial fortunes and leave the production of nuclear weapons to the United States.[46]

Despite the intellectual rigour of Blackett's approach, his views were quickly dismissed by both the Chiefs of Staff and the prime minister because they did not fit in with the 'deterrence habit of mind' that was developing. Little attempt was made to provide a detailed rebuttal of the Blackett memorandum. The COS simply argued that they disagreed fundamentally with his conclusions and assumptions, and Attlee expressed the view that 'the author, a distinguished scientist, speaks on political and military problems on which he is a layman'.[47] These views reflected the consensus which existed at the time within the political and military establishment, namely that Britain needed its own nuclear capability. Atomic weapons were seen as being of critical importance in achieving deterrence and securing Britain's political and security interests. Apart from the July 1946 JTWC Report and the Blackett Report, the first 'comprehensive' survey of the requirements of deterrence did not come until July 1947 when Tizard's Defence Research Policy Committee (DRPC) argued that a stockpile of 1,000 bombs would be needed. This figure was based on the conclusions of the Home Defence Committee, which had reported that twenty-five atomic bombs would be sufficient to knock Britain out of a war. The DRPC concluded that because the Soviet Union was roughly forty times the size of the United Kingdom, a deterrent force could be worked out on the basis of twenty-five bombs times forty, making a figure of 1,000! However, as Margaret Gowing has concluded, this 'methodology was so ridiculous' that its conclusions were worthless.[48]

The Decision to 'Go Nuclear' and Issues of Political Identity

One of the puzzles of British nuclear policy in the immediate post-war period is that, despite the rapid development of a 'deterrence habit of mind' amongst many of those involved in strategic planning, the government did not take the formal decision to produce atomic weapons until January 1947. This is even more surprising given the prime minister's apparent determination, on taking office, to make a decision quickly on the issue. On 10 August 1945 Attlee set up an ad hoc committee, known as Gen 75, to act as a 'forum for decision-making on atomic energy policy'. On 29 August he told the committee that 'A decision on major policy with regard to the atomic bomb is imperative. Until this is taken, civil and military departments are unable to plan.'[49] This implied that the first step should be to decide if Britain was going to develop atomic weapons. This would then be followed by a series of further decisions on how this was to be achieved. In practice, however, this process seems to have been reversed. Following the decision in October 1945 to set up the research establishment at Harwell, in December ministers decided that a single pile should be built to produce plutonium. Plutonium was preferred to Uranium 235 on the grounds that it was superior 'for military applications'. In January 1946, Marshal of the Royal Air Force, Lord Portal of Hungerford, was appointed Controller of Production of Atomic Energy within the Ministry of Supply, further confirming the military orientation of the atomic energy programme. The momentum towards atomic weapons production was taken a stage further in the summer of 1946. The JTWC produced 'a comprehensive initial guide to atomic warfare' in July, and in August the Chief of the Air Staff placed a formal requisition for an atomic bomb with the Ministry of Supply, even though as yet no decision had been made by the government to develop atomic weapons. The Official Royal Air Force Historian, Humphrey Wynn, sums up these developments in the following terms:

> by mid-1946 the Chiefs of Staff had recommended that a stock of atomic bombs be built up; an atomic energy production organization had been formed and a controller of production and director of research had been appointed; an Atomic Energy Bill had been published; the Americans had started peacetime testing of atomic weapons, had given Strategic Air Command the responsibility for delivering them and had passed the McMahon Act, designed to secure a US monopoly of atomic weapons until international control of them could be achieved; the Cabinet had accepted COS proposals for the inclusion of atomic weapons, and the means of delivering them, in Britain's future military plans; financial provision for atomic energy R & D had been approved; and the Air Staff had written down its requirement for an atomic bomb. *Yet the Government had not yet authorized the development of atomic weapons, and it was not until early 1947 that it did so.*[50]

The initiative which led to this anomalous situation being rectified came from Lord Portal. On 19 November 1946 he wrote to the prime minister, arguing that a decision was required on the development of atomic weapons. As a direct result of this letter a special ad hoc meeting (Gen 163) of selected government ministers met on 8 January 1947 to consider a paper from Portal. In his submission Portal argued that three courses of action were possible. The first was that Britain should not develop a bomb at all. The second was that a weapon should be produced by means of the ordinary agencies within the Ministry of Supply and the service departments. The third was that a weapon should be produced, but 'under special arrangements conducive to the utmost secrecy'. He went on to argue that he assumed that the first option would not be favoured by the government. If the second option was accepted he warned that the British programme would soon become known and this might diminish the chances of reopening cooperation with the United States. The preferred option, in Portal's view, was a decision to develop atomic weapons in secrecy. He pointed out that the Chiefs of Staff were in agreement with him and he asked for direction on two points: first, whether research and development on atomic weapons was to be undertaken; and second, if so, whether the arrangements outlined in option three were to be followed.[51]

In the debate that followed there seems to have been no opposition to Portal's proposal. The Foreign Secretary stressed that in his view it was vital that Britain pressed on with the study of all aspects of atomic energy because 'she could not afford to acquiesce in an American monopoly of the new development'. This was a view which was supported by all of the ministers present. It was agreed that (a) research and development on atomic weapons should be undertaken and (b) special arrangements should be put in place to make sure that the programme remained secret.

Margaret Gowing has argued that this crucial decision did not emerge as a result of a perception of an immediate threat, but was rather the result of:

> something fundamentalist and almost instinctive—a feeling that Britain must possess so climacteric a weapon in order to deter an atomically armed enemy, a feeling that Britain as a Great Power must acquire all major new weapons, a feeling that atomic weapons were a manifestation of the scientific and technological superiority on which Britain's strength, so deficient if measured in sheer numbers of men, must depend.[52]

Here we see deep-seated ideas inherent in British strategic culture. Great Power status, major weapon systems to deter threats, and the importance of scientific and technological superiority to offset deficiencies in manpower were all important attributes of Britain's traditional military policy. What is intriguing, given what appears to be the almost inevitable nature of the decision to develop atomic weapons, is why it was not taken earlier. In part it may have been the result of the pressure of events facing the government. With the immense tasks of reconstruction at home and the growing difficulties of international relations in the immediate post-war period, it is perhaps not surprising that it took the government some time to get around to tackling the issue formally. It could be argued that, strictly speaking, it was not necessary to make a decision before this date. It was only in late 1946 that military planning had reached the point at which specific decisions on things like the numbers of weapons to be produced and issues relating to the ordnance part of the programme required the authorization of the military programme. It may also have been the case that Attlee's own ambivalent attitude towards international control and a national nuclear programme contributed to the delay. In 1945 the prime minister had argued that a swift decision was necessary. At the same time, however, as we have argued, he had initiated proposals to try and see if some form of international control over atomic weapons could be achieved. It could be that this 'sensitivity on the issue of international control' contributed to a reluctance by the Attlee government to make a firm commitment to the nuclear programme—even though the implications of the decisions taken so far were very much in this direction. Although it is a matter of speculation, in the absence of clear documentary evidence, it seems likely that Attlee was attempting to keep his options open in case of a breakthrough in the negotiations on international control. By January 1947, however, the chances of such an agreement were rapidly declining and, faced with the 'ultimatum' from Portal, it seemed preferable to pursue the goal of an independent nuclear deterrent.

One of the key reasons for the decision to develop atomic weapons was a determination, after the McMahon Act of 1946 (which ended Anglo-American wartime collaboration), to be independent of the United States. The Foreign Secretary in particular was annoyed at the rather dismissive way he was being treated by the US Secretary of State, James Byrnes. He saw atomic weapons as a way of getting the United States to take Britain more seriously. In October 1946 he told his colleagues that:

> We've got to have this. I don't mind for myself but I don't want any other Foreign Secretary of this country to be talked at, or to, by the Secretary of State of the United States, Mr Byrnes. We've got to have this thing over here, whatever it costs... We've got to have a bloody Union Jack flying on top of it.[53]

Attlee also felt that nuclear weapons were essential to hold Britain's position vis à vis the United States. Some years later he expressed the view that 'We couldn't allow ourselves to be wholly in their hands, and their position wasn't awfully clear always... We couldn't agree that only the Americans should have atomic energy.'[54]

Part of this determination to develop atomic weapons so as to be able to pursue a more independent path to the United States, if that became necessary, was due to a continuing belief that Britain remained a Great Power in the world. There were those who felt that Britain's power was declining given the economic strains caused by the exertions of the war. However, this was not something that the government was prepared to accept. Ernest Bevin told the House of Commons on 16 May 1947 that:

> His Majesty's Government do not accept the view... that we have ceased to be a Great Power, or the contention that we have ceased to play that role. We regard ourselves as one of the Powers most vital to the peace of the world and we still have our historic part to play. The very fact that we have fought so hard for liberty, and paid such a price, warrants our retaining this position; indeed it places a duty upon us to continue to retain it. I am not aware of any suggestion, seriously advanced, that by a sudden stroke of fate, as it were, we have overnight ceased to be a Great Power.[55]

Atomic weapons were believed to be vital for Britain to go on playing its traditional role of protecting universal values of international peace and freedom. This is what Britain did.

The Bureaucratic Context

Rhetoric was one thing, but developing a government structure to deal with the unique and complex task of achieving that desired nuclear status proved to be far from straightforward. The failure to make a formal decision to develop atomic weapons until January 1947 meant that there was a lack of clear political direction in the immediate post-war period which was reflected in organizational weaknesses in the atomic energy programme. The system which emerged from 1945 operated on two main levels. At the highest level, the major responsibility for atomic energy lay with the prime minister and the ad hoc committees he established specifically to deal with key issues. Rather than involving the full Cabinet, or even the Cabinet Defence Committee, which was responsible for high-level military matters, Attlee preferred to gather around himself key ministers meeting in informal committees. The membership of these committees tended to vary from time to time, with the prime minister, Foreign Secretary, the Lord President of the Council, and defence minister as the core members who were joined on occasions by the president of the Board of Trade, the Chancellor of the Exchequer, the Lord Privy Seal, or the minister of supply. Although these (Gen) committees had a secretariat, the papers were not distributed to other members of the Cabinet, who remained unaware of the deliberations that took place and the decisions that were made. In February 1947 it was decided to replace these committees with a proper Ministerial Atomic Energy Committee, which was asked 'to deal with questions of policy in the field of atomic energy which required the consideration of Ministers'. As useful as this committee proved to be, in practice it met fairly infrequently and key decisions continued to be taken by the informal committees.

Below this higher level there were a wide range of committees, boards, councils, and departments that had responsibilities for different parts of the atomic energy programme (see Appendix 7). In the early stages, the prime minister himself was heavily involved in atomic issues, particularly the formal decision to develop atomic weapons and the question of international control which 'moved him profoundly'.[56] In time, however, although he continued to chair key committees, his personal involvement seems to have declined, raising questions (which will be touched upon later) about the effectiveness of the political guidance given to the military planners. In the early period, even when Attlee 'exercised especially close personal surveillance', other problems arose, particularly over his choice of Sir John Anderson to chair an Advisory Committee which he set up to report to him directly on atomic energy matters. Anderson was an Independent MP for the Scottish Universities who sat on the opposition front bench in 1945. His wartime experience with the atomic project, however, and his good relationship with the prime minister, made him the ideal person to lead a committee consisting of service personnel, officials, and scientists who could provide the expert advice that Attlee needed. The terms of reference of the Advisory Committee included 'investigating the implications of the use of atomic energy and advising the government on the steps to be taken in the military and industrial fields', as well as bringing forward 'proposals for the international treatment of the subject'. In the period through to the autumn of 1946 the Anderson Committee was central to the key decisions taken. However, concern about the lack of any ministerial responsibility for the committee and Anderson's growing antagonism towards other government policies led to a gradual decline in its role. The committee was finally wound up in December 1947.

The second level in the decision-making structure centred on the two key ministries directly involved in nuclear matters: the Ministry of Supply and the Ministry of Defence. One of the main problems with the Anderson Committee was that it had no formal links with these two ministries, even though the administration of the atomic energy programme was largely their responsibility. The situation was made even worse by the lack of any mechanism to coordinate the work of the Ministry of Supply and the Ministry of Defence. As will be seen, personal differences between key individuals in each ministry did not help matters. There were also problems arising from a lack of control and coordination within the Ministry of Supply itself.

In 1946 the Ministry of Supply was belatedly given administrative responsibility for the atomic energy programme. As we have seen, in early 1946 Lord Portal was appointed as Controller of Production to coordinate research and development work within the ministry, with overall responsibility for the production of nuclear weapons. In some ways Portal's wartime experience and post-war work in the atomic energy field made him an ideal person for this position. As Margaret Gowing has shown, however, his appointment was far from successful. Portal had been 'drained by the war' and 'had little taste for the atomic energy project'. He is described as being 'remote and unbending' and lacking the necessary administrative skills to achieve the kind of coordination required, not only between the research, production, and weapons development sections of the programme within the Ministry of Supply, but also between his own ministry and the Ministry of Defence.[57] To make matters even more confusing, his primary responsibility was to the prime minister and not to the minister of supply in whose ministry he was located.

The other ministry primarily concerned with nuclear policy was the Ministry of Defence, which was set up in 1946. Responsibility for planning within the MOD centred on the Chiefs of Staff and their various committees. Of particular importance were the Atomic Weapons subcommittee of the Deputy COS Committee, the JTWC, and the Joint Planning Staff. The Defence Research Policy Committee (DRPC) under Sir Henry Tizard was also set up in January 1947 to advise the Chiefs of Staff and the minister of defence on scientific policy. Problems arose, however, because no one seemed clear about the responsibility of the Chiefs of Staff for providing the strategic guidance which would govern the production of atomic weapons. And without clear guidance from the COS the various committees proved to be rather less effective than they might have been. Although they were directly responsible for advising the minister of defence and the Cabinet on the strategic issues associated with atomic energy, in practice the advice given by the military chiefs was very limited indeed. In the immediate post-war years they were so preoccupied with the pressing military problems left over from the war that they had little time to focus on the major strategic issues associated with the development of atomic weapons. Their contribution to the debate about atomic energy in 1945–6, therefore, did not go much beyond advising the government that they should develop nuclear weapons as quickly as possible for the purpose of deterrence just in case a system of international control should prove to be unobtainable (as they thought it would).

The lack of coordination between the key committees responsible for the atomic energy programme was clearly apparent in the exclusion of the Defence Research Policy Committee from the decision to develop atomic weapons. As late as June 1947 Tizard and his colleagues were still unaware that in January the government had decided to develop atomic weapons. Despite the fact that he was the Chief Scientist in the Ministry of Defence, Tizard had not been informed. Not surprisingly, this was a situation that he found intolerable. Expressing his growing frustrations with the cumbersome bureaucratic system, in 1947 he wrote: 'If I were the only one who was confused about these matters

I should think it was merely due to my own stupidity, but the Minister of Defence is himself uncertain where responsibility lies.'[58]

Even when attempts were made to improve the bureaucratic arrangements for coordinating policy by setting up two new committees at the end of 1947, in practice little was achieved. The Atomic Energy (Defence Research) Committee was established under Tizard to review and report on relations between defence research programmes as a whole and on atomic energy research. At the same time the Atomic Energy (Review of Production) Committee was set up under Portal to review the scale of atomic energy production in relation to the requirements of defence. The two committees were designed to be complementary, but it was not long before the Review of Production Committee took precedence and the problem of coordinating the production of fissile material with strategic policy remained largely unresolved.

Matters were not made any better by personality clashes within the Chiefs of Staff Committee itself, especially when General Montgomery joined the committee. According to Sir George Mallaby, the Secretary of the Joint Planning Staff, these clashes made any coordination of policy virtually impossible. He argues that when Monty succeeded Brooke as Chief of the Imperial General Staff (CIGS) in 1946, the achievement of unified aims and harmonious cooperation became impossible, and that the main reason for this was that Monty was not in the habit of listening to anybody except his closest advisers. He was not interested in what the Air Chief (Tedder) thought, and hardly disguised his contempt for the somewhat melancholy interventions of the Naval Chief (Cunningham). As for the Joint Planning Staff, 'they were a pack of fools whose reports should be completely ignored'.[59]

These personality clashes in the Chiefs of Staff Committee and the confused nature of the bureaucratic structure set up to deal with the atomic energy programme meant that there was a lack of coordination within the atomic energy project itself and between the atomic weapons programme and other defence affairs with which it was so closely related. This was not helped by civil–military differences over the Soviet Union and important aspects of British strategy.

Contending Attitudes Towards the Soviet Union

Differences arose in the early post-war period between the political leadership and the Chiefs of Staff over whether the Soviet Union should be identified, for strategic planning purposes, as the potential enemy. This clearly had important implications for the coordination of 'High Policy' and 'Strategic Planning'. During the Second World War 'a fundamental cleavage' emerged between the Chiefs of Staff and the Foreign Office over how to interpret the implications of the growing difficulties with the Soviet Union for post-war planning. From 1944 onwards the military chiefs warned that the proposed world organization might break down, and that Russia might then pursue its goal of world domination. In a Post-hostilities Report in November 1944 they pointed out that threats might emerge from a rearmed Germany, the USSR, or—'worst of all'—both. Russia, they warned, had emerged as the 'greatest land power in the world' and to balance its overwhelming military potential Britain would need—'as never before'—powerful allies (particularly the United States), defence in depth on the Continent, and technical superiority in the application of science to warfare.[60]

For Foreign Office officials, although the dangers of Soviet intransigence were becoming increasingly clear, there were great dangers in planning on the basis of a Russian threat which might become self-fulfilling. The Foreign Secretary, Anthony Eden, warned the Chiefs of Staff that trying to maintain friendship with the Soviet Union would be of crucial importance to Britain's post-war security interests, and hence everything had to be done to avoid being seen to be 'ganging up' on Russia. As far as the Foreign Office was concerned the 'anti-Russian extravagances' of the Chiefs of Staff were likely to 'precipitate the evils against which it was intended to guard'.[61] This reflected Foreign Office sensitivity to the 'security dilemma' in which states often find themselves.[62] It was important, the Foreign Office believed, not to do things which might be seen by the Soviet leaders as threatening and which might cause them to react in a way which would undermine British security interests. The Chiefs of Staff, however, remained less susceptible to these sensitivities.

The ambiguous nature of these attitudes towards the Soviet Union continued into the post-war period. While the COS pressed for the Soviet Union to be formally identified as the major threat to British worldwide security interests, the Foreign Office, despite its growing anxieties about Russian policies, urged a continuation of cooperation with Russia. This latter approach was spelled out in a report entitled 'Stock-Taking after V-E Day', which was written in July 1945 by Orme Sargent, the Deputy Under-Secretary of State in the Foreign Office.[63] In his report Sargent suggested that Britain should 'ceaselessly' pursue the goal of three-power cooperation. Despite all of the difficulties which had emerged in dealing with the Russians, he argued that it was unlikely that Stalin would risk war. What was needed was a firm policy, coordinated with the United States, to persuade the Soviet Union of the merits of cooperation.

Even when some Foreign Office officials became convinced in 1946 and early 1947 that the Soviet Union was practising 'the most vicious power politics' which might lead to conflict (thus joining forces with the military 'advocacy coalition'), Bevin and Attlee continued to refuse to allow the Chiefs of Staff to plan formally on the basis of a Russian threat.[64] Even though the Foreign Secretary and the prime minister acknowledged the hostile nature of Soviet policies they castigated officials for 'loose talk' about anti-Soviet groupings which they felt might undermine continuing efforts to achieve an accommodation with Moscow.[65] It was only after the collapse of the London Foreign Ministers' meeting in December 1947 that the Foreign Secretary gave up all hope of reaching an agreement with the Soviet leaders. It was then that the military leaders were given the green light to plan on the basis of the Soviet Union as the major threat to Britain's security interests. In practice, however, they had been doing this informally for some considerable time. In a major review of British strategy produced in May 1947, the Chiefs of Staff quite specifically identified the Soviet Union as 'the primary and only conceivable threat to British interests'. They argued that calculations of national interest would determine whether the Soviet Union would use atomic weapons against Britain when it acquired them. This led them to the view that:

> The only means whereby we can prevent her using them... is by facing her with the threat of large scale damage from similar weapons if she should employ them. This threat can only be achieved by evidence of our ability to use weapons of mass destruction on a considerable scale from the outset. In addition we believe that the knowledge that we possessed weapons of mass destruction and were prepared to use them would be a most effective deterrent to war itself. The decision of whether or not to use these weapons obviously cannot be taken now. The one certain point is that it must be a cardinal principle of our policy to be prepared, equipped and able to use them immediately.[66]

However, such an endorsement of deterrence directed firmly at the Soviet Union was not one that Attlee and his colleagues were willing to accept at the time. The prime minister believed that the planning assumptions behind the 1947 review, which emphasized the Soviet 'threat', were 'dangerous'. He was soon to change his mind as the Cold War gathered momentum.

The Middle East in Britain's Early Atomic Strategy

Apart from these differences between political and military leaders over the Soviet 'threat', there were also major disagreements during the early post-war period over the importance of the Middle East in British strategy. In early 1946 the prime minister challenged the Chiefs of Staff on the central focus given in their strategic deliberations to the Middle East and the Mediterranean. In his view this reflected old 'imperialist' thinking which required a reassessment. In reply the COS produced a paper in April justifying the need to retain bases in the Middle East, particularly in the context of their new policy of deterrence against the Soviet Union. They emphasized that important targets in the Soviet Union could not be reached from the United Kingdom, and the Middle East bases were essential as part of an air campaign which would have to be conducted if deterrence broke down.[67]

The prime minister, however, remained sceptical about the arguments put forward by the military chiefs and in July the COS felt it necessary to reinforce their earlier arguments. Once again they stressed that bases in the Middle East were a vital part of the defence of the United Kingdom itself: 'It is only from the Middle East area that effective air action can be taken', they told the prime minister. The area was essential for deterrence, and if war came it would also help to divert Russian resources away from attacks on Britain itself. Attlee, however, was still not convinced.[68] On 5 January 1947 he sent a memorandum to Bevin in which he argued that the atomic strategy developed by the Chiefs of Staff was 'one of despair'. He did not believe, he wrote, that such a strategy was a credible deterrent against an attack by the Soviet Union, and in his view it was more likely 'to provoke rather than deter Moscow'. The prime minister conceded that there was real uncertainty about Soviet behaviour but, in his opinion, it remained far from clear that the Soviet leaders were intent on world domination. It might be that 'changes in British strategic doctrine and posture would convince the Soviet leaders that the United Kingdom had no offensive intentions against them'.[69] Attlee did not push the matter further, but the memorandum provides clear evidence of his continuing ambivalence about an atomic strategy and his sensitivity about the security dilemma.

What is interesting about this debate, apart from the prime minister's criticisms of the strategic ideas developed by the COS, is that the military planners themselves had clearly not considered, at this early stage, the question of whether nuclear weapons were primarily required for deterrence or for war-fighting. Were these notions separate or were they related? No real thought seems to have been given to this question. At times they seemed to be espousing a concept of 'deterrence through punishment' (by threatening Soviet cities), while at other times more emphasis was given to a concept of 'deterrence through denial' (which involved the threat to attack Soviet military and war-making capabilities). The Middle East bases were appropriate for attacking Soviet oil installations in the Caucasus, while the main thrust of strategic planning focused on the primacy of city targetting. As Clark and Wheeler have rightly argued, 'although in theory the Chiefs made a distinction between deterring war and conducting war that had already broken out, their arguments for retention of air bases in the Middle East drifted back and forth between a deterrent and operational war-fighting role'.[70] These problems were to be a recurring theme.

Conclusion

At the end of 1947 British thinking about nuclear weapons in both military and political circles remained in a state of uncertainty. Work was progressing steadily on establishing a wide range of atomic research and production facilities with a view to developing an independent nuclear capability.[71] Based on the acknowledgement that Britain was particularly vulnerable to atomic attack a widespread consensus had been established in favour of deterrence. By this stage, the prime minister's earlier hopes for 'a better ordering of human affairs'[72] were beginning to fade and civil–military differences over the Soviet 'threat' and Middle Eastern strategy were much less acute than they had been in the first half of the year. However, two problems remained largely unresolved. The first of these centred on the lack of clear political guidance for future nuclear strategy. On issues such as international control the prime minister played a key part in the decision-making process, as he did on the key decision in January 1947 to develop atomic weapons. This confirms Hyman's thesis about the critical role of top political leaders in decisions to 'go nuclear'. The thesis, however, ignores the role of other important members of the ad hoc committees and other members of the 'nuclear advocacy coalition'. On most other issues, especially those relating to strategic planning, Attlee seems to have played almost no part beyond the occasional criticism of what he described as the Chiefs of Staff's 'strategy of despair'. Little attempt was made to establish agreement on the numbers of atomic weapons that would be required (given the differences between military planners on the subject) or to provide political guidance on the kinds of strategic targets which might be most appropriate (on which there was also some disagreement between defence officials). Questions therefore remained with regard to whether such issues were the primary responsibility of the military chiefs or the political leaders. At the time these issues seem to have been regarded as largely technical matters, better left to the military chiefs and their committees, whereas in fact they were matters of 'High Policy' which required clear political direction. This meant that a wide range of other groups (departments, boards, committees, and subcommittees) and individuals that supported the atomic weapons programme played a significant role in the planning and execution of policy. Such an approach has remained very much a feature of nuclear decision-making in Britain ever since. Apart from the military chiefs, as Tanya Ogilvie-White has argued, while a select group of ministers take the ultimate decisions,

> the information and analysis on which those decisions are based, and in fact recommendations on the most appropriate course of action, are provided by the

policy directors and the highest-ranking civil servants in the Ministry of Defence and Cabinet Office, with varying degrees of input from their counterparts in the Foreign and Commonwealth Office and the Treasury.[73]

The second (and related) problem which remained largely unresolved centred on the difficulty of coordinating the different aspects of nuclear strategy. The absence of firm political guidance exacerbated the problems associated with the complexities and inadequacies of the organizational 'structure' set up to develop atomic weapons and coordinate weapons production with the requirements of strategy. The use of informal ministerial committees, a Chairman of the Advisory Committee who was a member of the Opposition in Parliament, personality clashes within the atomic energy bureaucracy (as well as amongst the Chiefs of Staff), and a division between the Ministry of Supply and the Ministry of Defence meant that it remained extremely difficult to bring together all the parts of the atomic energy programme and related areas of defence. The frustration which these organizational inadequacies caused in defence circles is evident in the question asked by Sir Henry Tizard in 1947: 'For what war are we supposed to be preparing?'[74] This difficulty was to feature prominently in the ongoing debates which took place about what kind of nuclear strategy Britain should adopt. This reflected differences within parts of the 'nuclear advocacy coalition'.

2

The Chiefs of Staff, Nuclear Weapons, and Global Strategy

> *The Global Strategy Paper (of 1952) in due course strongly influenced the evolution of strategic doctrine in the West. It eventually led Britain to become the first nation to base its national security planning almost entirely upon a declaratory policy of nuclear deterrence.*
>
> Andrew Pierre[1]

The Chiefs of Staff were perhaps the most important group in the 'nuclear advocacy coalition' in Britain in the late 1940s and early 1950s. As the main military advisers to the government their beliefs were crucial to the development of an operational nuclear deterrent strategy. However, as the last chapter suggests, it would be wrong to conclude that there was no disagreement amongst them on the operational nature of that strategy. This chapter focuses on the debates between Britain's senior military officers that led to the Global Strategy Paper of 1952 which, as the American writer Andrew Pierre has argued, had a significant impact upon the nuclear strategies of the United States and NATO, and led to Britain becoming the first nation to put nuclear weapons at the forefront of its defence planning.

British Strategic Planning, 1947–50

As we have seen, the Chiefs of Staff had for many years been thinking in terms of deterrence.[2] As early as October 1945 they had stated that 'the best method of defence against the new weapon is likely to be the deterrent effect that the possession of the means of retaliation would have on a potential aggressor.'[3] The same theme was present in the Overall Strategic Plan of 1947, which contained not a strategy for fighting a war against the Soviet Union, but rather one for preventing it.[4] This reflected a widespread perception within British defence circles that the United Kingdom was peculiarly vulnerable to atomic air attack, making it essential that atomic war did not break out at all.[5]

However, as well as necessitating a policy of war prevention, atomic weapons also made it possible. The Chiefs realized that although these weapons could devastate Britain, the British and their allies could, with atomic air forces of their own, inflict huge destruction on others. By threatening to do so they could hope to achieve the aim of war prevention. In their 1947 Plan they stressed again that the knowledge that the West possessed and was 'prepared to use' atomic weapons 'would be a most effective deterrent to war itself'.[6] Although nuclear deterrence was recognized as a vitally important policy by British defence planners, early thinking on the subject had assumed that Britain would acquire its own nuclear weapons before the Soviet Union. This assumption was undermined by the first Soviet atomic test, late in 1949, in the shadow of which a strategic review was conducted. In the 1950 Global Strategy Paper which resulted, one of the two main changes in the strategic situation identified by the Chiefs of Staff since their previous review in 1947 was 'the discovery by Russia of the atomic bomb'.[7]

The 1950 Paper reflected the impact of this shock development. Although it set great store on the importance of the Western deterrent, it also emphasized the vital need for an efficient air defence system to protect a Britain made vulnerable to Soviet atomic attack unexpectedly early. It was hoped that advances in guided missile technology would be able to provide some defence against atomic air attack (and it was even predicted that the time could come when such missiles would make the manned bomber and the main deterrent obsolete).[8] The Chiefs were willing to slow down their own atomic weapons programme in order to devote greater resources to guided missiles.[9]

To some extent this focus on defence against atomic weapons implied a dilution of the importance of deterrence. The Chiefs also displayed some caution about the power of nuclear weapons in the 1950 Paper, warning that these weapons should not be seen as 'an easy short cut to victory'.[10]

The Origins of the 1952 Global Strategy Paper

Shortly after the election of October 1951, the new Churchill government concluded that Britain's defence policy was in need of revision. Two reasons in particular informed this belief. First, it was felt that the deterioration in Britain's economic position over the past year required savings to be made in the defence budget. Specifically, the ambitious rearmament programme begun by the Attlee government two years previously could no longer be sustained, and the improvements in conventional forces agreed by the North Atlantic Treaty Organisation (NATO) at its February 1952 Lisbon meeting could no longer be afforded.[11] Second, Winston Churchill, in his second stint as prime minister, held a strong belief that insufficient account was being taken in current British (and Western) defence planning of the value of nuclear weapons. This conviction had been reinforced at the start of the year when Churchill was briefed in Washington on the American strategic air plan.[12] Taken together, these factors persuaded the Churchill government to instruct the Chiefs of Staff to review British strategy. It was their belief in the need for a nuclear deterrent strategy which was at the heart of the Global Strategy Paper that emerged as a result of their review.

The Chiefs took their task seriously. Between 28 April and 2 May 1952 they reconsidered British strategy in the calm of the Royal Naval College, Greenwich, away from their daily routines.[13] The eventual result of their deliberations was a report on Defence Policy and Global Strategy, which remains perhaps the best-known, the most often discussed, and also one of the most highly regarded British defence documents of the Cold War period. The 1952 Global Strategy Paper, as it is usually titled, has been described as 'an important innovation in military thought', and, by Churchill himself, as 'a state paper of the greatest importance'.[14] While some commentators have questioned the significance and innovatory character of the Paper, the majority view it as 'a classic among military documents'.[15]

Those who subscribe to this view stress that the Paper was both important and influential. It was important, they argue, because it made Britain 'the first nation to base its national security planning almost entirely upon a declaratory policy of nuclear deterrence', and in so doing 'set out the basis of British strategic ideas in the nuclear age'.[16] The Paper is said to have influenced not only the future development of British strategy, but also 'the evolution of strategic doctrine in the West' as a whole.[17] In particular, it has been credited by some with influencing the Eisenhower administration's 'New Look' at defence policy in 1953, which put nuclear weapons at the heart of the US strategy of Massive Retaliation.[18]

Key Themes in the 1952 Global Strategy Paper

1. *Political and Economic Factors*

The Paper comprised two main parts: one on 'The Problems facing the Free World' and the other on 'The Problems facing the United Kingdom'.[19] It did not specifically emphasize nuclear weapons and deterrence by affording them major sections in the Paper. Indeed, by looking at British strategy in the context of Alliance strategy, the organization of the Paper, like that of 1950, illustrated Britain's awareness of its dependence on allies for its security.

This awareness was not new. It is evident from various defence documents of the early post-war period (and indeed of the wartime years) that contemporary policy-makers believed that alliances would be of major importance to Britain in the future.[20] In the 1947 Overall Strategic Plan, the Chiefs of Staff stressed that only with the aid of allies—and primarily the United States—could Britain hope to combat Soviet military strength.[21] The emphasis on Alliance considerations, however, was especially pronounced in the 1952 Paper because of the changes which it recommended in British and NATO strategies. The Chiefs of Staff were keenly aware of the need to convince their allies of the weaknesses of the existing strategies and the need for reform. At the same time, they warned that the task of informing the allies of British plans would need 'careful consideration' and stressed the importance of securing American backing.[22] The Paper therefore has to be read partly as a political document intended to persuade Britain's allies of the necessity for change.

In outlining why alteration of NATO strategy was necessary, the Chiefs reflected the government's concerns. They identified two key factors: 'the notable increase in United States atomic power and the economic situation'.[23] Regarding the former, the Chiefs felt that NATO planners had not sufficiently recognized the value of nuclear weapons. There was in the 'background' of NATO strategy a 'vague assumption' that the Americans had the capability to attack the Soviet Union with atomic bombs. Of the NATO states, however, only the US, Britain, and possibly Canada knew much about the atomic bomb. The other Alliance members could not 'estimate for themselves its full potentialities' and thus could not 'assess its possible strategic effects in war'.[24]

Because of this, NATO planning for the defence of Western Europe did not take sufficient account of the power of atomic weapons.[25] After their visit to the United States with Churchill, the Chiefs of Staff had 'reason to rate much more highly than previously' the size of the American nuclear arsenal and the ability of the US Strategic Air Command to attack targets in the USSR.[26] Their assessment was that, in the event of Soviet aggression, Russia would over the following few weeks 'be subjected to such a devastating attack upon so high a proportion of her vital centres that she would be unlikely to survive it as a Power capable of waging a full scale war'.[27] It was clear to the Chiefs of Staff that NATO strategy needed to be revised in the light of this American power.

Changing economic circumstances were the second factor identified by the Chiefs as requiring a revision of strategy. When the West's rearmament programme had been initiated eighteen months previously the economic situation had been 'comparatively rosy'.[28] Since then various developments had combined to undermine the economic strength of Britain and Western Europe. These included unprecedented rises in the costs of materials and labour and a general deterioration in the financial positions of Britain, the Commonwealth countries, and Western Europe. By early 1952 the British economy was in crisis. The critical balance of payments situation necessitated an increase in the export programme, particularly in the metal-using industries, and a cut in overseas expenditure on the services. The danger was that if nothing was done to meet the financial crisis, a further drain of gold and dollar reserves could force the United Kingdom to withdraw forces from the continent. The economies of the Western European states would also be crippled, undermining their defence efforts. The Chiefs feared that this would result in a 'bloodless victory' for the Soviet Union.[29]

Yet, as recently as February 1952, NATO had agreed in its Lisbon force goals to build up a force of 96 divisions and 9,000 aircraft by 1954 to counter the perceived Soviet superiority in conventional forces.[30] This commitment to conventional rearmament reflected the aims of the American NSC-68 document of April 1950.[31] Given the severe economic problems facing Britain and the countries of Western Europe, however, this was viewed as increasingly unrealistic by the British government and the Chiefs of Staff. Even with increased and continuing American aid (which the Chiefs did not believe would be forthcoming) there was no possibility whatsoever that the continental allies would be able to live up to 'their scheduled contributions of land and air forces fit to fight and in time'.[32] Moreover, it was a central argument of the Paper that the West had to now prepare to face a protracted Cold War rather than an immediate threat of 'hot war'. The logic of this position, argued the Chiefs, was that defence spending had to be kept to a level which the economies of Western Europe could continue to bear for many years. This would involve taking recent technical advances fully into account, which had not been done when the Lisbon force goals had been decided. As a result, the Chiefs warned, the Alliance was in danger of committing the serious error of attempting 'to superimpose a new atomic strategy upon the old traditional strategy'. NATO could not afford to make this mistake. It would be better advised to formulate a new strategy that integrated atomic and conventional forces.[33] The Chiefs did not explicitly state whether strategic or economic factors were more important, and since both pointed to the same sort of change—greater reliance on atomic power and less investment in conventional forces—it is difficult to determine which weighed more heavily in their deliberations. However, on reading the Paper one is left with the distinct impression that economic pressures were decisive in forcing a rethink of policy. In the second section of the Paper, for instance, the Chiefs stated that 'This review of British global strategy originated in instructions...to reconsider the United Kingdom rearmament programme on the assumption that it would be necessary for economic reasons to accept drastic cuts in planned defence expenditure in the coming years.'[34] Moreover, in a covering letter submitted to the Defence Committee with the Report, the Chiefs made no mention of the rise of American atomic power, but did explain that their recommendations resulted from 'the new situation that has been produced by economic necessity'.[35]

2. The Threat to the West

If the primary cause of the 1952 defence review is uncertain, the 1952 Paper, like previous policy statements, was absolutely clear about the threat posed to the West by 'the implacable and unlimited aims of Soviet Russia'. The Chiefs were convinced that the Soviet Union's ultimate goal was no less than 'world-domination'.[36] On the threat posed by China, however, there had been some change in thinking since 1950. In the 1950 Paper, the Chiefs of Staff dealt with China only in those sections relating to the Cold War in the Far East. A careful distinction was made between an anti-communist and an anti-Chinese policy in the region. The Chiefs felt that Chinese xenophobia would make Sino-Soviet relations awkward, and while they opposed appeasing China, they were keen not to drive her into the 'arms of Russia'.[37] By 1952, following Chinese intervention in the Korean War, the Chiefs were more pessimistic. China was mentioned along with the USSR in the introduction to the 1952 Paper on the basic problem facing the West, and was reassessed as 'a potentially great military power'. The Chinese were also now thought to be working 'hand-in-glove' with the Soviet Union to extend communist influence. Differences existed between the two states, which the West should try to exploit, but the Chiefs now feared that 'the community of military interests of Russia and China—at any rate in the short term—outweighs potential clashes of interest between them'.[38]

The Paper also reveals a change in thinking about the nature of the Soviet threat. The Chiefs revised their view of the risk of all-out war, taking issue with the assumption underpinning the existing Alliance strategy that there was a strong possibility of a Soviet attack on the West in the near future.[39] The Chiefs argued, as they had in their 1950 review, that traditional Russian policy was in practice defensive, involving 'a tactical withdrawal when faced with determined opposition'.[40] But now that Western strength had increased to the point where Russia faced the prospect of devastation in the event of aggression, it had missed its best chance 'for using war as a means of furthering her aims'.[41] Moreover, the mood of 1950, when the intervention of Chinese forces in Korea had 'made world war seem much more imminent', had passed.[42] The Chiefs now felt able to assert that 'the likelihood of war is more remote than was thought two years ago' (which was another, though less important, factor requiring a review of strategy).[43] In 1952 it was believed that the much more serious and immediate threat came from the Cold War, which seemed certain to be long and drawn out.[44] In the subsequent debates within the Alliance, especially with the Americans, this emphasis on the need to focus more attention on fighting the Cold War with the Soviet Union was a distinctive feature of the British attempt to revise NATO strategy.[45]

3. Nuclear Weapons and Deterrence

The Chiefs of Staff emphasized, however, that their Cold War policy could only be successful under the cover of the 'great deterrent'.[46] This deterrent would primarily be 'the knowledge on the part of the Kremlin that any aggression on their part will involve immediate and crushing retaliation by the long-range Air Striking Force with the atomic weapon'.[47] It should be the 'first essential' of allied policy 'to establish and maintain as long as may be necessary' the atomic force which would constitute 'a really effective deterrent against war'.[48] This stress on the development of deterrence thinking is one of the features of the 1952 Global Strategy Paper which is most often noted. Certainly, one of the main purposes of the Paper was to provide the strategic rationale for British negotiators in their dealings with their NATO allies, and especially the Americans, who in 1952 were pressing the European allies for greater contributions to Alliance conventional defence in line with the Lisbon goals.[49]

The Chiefs understood that nuclear weapons were not the answer to every problem which might confront the West. It is noteworthy, for example, that they did not see nuclear weapons as the best deterrent to China, as they did to Russia. They opposed the use of atomic weapons against China partly because the attack on Russia would require the bulk of available forces, so that the remainder would not have the desired military effect, and partly as atomic attacks on China would succeed only in turning public opinion in Asia against the West.[50] Also, in the case of certain minor aggressions it was recognized that the Western response would have to be conventional. The Paper states that 'Local actions—for instance the Greek, Indo-Chinese and Korean Wars—in which for political reasons the atom bomb is debarred, cannot be won without soldiers on the ground.'[51] The Chiefs of Staff therefore recognized in the 1952 Paper that there were limits to the value of nuclear weapons and deterrence. Nevertheless, their estimate of the utility of these weapons remained high.

Moreover, in contrast with the consensus in the United States, the Chiefs did not believe that the deterrent value of nuclear weapons would be greatly lessened as the Russians built up their own nuclear stockpile, provided that two conditions were met.[52] First, the intention of the allies to use atomic weapons immediately in the event of aggression had to be made 'unmistakably clear to the Russians'.[53] Second, irrespective of the relative size of the nuclear stockpiles on each side, the allies had to have the capability to carry out their own atomic air strike. As the Chiefs of Staff put it: 'The world is passing out of the era when the number of atom bombs is the crux of the matter and is entering an era when the main problem will be to ensure by all means that the weapons can be delivered without prohibitive loss to the attacker.'[54] For this to be achieved, they argued that it would be necessary for the West to keep one step ahead of the Russians in a wide variety of fields of scientific development.[55] That there was a degree of ambiguity on this matter, however, is suggested by one of the conclusions to the report, which argued that 'the Western Allies must keep their lead in atomic weapons'.[56] This echoed remarks from the 1950 Paper which stressed the importance of 'Western superiority in atomic air power', and warned of the possibility that once the Soviets had built up a large stockpile of their own, Western policy might be weakened by the 'fear of precipitating a war'.[57] This problem could best be countered by providing adequate defences against atomic attack. By 1952, on the other hand, although such defences were considered unattainable, the Chiefs on the whole saw little reason to doubt the effectiveness of the deterrent.

4. *The Idea of 'Deterrence in Concert'*

In the 1952 Paper the Chiefs wrote that in the event of war 'Britain was likely to be the first and principal target of the Russian atomic attack'.[58] War therefore had to be prevented by emphasizing nuclear weapons. For economic reasons, the major responsibility for providing the deterrent had to lie with the United States. But the Chiefs believed that it would be 'quite wrong for the United Kingdom to take no share' in the Western deterrent force. Despite the need to rely on the United States, British and American interests were not identical. This meant that it would not be 'possible to rely on the American Air Force to deal adequately with targets which are not of such direct strategic interest to the United States'. Some British contribution to Western nuclear forces was, in the view of the Chiefs of Staff, essential in order to deal with Soviet forces which would directly threaten Britain, such as 'the bases of enemy long-range bombers and U-boats'.[59]

The idea of using a British contribution to the Western deterrent to attack such targets was not new. It had been present in British thinking since at least late 1949, and, it has been argued, even earlier than that.[60] Following the Soviet atomic test, more attention was devoted to the issue of striking at Soviet atomic bomber bases as a means of reducing the scale of assault Britain would suffer in the event of an attack.[61] The 1952 Paper endorsed the view that the British nuclear force would constitute 'an essential defensive factor in the form of attack at source'.[62] The Air Defence Committee had apparently estimated that such an attack at source could reduce the threat posed by atomic air attack by 50 per cent. While the Chiefs regarded this as 'somewhat optimistic', once air defence against atomic attack had been abandoned, a counter-military strike offered the only means of defence available.[63]

There were, therefore, sound strategic grounds for a British nuclear force. However, Britain's contribution to the Western deterrent force was necessary for other purposes too. In particular, it had a political rationale: to influence American policy in war and in peacetime. The Chiefs believed that:

> to have no share in what is recognised as the main deterrent in the Cold War, and the only allied offensive in world war, would seriously weaken British influence on American policy and planning in the Cold War, and in war would mean that the United Kingdom would have no claim to any share in the policy or planning of the offensive.[64]

This point was reinforced later in the Paper when the Chiefs argued that 'we consider it would be most unwise for the United Kingdom to be completely dependent on the United States and to accept the serious political disadvantages of not having a stock of atom bombs under its own control'.[65] This meant that Britain had to press ahead urgently with its own research programme and build up its medium bomber force. Despite this stress on independence, the Chiefs were clearly not interested in the development of a wholly independent British nuclear deterrent. Britain had to play its part 'in concert' with the United States. The Chiefs even hoped that supplies of American atomic bombs would be made available to Britain in an emergency. They believed that Britain had been close to reaching an agreement with the Americans in 1949 which would have provided a stock of American-made bombs held under British control in this country. The Fuchs affair had put paid to this agreement.[66] However, following their recent contact with their counterparts in the United States, the Chiefs of Staff were confident that, after the forthcoming American election and the first British atomic explosion, the abortive agreement of 1949 could be revived. In any event, they felt that it was 'probable that if war came a stock of American atom bombs would be made available for use by the Royal Air Force'.[67]

5. *COS Views on Disarmament*

An alternative to the chosen policy of nuclear deterrence and preparation for war would have been to press for disarmament. However, the Chiefs of Staff took a firm stand in the 1952 Paper (as they had in the 1950 Paper) against what they regarded as an overly emotional approach in some sectors of society towards nuclear disarmament. This concern was summed up in their warning that: 'The idea of outlawing atomic warfare naturally appeals to the best sentiments of all decent people, as well as to the unreasoning instinct of self-preservation. Therein lies its danger.'[68]

The Chiefs of Staff argued that it would be impossible for the Western states to contain the Soviet Union and China by conventional means. What was needed was the application of science—in which the West had a distinct advantage—to offset the inherent manpower advantages of the communist states. This meant that the pressure for disarmament had to be resisted in order to preserve the deterrent to war, which could be justified on moral grounds. The Chiefs averred that 'the existence of the great atomic deterrent is of vital importance to humanity'. For deterrence to work, and for security to be maintained, it was important, they believed, that the West retained the freedom to use nuclear weapons. This represented an important recurring theme in British deterrent thinking down to the present day. For deterrence to work, it was necessary to have plans for nuclear use. The Chiefs believed that because of this, public opinion had to be educated to 'see beyond emotion and to appreciate the reality' of international security requirements.[69]

It is of some interest that certain paragraphs of the Cabinet version of the 1952 Paper relating to disarmament were removed before declassification.[70] Scrutiny of other Chiefs of Staff documents, however, reveals that these paragraphs refer to Britain's policy on the sensitive issue of chemical and bacteriological warfare. In a Chiefs of Staff paper written on 15 July 1952 reference is made to the missing paragraphs, and government policy on the matter is spelled out quite explicitly in the following terms: 'The Allies should not take up a position which would deprive them of their ability to use Chemical Warfare or Bacteriological Warfare in retaliation, if this were to their advantage.'[71] It appears from the Chiefs of Staff paper that this statement represented an amendment to the views expressed in the original Global Strategy Paper. Precisely what was said in the original, however, remains unknown.

What this does reveal, however, is that the Churchill government was not only prepared to sanction the use of nuclear weapons in the event of war, but was also prepared to contemplate the use of chemical and bacteriological weapons if this proved necessary. Whether this would be in retaliation to the use of similar weapons by the Soviet Union or simply in retaliation to a Soviet attack on the West using conventional forces is not clear.[72]

COS Differences About the Nature of Future War

Disarmament having been rejected as an approach to security in favour of maintaining and enhancing Western military strength, plans had to be made for the possibility of war. While the 1952 Paper was firmly based on the belief that all-out war was not imminent and could be prevented, the possibility of war could not be entirely discounted. Western planning had to proceed on the basis that war might still occur. Should it do so, the Chiefs of Staff predicted that the Soviet Union would attempt to overrun Western Europe and neutralize US atomic bases in Britain by atomic attacks. They did not believe that Russia would have the capability in the near future to deliver a decisive atomic attack on the United States. It was thought highly likely, though, that the Soviets would 'make a limited atomic attack on that country for diversionary effect and in the hope of locking up considerable American forces'. In reply the United States would certainly react with an all-out atomic attack on Russia, designed to 'cripple her war-making capacity and her ability to support her forces in the field'.[73] All this would add up to an opening phase of 'unparalleled intensity' in a future world war.[74]

One of the interesting features of the Paper is the way it reflects the inter-service disagreements of the time. One such disagreement centred on the question of how war would develop after the initial nuclear phase. There is considerable discussion in the secondary literature about the inclusion in the Paper of a section on 'broken-backed' warfare. Most accounts conclude that while Marshal of the RAF Sir John Slessor, the Chief of the Air Staff, did not believe that much military activity would take place after the nuclear phase, he allowed—as a concession to the First Sea Lord, Admiral Sir Rhoderick McGrigor—a passage stating that there would be a subsequent phase in which both sides would continue to fight with their remaining forces. This 'broken-backed' warfare would be waged more at sea than elsewhere. This would guarantee a role for the Royal Navy, vital if McGrigor was to support the rest of the Paper.[75] Inspection of the Paper shows that the term 'broken-backed' is not in fact used in this context;[76] nevertheless, the essence of the conventional account is confirmed by the Paper. The Chiefs asserted that it was both 'difficult and dangerous' to forecast the length of a future war, a point illustrated by their subsequent conflicting remarks.[77] At one point it was argued that war 'may last only a few weeks: but at the end of that period it seems certain that both sides, particularly Russia and the United Kingdom, will have suffered terrible damage'.[78] Later, however, the Paper states that war might also involve a long-drawn-out period of chaos 'with an intermittent struggle gradually spreading world-wide'.[79] The point is also made that if the atomic offensive in the opening phase had not already been decisive, its effects would be apparent and the following phase, if war continued, would be at a greatly reduced intensity, 'though perhaps less at sea than elsewhere'.[80] The first statement reflected the views of Sir John Slessor; the others were closer to those of Sir Rhoderick McGrigor.

This significant ambiguity in the Chiefs' thinking was further evident in the discussion in the Paper about what preparations should be made for a 'hot war'. One argument advanced was that the logical conclusion of the picture of future war painted by the Paper must be that the allies would have to concentrate on the measures that would best contribute to their defence 'in the opening phase and to the violence of the initial assault upon the enemy'.[81] However, the Chiefs then conceded that it was not possible for the allies to go 'all the way in giving effect to this conclusion'. The Alliance should not plan 'exclusively for a short war'.[82] Compounding the confusion, they go on to reverse the argument once more by saying that: 'Nevertheless, we think that... the fact that it is economically impracticable to make the preparations necessary for a long war should be faced, and a guiding principle of the rearmament programme should be to ensure survival in the short opening phase.'[83]

The Chiefs therefore remained divided over whether it was necessary to plan for a long war or a short war, but, as in 1950, they gave priority to surviving the initial onslaught.[84] There is perhaps additional evidence of this ambiguity in the Chiefs' thinking in those sections of the Paper that discuss the 'mortal threat' to Britain's sea lines of communication posed by the prospect of an intense Soviet mining and U-boat campaign, along with atomic attacks on British ports. Even in the opening intense phase of war this would be a major problem. The provision of a variety of countermeasures was thus a 'high priority commitment'. Yet it is hard to see how such Soviet measures could force Britain to starve in a war which lasted only a few weeks: surely attacks on sea communications would only become a serious threat in a longer struggle? The Paper noted that the commitment to measures to counter this threat 'must be conditioned by the probable nature and duration of a future war', but did not elaborate on the implications of this remark.[85]

The 'Complementary Deterrent'

If the Chiefs of Staff were not entirely in agreement about what forces should be provided for fighting after the initial phase of a war, they did nevertheless emphasize the need for land and air forces at a high state of readiness in Western Europe. Such forces would complement the nuclear deterrent, for if they were maintained at a high enough level the Russians would realize that the allies had the capability of making any Soviet advance across Europe slow and difficult. This delay itself would be important in deterring the Soviet Union. But it would also serve the purpose, if deterrence broke down, of enabling 'the Allied air offensive to be effective before Europe has been overrun'.[86] (The Chiefs stressed the importance of defending Europe as far east as possible, for Russian occupation of Western Europe would have an 'appalling' effect on European civilization.[87]) This emphasis on conventional capabilities is something which has not been recognized in some of the secondary accounts, which tend to stress the priority given to nuclear deterrence in the Paper.[88]

The Chiefs of Staff, nevertheless, identified a problem in the provision of 'the complementary deterrent'. Although some increase in Alliance conventional forces had already occurred, there was still room for improvement. Until this was achieved the Soviet Union might be tempted to take advantage of allied weakness by confronting the West with local 'faits accompli'.[89] The key question which the Chiefs did not address, however, was exactly how these increases in Western conventional forces were to be achieved. In particular, how were Britain's Western European allies to be convinced of the need to increase their forces when the British were simultaneously recommending that their own conventional contribution to the build-up of Alliance forces should be reduced?

These reductions were spelled out in the section of the Paper covering the British contribution to Western defence. Given that there was no immediate danger of war, it was argued that certain risks might be taken 'in the light of the present economic situation'. This meant that the expansion of British conventional forces initiated by the previous Labour government could be cut back.[90] The planned RAF force of 1,550 aircraft was now both 'economically unattainable' and 'strategically unsuitable'. Major reductions to around 800 front-line aircraft were envisaged, with a change in emphasis away from tactical aircraft to medium bombers. There could also be cutbacks in other areas of air defence (including medium anti-aircraft forces) which seemed increasingly redundant.[91] Because naval forces had an important role to play in the Cold War and in dealing with the threat of the U-boat and the mine in war, savings could only come in the longer term in this area.[92]

On the other hand, substantial savings could be realized by cutting British forces in West Germany. However, the Chiefs conceded that 'any withdrawal of these forces in the near future would have a grave effect on NATO and in the United States and is therefore out of the question'.[93] Instead they decided to cut back on the reserves of the planned build-up of forces in war. This involved cancellations, reductions, and deferment of re-equipment programmes, which meant that in practice the UK would not be able to fulfill its commitments to NATO under the Lisbon force goals.[94] In short, even though Britain had committed herself to making a contribution to continental defence in

1950, the reluctance of British military leaders to honour that role remains clear in the 1952 Paper.[95]

It has been argued by some commentators that the 1952 Paper stressed that the West's deficiency in conventional forces could be made good through the deployment of tactical atomic weapons.[96] The Paper does indeed note that one of the developments leading to the revision of Western strategy was American possession of a 'substantial and increasing number of the smaller atom bomb', a weapon which 'can add materially to the strength of the tactical defensive'.[97] Furthermore, one of the Paper's conclusions was that the allies needed to reassess the forces needed for war, especially in Western Europe, 'taking into account the effect of atomic attack in Russia and also the tactical value of the small atom bomb'.[98] Overall, however, the Paper devoted very little attention to tactical atomic weapons and did not emphasize their value to any significant extent. In considering those developments which were held to have enhanced the ability of the Alliance to defend Western Europe, the Chiefs cited the establishment of the Supreme Headquarters Allied Powers Europe (SHAPE), the increased size and efficiency of land and air forces, and higher morale.[99] Small atom bombs were omitted at this point. Thus, while the Paper argued that tactical atomic weapons, designed for use on the battlefield, could compensate for conventional weakness, it did not premise calls for reductions in NATO force targets exclusively or even largely on the contribution which these weapons could make to the defence of Europe.

Germany: Rearmament and Reunification

Since 1950 it had been accepted by the British and American governments that one way to bolster the conventional defences of Western Europe was to involve Germany in European defence.[100] It must be remembered that the 1952 Global Strategy Paper was written at a time when the implications of the Lisbon force goals were being digested by Western governments and West German rearmament remained a topic of major political debate within NATO. The Paper was also written just as Stalin made his extraordinary offer in March 1952 to negotiate the reunification of Germany, provided that the West accepted that the new German state should be neutral.[101] In common with other Western governments, Britain saw Stalin's offer as an attempt to prevent West German rearmament. The offer was therefore firmly rejected.[102] What the 1952 Paper reveals, however, is that the Chiefs of Staff themselves were not averse to a reunified Germany 'independent of the defence orbit either of Russia or the West'. Indeed, they saw this as a way of limiting British involvement in continental defence, which had been a traditional feature of

British foreign and defence policy. They recognised that the division of Germany—and Berlin in particular—was a major source of friction and could easily become a cause of war.[103] They also argued that 'if the Allies adopt measures which seem likely to make unification impossible, the Russians will hold it out as a bribe and entice the Germans to throw in their lot with Russia rather than with the Allies'.[104]

It was therefore vital that the West should keep open the option of unification. If unification was achieved, however, the Chiefs pointed out that two things would need to be guarded against: first, 'Germany precipitating another war by attempting to regain lost territories'; and second, 'a re-armed Germany becoming a make-weight in Europe by throwing her military influence on one side or the other'. The key to preventing a unified Germany from becoming 'a seriously disturbing element', the Chiefs believed, would be the continued American presence in Europe.[105] More than this, however, they urged the government to consider an Anglo-American nuclear guarantee 'given equally to Russia and her Polish and Czechoslovakian satellites, to Germany and to Austria, and to the Western continental Allies, making it clear that an attack by any one of them against another would automatically result in the use of the atomic weapon against the aggressor'.[106]

COS Views on the Cold War

With deterrence in place and all-out war unlikely, waging the Cold War took on great importance. The British Chiefs calculated that the Soviet approach would be to shrink from direct confrontation in Europe and instead try to exploit the West's weaknesses elsewhere. Probably for a prolonged period, the Free World would have to face the challenge of the Cold War around the world, and it was on this dimension of the East–West conflict, the Chiefs believed, that the allies should focus their attention. This emphasis on the Cold War was one of the key features of the Paper. The Chiefs of Staff argued that the Western states would have to adopt a broad and coherent strategy which did not bankrupt them in dealing with the indirect threat.[107] To aid the establishment of such a strategy, they proposed a scheme as controversial as their ideas on German unification, this time regarding France. They felt that the United States was too preoccupied with 'the NATO concept to the exclusion of some other equally important strategic areas elsewhere', including the Middle East and the Far East. Greater coordination and central direction of global strategy was necessary, the Chiefs believed, not only between Britain and the United States, but also involving France. Its 'weakness and inefficiency' notwithstanding, France was a world power with a considerable stake in the Far East and Africa. She therefore had to be associated with any worldwide system of defence coordination.[108] The Chiefs recommended that 'the allied aim should now be to establish a tripartite body under which each theatre would have its own defence organisation designed specifically to meet its own peculiar needs and problems'.[109] What is of interest about this proposal is that a similar idea was to be advanced in 1958 by President de Gaulle, only to be rejected by the Eisenhower and Macmillan governments.[110]

In the absence of a coordinated Western strategy the Chiefs of Staff recorded their own views on how the Cold War should be fought. Their proposals were similar to those expressed in the 1950 report. The first task of the Free World, they wrote, was to 'establish firmly the anti-Communist front' in those states outside the Soviet sphere of influence. Later, as the Free World grew in strength, the aim would be to reduce the Soviet Union's hold on its satellite states, with the ultimate objective of making them independent but 'benevolently neutral' to the West. In the East, Chinese expansion would have to be resisted, and efforts made to 'drive a wedge between Russia and China'. Militarily, any aggression by either China or the Soviet Union would have to be countered, making the role of troops on the ground essential.[111]

However, successful prosecution of the Cold War would require more than just military strength. In a few paragraphs with a rather woolly feel to them, the Chiefs counselled that the West would also need 'self-confidence and moral force'. It should pursue a 'strong and consistent policy', and should not be 'unduly anxious about provoking Russia'. The West should aim to develop 'a united and confident public opinion' through 'an extension of the various agencies which are at work in the Free World to increase the cohesion and stability of public opinion and to undermine the morale of the enemy'. Britain in particular had the 'experience and the knowledge of the world' needed to lead such a campaign, the Chiefs felt.[112]

As we saw in the preceding chapter, the Chiefs believed that the Middle East was of 'great importance' in the Cold War. There were several reasons for this assessment, including the value of the oil and bomber bases in the region. There were, in addition, traditional British interests in the region which had to be safeguarded. It would therefore be a large prize for the Soviets, and so it was vital for the allies to retain their influence in the region and to defend it in the event of war. Western forces in the Middle East could not be greatly reduced if its stability was to be maintained, and if it was to be defended in war. At the same time the Chiefs argued that Britain could not afford to maintain its present forces in the region. The UK Middle East peacetime garrison might be cut to around one division and 160 aircraft, they thought. There was a certain amount of risk attached to these cuts, the Chiefs recognized, though it was hoped that the proposed Middle East Defence Organisation (MEDO) would strengthen the Free World in the region.[113]

Important though the Middle East was, it faced no direct military threat at that time. Rather, the Chiefs saw a shift of emphasis in the Cold War away from Europe and towards Asia. It was in East Asia that the Cold War had so far 'taken its most violent and aggressive form'. It was feared that 'the road to Paris might well be via Peking and Delhi', and presumably for this reason the Chiefs concluded that the Far East was 'of greater importance' in the Cold War than the Middle East. The fate of Indo-China was seen as crucial to the future of the region. The French would have to be offered assistance there to ensure that communism did not triumph.[114] Communism in this area was sponsored by the Soviet Union, the Chiefs argued, but the 'direct military force' behind it was China. Although the Chiefs made it clear that China was a threat on its own and not merely a Soviet satellite, they believed that it would not be in the interests of the West 'to get involved in war with China'. The Chinese therefore had to be deterred from aggression. As has been mentioned, the Chiefs saw the presence of ground forces as the best deterrent to Chinese aggression (though where these forces were to come from was far from clear).[115] While there were also special UK Commonwealth interests in the Far East, and despite their ranking it higher than the Middle East in Cold War terms, the Chiefs argued that in a 'hot war' whatever effort was devoted to the Far East should not be at the expense of provision for the more important region: Western Europe.[116]

Conclusion

The 1952 Global Strategy Paper did not constitute a clear and categorical break with past thinking. In many ways it reiterated some of the ideas that had been included in the reviews of 1947 and 1950. However, the 1952 document does differ in some important respects from earlier statements, due to the changing political, economic, and strategic circumstances of the period. In particular, there was greater stress given to nuclear deterrence and a greater commitment to nuclear weapons than in the 1950 Paper. With defence against atomic air attack relatively neglected, and some information about American atomic air power available, deterrence took on new importance. The 1952 Paper put greater stress on economic factors than previous reviews, as the cost of the Korean rearmament programme became increasingly unbearable. At the same time, the Korean War raised the importance of the Far East in the Cold War and led to a reassessment of the perceived Chinese threat.

The 1952 Paper's significance may also be measured by its impact on future policy. It was intended to provide a long-term, affordable strategy for Britain and the Alliance. However, it certainly did not have the immediate desired effect. At the end of their review the Chiefs of Staff promised that their recommendations would produce 'substantial savings in the United Kingdom rearmament programme'.[117] However, in a final paragraph rendered in bold type, they warned that 'The reductions which we recommend in the build-up and equipment of the forces can be undertaken only by incurring real and serious risks. These risks are only justifiable in the face of the threat of economic disaster.'[118] But in practice the reductions which ensued were not sufficient to meet the economic demands of the government. Within six months of the Chiefs of Staff presenting their Global Strategy Paper the government would undertake another Radical Review of strategy, again designed to bring defence spending under control.[119] In part the 1952 review failed to square military strategy with the economy because not all of its conclusions were put into practice. Nevertheless, the Paper did set the foundations of declaratory British strategic policy for many years to come. The stress on nuclear weapons contained in the Paper can be found later, especially in the Defence White Paper of 1957—which arguably went much further in converting declaratory policy into actual policy.[120] It follows that the conclusions in the 1952 Paper on the need for economy and the value of nuclear deterrence, which received far more emphasis than in the 1947 and 1950 reviews, both played a large role in future British policy.

The 1952 Paper also represented 'the first full-dress critique' of NATO strategy.[121] It formed the basis of the British attempt to change Alliance military policy, beginning in mid-1952 when Sir John Slessor travelled to Washington to attempt to gain American backing for British plans.[122] The Chief of the Air Staff failed to do so, yet there is evidence that the Paper found favour at least with the US Air Force. Charles Murphy, who was closely associated with the US Air Force, praised Slessor's ideas in his January 1953 *Fortune* article.[123] Later that year the Eisenhower administration, facing similar economic pressures to the British, adopted the 'New Look' defence policy which, like the 1952 Paper, emphasized the utility of nuclear weapons.[124] While it is difficult to prove that the Global Strategy Paper directly influenced the new administration, there can be no doubt that the American Joint Chiefs of Staff had a clear understanding of the British desire to change Alliance strategy in a more nuclear direction from the summer of 1952 onwards.[125]

3

From Atomic Weapons to Thermonuclear Weapons

> *The discriminate test for a first class power is whether it has made an atomic bomb.*
>
> William Penney*
>
> *[W]e are a major power again.*
>
> Randolph Churchill**

Apart from the key role of the Chiefs of Staff in the development of a 'deterrence habit of mind' in Britain, there were other individuals and groups who also formed part of an advocacy coalition in favour of nuclear weapons. This coalition included defence and scientific officials, government advisers, scientists, engineers, weaponeers, and politicians. Covertly, because of the 1946 McMahon Act, it also included scientists and engineers from the United States. The critical role of this coalition can be seen in the nuclear testing programme which led to Britain's first atomic test in 1952 and subsequently to the development of thermonuclear weapons in 1957–8.

The Development of the British Atomic Capability

As the Controller of Production, Atomic Energy, Lord Portal had the task of putting together a team that would implement the government's January 1947 decision to develop atomic weapons. To achieve this, he appointed a number of top scientists and engineers who were to be at the heart of the atomic programme. His initial appointments included the nuclear physicist and Nobel Prize winner John Cockcroft, as Director of the Atomic Energy Research Establishment based at Harwell; Christopher Hinton, a senior ICI engineer who was chosen to design and construct the atomic pile, and who based himself at Risley; Michael Perrin, another former ICI man, acted as his technical adviser; and Sir James Chadwick, another Nobel Prize winner and described as 'one of Britain's greatest living scientists', also provided him with scientific advice.[1] A little later he appointed William Penney—the Chief Superintendent of Armament Research, who had played an influential role in the Manhattan Project—to oversee the vital work on the military applications of atomic energy. All had a firm belief in the importance of Britain developing atomic weapons.

Their task, however, was to be far from easy or straightforward. A range of industrial complexes had to be built up:

> one, to extract and refine uranium metal from ore, which was to be built at Springfields, near Preston in Lancashire; the pile itself at the Sellafield site, soon to be renamed Windscale; and a third to extract and refine plutonium which was manufactured in the course of the nuclear reaction inside the pile.[2]

Scientists and engineers had to be recruited, which proved extremely difficult in the early years after the Second World War. All of the various organizations had to be effectively coordinated. And only limited knowledge about how to design and develop a bomb was available, from a small number of scientists and engineers who had taken part in the American Manhattan Project during the war. Brian Cathcart has summed up the range of difficulties faced by William Penney and his colleagues as follows:

> The story of the making of Britain's first atomic bomb is one of improvization and struggle, of hesitation and last minute rush, of high stakes and low cards...the atomic project [was]...characterized by a somewhat evolutionary approach to organization and by a desperate struggle for resources. The right man [William Penney] was put in charge...but he found his path obstructed by many obstacles, from official secrecy to bureaucratic obstinacy.... many mistakes were made and it was by luck as much as judgement that failure was avoided. All this confusion and haste was owed in large part to the circumstances of the country, exhausted by six years of war and groping to define its place in a changed world.[3]

Despite all the difficulties, Penney proved to be highly effective in coordinating all of the complex elements of what was largely an indigenous programme. Given his previous important role in the Manhattan Project, however, he received 'a lot of stuff under the counter' from former scientific colleagues in the United States, despite the 1946 McMahon Act in the United States (which forbade such cooperation).[4] This began what might be described as the 'transatlantic advocacy coalition' of UK and US scientists and engineers who were to play an important part in the British nuclear programme in the future.

The first British test of an experimental plutonium device (Operation Hurricane) took place in the Monte Bello Islands off the north-west coast of Australia in October 1952.[5] In the circumstances, whatever views one holds about the morality of the project, the *Hurricane* test was a major success for British science and engineering. Nevertheless, Britain did not immediately possess an atomic weapons capability. Various technical problems still had to be overcome before an operational weapon system (Blue Danube) became available. There were also problems associated with matching weapons to aircraft, especially as the V-bombers, designed to carry Britain's atomic weapons, were not scheduled to enter service until 1955.[6]

Further tests took place in October 1953 at Emu Field, south-west of Woomera in Australia (Operation Totem), with the first Blue Danube atomic bombs delivered to RAF Bomber Command's Armaments school at Wittering between 7 and 14 November 1953. It was hoped that five bombs would be ready by the end of 1953, with three to be delivered in November and a further two in December.[7] However, trials to match the new weapons to the Valiant bombers which were to deliver them did not begin until July 1955. The first assembly of live radioactive components of atomic weapons took place on 28 July. This date marked the moment when 'the RAF had an atomic bomb capability' for the first time (though the first live drop from an aircraft did not in fact take place until 11 October 1956 at Maralinga in South Australia).[8] Nevertheless, the RAF had an 'emergency' operational capability from mid-1955 onwards.

Another set of trials took place at Monte Bello between January and June 1956 (Operation Mosaic) and at Maralinga from July to November 1956 (Operation Buffalo). The main purpose of the Mosaic tests were to study the boosting of fission devices with 'light materials'. These tests, comparable to the US *George* shot, were Britain's first steps into the thermonuclear area.

The Decision to Develop Thermonuclear Weapons

While this atomic weapons capability was being developed, the government had taken the decision to develop thermonuclear weapons. On 16 June 1954 the Chiefs of Staff recommended to the Cabinet Defence Committee that 'following the US and Soviet H-Bomb tests in 1952 and 1953, Britain should produce its own thermonuclear weapon'.[9] Despite modifications of the McMahon Act in 1948 and 1951, and indications earlier in 1954 that Britain would receive more information about atomic weapons from the United States, it remained clear that there was little likelihood of a major breakthrough in cooperation between the two countries. The Chiefs of Staff had received reports from a Working Party on the 'Operational Use of Atomic

Atomic Weapons to Thermonuclear Weapons

Weapons' and from their Joint Planning Staff, both of which recommended that Britain should follow the United States and the Soviet Union and develop H-bombs.[10] The Chiefs of Staff concurred with these views, arguing that Britain must 'possess the means of waging war with the most up-to-date nuclear weapons'.[11] They also strongly believed in the need to maintain Britain's role in the world. The First Sea Lord, Sir Rhoderick McGrigor, reflected this view when he argued that:

> The United Kingdom, as the recognised leader of the Commonwealth, and as a leading world power, had a position to maintain in world affairs. If our influence were to decline it would be virtually impossible to regain our rightful place as a world power. It was essential that the United Kingdom should have the ability to produce the H-Bomb in order that she could claim membership of the Allied H-Club.[12]

At the same time that the Chiefs of Staff were advising that thermonuclear weapons should be developed, the Churchill government was under pressure from the United States and from Labour backbenchers to accept a moratorium on nuclear testing. The Eisenhower administration had recently completed its own *Castle* series of thermonuclear tests and was aware that the device exploded by the Soviet Union in 1953 was only an 'intermediate' thermonuclear device; more R&D and more testing would be needed in order to achieve a true H-bomb. A test moratorium would therefore 'freeze' Soviet inferiority in the development of thermonuclear weapons.

The idea of a moratorium was also supported by a group of Labour backbenchers on moral rather than political or strategic grounds. Following the 'Lucky Dragon' incident in 1954, opponents of nuclear weapons in the Labour Party put down a motion in the House of Commons demanding the immediate cessation of testing.[13] Trade unions also passed resolutions condemning testing, reflecting a growing unease in parts of British society about the morality of the new weapons and an anxiety about contamination and radioactive fallout.[14] Faced with domestic and American pressure, the government had to decide whether to push ahead with its own H-bomb programme, as the COS recommended, or support a moratorium which would restrict further developments by the Soviet Union (and the UK). The issue was discussed at the Cabinet Defence Committee in June and by the full Cabinet in July 1954.[15] The consensus at these meetings was that Britain should go ahead with the development of thermonuclear weapons for a combination of political and strategic reasons.[16] Prime Minister Winston Churchill and the majority of his colleagues believed that in order to remain a Great Power Britain had to possess the 'best weapons available'. There was also concern that without such weapons Britain would not be in a position to influence the American government and prevent impatient elements in Washington from plunging 'the world into war, either through a misguided intervention in Asia or in order to forestall an attack by Russia'.[17] The Cabinet also took notice of the strategic arguments put forward by the Chiefs of Staff, who argued that thermonuclear weapons enhanced deterrence because they helped to overcome the 'problem of terminal accuracy' which afflicted atomic weapons.

The power of the H-bomb was such that it was not as important to hit the target directly in order to destroy it. This increased the credibility of the threat, they argued, and also improved the ability to destroy targets which were particularly threatening to Britain should war break out. In their view, thermonuclear weapons were great 'equalizers' in the sense that the Soviet Union and the United States were now just as vulnerable as Britain.[18] Another consideration was that thermonuclear weapons would allow the government to make the reductions in airpower needed to deliver the weapons to their targets. At a time of great financial pressure on the defence budget this seemed an attractive option.

The Role of Scientists and Weaponeers

However, at the time that the Cabinet took its decision (July 1954), weapons scientists at Aldermaston were still a long way from knowing how to make thermonuclear weapons. William Cook had been asked in September 1954—by William Penney, who was now the Atomic Energy Authority (AEA) Member of Weapons Research and Director of Aldermaston—to take over responsibility for managing the thermonuclear research, development, and testing programme. A Weapon Development Committee was set up, under Cook's direction, and he set about the task of selecting a team to uncover 'the secret of the Ulam-Teller invention'. When this was achieved, and by whom, however, remains largely unknown. One of the scientists involved, J.C. Ward, claimed in 1985 that the key breakthrough was made by himself. In a letter to Prime Minister Margaret Thatcher on 13 May 1985, Ward said that he was recruited by Cook in the spring of 1955 and that at this stage 'the secret' of the H-bomb was unknown. It was, he claims, 'far beyond the talents of the personnel at Aldermaston'. He then goes on to make the following claim: 'Under great stress, and with no assistance whatever, I came up with the correct scheme within six months, minor modifications excepted (and also obvious precautions).'[19] However, he says that his contribution was not appreciated by either Penney or Cook, and he left Aldermaston after a short period to work in the United States. Substantiating Ward's claim is not easy because a number of the key participants, including William Penney and William Cook are dead. Where the true paternity of the British H-Bomb lies therefore remains somewhat uncertain. What seems clear, however, is that the calculations and design of Britain's first thermonuclear devices (tested in May 1957) were far from completion when Ward left Aldermaston in late 1955. That work was completed by I. Corner, K.V. Roberts, J.B. Taylor, H.R. Hulme, and K.W. Allen and others, all of whom made significant contributions to the development of the British H-Bomb. During the period from 1955 to 1957 different ideas on a two-stage ('Tom' and 'Dick') and even a three-stage ('Tom', 'Dick', and 'Harry') device were explored until the two-stage *Short Granite* and *Purple Granite* were chosen for testing.[20] It appears that British scientists were helped in their work by information derived from a 'sanitized' transcript of the Oppenheimer trial that was taking place in the United States at the time. They were also assisted by techniques which had been developed for 'interpreting the radiochemical data obtained by analysis of samples of weapons debris'.[21]

The Grapple Tests, May–June 1957

Having received political authorization for the development of thermonuclear weapons, the Chiefs of Staff decided on 6 April 1955 to develop 'as a first priority a weapon with a yield of about one megaton'.[22] In line with this, on 28 July 1955 the Ministry of Supply received 'Operational Requirement' (OR) 1136 for the production of a thermonuclear weapon, code named *Yellow Sun*. As shown in Table 3.1, while the Mosaic and Buffalo atomic tests were taking place in 1956, the Atomic Weapons Trials Executive began its preparations for a series of megaton tests, which it was hoped would take place off Christmas Island in the Pacific Ocean in May/June 1957.[23]

Announcing the tests to the House of Commons on 7 June 1955, Churchill's successor, Anthony Eden, sensitive to the opposition building up against testing, emphasized the isolation of the test ground and the safety precautions being undertaken:

> In the Statement of Defence, 1955, Her Majesty's Government announced their intention to manufacture thermonuclear weapons. As I have previously stated, the holding of tests is an essential part of the process of providing ourselves with such weapons. The United States of America and the Union of Soviet Socialist Republics have already held such tests and Her Majesty's Government have decided to carry out a limited number of nuclear test explosions in the megaton range. These will take place during the first half of 1957 in a remote part of the Pacific Ocean. The explosions will take place far from any inhabited islands and the tests will be so arranged as to avoid danger to persons or property. The tests will be high air bursts which will not involve heavy fall-out. All safety precautions will be taken in the light of our knowledge and of experience gained from the tests of other countries.[24]

Table 3.1. UK atmospheric nuclear weapons tests in Australia and the Pacific Ocean, 1952–1958

Operation Name	Round and	Location	Date of Firing	Yield
Hurricane		Off Trimouille Island, Monte Bello Islands, Western Australia	3 Oct 1952	25 kt
Totem	1	Emu Field, South Australia	14 Oct 1953	10 kt
	2	Emu Field, South Australia	26 Oct 1953	8 kt
Mosaic	1	Trimouille Island, Monte Bello Islands, Western Australia	16 May 1956	15 kt
	2	Alpha Island, Monte Bello Islands, Western Australia	19 June 1956	60 kt[†]
Buffalo	1	One Tree, Maralinga Range, South Australia	27 Sep 1956	15 kt
	2	Marcoo, Maralinga Range, South Australia	4 Oct 1956	1.5 kt
	3	Kite, Maralinga Range, South Australia	11 Oct 1956	3 kt
	4	Breakaway, Maralinga Range, South Australia	21 Oct 1956	10 kt
Grapple	1 Short Granite	Off Malden Island, Pacific Ocean	15 May 1957	0.3 Mt*
	2 Orange Herald	Off Malden Island, Pacific Ocean	31 May 1957	0.72 Mt*
	3 Purple Granite	Off Malden Island, Pacific Ocean	19 Jun 1957	0.2 Mt*
Antler	1	Tadje, Maralinga Range, South Australia	14 Sep 1957	1 kt
	2	Biak, Maralinga Range, South Australia	25 Sep 1957	6 kt
	3	Taranaki, Maralinga Range, South Australia	9 Oct 1957	25 kt
Grapple X		Off Christmas Island, Pacific Ocean	8 Nov 1957	1.8 Mt*
Grapple Y		Off Christmas Island, Pacific Ocean	28 Apr 1958	3 Mt*
Grapple Z	1 Pennant	Christmas Island, Pacific Ocean	22 Aug 1958	24 kt*
	2 Flagpole	Off Christmas Island, Pacific Ocean	2 Sep 1958	1 Mt*
	3 Halliard	Off Christmas Island, Pacific Ocean	11 Sep 1958	0.8 Mt*
	4 Burgee	Christmas Island, Pacific Ocean	23 Sep 1958	25 kt*

[†] It was suggested at the Royal Commission on the Australian tests in 1985 that the yield of this test may have been as high as 98 kilotons.
* MOD estimates made available in October 1993.

Source: The National Radiological Protection Board (NRPB 266) ICRF, Second Report, Dec. 1993.

Eden also indicated that the government was prepared to talk to other governments on the regulation and limitation of nuclear testing. Concern about growing opposition to testing was also evident in official defence planning circles. The Atomic Energy Sub-Committee of the Defence Research Policy Committee told the Chiefs of Staff that the earliest possible achievement of a megaton explosion was necessary to demonstrate the ability to make thermonuclear weapons. Given the increasing political pressure against the megaton trials, they argued that it was essential 'to safeguard the future by obtaining the greatest possible amount of scientific knowledge and weapon design experience' as the foundation of Britain's megaton weapons development programme.[25]

The need to compress the megaton test programme as much as possible and to minimize fallout contributed to the decision to take a major gamble in the first test by having a high burst rather than a surface or tower-mounted burst. In their initial tests the United States and the Soviet Union had opted for a ground burst of the experimental devices used. It took the United States from 1952 until 1956 before they tested an air-dropped megaton device. In contrast, Britain decided to undertake the more technically demanding task of an air drop in their first test on 15 May 1957.[26] There were also two further air drops on 31 May and 19 June 1957. How successful these ambitious tests were is a matter of some debate. While they undoubtedly provided important information on the performance of a number of different types of megaton warhead—including a high yield fission warhead and the two-stage thermonuclear (*Granite*) bombs—it is apparent that the tests did not provide sufficient data to enable a firm decision to be made regarding the warhead to be chosen for *Yellow Sun*, the specifications for which had been laid down in OR 1136 in July 1955.[27] This was perhaps not surprising given the difficulties of transferring theoretical calculations on paper to practical experimental conditions. The Chief Scientific Adviser to the MOD, Sir Frederick Brundrett, was certainly satisfied with the results. He described them at the time as 'an immense achievement of which I think we can be proud'.[28] However, the scientific director of the series, William Cook, was less happy. He told the task force commander, Air Vice Marshal Oulton, that unfortunately they had not got it quite right and would have to try again later in the year. From the documents available it seems that the test of the 'fall-back' fission weapon, *Orange Herald* was successful, while the two thermonuclear (Short Granite and Purple Granite) shots were disappointing.[29] (Nevertheless, a yield of 0.72 megaton from a fission warhead was in itself a remarkable technical achievement.)

There seem to be two main reasons for the disappointing results of the first Grapple shots. The first was that there were some disagreements between the scientists involved about the most appropriate design for the weapon. The second was the pressure from the government on AWRE to test a thermonuclear device as soon as possible before the United States and the Soviet Union agreed on a moratorium. According to Professor K.W. Allen:

> There was some divergence of view in AWRE at the time about the best approach to the thermonuclear tests. Almost all the designers were applied mathematicians who were confident of their computer calculations and felt they could design a device from first principles. I, as an experimental physicist, who had studied the results of the US tests, was less happy about the general principles and felt there were two major areas of uncertainty. One of these concerned the hydrodynamics and the other was the nuclear physics of the system proposed. I would have much preferred tests which examined these aspects separately. However, time was short and it was decided to test the rather complex *green granite* design.[30]

The 'Interim' Megaton Weapon

It had been decided in October 1956 that the quickest way to achieve a 'form of megaton warhead' would be to develop an 'interim' weapon.[31] Following the May/June tests it was decided to develop a large-yield fission weapon, known as *Violet Club*, with a *Green Grass* warhead based on *Orange Herald*. It was this weapon which was issued to the RAF in March 1958. The aim was to provide the RAF with a megaton capability at the earliest possible moment.[32] Its actual yield was 0.5 MT.

The question of why Britain introduced *Violet Club* has been the source of some controversy. According to Norman Dombey and Eric Grove the main reason was to try and convince the United States that Britain was further ahead than she really was in order to open up nuclear collaboration between the two countries. Dombey has been quoted as saying that: 'We were only a year or two away from making...full hydrogen bombs—but could not wait. Essentially, we bluffed the Americans into thinking we had arrived at making hydrogen bombs, but hadn't quite.'[33] This argument has also been supported by the American expert on nuclear weapons, Robert S. Norris. Having achieved the desired cooperation with the Mutual Defence Agreement of 1958, Norris argues that Britain gave up its independent attempt to design warheads and relied instead on US designs for the *Yellow Sun 2* weapon which was introduced in 1961.[34]

These arguments, however, can be contested. As far as Anglo-American relations are concerned, the argument by Dombey and Grove ignores the scale of cooperation which had been achieved by this time. As Chapter 4 demonstrates, detailed discussions were underway in 1957 about a combined strategic targeting plan and both countries had been collaborating closely on atomic intelligence matters for some time, including the sampling and monitoring of Soviet tests.[35] American observers, such as Dr Herbert York of the Lawrence Livermore Laboratory, were present at some of the Grapple tests and made their own estimates of the yield of the tests. We know also that British and American scientists were engaged in a regular exchange of data at this time. Sir Frederick Brundrett, the Chief Scientific Adviser at the MOD, revealed the closeness of the partnership which existed when he told the Chief of the Air Staff on 16 May 1957: 'So far as I am able to judge from American reports as well as our own preliminary assessments, we have fulfilled our expectations.'[36] Meetings also took place between the US and UK weapons scientists from the autumn of 1957—long before the 1958 Mutual Defence Agreement was signed.[37] American documents have revealed that the latest British thinking was discussed at these meetings. It is known that the American scientists were impressed by the progress made by the British. Further meetings also took place in Albuquerque, New Mexico, in 1958 to discuss the outcome of the new round of tests being undertaken. The most important of these meetings occurred in August and September, when the British provided information on their high yield fission bomb, 'now in the stockpile', and megaton designs were exchanged. This became possible as a result of the success of the Grapple X, Y, and Z Tests.[38]

The Grapple X, Y, Z Tests, October 1957 to September 1958

After the disappointment of the tests in May/June 1957 it was decided to undertake further tests to solve some of the scientific problems which still remained unresolved. Grapple 'X' (one shot) took place in October/November 1957, Grapple 'Y' (one shot) in April 1958, and Grapple 'Z' (four shots) in August/September 1958.[39] According to the Assistant Chief of the Air Staff these tests were 'not directed at any specific weapon because the disappointing results obtained from this type of device in shots 1 and 3 at Grapple last May have forced scientists into attacking the problem in a purely scientific manner'.[40] It may be significant that just before the Grapple 'X' test Britain acquired an IBM 704 computer from the United States which enabled the weapon scientists to test some of the principles on which their designs were based. This increase in computing power may have made an important contribution to the success of the tests that followed.[41] Grapple 'X' produced a yield of 1.8 MT and Grapple 'Y' a yield of 3 MT. Taken together, Grapple 'X', 'Y', and 'Z' reflected the lessons which had been learned from earlier tests and represented the highly successful culmination of a process which began in 1954. Professor K.W. Allen has argued that after the comparative failure of the Green Granite design, 'a much simpler device was successfully tested in November 1957. This sorted out the hydrodynamics, and was followed in

May 1958 by Grapple 'Y' which got the nuclear physics right and was the basis for a megaton weapon.'[42] (See Appendix 1.)

The H-Bomb Myth, Great Power Status, and Political Influence

What this account suggests is that the public announcement of successful thermonuclear tests in the summer of 1957 was accurate, but it did not lead to the introduction of a thermonuclear weapon into service until 1961. As with the 'bomber gap myth' and the 'missile gap myth' which were being perpetrated at much the same time, it has been argued that there was a 'H-bomb myth' in Britain between 1957 and 1961 designed to enhance the country's status and reinforce its strategic interests at a time of great tension in East–West relations. Behind the claims to thermonuclear status an 'interim' weapon system was produced which was extremely 'delicate' and had to be kept 'exclusively under the control of the Atomic Weapons Research Establishment'.[43]

Not surprisingly, perhaps, the RAF could not wait to get rid of the weapon as soon as they possibly could, even though it provided them with a 'near megaton capability' which could have been used in emergency circumstances. As we argued earlier, it was not likely that the Americans would have been fooled into believing that Britain was more advanced than she was in 1957. American scientists undoubtedly had a reasonably clear picture of the advances being made in Britain through the different kinds of cooperation that were taking place. The United States and the Soviet Union had passed through the phase of initially developing 'interim' weapons, and Britain's Grapple Tests provided an indication not only that she was intent on developing the H-bomb, but also that the scientific and technological expertise existed to achieve an operational thermonuclear capability in due course.

The rhetoric of thermonuclear status, however, was very important to the Conservative government of the day. The Suez crisis of 1956 had been a great humiliation, and for many members of the ruling party catching up with the technological achievements in weapon design of the United States and the Soviet Union demonstrated that Britain had recovered its Great Power status once again. Randolph Churchill told the American Chamber of Commerce in November 1958 that 'Britain can knock down twelve cities in the region of Stalingrad and Moscow from bases in Britain and another dozen from bases in Cyprus. We did not have that power at the time of Suez. We are a major power again.'[44]

Similar sentiments were expressed by another Conservative politician, Julian Amery. Speaking in the House of Commons, he argued that:

It would seem that the Hydrogen bomb... will make us a world power again. The atom bomb rather put us out of the race because only big territorial expanses like the United States or the Soviet Union could stand up to atom-bombing and hope to survive. We should have been obliterated very quickly. But the hydrogen bomb is a great leveller. It cancels out the disparity between population and the big areas of territory and smaller ones. It would be just as dangerous for the Soviet Union, or the United States to incur thermonuclear nuclear bombardment as it would be for us.[45]

This belief in a Great Power identity for Britain associated with thermonuclear status was closely linked to a perceived need to have influence in Washington. The prime minister at the time of the Grapple Tests, Harold Macmillan, was very concerned that thermonuclear weapons meant that Britain did not have 'to surrender our power to influence American policy'. The fact that these weapons were independently developed meant that it gave Britain a better position in the world, but it also gave her a better position with respect to the United States. According to the prime minister: 'It puts us where we ought to be, in the position of a Great Power. The fact that we have it makes the United States pay a greater regard to our point of view, and that is of great importance.'[46]

CND and Public Opposition to Nuclear Weapons

This belief in the importance of nuclear weapons for security and Great Power status was not, however, supported by all of the British public. During the 1950s the British Peace Committee and the Direct Action Committee campaigned against nuclear weapons. The nuclear testing programmes of the United States, the Soviet Union, and Britain in particular caused growing anxiety about nuclear war breaking out, as well as the health and environmental damage caused by the atmospheric tests. For many, nuclear weapons and nuclear deterrence which threatened the lives of millions of people were morally unacceptable. This reflected a very different moral belief to that held by the government. An article by the respected author J.B. Priestly in the *New Statesman* magazine on 2 November 1957 entitled 'Britain and Nuclear Weapons' led to a meeting in the rooms of Canon John Collins of St Pauls Cathedral when the Campaign for Nuclear Disarmament (CND) was set up. An inaugural meeting took place in the Central Hall, Westminster, on 17 February 1958 which attracted 5,000 people, as well as considerable public attention. This was followed by the first march (of fifty-two miles) from London to the Atomic Weapons Establishment at Aldermaston at Easter to protest against the British nuclear programme and to call for unilateral disarmament. All sections of society were involved in the march, including religious leaders, academics, journalists, writers, actors, musicians, Labour Party members, and trade unionists. The march was organized by the Direct Action Committee and supported by CND.

By 1959 CND had become a significant social movement, with 60,000 people taking part in the annual Aldermaston march, and by 1961 the marchers had grown to over 150,000. The leaders of the movement contained a number of eminent individuals, including Bertram Russell, Michael Foot, J.B. Priestly, Kingsley Martin, and Cannon John Collins. Their aim was to work through the Labour Party to achieve a fundamental change of Britain's defence policy, which they believed was both dangerous and immoral. In 1960, CND achieved a breakthrough when the Labour Party voted at its annual conference for unilateral disarmament, despite the opposition of its leadership under Hugh Gaitskill. Gaitskill, however, vowed to 'fight, fight and fight again' to reverse this policy and at the 1961 conference Labour reversed its decision and voted against unilateral disarmament. This led to a gradual decline in the fortunes of CND, which resulted in some conflict within the movement between those such as Bertrand Russell, who wanted to start a programme of direct action against the government's nuclear policies, and those such as Canon John Collins, who wished to keep to lawful protests. Russell subsequently left CND in 1961 to form the Committee of 100. Despite this demise in the prominence of CND it retained some minority support from that section of the population whose beliefs about the utility of nuclear weapons and nuclear deterrence were very different to those of the Conservative government. As we will see, the movement had another period of raised public support in the 1980s.

Conclusion

Despite the rise in support for CND in the late 1950s, it never had the support of the majority of the public. Gallop Polls for the period from 1958 to 1961 show a dip in support for government policy in 1959, but even then a healthy majority still favoured retaining the H-bomb. Asked if they would approve or disapprove if Britain gave up its thermonuclear weapons even if other countries did not, in April 1958 61 per cent disapproved and 25 per cent approved; in March 1959 50 per cent disapproved and 30 per cent approved; and in September 1961 62 per cent disapproved and 21 per cent approved.[47] In this sense, the elite nuclear advocacy coalition of leading politicians, officials, military leaders, as well as scientists and engineers involved in the programme, continued to have broad democratic support. Looking back on this period, Andrew Pierre has argued that the clash of beliefs on the utility of nuclear weapons during this period, from the atomic bomb tests to the

H-bomb tests, with government policy continually supported by the majority of public opinion, meant that a great opportunity was missed for serious attention to be given to the consequences of the British programme for future nuclear proliferation.[48] However, it was the government's belief, shared by the leaders of the opposition Labour Party, that other states were unlikely to follow Britain's example and, in the dangerous world of the Cold War, that Britain's place in the world and her security were better served by retaining and improving the nation's nuclear capability.[49] In particular, it was believed that the country's security required a close nuclear partnership with the United States.

4

Forging the 'Special' Anglo-American Nuclear Relationship

Dulles came to luncheon at the Embassy. We had a talk afterwards, and he produced the draft of a declaration to be called the Declaration of Common Purpose. 'I glanced at it, and saw, embodied in a lot of verbiage, para. 3—the end of the McMahon Act—the great prize!

Harold Macmillan, 24 October 1957[1]

It has been argued that 'Britain's nuclear ties with America run very deep and constitute a core feature of the "special relationship" so central to Britain's international identity.'[2] This chapter describes the background to the Anglo-American nuclear relationship, from a period of bitterness and frustration in the late 1940s and early 1950s, when Britain struggled to re-establish the close wartime cooperation with the United States in the atomic energy field, through to the breakthrough and final stages of negotiations in 1957 and 1958 when the Cooperation on the Uses of Atomic Energy for Mutual Defense Purposes Agreement (MDA) was signed. What emerges is a story of consistent, patient, and determined (but not always successful) diplomacy by British policy-makers in the late 1940s and 1950s, designed to gain access to American nuclear secrets and to influence US strategic decision-making. In contrast, American policy was much less coherent, even though there was a consistent attempt to maximize American security interests in a constantly changing strategic environment. The reluctance of many officials to share nuclear secrets with Britain, together with the fragmented and competitive political system in which they operated, meant that progress toward greater Anglo-American nuclear cooperation was achieved only when international circumstances were perceived to be more threatening and when it was believed that the British could make a useful contribution to the American nuclear programme.

In line with Hyman's argument, the chapter also suggests that the political leadership of the British prime minister and the US president was of crucial importance in opening up close nuclear cooperation between the two countries. President Eisenhower, in particular, was decisive in overcoming domestic obstacles to greater nuclear cooperation between the United States and its European allies, especially Britain.[3] Anglo-American nuclear cooperation was initially perceived by the president as part of a broader strategy to coordinate the policies of the NATO states to deal more effectively with the perceived threat from the Soviet Union and to ease the pressure on the American economy. It later turned into an 'exceptional' bilateral relationship, largely because of growing domestic fears about the dangers of nuclear proliferation and an awareness that cooperation with Britain brought important mutual benefits. The patience and determination of Harold Macmillan was also of great significance. The British prime minister strongly believed that close ties between the two countries, especially in the nuclear field, was not only mutually beneficial, but also contributed to important universal values. For him, a return to the close nuclear partnership of the Second World War was truly 'the great prize'.[4]

One of the central arguments developed in this chapter is that the Anglo-American nuclear partnership that developed from 1958 went further than is often supposed and was based on an exchange of nuclear secrets rather than on a simple transfer of nuclear information from the United States to Britain. While the Anglo-American nuclear partnership was to become one of the core elements of the 'special relationship' between the two countries from the late 1950s onwards, it was to be maintained primarily as a result of reciprocity rather than sentimental attachment or vague notions of kinship. It was also to become an important part of Britain's self-identity.

Background: The Years of British Frustration

The end of the Second World War brought great disappointment to the British government. As we saw earlier, despite close collaboration in the Manhattan Project and a series of wartime agreements (at Quebec in August 1943 and Hyde Park in September 1944) that promised continuing post-war cooperation in the atomic energy field, in August 1946 the United States passed the McMahon Act, which prohibited the passing of classified atomic energy information to all foreign countries, including Britain, '*on pain of life imprisonment or even death*'.[5] This reflected a combination of both internationalist and nationalist opinion in favour of the United States maintaining a monopoly of atomic weapons (until some system of international control could be established, in the case of the former).

Believing itself to be a Great Power and entitled, through the wartime agreements and its own very significant contribution to the Manhattan Project, to the most powerful weapons available, as we have seen, the Attlee government initiated its own independent nuclear weapons programme in January 1947.[6] As the Cold War gathered momentum, it was felt that atomic weapons were essential to maintain national security and enhance British political influence. Among those ministers involved in the decision, there was also a strong conviction that an independent British atomic energy programme was essential if the desired objective of reopening nuclear cooperation with the Americans was to be achieved. Much to the frustration of both Labour and Conservative governments in the period from the late 1940s to the mid-1950s, however, it was to prove impossible to re-establish the intimacy of the Manhattan Project. Atomic energy cooperation stood apart from the close diplomatic and military partnership that was otherwise developing between the two countries at the time.[7]

American attempts to maintain their nuclear monopoly and unfettered control over their nuclear weapons were clearly evident in the *Modus Vivendi* agreement of January 1948 and the 'Truman–Attlee Understandings' of October 1951. The *Modus Vivendi* ended Britain's right of veto over the American use of atomic weapons agreed at Quebec in 1943, in exchange for a range of non-military atomic energy information.[8] The October 1951 agreement (later confirmed by Churchill in January 1952) provided a rather vague 'understanding' that the use of American aircraft from British bases (sent there during the Berlin Blockade in 1948–9) should be a matter for joint agreement between the US president and the British prime minister 'in the light of the circumstances prevailing at the time'.[9] The British were made aware that, while the United States had every intention of consulting Britain before launching aircraft equipped with nuclear weapons from UK territory, there might be circumstances when there would be no time for consultation.[10]

By 1953, when President Eisenhower came to office, growing worries about Soviet technological developments led to attempts to achieve a new era of closer nuclear cooperation. The new American president believed that in the longer term Europe should become 'a third great power bloc', closely aligned with the United States but capable of looking after its own defence. This would allow the United States to gradually withdraw its troops (which had only been deployed as a temporary expedient) as Europe built up its own conventional and nuclear forces to counter those of the Soviet Union. Until this happened, Eisenhower thought that the best thing would be for the United States to treat the NATO countries as 'true allies' and supply them with the weapons and technology they needed to counter the perceived Soviet superiority in conventional military capabilities and the rapid developments being made in the nuclear field. This included a plan for nuclear sharing between the NATO states.

The Soviet thermonuclear test in August 1953 (*Joe 4*) caused the president to tell Congress that the McMahon Act was now obsolete.[11] In his view it was a 'terrible piece of legislation' that seriously undermined the United States' relationship with its NATO partners. Despite the approval of a new Atomic Energy Act in August 1954, designed to open up greater cooperation with US allies, congressional opposition and interagency disputes (especially between the Congressional Joint Committee on Atomic Energy [JCAE] and the executive Atomic Energy Commission [AEC]) made the negotiation of agreements difficult to achieve. Even when an agreement was eventually signed with Britain in 1955, it proved difficult to fully implement. It did enable the RAF and the USAF to cooperate more effectively through an arrangement known as 'Project E', which permitted the transfer of nuclear weapons to British forces for use in an emergency.[12] (See Appendix 2.) Worries were expressed in Congress, however, particularly about the dangers of encouraging proliferation and about the possibility of the Soviet Union gaining access to US nuclear secrets as a result of weaknesses in British security arrangements.[13] Even before the frustrations associated with the implementation of the 1955 agreement, in 1954 the Churchill government had taken a series of decisions to not only develop thermonuclear weapons, but to also expand the production of plutonium and highly enriched uranium by building six new nuclear reactors and extending other production plants. By doing so, Britain was, in part, attempting to demonstrate to the United States that it was an ally worthy of collaborating with and that it intended to remain a nuclear power.

Eisenhower Takes the Initiative

This approach seemed to be paying off in early 1956. Instead of waiting for the different federal agencies to reach a consensus on the need for greater Anglo-American nuclear cooperation, President Eisenhower began to provide more vigorous leadership in the nuclear field. On 22 March the US Joint Strategic Survey Committee (JSSC) sent a memorandum to the Joint Chiefs of Staff warning that

> if in time of tension with the Soviets the United States tried to launch the Intermediate Range Ballistic Missiles (IRBMs) from allied soil for the resolution of issues not considered vital to allied officials, allied governments might protest or even try to prevent the launching for fear of retribution against the missile bases or other targets on their soil by the Soviets.[14]

It was therefore vital, Eisenhower believed, to secure the cooperation of the allies, and this required greater sensitivity about their anxieties. In April the Department of Defence sent a draft amendment to the June 1955 agreement to the AEC (without informing the JCAE), permitting the transmission to Britain of nuclear submarine propulsion information.[15] At the same time, the administration opened negotiations with the British that led to a new agreement being signed on 13 June.[16] Announcing the new arrangement on 20 June, the British foreign secretary, Selwyn Lloyd, said that it would 'permit a broader exchange of materials in the Atomic Energy programmes of the two countries' and would 'also provide for the exchange of information concerning military package power reactors and other military reactors for the propulsion of naval vessels, aircraft and land vehicles'.[17] Despite disappointment over the limitations of the 1955 agreement, it seemed to the British government that greater nuclear cooperation with the United States was now within their grasp. Once again, however, bureaucratic disputes were to intervene to thwart British aspirations.[18]

When the administration revealed its plans to the JCAE on 8 June, the members protested that they had been kept completely in the dark by the administration and argued that the 1954 Atomic Energy Act did not allow for the exchange of nuclear submarine propulsion information with the British.[19] Such was their anger that they insisted that the president should suspend the new agreement. As a minority president, and faced with an imminent election campaign, Eisenhower had little choice but to agree.[20] For the British, the unfulfillment of yet another Anglo-American agreement was 'almost too much to bear'.[21] All the government could do was press ahead with its own independent nuclear programme and continue its patient diplomacy. In May 1956 the first two atomic tests (Mosaic) for two and a half years took place, and a further four were planned for the autumn. Preparations also continued for Britain's first thermonuclear test (Grapple) in the spring of 1957.[22] The advice from Sir Harold Caccia, the British ambassador in Washington, was that American acceptance of Britain as a Great Power and the possibility of exercising influence on US policy rested on having a military nuclear programme with 'megaton as well as kiloton weapons'.[23]

The Impact of Suez and Sputnik

What was needed, from the British point of view, was a dramatic turn of events that would transform congressional thinking about the need to cooperate closely with Britain in the nuclear field. Fortuitously (from Britain's point of view), in late 1956 and late 1957 two events took place that encouraged Eisenhower 'to use his vast prestige as a popular president, a sound strategist, and an admired war hero' to override congressional opposition and achieve the kind of nuclear partnership he had been advocating for some time.²⁴ Ironically, it was to be the Suez crisis of October–November 1956 and later the launch by the Soviet Union of Sputnik in October 1957 that created the circumstances that finally transformed rhetoric into reality.

Suez, which was without doubt the lowest point in Anglo-American relations in the post-Second World War period, produced the conditions for a major surge forward in nuclear cooperation. In the aftermath of the crisis, and with Britain humiliated largely as a result of US actions, Eisenhower recognized the need to take the first steps to restore the relationship. With a new government in power in Britain led by Harold Macmillan (a close wartime friend of the president), in January 1957 Eisenhower directed the US Embassy in London to invite the prime minister to a conference in Bermuda in March.²⁵ With a growing threat perceived from the Soviet Union, increased defence cooperation was chosen as the symbol for the restoration of the close bilateral relationship between the two countries. By way of preparation for the summit meeting, the British minister of defence, Duncan Sandys, visited Washington on 29 January for talks with his opposite number, Charles Wilson. The advice given to Sandys by the Foreign Office prior to his visit was 'to avoid giving the appearance of running after the Americans'—but he was also told not to appear 'too resentful'.²⁶

In their talks, Sandys and Wilson set out the framework for the Bermuda meeting and a series of wide-ranging defence negotiations to follow. The issues they discussed included the adaptation of British bombers to carry US nuclear weapons (under the terms of 'Project E'), the storage of American nuclear weapons on British territory, and greater coordination between the RAF and the US Strategic Air Command (SAC) on strategic bombing targets. The United States also undertook 'to do something special' for Britain should an international agreement be reached on ending the production of fissile materials. The most significant US proposal, however, was that American Intermediate Range Ballistic Missiles (IRBMs) should be based in Britain. Under the plan, Britain would receive four squadrons of *Thor* missiles (60 missiles in all). The warheads would remain under American control, as US law required, but a joint Anglo-American decision would be required before the missiles were launched. From the United States' point of view, the missiles would improve the West's response to recent Soviet developments in the thermonuclear and missile fields and would provide psychological assurance to Britain and the other NATO allies that the United States was committed to the defence of Western Europe. The United States also had plans to deploy *Jupiter* missiles to Italy and Turkey. For Britain, Thor missiles were an important breakthrough in the further development of a close Anglo-American nuclear partnership. They also fitted in closely with Sandys' desire to place more emphasis in British defence policy on nuclear deterrence (shortly to be announced in his Spring 1957 Defence White Paper). They would provide Britain with partial responsibility for a thermonuclear IRBM capability long before the UK's indigenous *Blue Streak* IRBM was scheduled to be deployed in 1960.[27]

Despite continuing opposition from the JCAE, after Sandys' successful visit to the United States, on 5 February 1957 President Eisenhower ordered the AEC, DOD, and State Department to implement the June 1956 agreement with Britain. The president was determined to play a more vigorous role in achieving closer Anglo-American nuclear partnership. At Bermuda, between 21 and 24 March, Eisenhower and Macmillan agreed on a wide range of areas of defence cooperation, including IRBMs, nuclear materials, combined intelligence operations, and joint military planning. The president also directed Lewis Strauss and the AEC, at long last, to brief the British on the dimensions and weights of American nuclear weapons so that British aircraft and bombing mechanisms could be adjusted to carry US nuclear weapons.[28]

Despite the major step forward in Anglo-American nuclear cooperation at the Bermuda meeting, a number of problems arose in the following months that dampened the renewed optimism in London. Although British scientists successfully detonated a hydrogen bomb near Christmas Island in the Pacific on 15 May, the yield of the device was disappointing.[29] Shortly afterwards, Harold Stassen, Eisenhower's special assistant on disarmament, put a proposal before the London Disarmament Conference designed to achieve an early end to the production of fissile material for military purposes. This led Labour MPs in the House of Commons to ask the government if it would adhere to the American call for disarmament.[30] An angry Macmillan wrote to Eisenhower in June pointing out the political embarrassment Stassen had caused for his government and recalling Wilson's offer to Sandys in January that the United States would do something 'special' for Britain in the event of an international moratorium on testing.[31] In his reply, Eisenhower effectively repudiated Stassen's initiative. He assured the prime minister that 'there is no agreed upon American position which is to be interpreted as a basis for negotiations with the Soviets'.[32]

Although the president's reply helped to allay British fears that the Americans might be interested in preventing the accumulation of a larger stockpile of nuclear weapons, continuing negotiations on the deployment of Thor missiles created renewed difficulties.[33] By the summer of 1957 a wide range of differences had arisen between British and American officials over issues such as the custody of missiles deployed in Britain, the division of costs, the selection of targets to be attacked, the terms under which the British might replace the missiles and the warheads with British-built missiles and warheads, and the conditions under which the IRBMs would be used. Given the largely unresolved problem of the use of American bombers based in Britain, the government continued to 'insist on a strong right of consultation, if not veto, over the use of any American IRBMs on British soil'.[34] By autumn the negotiations had stalled. The impetus and optimism that had been created by the Bermuda conference in March had long since 'dissipated in a morass of details and disagreements'.[35]

At this point, another event occurred that led to new initiatives in the field of Anglo-American nuclear relations. On 4 October *Sputnik I* was launched by the Soviet Union. This was a major psychological shock to the American public, politicians, and scientific community, changing the prevailing perception of Soviet technological inferiority. Suddenly the Soviet Union seemed to be ahead. As James R. Killian argued: 'Overnight there developed a widespread fear that the country lay at the mercy of the Russian military machine and that our government and its military arm had abruptly lost the power to defend the homeland itself, much less to maintain US prestige and leadership in the international arena.'[36] For Britain, Sputnik was a shock, but it also provided an important opportunity for British diplomacy. On 7 October Harold Caccia sent a telegram from Washington to the Foreign Office arguing that the time was ripe for a high-level approach to repeal the McMahon Act. This view was supported by senior officials in the Foreign Office, as well as by Sir Edwin Plowden, the head of the Atomic Energy Authority, Sir Richard Powell, the Permanent Secretary in the Ministry of Defence, and Sir Frederick Brundrett, the Chief Scientific Adviser in the MOD.[37] On 10 October Macmillan wrote to Eisenhower to suggest a meeting with the president, and on the same day Sandys told the Conservative party conference that American officials 'would get a ready response if they now brought forward a proposal for greater Anglo-American exchanges of information'. Such exchanges, he argued, would eliminate wasteful duplication and permit the accelerated development of nuclear forces to match Soviet technological advances.[38]

Unfortunately for the prime minister, on 10 October a fire broke out at the Windscale nuclear reactor in Cumberland. The fire lasted for three days, releasing substantial amounts of radioactive material which spread across the UK and Europe. There was considerable anxiety in the British government at the time that the incident would have a detrimental effect on negotiations with the United States, which had reached a critical juncture. Despite the fire, however, the prime minister's initiative was well received in the United States, especially by those officials (such as General Herbert Loper, assistant to the Secretary of Defense) who had long supported greater Anglo-American nuclear cooperation against congressional opposition. An invitation was sent to Macmillan to visit Washington for talks with the president on 24 and 25 October. Just before the meeting took place, the Secretary of State, John Foster Dulles, told Livingston T. Merchant, the ambassador to Canada, that the president was ready to go 'pretty far' with the British.[39] What Eisenhower had in mind was revealed on the first day of the conference when Dulles proposed a 'Declaration of Common Purpose', advocating greater interdependence between the two countries. In line with this, the president promised to ask Congress to amend the atomic energy legislation, and two study groups were set up to work out the details of a more intimate nuclear partnership.[40] One group, headed by Strauss and Plowden, was asked to discuss overall nuclear cooperation and exchanges of nuclear information. The other group, headed by Sir Richard Powell, was asked to look at defence cooperation, particularly in the missile field. Following their initial successful meetings, on 25 October it was decided to set up a series of technical meetings over the following two months to take the discussions further.[41] The personal relationships established at these technical meetings were to prove an important element in laying the foundations for greater cooperation in the months and years that followed.

Part of the reason for the American decision to help Britain in the nuclear field was a desire to encourage the Macmillan government not to implement the deep cuts in conventional forces that had been announced in the 1957 Sandys White Paper. Both the president and Secretary of State Dulles were concerned that such cuts would have a detrimental effect on alliance cohesion and encourage other allies to follow suit. It is also clear that the US administration saw nuclear cooperation as a way of securing British support for American foreign policy in a number of areas. It was concerned that the UK should not push for a change in the representation of China in the United Nations. American briefing papers for Macmillan's visit to the United States also reveal that US officials wanted the British to maintain their position in the Persian Gulf, as well as an assurance that they would not try to undermine the progress towards European integration recently made with the Treaty of Rome.[42]

Despite these attempts to link nuclear cooperation (albeit indirectly) with support for US foreign policy objectives, the British were delighted by the outcome of the Washington conference. Unknown to them, however, disagreements still existed among American officials over how far cooperation with Britain should go. Dulles supported increased nuclear support for Britain, but he was concerned that an exclusive 'special relationship' would complicate relations with the United States' other allies. As Jan Melissen has argued: 'An important undercurrent in US nuclear policy conceived of the Anglo-American relationship in the wider context of US-European relations, which was at odds with the British conception of an exclusive bilateral alliance.'[43] Following Sputnik, many West European states perceived a weakening of the US nuclear guarantee to Europe and pressed for a greater say in US nuclear decision-making. For Eisenhower, with his long-term goal of handing over more responsibility for their own defence to the Europeans, the answer lay in a liberal system of nuclear sharing not only with Britain, but with the other

NATO allies as well. Cooperation with Britain in 1957, therefore, was seen, initially at least, as something that could eventually be broadened to include other alliance members.[44]

Although Strauss had finally been converted to the idea of providing information to Britain about the external characteristics of atomic weapons (partly due to the close personal relationship he had developed with Plowden), he remained unconvinced about telling the British about the 'inner geometry' of the weapons. Faced by the strong determination of the president in October to collaborate closely with the British, he considered resignation, arguing that he was not in favour of turning everything over to them irrespective of whether or not this involved information of a very secret character and whether or not there was, on the part of the British, a real 'need to know'. The Joint Chiefs of Staff also grumbled about putting too much confidence in the British. Such was the confusion on the American side over how much information to reveal that a meeting had to be called just after the Washington conference among Dulles, Strauss, and the president in order to achieve 'a clarification in our minds, the president's mind, and maybe Macmillan's, as to the scope of the reservations regarding weapons information exchanging'.[45]

Whatever the disagreement among American officials, the British had a very clear idea about what they wanted. The aim was to secure design and fabrication information on both atomic and hydrogen weapons that would save them millions of pounds and also help avoid the continuing domestic political difficulties they were facing over the question of a moratorium on nuclear testing. Specifically, they wanted 'information about the weight, dimensions and yield of American hydrogen weapons together with safety features, the vulnerability of weapons, fusing and firing features, loading checks and in flight procedures'.[46] Such information would allow British scientists to design delivery systems that would be compatible with American warheads.

As we have seen, the British Grapple tests of two thermonuclear devices in May and June 1957 had not been wholly satisfactory. Certainly they had provided a proof of principle and operationally had been very successful, but the yields had been much below the expected megaton. A further test in November (Grapple X), however, yielded 1.8 megatons, and further successful tests of other designs were to be carried out in 1958. This helped to provide further confirmation to those officials in the United States who wanted assurance that Britain had something to offer. In US–UK technical talks on 23 and 24 November and 3 and 5 December, rapid progress was made on a wide range of issues. American scientists were willing to exchange information on nuclear materials, anti-submarine detection, nuclear warheads, delivery systems, military propulsion and power reactors, and defence against ballistic missiles, as well as chemical and radiological warfare, infrared research, and thermionic valve research.[47] Despite this progress, two key problems continued to haunt the negotiations. These centred on the ongoing disagreements over the transmission of nuclear submarine propulsion information and negotiations on the Thor deal.

Eisenhower's directive in February 1957 to implement the July 1956 agreement with Britain led to a visit to Britain by the head of the US Navy's nuclear program, Rear Admiral Rickover, in May 1957.[48] In turn, this led to Royal naval officers being sent to the United States to study the navy's submarine programme. By October, however, Rickover had become worried that the presence of British officers was slowing down preparations for the Polaris sea trials at a time when the US Navy was competing with the other services for resources on strategic nuclear systems. By December 1957 relations had become strained, and British officers were complaining that they were not getting the information they had been promised. The situation was finally resolved when Rickover suggested that Britain should be allowed to buy a nuclear submarine reactor (the S5W) from the American company Westinghouse. This would allow the British to build their own nuclear submarines, it would save them money, and he would be able to get on with his work with Polaris without interruption.[49]

By late December most of the outstanding difficulties in the Thor negotiations had also been resolved.[50] With the successful US test of the Atlas ICBM on 17 December and rapid progress being made on Titan ICBMs, Polaris SLBMs, and the solid-fuelled Minuteman ICBM, the case for Thor deployment had declined. However, from the point of view of Dulles and Quarles (the US Deputy Secretary of Defense), Thor had considerable political importance in providing evidence of US commitment to NATO at a time when the American nuclear guarantee to Western Europe was being questioned as a result of the development of a Soviet ICBM capability.[51] For Britain as well, the deployment of Thor was an important symbol of the new special nuclear relationship (and the special relationship identity) that was gradually emerging. As a result, the frictions that had characterized the negotiations since 1956 evaporated, and by the end of the year the framework of an agreement had been reached.

Despite progress on these two important areas of submarine propulsion and IRBMs, as the American Embassy in London told the State Department, for the Macmillan government it was the ability to modify US atomic energy legislation that had 'become the touchstone of American intentions' by the end of 1957. On 18 December, following the late November and early December technical talks, an interim report was signed between American and British officials and was to be sent to the president and the prime minister. Both governments, however, continued to face a number of additional difficulties that complicated the final stages of the negotiations.[52]

In Britain the Macmillan government was still facing pressure to agree to a moratorium on nuclear testing, especially after the Soviet Union announced a surprise unilateral end to testing in March.[53] The Labour Party also renewed earlier criticisms of the government's apparent inability to achieve a veto over American nuclear operations from British bases. In late 1957 and early 1958 the 'Reflex Action' exercises took place, which involved the rotation of nuclear-armed American B-47 aircraft across the Atlantic so that they could remain on 15-minute ground alert at RAF bases in Britain.[54] Faced with new anxieties about a surprise attack, the US Strategic Air Command was developing new arrangements that would allow aircraft already in flight to turn immediately to attack key targets in the Soviet Union if the US early-warning system detected an impending strike.[55] It was clear, Labour spokesmen said, that there could be no veto over US aircraft based in Britain operating such procedures.[56] The situation was made worse shortly after the Thor Agreement was finally reached on 22 February 1958, when a statement was made by a Colonel Zinc of the USAF, who claimed that he would be taking over 'operational command of the missiles' in Britain.[57] Even though the statement was repudiated by the US government, Macmillan faced renewed criticisms that there was no effective veto and that Britain had become dangerously dependent on the United States. The Conservative government rejected these criticisms but continued to press for an early agreement with the United States before the pressure to accept a moratorium on testing became too great. The prime minister remained privately concerned that the existing arrangements relating to American bases in Britain were far from satisfactory.[58]

Last Minute Problems

In the United States, despite growing support in Congress for increased nuclear cooperation with Britain, the president still faced a difficult task in persuading some members of the JCAE to accept his plans for amending atomic energy legislation.[59] When the JCAE Subcommittee on Agreements for Cooperation came to consider the amendments between 29 and 31 January, several members continued to express their opposition. Representative Chet Holifield (D-CA) stated that he 'genuinely held reservations that the administration was going too far, too fast in agreeing to give the British and other allies nuclear information, parts and materials without proper compensation or safeguards against an escalation of the arms race'. The former chairman of the JCAE, Senator Clinton P. Anderson (D-NM), a long-term opponent of nuclear cooperation with the British, was also anxious that the vagueness of the proposed amendments would allow the administration to pass on secrets about thermonuclear weapons as well as atomic weapons. Significantly, in terms of what was to follow, at the hearings he was assured by Quarles that 'there is no thermonuclear design that we now either have or contemplate that would be of a character that you could transfer under this plan'.[60]

Although the JCAE as a whole favoured increased cooperation with Britain by the summer of 1958, due to growing concerns about Soviet technological developments, difficulties continued over an AEC proposal to link the nuclear submarine reactor transfer to the transfer of British information about Calder Hall, a gas-cooled, graphite-moderated nuclear power station.[61] The JCAE was anxious that there should be reciprocity, and the one area where Britain was ahead of the United States was in the field of civil nuclear power. In their turn, the British government believed that this information would be passed on to private companies in the United States who would use it to undermine Britain's future commercial nuclear position. Despite continuous pressure from the State Department throughout June to accept the linkage, Macmillan dug his heels in and refused. Eventually, the administration was persuaded to drop the linkage.[62] With this final difficulty settled, the amendments to the Atomic Energy Act of 1954 were passed by Congress on 30 June.

To overcome JCAE worries about nuclear proliferation, the new act (under Section 6) authorized the president to give restricted data on atomic weapons only to those countries (such as Britain) that had made 'substantial progress' in the nuclear field in order to improve their atomic weapons design, development, and fabrication abilities. Such information could only be provided if, in the president's judgement, it would 'promote and not constitute an unreasonable risk to the common defense and security of the United States'. The act also allowed (under Section 1) the transfer by sale, lease, or loan of nonnuclear parts to an ally that had made 'substantial progress' in the nuclear field in order to improve that ally's state of training and operational readiness.[63] The act did not name any ally or allies, but in 1958 only Britain met the 'substantial progress' requirements.

The 1958 Mutual Defence Agreement (MDA)

The day after the act became law on 2 July, John Foster Dulles and Samuel Hood, the British minister in Washington, signed a new bilateral agreement for 'Cooperation on the Uses of Atomic Energy for Mutual Defense Purposes'.[64] Under Article 2a of the agreement, Britain and the United States promised to exchange information for:

> the development of defense plans, the training of personnel in the employment of, and defense against, atomic weapons and other military applications of atomic energy, the evaluation of the capabilities of potential enemies in the employment of atomic weapons and other military applications of atomic energy, the

development of delivery systems compatible with the atomic weapons which they carry, and research, development, and design of military reactors to the extent and by such means as may be agreed.

Article 2b also allowed for the communication of information by one party to the other to improve the recipients 'atomic weapon design, development and fabrication capability'. In addition, as Admiral Rickover had recommended, under Article 13, a private American company (Westinghouse) would be permitted to sell to the British government a complete nuclear submarine reactor and spare parts, together with 'information relating to safety features and information for the design, manufacture and operation of the reactor'. In deference to Congressional concerns that 'do-it-yourself' kits for nuclear weapons should not be provided to allies, the agreement did not allow for non-nuclear components to be passed on to the British. Eisenhower himself was unhappy about this restriction, and it was subsequently removed in a further agreement that was signed on 2 May 1959.[65]

In the literature on Anglo-American nuclear relations, there has been considerable speculation about the question of whether the 30 June 1958 Atomic Energy Act and the 3 July 1958 Mutual Defence Agreement allowed the United States to pass on to the British information about thermonuclear weapons. It will be remembered that at the JCAE Subcommittee on Agreements for Cooperation in January, Quarles had gone out of his way to reassure members that the administration had no intention of providing any allies, including Britain, with the designs of thermonuclear weapons. In his authoritative study *The Long Wait*, Timothy Botti argues that although the 1958 amendments to the 1954 Atomic Energy Act gave the Eisenhower administration the legal authority to provide information on both atomic and thermonuclear weapons, the JCAE 'made certain that the Administration did not agree to any exchange of hydrogen weapons data under the Anglo-American bilateral agreement of 3 July 1958'.[66] Botti goes on to argue that while it is unclear whether the 7 May 1959 agreement permitted thermonuclear data to be exchanged, it is likely that shortly after this agreement arrangements were made that did permit such an exchange to take place.

From the archival evidence available, it is clear that Botti is in error. On 10 August 1958 Macmillan wrote to Eisenhower expressing his concern about reports that the United States was once again seriously considering a moratorium on nuclear testing.[67] With the Grapple Z tests scheduled for late August and September, the prime minister wanted an assurance that, following the July agreement, Britain would receive the information it needed, especially on the essential technique of the weight reduction of warheads and their 'invulnerability'. In a document outlining the information to be initially exchanged with the UK, the AEC indicated a willingness to tell the British about certain thermonuclear weapons, as well as fission weapons. Yet the paper also highlights certain information about these weapons that should not be revealed to the British.[68] In a meeting on 20 August to discuss Macmillan's request, the president was told by Donald Quarles that the plans drawn up for the initial exchange did not 'go as far as to provide what the British requested'. In response to this the president 'stated most strongly' that the United States could not conduct its operations on such a basis. It had to be prepared, he said, to provide the British with such information as they needed for their further weapons development.[69] On the following day he went out of his way to see Dr Willard Libby, the chairman of the forthcoming technical talks with the British, in order to explain his 'philosophy' regarding the exchange of atomic information with the UK. Eisenhower told Libby that the United States owed Britain a debt from the Second World War. Any exchanges, he argued,

> should be full and generous: any attempt to do otherwise with true allys [sic] is bound to alienate them. The President cited the British assistance to the US in World War 11 through making their intelligence available to us (when we had no intelligence of our own, not having maintained intelligence sections between the wars); he further cited their assistance to us in getting work started on atomic weapons, in providing us information about radar, and information on the design and development of jet engines.[70]

In line with this sentiment, he replied to Macmillan, agreeing to pass on the information the prime minister had requested, arguing that he had no desire 'to push Britain, either politically or technically into an isolated position'. On this basis (which clearly implied a promise to pass on the specific information on thermonuclear weapons that the British wanted), both governments agreed that a moratorium could begin on 31 October.[71]

Anglo-American Technical Meetings: The Exchange of Nuclear Secrets Begins

At the first of the technical meetings between scientific officials, which took place in Washington on 27 and 28 August, the British participants were given a wide range of information on the external characteristics of different thermonuclear weapons, as well as the amount of special materials they contained, safety features, mechanical and electrical design, and vulnerability. At the meeting two documents were formally exchanged, and the British were told on a personal basis about nine American weapons, including three megaton warheads (the Mark 27, Mark 28, and Mark 15/39).[72] On the basis of the information provided by the British on their own fission and thermonuclear weapons research, it was recognized in the United States that Britain had something significant to offer the partnership.[73] According to an assessment of the meeting sent to the president shortly afterward, British scientists were 'judged to be of outstanding calibre by their US counterparts'. It was also apparent to the US scientists involved that 'substantial advances made by the United Kingdom would be of great benefit to the United States' and that British 'weapons development personnel have manifested a high degree of ingenuity in designing their weapons, and they have certain theoretical designs of great potential value'. The Americans were particularly interested in the forthcoming Grapple Z tests, which they felt might contribute usefully to the American programme.[74] Reflecting this, Macmillan wrote with great satisfaction in his diary on 1 September that

> we are as far, and even further advanced in the art than our American friends. They thought interchange of information would be all give. They are keen that we should complete our series, especially the last megaton (Halliard 1, September 11), the character of which is novel and of deep interest to them.[75]

The Washington meeting was followed by another from 15 to 17 September at the Sandia Laboratory in Albuquerque, New Mexico. At this meeting the US AEC gave 'the British fabrication (and design) prints, material specifications, and relevant theoretical and experimental information related to the specific designs and individual components of certain specific weapons'.[76] The British were particularly interested in two American warheads. The Mark 28 was seen as 'economical and versatile' and 'the most impressive of the American warheads': it could be used as a free-falling bomb, a powered bomb, a tactical bomb, and an IRBM warhead, with yields varying from 10 kilotons to 1.1 megatons. They were also interested in the Mark 47 (initially viewed as a 'scrappy assembly') which was suitable for ballistic missiles (and was later used in the Polaris system). At the end of the meeting, Sir William Cook, the head of the UK delegation, cabled to London to say that there was 'no doubt that our technical achievements in thermonuclear warheads, invulnerability and component techniques, with our resources and timescale, have considerably impressed US delegates and [have] been reason for more forthcoming attitude than formal procedures would dictate'.[77] A US report on the meeting reveals equal satisfaction with the outcome. 'The United States', it was argued, 'emerged with a clear understanding of the progress the United Kingdom has made in research and design and a recognition of certain areas where the United Kingdom has underway effort which should, if directed in lines complementary to the US effort, lead to greater overall combined progress'.[78] At Sandia, it has been said that 'twelve years of history unrolled in a few hours'.[79]

By the autumn of 1958, freed from the political constraints that had characterized the Anglo-American nuclear relationship for many years, 'information streamed across the Atlantic at a breathtaking pace'.[80] Between 17 and

25 November, American scientists visited Aldermaston and discussions took place on the production by Britain of 'the first mass-produced thermonuclear weapon in the US stockpile'.[81] These discussions on the Mark 28 bomb were continued from 8 to 17 December, when a group of British scientists visited a number of AEC facilities, including the Livermore Laboratory in California. 'Here they received detailed information on tools and techniques, and the Americans showed them pertinent documents and drawings of weapon parts.'[82] Further meetings were held in the first quarter of 1959, when Britain received 'fabrication prints, design prints, and material specifications on the Mark 28 bomb'.[83] At the end of February, 'four crates of drawings and papers were handed over by the AEC to the British staff in Washington'.[84]

Between 13 and 14 April a 'Stocktake' meeting was held in London to evaluate what had been done since the 1958 agreement and to look forward to widening the scope of future nuclear collaboration. At the meeting, twenty specific subjects for exchanges of information were identified, including diagnostic methods and interpretation, radio flash, health physics, mechanical safing, interpretation of yield measurements, and physical metallurgy of plutonium. This information was to be exchanged by a system of exchange visits and reports (EIVR). At the meeting it was also agreed to set up fifteen joint working groups (JOWOGs) that would focus on areas of common interest. These would deal with subjects such as antimissile defence systems, a lightweight (500–600 lb) megaton warhead, external neutron sources, safety of high explosives, compatibility of materials, vulnerability, and underground and outer space testing.[85] At the same meeting the UK delegates asked for, and received, full information on the American Mark 47 warhead.[86]

Thus, contrary to Botti's claims, it is clear that Britain did receive a wide range of information about American thermonuclear weapons, and many other aspects of the US nuclear programme, following the 1958 MDA and long before the follow-up agreement in May 1959. What the 1959 agreement did was to widen the range of cooperation to include the exchange of materials (British plutonium for US uranium 235, tritium, and lithium) and the sale of non-nuclear components to Britain. As a vital material in the development of thermonuclear warheads, tritium was especially important to Britain. It would have been very expensive for Britain to have produced its own facilities for producing tritium. What emerged from the scientific exchanges in the aftermath of the bilateral agreement was a mutual respect between the British and American scientists involved and the beginning of a system of JOWOGs and EIVRs back and forth across the Atlantic that provided the framework for a quiet, highly complex, flexible, and largely secret nuclear relationship that has remained in place ever since. At various times JOWOGs were added, cancelled, or modified to meet the changing technical and scientific requirements of the day. Writing in 1994 Robert S. Norris, Andrew S. Burrows, and Richard W, Fieldhouse highlighted the complexity and the long-term significance of the JOWOGs and EIVRs in maintaining the close nuclear partnership between Britain and the United States. They pointed out that the remarkably wide range of topics discussed and the kinds of information exchanged had grown over the years to include subjects such as:

> one-point safety, computer codes, metallurgy and fabrication technology for beryllium, uranium and plutonium, corrosion of uranium in the presence of water vapour, underground effects tests, outer space testing, clandestine testing, the technology of lithium compounds, high explosives, deuterium monitors, extinguishing plutonium fires, high-speed cameras, mechanical safing, liquid and solid explosive shock initiation, environmental sensing switches, neutron sources, tritium reservoirs, telemetry.[87]

Although the United States was to develop nuclear relationships with other allies during the Cold War, there can be no doubt that the scale and depth of the exchange of nuclear secrets with Britain under the 1958–9 agreements were qualitatively different.[88]

The Significance of the Mutual Defence Agreement

The Mutual Defence Agreement reached between Britain and the United States on 3 July 1958 is one of the most remarkable agreements ever reached between two sovereign states.[89] It provided for the unprecedented exchange of a wide range of vital nuclear secrets and established a framework for an Anglo-American nuclear partnership that remained in force throughout the Cold War period and which continues today. The significance of the Agreement, however, remains a matter of debate, especially the reasons why, after a considerable period of reluctance to engage in a close nuclear partnership, the Eisenhower administration agreed to a major amendment of the 1946 McMahon Act. Two distinctively different arguments have been put forward to explain the decision to share many of its most vital nuclear secrets with Britain from 1958 onwards. One argument focuses on effective (or perfidious, according to some American judgements) British diplomacy. According to this view, the British used the concept of the 'special relationship' as a 'tool of diplomacy', exploiting the close wartime relationship between Eisenhower and Macmillan to gain preferential treatment and secure influence over US decision-making.[90] The other, contrasting argument is that the Americans had a clear view of what Britain was trying to achieve and used the nuclear partnership themselves to secure British dependence on the United States and unconditional support for US foreign and defence policy during the Cold War.[91]

It would seem, however, that the reasons for American nuclear assistance to Britain are more complex than either of these two interpretations suggest. While there is probably some truth in both, neither provides a convincing explanation for the 1958 agreement and the nuclear partnership that followed. After the setback of the 1946 McMahon Act, one of the principal objectives of both Labour and Conservative governments was to resume the intimacy of the wartime nuclear partnership. They believed that in the context of the Cold War, British security interests were best served through the development of a national nuclear deterrent force and a close nuclear alliance with the United States. This they pursued with doggedness and patience, despite the disappointments of the 1948 *Modus Vivendi* and the 1955–6 agreements. For reasons of national security, Great Power status, and a perceived need to influence US decision-making, Britain did seek to establish and exploit a preferential 'special relationship' with the United States in order to gain access to the vast American nuclear programme. Despite Suez, no opportunity was lost (especially after Sputnik) to emphasize the need for greater interdependence in the security field to deal with the growing strategic power of the Soviet Union. With the 1958 agreement this crucial objective was finally achieved.

The fact that Britain succeeded in many of its objectives seems to be confirmed by complaints from American diplomats, such as Undersecretary of State George Ball, about the way the British deliberately used sentimentality to the detriment of US interests. Ball claims that 'the emotional baggage of the "special relationship" got in the way of cooler American judgement', and, by helping Britain in the nuclear field, US interests in preventing the proliferation of nuclear weapons and maintaining alliance cohesion was undermined.[92]

At the same time, despite these successes of British diplomacy, a case can also be made that there was a price to pay for the continuous help Britain received from the United States. In many ways, Ball exaggerates the extent to which Britain has been able to exploit the concept of the 'special relationship' and the detrimental effects it has had on US diplomacy and security policies. In explaining the reasons why the United States agreed to give Britain such generous nuclear support under the 1958 and 1959 agreements, it is clear that President Eisenhower and many of his close advisers believed that US security and diplomatic interests were significantly enhanced by the close relationship with Britain. From the late 1950s, as Andrew Pierre has argued, Britain often 'tied herself to the American order of priorities in research, development and production and in some respects at least became partially dependent on American satellite intelligence, navigation and radio communications systems'. Pierre, a former State Department official, is probably right in his claim that, as a result, Britain 'undoubtedly lost a measure of her strategic independence' and the United States secured a measure of control over British nuclear policies.[93] The United States also sought, with some success, to link cooperation in the nuclear field with broader British support for US foreign policy objectives, especially in the United Nations, the Middle East, and Europe. A case can therefore be made that the overall benefits were rather more equal than is often supposed. (See Appendix 5.)

One of Eisenhower's key objectives while he was in office was to reduce the economic burden of American defences. He saw the US military presence in Europe as temporary, designed to provide the necessary protection while the Europeans developed their own political institutions and defence capabilities. By the late 1950s, however, he was increasingly concerned by the overdependence of the Europeans on the United States and saw the sharing of nuclear secrets with US allies as being an important way to help build confidence and contribute to the establishment of a European nuclear force. As Marc Trachtenberg has shown so convincingly, the arrangements with Britain in 1957–8 were seen not as a contribution to the development of a 'special relationship' with Britain, but as a kind of 'opening wedge' for a broader sharing of nuclear information with US NATO allies in general.[94] Although this conflicted with Britain's desire for an exclusive bilateral partnership, Eisenhower believed that US (and Western) interests were best served through the development of a 'third great power bloc', working closely with the United States to contain the Soviet Union. This would also allow the withdrawal of American military forces from Europe. Although there was a shift in US policy towards greater centralized control over nuclear weapons in 1960 (leaving a de facto 'special nuclear relationship' with Britain as the legacy of the nuclear sharing policy), it remains the case that Britain did not manoeuvre the United States into that relationship as a result of some sort of sentimental blackmail, as Ball implies.[95] The US had its own distinct interests, which it was trying to pursue.

It is also clear that, in order to protect its own interests in a number of areas of the nuclear relationship, the United States was not as forthcoming as Britain might have wished. There was a continuing reluctance, even on Eisenhower's part, to pass on to British officials the latest information of the highest secrecy, which they did not need to know. Also, despite the sale to Britain of a submarine nuclear propulsion plant under the 1958 agreement, British hopes of continued collaboration in this field went unfulfilled. After 1958 Admiral Rickover stubbornly refused to include the British in any subsequent improvements in US submarine technology. As a result, later British submarine reactors were produced independently by Rolls Royce.

For the United States, its nuclear bases in Britain were also a very important part of its strategic plans against the Soviet Union, especially in the era before the development and deployment of intercontinental ballistic missiles. These bases created a number of problems for Britain, including the dangers associated with nuclear accidents. In July 1956 an American B-47 bomber crashed into a nuclear storage facility at the US Lakenheath Air Base in Suffolk. According to one bomb disposal officer who undertook an examination of the incident, 'it was a miracle that one of the Mark 6 (nuclear bombs) with exposed detonators sheared didn't go'. According to Eric Schlosser, 'the nuclear cores of the weapons were stored in a different igloo. If the B-47 had hit that igloo instead, a large cloud of plutonium could have floated across the Suffolk countryside.'[96] Also in February 1958, another B-47 aircraft based at Greenham Common and loaded with nuclear weapons caught fire and burned out. In 1960 signs of high-level radioactive contamination were detected by AWRE scientists, although there was no official confirmation that the incident had involved nuclear weapons.[97]

The issue of consultation over the use by the United States of nuclear weapons in general, as well as the use of American bases in Britain, also remained a bone of contention (at least in private) between the two states. Faced with the danger of nuclear attack, throughout the 1950s British governments sought an arrangement with the United States to ensure that Britain retained a veto over the use of UK-based American nuclear aircraft (and later missiles). Successive British governments also tried to manoeuvre American presidents into accepting the principle of consultation before any decision was made to use nuclear weapons. In both areas, the British were largely unsuccessful. Although American officials accepted the need to consult before using bases in Britain, they stuck to the position that this could only take place if the necessary time was available. They refused to accept any British veto over the American use of nuclear weapons in general, even though Britain would certainly be in the front line of any nuclear conflict with the Soviet Union. Even though Macmillan argues in his memoirs that a secret agreement was reached in June 1958 (known as the Murphy-Dean Agreement) to tie up the 'loose arrangements' made between Attlee and Truman in October 1951 and Churchill and Truman in January 1952, it is now clear that the United States did not modify its position to any great extent in this agreement. When public concern over US bases in Britain periodically re-emerged in later years, the government response was always to refer back to the 'understandings' of the early 1950s, without any mention of the 1958 agreement.[98] Successive British governments recognized that there were limits on how far they could press the United States on this matter.

Conclusion

It would be wrong to conclude from this, however, that the United States pursued a clear single-minded policy designed to secure British dependence. The competitiveness and rivalries between, and within, the federal agencies meant that American policy was often incoherent, emerging as a result of bureaucratic compromises, domestic political circumstances, or shock external events. From 1953, when Eisenhower became president, there was a discernible shift in US policy in favour of greater nuclear cooperation with America's allies, and especially with Britain. Initially the president had to balance competing political demands, and this meant that progress in the negotiations was slow. By 1957, however, the president had managed to convince a majority in Congress and the JCAE that the deteriorating strategic relationship with the Soviet Union required more cooperation with allies in the nuclear field, and especially with Britain. The fact that Britain was already a nuclear power meant that, for the president, fears of encouraging further proliferation were secondary. Although there were some anxieties within the administration about the effects of close relations with Britain on other allies, Eisenhower himself believed that alliance cohesion would be strengthened as a result of a close Anglo-American nuclear relationship. Ultimately, therefore, it was the president's perception of the requirements of American national interests (no doubt coloured by his wartime experiences), as much as effective British diplomacy, and changing international events that finally overcame powerful bureaucratic opposition and brought about the successful completion of the Anglo-American atomic energy negotiations.

Despite the president's leading role, there were others who played an important part in laying the foundations for the nuclear relationship. Even though the British have undoubtedly gained far more from the nuclear partnership, in scientific and technical terms, than the United States, the 1958 agreement was based on an American belief, especially within the scientific community, that Britain had something to offer the United States. It is clear that American defence officials, together with scientists and engineers working in the atomic energy field, welcomed the contribution that they believed British scientists could make to their own programme. In July 1958 Frederick Jandrey, the Deputy Secretary for European Affairs, told the US JCAE that:

> for us, the merging of British information and know-how in a common fund with our own ... should provide two direct benefits. Since nuclear weapons programmes have been carried out independently by each country we stand to gain from techniques developed by the British where they have solved the same problems which we faced by methods different from our own. For the same reason, where we find that British techniques developed separately are closely similar to those we have evolved, we can have added confidence in the evolution of our own program. Thus our weapons program should profit measurably through the stimulation which inevitably results from the cross-fertilization of ideas.[99]

This was very much the view of the US scientific community, and it was their very close professional and personal relationship with their British counterparts that reinforced the president's own determination to develop an intimate nuclear relationship with Britain. They formed part of what might be called a 'transatlantic nuclear advocacy coalition'.

For the government the fact that Britain had something to offer the United States was very important. Reciprocity helped to achieve what Macmillan called the 'great prize', after many unsuccessful years of trying to amend the McMahon Act.[100] It also ensured that Britain was able to develop a unique nuclear partnership, not available to any other US ally, and, with intelligence collaboration, became the basis of what governments ever since have called 'the special relationship'. It was believed to enhance Britain's Great Power status, reinforcing her self-identity as a nation apart, one that could act independently, but which also had close, preferential relations with one of the two world superpowers. Ritchie makes much the same point when he argues that:

> Being close to the United States [has been]...intrinsic to the defence and wider political establishment's identity. Possession of nuclear weapons [has been]...perceived to be part of what enables Britain to maintain political and military credibility in Washington, gain access to the highest levels of policy-making to support the 'special relationship', and to keep America engaged in the world.[101]

5
Polaris, Independence, and Interdependence

> We were really between the two worlds, the world of independence which was now ceasing to exist and the world of interdependence which we had not yet reached, though we were moving towards it. The nearer we got to it the more surrender of sovereignty there would have to be in practice, but until our design for interdependence was completed, we must be able in the last resort to control our own forces.
>
> Harold Macmillan, 1962[1]

The 1958 MDA created something of a paradox for Britain. On the one hand, the Conservative government of the day wished to maintain an independent nuclear deterrent. On the other hand, it also wanted to get the benefits, both political and military, of a close interdependent nuclear relationship with the United States. Increasingly it seemed that Britain's desire for Great Power status and independence of action in foreign and defence policy could only be achieved through a technological interdependence with the United States that resulted in some political and strategic dependence. The nature of this paradox can be seen in the Polaris Sales Agreement of 1963 and the subsequent efforts to improve Britain's strategic nuclear forces.

Interdependence and Nuclear Delivery Systems

In March 1957, four months after the Suez Crisis had ended and the same month that the Treaty of Rome was signed in Paris, British Prime Minister Harold Macmillan met President Eisenhower on the island of Bermuda, ostensibly to discuss the pressing issues of the day in one of their periodic Cold War summit meetings. As we have seen, at Bermuda the British government sought to repair some of the damage caused by Suez by agreeing to a public undertaking for America to station *Thor*, an intermediate range ballistic missile (IRBM) with a maximum range of 1,500 nautical miles, alongside the air bases in Britain that America was already operating for their medium bomber force.[2] Suez had demonstrated, in a most public fashion, the limits of Britain's post-war international position.

The Thor agreement, however, had its genesis three years prior to the Bermuda meeting, with the Wilson–Sandys Agreement which provided for 'close collaboration, exchange of information, mutual planning of development programs, joint discussion of technical questions and encouragement of firm to firm collaboration'[3] following the 1954 amendment to the McMahon Act of 1946.[4] This partial restoration of nuclear collaboration was warmly welcomed by the British. It was decided that, with America developing a missile of intercontinental range, Britain should develop a Medium Range Ballistic Missile (MRBM) programme of its own—a programme that eventually led to the development of *Blue Streak*, which in turn built on earlier work conducted in the UK and Australia.[5] The new arrangements gave Britain access to some of the latest American technology and helped pave the way for the Thor agreement and, later, the sanctioning of the sale of both the *Skybolt* and *Polaris* systems.

Britain's indigenous Blue Streak project, however, was to suffer from many of the strategic problems that troubled Thor, and it was cancelled in April 1960 in favour of the American Air Launched Ballistic Missile (ALBM), Skybolt.[6] The fault with Blue Streak lay not in the missile itself, which was better than anything yet produced and a glowing testament to the technological prowess of the team of scientists and engineers working on the project both in this country and at the Woomera test sites in Australia. Rather, it was a victim of escalating costs, a changing strategic landscape, and bureaucratic politics.[7] The missile was thought to be vulnerable to Soviet attack, but the RAF was also somewhat ambivalent about moving from manned bombers to missiles.[8] Significantly, the front-end of Blue Streak would have had a number of penetration aids (Penaids) and incorporated radar absorbent materials that made detection and discrimination a difficult process, research that would later feed into the *Chevaline* project.[9]

The agreement to purchase Skybolt from the United States, agreed between 27–31 March 1960 in Washington, with Britain supplying its own warheads, allowed the government to announce the cancellation of Blue Streak in Parliament on 13 April.[10] This meant that Macmillan could claim to have secured the maintenance of the independent aspect of the British nuclear deterrent even though Britain was now relying on a foreign power to maintain the credibility of its deterrent force into the mid-1960s. Skybolt, however, was still in development when the Washington Agreement was signed. It was only ever envisaged as a stopgap measure, but there was no other effective alternative system in the offing at the time of the cancellation of Blue Streak.[11]

Britain had one other delivery system to enhance the credibility of the nuclear deterrent into the 1960s, which was then carried exclusively by the Royal Air Force through the V-bombers, with an indigenous 'cruise missile' called *Blue Steel*.[12] Blue Steel began development during the late 1950s and was due to enter service with the RAF by 1961 or 1962. However, it was beset by delays, eventually operating from early 1963 until 1969. In the meantime Skybolt, which the RAF and Conservative government had invested with so much importance, was also suffering development problems at a time when manned bombers were becoming increasingly vulnerable to the growing numbers of sophisticated air defences the Soviet Union were deploying around their borders.

The US Department of Defense (DOD) headed by Robert MacNamara had for some time debated Skybolt's strategic merits and had only decided to continue to fund the project because of the sales agreement with the UK. Despite wanting to show solidarity with the British, Skybolt was cancelled in November 1962. There had been several official warnings from both the State Department and DOD regarding cancellation. Nevertheless, the British government was shocked at the manner of the cancellation and this precipitated a crisis in Anglo-American relations.[13] Despite a late offer to continue with the project with Britain taking a much larger proportion of the costs, Britain refused. By the late 1950s it was clear that Soviet anti-aircraft defences meant that the bomber would no longer always get through, as Stanley Baldwin had famously claimed 30 years before.[14] What the Conservative government of Harold Macmillan chose to pursue as a replacement was the submarine launched missile system Polaris.[15]

Negotiating the Polaris Agreement

When Prime Minister Harold Macmillan met his American counterpart John F. Kennedy in December 1962 at Nassau in the Bahamas, the key item on the agenda was the Skybolt cancellation. It was a crisis that many felt could bring down the British government. Macmillan, half American by birth, believed that it was imperative to breathe new life into the flagging 'special relationship'.[16] The prime minister believed that in order for deterrence to remain effective, Britain needed a submarine-based ballistic missile. He therefore vigorously pursued the US Polaris system at the Nassau Conference as an effective substitute for Skybolt. Following a tense meeting between the president and the prime minister and their key advisers, a joint communiqué was issued which committed the United States to sell to Britain complete Polaris missile systems and to provide the designs for the missile compartments.[17] By April of the following year the terms of an agreement had been hammered out, with the government opting to buy the vastly upgraded version of the missile, the A-3, which was still in development in the United States.[18] As Ian Clark comments:

> From the American point of view, the outcome of the meeting was hostage to wider policy issues. In particular, there was concern about the impact of Nassau upon the two elements of European strategy, namely Britain's application for membership of the Common Market, and also the projection of the Multilateral Nuclear Force (MLF).[19] Kennedy had to reconcile his political stake in the Macmillan Government, and in the special relationship more generally, with these wider foreign-policy concerns.[20]

Under the Nassau Agreement, Britain maintained its cherished asset 'at a knock-down price' that cost less than 2 per cent of the total British defence budget, whilst France had to struggle painfully and expensively to construct her own underwater deterrent without American assistance.[21] Furthermore, 'the whole business highlighted the extent of the dependency Britain had entered into after the cancellation of Blue Streak, and there was no disguising the fact that she was now firmly tied to the American order of priorities rather than to her own'.[22]

In many ways, as Andrew Pierre has argued, 'Nassau was a great turning point in the history of the British nuclear force. Before the conference a mix of events and ideas seemed to be forcing out the "independent deterrent"; after the conference the continuation of an independent capability was assured for perhaps another twenty years.'[23] At the same point, however, for the first time Britain accepted that it was not able to produce a credible means of delivering its nuclear weapons itself. The government claimed the virtues of both 'interdependence' and 'independence' simultaneously. Whilst the UK was now dependent on the United States to maintain a fully effective and economical means of nuclear delivery for its strategic deterrent, it would maintain operational independence through a UK-only command and control chain and at the same time manufacture its own warheads at the Atomic Weapons Research Establishment (AWRE) at Aldermaston.

AWRE's work was at the cutting edge of nuclear warhead design and development and was conducted with the benefit of exchanges (on specific issues) with the American nuclear weapons facilities at the Lawrence Livermore National Laboratory, Sandia, and at Los Alamos, along with a small number of civilian contractors.[24] As noted earlier, these exchanges at the technical 'working level' were conducted through Anglo-American Joint Working Groups and exchange visits (JOWOGs and EIVRs) created following the 1958 Mutual Defence Agreement (MDA).[25] After the 1963 Polaris Sales Agreement (PSA) these activities became linked to the strategic nuclear weapons programmes of the US Navy and their Special Projects Office (SPO) through the Department of

Defense, Atomic Energy Commission (AEC), and Lockheed Missile and Space Company (LMSC)—the manufacturers of Polaris, and later *Poseidon* and *Trident* missiles.[26]

By late 1964, the 1958 MDA and 1963 Polaris Sales Agreement (PSA), therefore, had fundamentally altered the entire basis of British nuclear weapons policy. No longer was there a truly independent British nuclear deterrent in all its aspects as had existed in 1958. Instead, there was a cooperative nuclear alliance with the Americans based on what Harold Macmillan liked to call 'interdependency'.[27] This 'interdependency' functioned within the multilateral alliance structure of NATO, but in many ways it resulted in a 'special nuclear relationship' which excluded other allies in the Western alliance.[28] (See Appendix 5.)

Polaris: Targetting Issues and the 'Moscow Criterion'

In the years after the Nassau Agreement, while the 'deterrence habit of mind' continued to dominate thinking within the political and military elite, there were constant debates about nuclear targetting, which eventually led to important changes in subsequent years in thinking about the operational role of nuclear weapons should deterrence ever break down. At the same time, the command and control arrangements for Polaris were being established to permit operational control over the strategic deterrent and allow for withdrawal from NATO operations to which they were normally committed in circumstances 'where supreme national interests were at stake'.

Polaris raised important questions about operational planning and how the force would be used. In order for it to be effective as a deterrent, the UK Chiefs of Staff (COS) decided that it was imperative that the British nuclear force should be able to attack Moscow with an assurance of destruction.[29] The 'Moscow Criterion', as it became known, was based on a Joint Intelligence Committee (JIC) assessment from 1962. (See Appendix 4.) This assessment was based on what they believed the Soviet Union would consider 'unacceptable damage'. The aim was to 'severely reduce the Soviet Union's economic and military strength in its struggle to overtake the United States and dominate the world'.[30] It was felt that it would not be unreasonable to assume that the Soviet leaders would consider that the certain destruction of their five largest cities would put them at an unacceptable disadvantage in relation to the United States. The selection of the five largest cities was made on a points system, points being awarded for the following:

a. Size of population.
b. Civil and administrative centres.

c. Centres of economic control.
d. Military command posts.
e. Telecommunications centres.

On this basis Moscow was the most important one of the five, and because of this the JIC assessment came to be known as the 'Moscow Criterion'.[31] By the time Polaris began to be deployed in the North Atlantic in 1968 the target set had been revised again, with an additional 7–11 Soviet cities chosen for targetting. These again included Moscow and Leningrad (the two most populous cities of the USSR), with a requirement of a minimum level of destruction of 50 per cent.[32] Of these 7–11 cities, the remainder had to have populations exceeding 300,000. These were the parameters, it was believed, for *independent* strategic nuclear targetting by the British Polaris force.[33]

As Sir Michael Quinlan, a former Deputy Under-Secretary in the Ministry of Defence (MOD), later indicated: 'to allow the Soviet Union (a state system very much based upon central governmental authority) to enjoy perceived sanctuary for their capital and a considerable area around it would risk weakening whatever concern they might feel about the UK capability and resolve'.[34] With the 'Moscow Criterion' at the centre of independent strategic targetting it became essential to make sure the deterrent force could get through the developing Soviet anti-ballistic missile (ABM) screen.[35]

Nuclear deterrence was not something that could be conclusively demonstrated.[36] There was no historical precedent to call upon, given the destructive potential of nuclear weapons (particularly thermonuclear weapons). Instead, the Chiefs of Staff (COS) had to rely on their own judgements based on their experiences of conflict in World War Two and their differing beliefs over what forces would be sufficient to deter a likely enemy from hostile action. This led to some differences between them about the emphasis to be given to 'independence' and 'interdependence'. The RAF favoured more emphasis on 'independence' while the Army and Navy stressed 'interdependence', which would involve more partnership with the United States. In September 1958 the Chief of the COS Committee, Sir William Dickson, had told the then Minister of Defence, Duncan Sandys:

> When the First Sea Lord and the CIGS state that they are absolutely opposed to the concept of an 'independent UK nuclear deterrent', they mean that they are opposed to attempts to possess ourselves with an 'unrestricted' deterrent which is powerful enough by itself to inflict unacceptable devastation on Russia. They do not think that there is a 'military' requirement for an 'independent' deterrent, but accept that 'political' reasons require us to have a contribution to the western deterrent which is not controlled by US strings. CAS agrees that our 'independent deterrent' does not have to be of a size capable by itself of defeating Russia but that

it must be of such a size and capability as to cause Russia to think twice before attacking this country and British vital interests.[37]

These differences of view between the members of the COS about 'independence' and 'interdependence' continued into the 1960s and had an impact on Britain's nuclear capability, especially in terms of the size of Britain's V-Bomber force. In 1955 it had been planned that 240 aircraft would be developed. By 1956 this had been reduced to 184, and then in 1963 to 120. By 1965, prior to the deployment of Polaris, the number had dropped to 88.[38]

Polaris and the 1964 Election

The most important element of the operational factors relating to Polaris was that national importance was attached to the maintenance of at least one submarine always on station (now known as Continuous At-Sea Deterrence [CASD]). In the run-up to the General Election of October 1964 the Conservative government under Douglas-Home maintained the traditional belief in the utility of its nuclear deterrent force. He told *The Times* that 'We have decided that Britain must be equipped to be present in the councils of war and peace—and to be there by right. And this means nuclear power.'[39] On the eve of the election he pointed out the differences between the Conservative and Labour attitudes to nuclear weapons in the following terms:

> As Foreign Secretary and now as Prime Minister I know that the world is a dangerous place. It is just at this moment, when France and China are becoming nuclear powers, that the Socialists would propose to discard all control by a British government over Britain's nuclear arms... I must be sure that each of you recognizes the consequences of such a Socialist decision. It would mean that we should surrender all our authority in world affairs and hand over the decision about the life and future of Britain to another country. This I am quite sure you cannot allow.[40]

Douglas-Home was highlighting the impression that the Labour Party had created during the election campaign that, if elected, it would give up Britain's nuclear weapons. Despite Hugh Gaitskill's reversal of Labour's opposition unilateralist policy in 1961, the party had remained deeply divided over what it would do about nuclear weapons if elected to power. In its manifesto, the new leadership of Harold Wilson avoided these divisions by claiming that it would renegotiate the Nassau Agreement, but did not go as far as specifically saying it would abandon nuclear weapons. As Labour's manifesto argued:

> The Nassau agreement to buy Polaris know-how and Polaris missiles from the USA will add nothing to the deterrent strength of the Western Alliance... We

are not prepared any longer to waste the country's resources on endless duplication of strategic nuclear weapons. We shall propose the re-negotiation of the Nassau Agreement. Our stress will be on the strengthening of our conventional regular forces so that we can contribute our share to NATO defence and also fulfil our peacekeeping commitments to the Commonwealth and the United Nations.[41]

The Labour Party criticized the 'independent deterrent' as being neither 'independent', because of its dependence on the US, nor a 'deterrent', because they argued that it lacked credibility.

With Wilson's victory in the 1964 General Election, it appeared for a time that Britain had a new government with very different beliefs about the utility of nuclear weapons for Great Power status, deterrence, and political influence in the United States. In practice, following the election, Wilson and his Defence Secretary, Denis Healey, proposed that Britain's V-Bomber force and the Polaris submarines, together with US nuclear forces and a French contribution, should form part of an Atlantic Nuclear Force (ANF). This proposal was made to counter an earlier project sponsored by the US State Department to set up a Multilateral Nuclear Force (MLF), consisting of a fleet of twenty-five surface vessels, each armed with eight Polaris A-3 missiles. The force was to be 'mixed-manned', with each ship having at least three nationalities, designed to achieve a partnership in nuclear management to discourage other NATO countries, and particularly West Germany, from wanting its own independent nuclear capabilities.[42]

The US would retain a veto over the use of the nuclear forces involved. Britain had opposed the MLF since it was first proposed in the late 1950s, on the grounds that it might be a device to undermine Britain's independent deterrent by factions in the US State Department who were known to want this. The Nassau Agreement had provided for Britain to pool its Polaris force with NATO, but it also allowed the UK to withdraw its forces from Alliance control 'if supreme national interests were at stake'. Nassau did, however, have the effect of reviving interest in the MLF idea. Continuing its opposition to the idea, Wilson put forward the idea of the ANF as an alternative. There has been a great deal of debate about why the Labour government did this. Most commentators have concluded that it used the proposal to undermine the MLF project, which the American government itself was largely unenthusiastic about. It has been suggested that this was 'the first time in history that one non-existent fleet was used to sink another non-existent fleet'.[43] It also deflected attention from the government's promise to renegotiate Nassau.

Although the Multilateral Force and Atlantic Nuclear Force proposals remained on the political agenda, the British government and their advisers were already beginning to move away from 'hardware' solutions such as the MLF and towards a 'software' solution through consultation measures within the Alliance framework. The Atlantic Nuclear Force, like the MLF proposals, was allowed to drift into obscurity, and by February 1966 it was being publicly reported that the ANF was effectively dead. Although the ANF was a serious proposal aimed at finding a solution to satisfy the concerns of the non-nuclear members of NATO it was never a preferred solution and was intended to avoid a schism with the US over such a public issue.[44] The ANF became a British-led 'stalking horse' aimed at forestalling the MLF until a more acceptable command and control mechanism could be negotiated, as well as providing a smokescreen for Wilson's policy reversal over Polaris.[45]

When both the MLF and ANF proposals were quietly dropped the Labour government was left with the Polaris forces, projected to enter into service in 1968. Wilson was keen to reject the Conservative idea that it was an 'independent deterrent' and to emphasize that it firmly committed to the NATO alliance. He challenged the Leader of the Opposition in a debate about the Polaris force in the House of Commons in December 1964:

> We want to know what sort of war they are going to have the deterrent for. Obviously not some nuclear Suez. We acquit them of that. Obviously not as a contribution to a trigger mechanism to bring the American bomb into action when the American government did not want to do it. The argument we have had is that one day we may get some lunatic American President, who, when the crunch came, was prepared to retire to Fortress America and to leave Europe to its fate. We have now answered that point, because we have made it clear that this (the British nuclear force) is committed to NATO as long as the alliance lasts. So I put it to the leader of the Opposition—what are they voting about tonight? It is not a nuclear Suez. It is not a trigger for the American strategic deterrent. We are left with one possibility—that the leader of the Opposition is talking about embarking on a go-it-alone war with the Soviet Union when the rest of the alliance does not wish to do so. Is that it? Our credibility depends on this—it depends on the credibility of the Government. I want the leader of the Opposition to tell us, as a former Prime Minister, as the head of the alternative government, knowing that a go-it-alone war would mean a certain amount of posthumous revenge against the Soviet Union and total annihilation of all human life in Britain, whether he would be prepared to press the button in that kind of war. If he is not prepared to answer that... this has proved their argument is a charade.[46]

Wilson went out of his way to dispel what he called the 'myth' of 'independence' by arguing that in many important respects, including the supply of fissile material, Britain remained highly dependent on the United States for the continuing viability of the Polaris force. For Wilson, interdependence with the United States inevitably undermined the previous Conservative government's claims to continuing independence. The belief in nuclear weapons as a means to independent 'Great Power' status was less pronounced in the leadership of the new Labour government. However, although the rhetoric played down independence, the Labour government was to retain a commitment to preserving important indigenous elements of Britain's nuclear force.

Britain and NATO Nuclear Policy in the 1960s

During the Wilson government Britain also played an important part in the development of NATO's nuclear deterrent strategy. Britain supported the Alliance's strategic concept of Flexible Response which, as MC 14/3, was accepted by NATO ministers at their meeting on 14 December 1967. British officials also played a leading role in Alliance Nuclear Planning Group (NPG), also set up in 1967. The NPG was established to deal with the outstanding problem left by the demise of the MLF. To deal with the difficulty of non-nuclear members of the Alliance, especially West Germany, feeling left out of the debate and the formulation of NATO nuclear strategy, the NPG was introduced to enable discussion amongst the members of the Alliance on issues relating to nuclear weapon doctrines, policies, and deployments. In these discussions British officials, such as Michael Quinlan, played a central role in the development of the Provisional Political Guidelines for the Initial Defensive Tactical Use of Nuclear Weapons (PPGs) in 1969. The aim of the Flexible Response strategy was to achieve deterrence by providing the necessary conventional and nuclear capability for 'apt and credible application of minimum effective force to fit any possible scenario' associated with aggression by the Soviet Union and the Warsaw Pact. This required building up a substantial range of military options which would be available to the Alliance at a time of crisis. According to Quinlan, the members of the NPG accepted that: 'Deterrence required making it as hard as possible for any adversary to form the view that NATO would shrink from decisions on raising the conflict's breadth or severity, or to dare to act on such a view'.[47]

Faced with Soviet conventional superiority in Europe, British officials were of the firm view that although the use of nuclear weapons was not inevitable if war broke out, there had to be convincing plans for their use. Without such plans, an Alliance deterrent strategy would be incredible. With their support the Provisional Political Guidelines were drawn up, which envisaged the idea of using nuclear weapons on a limited scale if Alliance conventional forces were being overrun. The aim would be to send a strong political message, short of the ultimate strategic strike, to an aggressor that 'he had mistaken NATOs political tolerance and under-rated NATOs will to resist, and that for his own survival he must therefore back off'.[48]

Given the range of possible options by an adversary, the PPGs laid out a checklist of factors that would have to be weighed carefully, including how many nuclear strikes would be necessary, the yield of the weapons used, and the level of collateral damage that might be inflicted. A judgement would have to be made about how to achieve 'the right balance between doing too little to drive home the message and doing too much to provoke a ferocious reaction in rage, spasm, or misunderstanding'.[49] While such realistic plans had to exist, it was felt that whether the Alliance would in fact take the terrible decision to cross the nuclear threshold would be a matter for NATO at the time. Officials rejected the view that if the Alliance did decide to use nuclear weapons this would inevitably lead to uncontrollable escalation to the strategic nuclear level. It was argued that the adversary would be left with the very difficult decision to escalate the conflict further and that there would be a good chance that this would lead to the termination of the conflict. The main thrust of adopting such 'a tough minded' approach, however, was to strengthen the chances of deterrence working. For defence officials, like Quinlan, the aim of using tactical nuclear weapons, if deterrence failed was to reverse the initial Soviet calculation of the comparative advantage of aggression to persuade the aggressor that the likely benefits of continuing were outweighed by the likely costs and risks, above all the risk that the weight of military effort needed to pursue military success would reach the point at which NATO might respond with a major strategic strike.[50]

With these weighty issues in mind and Britain a major contributor to NATO, Polaris was not cancelled by Labour. Rather, it was to be subsumed (or 'internationalized') in NATO. In the years that followed, Wilson kept the deterrent off the political agenda as much as possible in an attempt to guard against divisions within the Labour Party on the issue—divisions that remained apparent during the 1970s and 1980s.[51] In assessing these major policy decisions—the retention of a British nuclear deterrent, the proposals for an ANF, as well as the number of submarines to be built—it is interesting to ask if there ever was any possibility that the Wilson government would have relinquished Britain's hard won nuclear inheritance? Was the British state politically (and economically) ready to take that momentous step? The answer is probably 'no'. Public opinion remained divided on the issue, but only a minority favoured unilateral nuclear disarmament and the government continued to see some utility in possessing a nuclear capability.

At the highest political levels, Wilson and other senior figures in the Cabinet felt that possession of the nuclear deterrent brought with it international importance that could not be claimed through conventional means. Although there are scant references to Polaris or nuclear weapons in his memoirs, Wilson later maintained that:

> I never believed we had a really independent deterrent. On the other hand, I didn't want to be in the position of having to subordinate ourselves to the Americans when they, at a certain point, would say, 'We're going to use it,' or something of

that kind—though in fact, I doubt anyone expected it ever to be used. It wasn't that we wanted to get into a nuclear club or anything of that kind. We wanted to learn a lot about the nuclear thing, and so on. We might need to restrain the Americans, if we learnt about new things that could happen of a devastating character.[52]

Similar points were made *post facto* by Denis Healey, Secretary of State for Defence throughout Wilson's first government. He commented in his memoirs that: 'they [the UK Polaris submarines] would give Britain more of an influence, particularly in Washington, during the coming revision of NATO strategy, and because they would tend to reinforce the credibility of the American deterrent'.[53] Healey also stated that it was 'essential that we had a system which could commit the Americans if *we* used it. It was a kind of insurance policy'—an insurance policy and 'catalytic deterrent' which offered Western Europe a 'second centre' of nuclear decision-making.[54]

Four days after the 1964 General Election the Chief of the Naval Staff, Admiral Sir David Luce, had put forward the case for five submarines based on the operational requirements needed to maintain the same level of strategic targetting as the V-bombers.[55] Luce based the need for five submarines on the need to destroy twenty Soviet cities, as put forward by the Joint Intelligence Committee (JIC), aided by Joint Intelligence Global Studies on Atomic War (JIGSAW), regarding the level of destruction necessary to maintain independent nuclear deterrence.[56] This led to a dispute over the size of the Polaris force and revealed some interesting aspects of the contemporary British approach to nuclear deterrence. Its claim to be a 'minimum' deterrent was founded upon economic and political pragmatism, rather than strict military criteria at either the strategic and operational levels—it was overwhelmingly a politically based decision, for strategy is not formed in a vacuum: it is shaped by the economic vitality and political values of the state as well as its strategic culture.[57] The size of the Polaris force was a compromise between what was militarily desirable, economically affordable, and politically acceptable—including the commitments the UK government had made to the US in relation to NATO at the Nassau conference in 1962. In a wider context the balance between capabilities and commitments meant that the country was becoming stretched, economically and militarily—sometimes close to breaking point. This was an issue which was to be a hallmark of UK defence policy through to April 1967.

The British Polaris programme would prove to be a remarkable achievement, completed in 1968 on time and within budget, and was seen by some as 'by far the most ambitious building project undertaken by the Navy since the last war'.[58] With running costs at around 2 per cent of the overall defence budget, the UK Polaris force was also perceived by the government to be a cost-effective and credible strategic deterrent. It was believed that it enhanced the British state's strategic credibility, and many senior politicians across the political spectrum felt that it enhanced its international status.³⁹ By the time the Polaris fleet was deployed operational independence had also been assured through a national command and control chain.

Operational Independence

By June 1966, although it was recognized that ongoing discussions on NATO nuclear decision-making machinery might impinge on the targetting of Polaris, the Chiefs of Staff decided that there was no reason why provisional target planning should not begin.⁶⁰ The scope of discussions was to include:

a. Establishing [the] extent of NATO targeting requirements.
b. Drawing up [a] detailed timetable of planning events and confirming our own views on the procedure.
c. Making provision for UK naval representation as required in the nuclear planning organisation of the targeting authority.
d. Drawing up a provisional target list.
e. Establishing the factors on which to base subsequent detailed planning for communications and release procedures.⁶¹

George Leitch, the Deputy Under-Secretary of State (Policy), noted that for operational purposes the UK Polaris deterrent would be under the direction of the British government since 'control of the firing chain will remain in UK hands'.⁶² This crucial point was also reinforced in a minute from Healey to the prime minister on 3 August 1967. Healey told Wilson that he would inform NATO 'of our intention to assign the Polaris submarines to NATO in terms which would retain ultimate United Kingdom control and which would not prevent the removal of the force from NATO command'.⁶³

This position was also agreed amongst the Ministerial Committee on Nuclear Policy (an executive inner-cabinet group containing the prime minister, Defence Secretary, Foreign Secretary, and Chancellor of the Exchequer) after prior consultation with the Foreign Secretary, George Brown. More importantly, the command and control (C²) arrangements were such that 'no submarine commander would be authorised to fire the Polaris weapons without the Prime Minister's specific authority'.⁶⁴ It also meant that Polaris could be redeployed out of the NATO area if the situation so demanded.⁶⁵ This effectively maintained a UK national veto over the use of the strategic nuclear deterrent, thus allowing the government to use their nuclear forces independently 'where supreme national interests were at stake' in accordance with clause IV of the Nassau Agreement.⁶⁶

Due to these specific C² arrangements, only the Polaris missiles were to be assigned to SACEUR for targetting, but the submarines were in practice to remain under UK control.⁶⁷ This was due to their being assigned to the Supreme Allied Commander Atlantic (SACLANT), based in Norfolk, Virginia, who in turn always had a Royal Navy officer in charge of his subordinate command, the Eastern Atlantic (EASTLANT).⁶⁸ Healey also revealed that the submarines would always patrol in the North Atlantic.⁶⁹ Patrol in the Mediterranean was not favoured by the RN on operational grounds, partly due to the transit times from their base at Faslane in the north-west of Scotland, and also because the Mediterranean theatre was controlled directly by SACEUR.⁷⁰ Due to the possibilities of Soviet espionage, the movements of Polaris whilst on patrol were on a strictly national 'need to know' basis.⁷¹

The actual terms of their assignment to SACEUR were drafted on 3 August 1967 as follows:

> In accordance with paragraph 8 of the Nassau Communiqué date 21st December, 1962, Her Majesty's government have in a separate memorandum assigned to SACEUR all the missiles of the UK Polaris force, for targetting planning, state of readiness, co-ordination and execution of strikes in accordance with his nuclear strike plan... For military and other reasons, however, Her Majesty's Government have decided that the submarines should operate in the Atlantic area. In order therefore to implement paragraph 8 of the Nassau Communiqué in respect of the submarines, Her Majesty's Government have earmarked them for assignment to you [SACLANT] in emergency... This assignment... will be subject to the following conditions:
>   a. The missiles of the force must be available at all times for SACEUR's nuclear strike plan...
>   b. You are requested to issue instructions that during the whole period of assignment up to and including missile operations, the operational command and control of the submarines is to be delegated to CINCEASTLANT: after missile operations are completed, you will be free to dispose of the submarines as SSNs as you think fit.
>   c. The logistics and support of the submarines, as well as of the missiles assigned to SACEUR, will remain a national responsibility.⁷²

By tasking Polaris in this way the British government maintained national control over the strategic deterrent and could 'safeguard US information to the UK'.⁷³ Still, Healey remained anxious that the terms of its assignment to NATO under the Nassau Agreement were ambiguous and needed clarification, and was concerned enough to ask the Foreign Secretary to visit the United States to spell out the commitment, given that possible deployment east of Suez to provide nuclear guarantees to Commonwealth nations was still on the agenda.⁷⁴ Moreover, he did not want to publicize these arrangements with NATO, or the veto Britain held, and he did not want to see these matters debated in Parliament: his intention was to merely confirm to Parliament that the Polaris submarines would be assigned to NATO.⁷⁵

The detailed terms of the assignment of Polaris to NATO meant that a high degree of secrecy could be maintained concerning the command and control of British nuclear forces and the close supervision of executive nuclear policy by Wilson's inner Cabinet. It further demonstrates that even with the formal assignment of Polaris to the NATO SACEUR, in practice the UK retained the final decision on its use. This was seen as necessary to safeguard against a decline in the US nuclear guarantee, which could necessitate threatening an independent nuclear strike by the UK against a small number of Soviet cities, including the heavily defended Moscow area.⁷⁶

This minute by Healey is also revealing for another reason. In it he stated that its assignment to SACEUR/CINCEASTLANT was also designed to protect strictly bilateral intelligence secrets between Britain and the US that could not be shared with their allies in NATO.⁷⁷ This demonstrates that even within the NATO alliance, there were intelligence secrets that could not be shared with allies.⁷⁸ It further reveals how the Anglo-American strategic alliance operated within NATO. This was not necessarily detrimental to the Alliance, but it illustrates wider concerns within Western Europe that they were being excluded from the C³I (Command, Control, Communications, and Intelligence) chain, and highlighted their national inability to guarantee their own security in the advent of potential or actual nuclear use.⁷⁹ These concerns persisted for the remainder of the Cold War, even after the formation of the NATO Nuclear Planning Group (NPG) and subsequent Provisional Political Guidelines (PPGs) on nuclear use introduced in 1969 following the Healey-Schröder Report.⁸⁰

By 16 August 1967 these arrangements still had to be agreed with Healey. He wanted to see the C³I measures for Polaris tightened up and operated with the same degree of efficiency as those for the V-bombers. As such, he instructed the Ministry of Defence to further examine these issues by mid-October.⁸¹ With the transition of the strategic deterrent from the V-bombers to Polaris due to take place in 1968, this was overdue. It was also under discussion in another highly secret group of senior ministers—the *Cabinet Committee on Nuclear Retaliation Procedures*.⁸² This committee wanted to examine more closely how communications links with the Polaris submarines and the chain of command would function following a nuclear attack on the British Isles.⁸³

The Command and Control of Polaris—The National Dimension

With the RN responsible for the day-to-day operations of Polaris, it was essential to determine in detail how the C² system would function between the Supreme Headquarters Allied Powers Europe (SHAPE) (which housed SACEUR), the military and political authorities in the UK, and the Polaris submarine captains. The chain of command and control would require SACEUR to be able to communicate directly with the Commander-in-Chief Home Fleet (CINC) based at Northwood.

In March 1967 Healey suggested to Wilson that Northwood, home to CINCEASTLANT (who under the existing naval 'double hat' arrangements was also CINC Home Fleet), then a national command and control centre for RAF Coastal Command, should become the 'firing headquarters' for Polaris. This would then make it possible 'both to pass the firing order and [provide] information that the order to release the weapons has been passed on'.[84] This also necessitated the provision of effective communications between SHAPE and Northwood. Healey felt that the most effective way of accomplishing this was for Northwood to be the hub for communications between SHAPE, 10 Downing Street, and the Polaris submarines, with firing orders communicated to the Polaris submarines from the VLF station at Rugby.[85] CINC would only be able to authorize release on the specific authority of the prime minister.[86]

In order to facilitate these arrangements, further work was being undertaken on the provision of a 'Survival System' as part of the broader picture for the 'machinery of Government in war'.[87] Although planning for the operations of the British government under both conventional and nuclear war existed prior to these discussions, members of the Cabinet Office were unsure if provisions already existed which specifically gave the prime minister the executive authority to authorize the use of British nuclear weapons.[88] Sir Burke Trend, the highly influential Cabinet Secretary, felt that Healey's recommendations should be adopted 'without more ado' and did not favour 'troubling' the Ministerial Committee on Nuclear Policy with this.[89] Harold Wilson did not comment on the recommendation but, in a minute to Healey, maintained that 'no submarine Commander shall be authorised to fire the Polaris weapons without my specific authority', emphasizing the critical role of the prime minister in nuclear decision-making.[90]

The precise arrangements included the setting up of a two-way, closed-circuit link for television and speech between 10 Downing Street and Northwood. These would build on existing communications links using the public services provided by the Royal Mail and television through public broadcasters such as the BBC.[91] The Navy Department felt it was essential that the Polaris Control

Polaris, Independence, and Interdependence

Officer at Northwood could visually see the prime minister (and vice versa) as the order to use Polaris was given. To this end, cameras would be placed at either end with a telephone and monitors. At 10 Downing Street this equipment would be placed in the prime minister's private office rather than the Cabinet Room. An ideal place was even suggested for the camera—on top of the existing television cabinet focused on the round table in front of the prime minister's desk. These arrangements would have to be tried periodically to test the functioning of the system.[92]

With Polaris due to take over the role of strategic deterrence from the V-bombers the following year, the C^2 aspects during the transition period (and into war) were also under detailed examination by the Official Cabinet Committee on Nuclear Retaliation Procedures.[93] It was subsequently decided to confirm these procedures and to conduct drills to test the system first thing in the morning, at lunch time or early evening. The Navy Department recommended that these drills should be conducted twice daily, taking no more than a minute or two 'with a little practise'.[94] It was recommended these should not be conducted by the prime minister but by the Duty Clerk, who would merely confirm 'all is well'.[95] The system had an operational in-service target date of 12 March 1968.

On 2 May the Navy Department, in consultation with the Cabinet Office, produced two pads (one for use and one in reserve) which would be used to produce the authentication codes for Polaris release in the event that the CCTV links with Northwood failed. They were to be housed in two separate combination-locked boxes, with the combinations known only by four people (two for each box). Neither would know the other's combination and these would be held in the inner or outer Private Office of No. 10. This would enable the 'two man rule' to take effect. This functioned all the way down the chain of Polaris command, with only a limited number of people even aware of the procedure.[96]

Under the 'two man rule' both the prime minister and the Chief of Defence Staff (or his representative) would have to be at 10 Downing Street in order for the firing orders for Polaris to be initiated. The combinations for one of the two safes would be held by 'the naval officer on watch at No. 10 Downing Street'.[97] In practice, not out of keeping with the film *Dr Strangelove*, the 1964 black comedy satirizing nuclear war, arrangements were being put in place to ensure that 'if the tester went haywire or indeed had a mental aberration someone else was present to deal with the situation'.[98] The instructions for the operational procedures themselves (as distinct from the drills) were to be held in a sealed envelope in a file in No. 10.[99] This could ultimately have been a decision forced on the prime minister in as little as a few minutes, if the Soviets had launched their nuclear weapons.[100]

By July 1968 these arrangements had been implemented through the appointment of a senior Royal Navy officer to a role known as *CTF 345*. CTF 345 was the RN Commander-in-Chief Western Fleet (CINCWF) who controlled all RN submarines including the SSBNs from his above-ground offices at Northwood, where he had a continuously manned operations room. He also wore a NATO hat, as Commander-in-Chief Allied Channel Command. CINCWF for Polaris' first deterrent patrol was Admiral Sir John Bush. CTF 345 would write the patrol orders, pass on intelligence updates, make adjustments to patrols, and pass orders to the Polaris submarines. Inside the MOD, the Assistant Chief of the Naval Staff (Operations)—ACNS(O)—had special responsibility for operational coordination of Polaris matters, with a Duty Clerk taking over outside of working hours (but with no operational authority). The patrol orders were held in the ACNS(O)'s 'Polaris' safe, in a sealed envelope which the Duty Commander was to open only under extreme circumstances and after consulting with CTF 345.[101] The Polaris boats would patrol for around fifty-six days, during which time they would maintain strict radio silence unless in an emergency. That would not be broken until the fifty fathom line had been crossed in the Londonderry area, about twelve hours out of their base at Faslane in North-West Scotland.[102]

It is interesting to ask what would have happened in the event of a pre-emptive attack on London. In these circumstances, it was highly unlikely that the orders for a retaliatory nuclear strike could have been issued from No. 10. It seems probable that members of the Cabinet would have been taken to 'TURNSTILE'.[103] From there the authorization to fire Polaris could be made, although as Peter Hennessy rightly states: 'The sheer horror of the decision can never be properly reconstructed'.[104] The fear that would have gripped decision-makers in Britain and across the world as nuclear Armageddon was faced would have been tangible. In those circumstances, what would pass through someone's mind? Perhaps an indicator can be found in the observation of Sir Edward Grey, the British Foreign Secretary, on the eve of the First World War. Fearing what lay ahead, he told the House of Commons on 3 August 1914, 'We are going to suffer, I am afraid, terribly in this war, whether we are in it or whether we stand aside'.[105] In both 1914 and 1939, Britain faced world wars that crisis management had failed to avert, although in both cases war had been postponed. In a situation where World War Three could have developed it was imperative to plan ahead. The experiences of both conflicts would have weighed heavily upon policy-makers and could well have influenced the 'letters of last resort' each prime minister since Wilson has written to instruct the SSBN captains in the event of a devastating nuclear strike which wiped out the command authority.[106]

Conflicting Ideas and Beliefs About Operational Nuclear Strategy

As the Soviet Union began a concerted programme to protect its capital with ABMs in the late 1960s, the COS believed that it remained necessary for the UK to continue to threaten Moscow with an absolute 'assurance of destruction'.[107] They were sceptical that full-scale deployment of ABM systems around Soviet cities would occur given the high costs and limited effectiveness, but they still believed that it was necessary to plan against the risk that the UK's deterrent would become ineffective against Soviet ABMs in the long term.[108] This sparked off a lively debate amongst defence officials about the future of Polaris.

Influential in this debate were the views of the dynamic Chief Scientific Advisor in the Ministry of Defence, Sir Solly Zuckerman. He was opposed to a Polaris improvement programme on strategic grounds. He regarded ABMs as a futile, politically inspired measure, both for the US and the USSR, because he believed they would be swamped by the large numbers of missiles both sides could and would launch if there was a nuclear war. In taking this stance, he incurred the hostility of many of those within the MOD and Atomic Weapons Research Establishment (AWRE) who had been central to the development of the UK nuclear weapons programme.

Zuckerman also felt the resources needed to improve Polaris could be ill-afforded by Britain, and that the Polaris fleet, which was assigned to NATO, 'was there to deter, not to fight nuclear wars'.[109] He argued that it was extremely unlikely that the UK deterrent would ever be launched independently of the United States, and therefore improving the UK Polaris force was unnecessary. For him, the UK reaction to the situation should be to engage in high-level diplomacy to prevent the deployment of ABMs.[110] Denis Healey and many other nuclear scientists did not share his views. Zuckerman, nevertheless, continued to insist that it was premature to engage in a Polaris improvement programme[111] until the possibility of talks between the United States and the USSR on strategic arms limitation had been explored further.[112]

Above all, Zuckerman remained implacably opposed to mounting a more concerted Polaris improvement programme to guarantee sustaining the 'Moscow Criterion'. Improvements to Polaris would be unnecessary if it was assigned to attack targets outside of the ABM defences. He felt that the real reason for beginning such an effort was to keep up with the technical developments of the 'American and Russian Joneses' driven by the strength of the military-industrial complex on both sides of the Atlantic.[113] Echoing a later debate, Zuckerman advocated changing British national targeting doctrine away from the 'Moscow Criterion' to instead target undefended areas of high military or political value such as other cities. However, senior members of the Wilson government were not persuaded that such a policy constituted an effective strategic nuclear deterrent.

The nuclear scientific community, in contrast to Zuckerman, were broadly in favour of mounting an improvement programme and new technical studies made it clear that countermeasures to Soviet ABM defences were necessary to guarantee the penetration of Britain's relatively small number of Polaris missiles.[114] In March 1967 a high-level team of the government's scientific advisers were invited to America as part of ongoing Anglo-American discussions regarding possible improvements to Polaris. There Zuckerman informed their US counterparts, without reference to the other members of the UK delegation, that Britain would not be developing a second generation deterrent beyond Polaris.[115] This was greeted with dismay by the American authorities.[116] As a result he found himself isolated on this issue against the considered views of the Joint Intelligence Committee (JIC), Chiefs of Staff, the Atomic Weapons Research Establishment, and some of his own technical advisers in the Ministry of Defence (MOD). There is little doubt that this partly contributed to his move to the Cabinet Office in the spring of 1967 to become government Chief Scientific Advisor. Thereafter, Zuckerman claims in his memoirs, he was kept in the dark about matters concerning nuclear weapons, although the declassified documentary record indicates that he continued to play a significant role until at least 1970.[117]

With the considerable obstacle of Solly Zuckerman largely removed from the picture the MOD began to look more seriously at what form a Polaris improvement programme would take. By then, interestingly, the issue of improvements to Polaris had become tied into discussions on the continued need for a UK nuclear deterrent at all, and led to a study on 'Britain's nuclear weapons policy' that was considered by the Nuclear Policy Committee in December 1967. In preparation for the meetings that followed, Sir Burke Trend, the highly influential Cabinet Secretary, was keen to highlight to Wilson the lack of interdepartmental consensus within the civil service. He felt that the 'considerations involved have, I think, been more exhaustively examined than ever before and the questions to which Ministers should address themselves are now as sharply pointed as they can be'.[118]

The MOD and the Foreign Office felt that abandoning the deterrent would be unsettling for its European allies at a time when doubts were again resurfacing regarding the American nuclear guarantee. They felt that:

> in these circumstances a decision to give up would be a major change of direction which would have revolutionary consequences for our entire defence policy; while a decision to stay in the business until we can see more clearly where we are going on various fronts, could be regarded as merely elementary prudence.[119]

Lined up alongside Sir Solly Zuckerman's continued opposition from his position in the Cabinet Office were the views of the Treasury and the Department for Economic Affairs. Both were opposed to the retention of the deterrent on the grounds of cost and the relevancy of British nuclear weapons vis-à-vis the superpowers (given the weight of US strategic forces which, through Article 5 of the North Atlantic Treaty, in their view, provided a nuclear guarantee to the UK).[120]

As a consequence, the government was divided on the way forward and not able to make a firm recommendation regarding improvements. There was, however, a 'tacit acceptance' that the deterrent should be retained, including all elements of the Polaris programme.[121] By the early summer of 1970, the scientists working on Britain's nuclear weapons programme were advising the government of the need to pursue improvements to the UK Polaris force.[122] Zuckerman once again cautioned against undertaking an open-ended Polaris improvement programme, telling Sir Burke Trend: 'What we know about Russian R & D is probably less than what the Americans know, and in our circumstances of financial stringency, we cannot use our ignorance as an excuse for spending money on studies, the primary purpose of which would be to keep the boys happy'.[123]

Decisions on improvements were made all the more difficult by strong opposition from the Royal Navy to modifying Polaris and a desire to keep in line with the US Navy, resulting in their persistent support for acquiring the new US Poseidon missile with its multiple independently targetable re-entry vehicles (MIRVs) which could dispense warheads from the upper atmosphere to widely spaced targets on the ground.

The arguments between Sir Solly Zuckerman and his former colleagues in the Ministry of Defence over national strategic deterrence resembled the arguments put forward by Professor P.M.S. Blackett in the 1940s with the 'nuclear advocates' at that time.[124] It remained the responsibility of senior civil servants such as Sir Solly Zuckerman and Sir Burke Trend to try to guide ministers through the available options as well as acting as an 'institutional memory' within government. However, each had different ideas and beliefs about nuclear strategy and how best to respond to these questions, based upon on their experience of these matters (with a tenure often outlasting the ministers they served). As Secretary to the Cabinet, Trend, in particular, exercised a high degree of influence over the prime minister on every aspect of government, including the key decisions on British nuclear policy. In Cabinet, there was, as before, little or no serious detailed debate on strategic nuclear policy. As a result, despite the opposition of those such as Zuckerman, the Polaris Improvement Programme continued largely unhindered into the 1970s.

Conclusion

The decade from the late 1950s to the late 1960s brought significant changes to British nuclear policy, but there were also important continuities. With the MDA, the cancellations of the Blue Streak and Skybolt missiles, and the 1962 Polaris Sales Agreement, the large degree of independence of the British nuclear programme was replaced by increasing interdependency with the United States, and in some important respects dependence on US technology and policies. While the Macmillan and Douglas-Home governments continued to stress that Britain retained independent control over its nuclear deterrent capability, the Wilson government played down ideas of independence. The emphasis was placed instead on Britain's nuclear contribution to the NATO alliance. Given divisions within the Party over unilateral nuclear disarmament there was also a commitment in public not to replace the Polaris force when its active life came to an end and there was less stress under Labour on the role of nuclear weapons in sustaining Britain's 'Great Power' identity.

At the same time, however, despite the rhetoric, there was considerable continuity in the beliefs at the highest level about Britain's nuclear capability. In particular, there remained support at the top echelons of the Labour Party for the need to improve the Polaris force for as long as possible and to sustain the deterrent credibility of Britain's nuclear force. This support for the Polaris Improvement Programme was closely linked to a continuing belief that effective deterrence required the ability to target Moscow, which had long been a key characteristic of British nuclear doctrine. Also, although there was an emphasis on the contribution to the Alliance, the prime minister and his Defence Secretary continued to highlight the 'let-out clause' which allowed Britain to withdraw its nuclear force should its vital national interests be at stake in a crisis. The Wilson government also put considerable energy into ensuring that the appropriate command, control, and intelligence arrangements for the deterrent were put in place. Although less stress was placed on Britain's 'Great Power' role in the world, the prime minister and his key political allies continued to believe in the utility that nuclear weapons could provide in enhancing British influence in Washington and other parts of the world. Despite some differences with President Johnson over Britain's failure to join the United States in the Vietnam War, Wilson still regarded close ties with America to be an essential element in British foreign and defence policy. This continuity, involving support for the 'special relationship' identity and the close nuclear ties with the United States, however, was to be challenged in the early years of the 1970s.

6

The Polaris Improvement Programme and Chevaline

> They didn't want to tell me because they knew I understood the issue perfectly well and would cancel...and that's one of the worries I think ministers must have about civil servants, that they will withhold information which they think will lead to a decision they don't like.
>
> Denis Healey, 2011[1]

One of the key questions for the new Heath administration between 1970 and 1974 remained whether to replace Polaris or to make improvements to overcome Soviet ABM defences. Under Edward Heath the British government looked seriously at changing the direction of its nuclear weapons policies, which until this point had been closely entwined with those of the United States. The new prime minister wanted to explore the possibilities of nuclear collaboration with France—an *entente nuclèaire*. His intention was to dilute the 'special nuclear relationship' with the United States, established through the 1958 Mutual Defence Agreement (MDA) and 1963 Polaris Sales Agreement (PSA), as part of a deeper political and economic reorientation towards Europe. The nuclear special relationship identity, however, remained firmly entrenched in the 1970s, with the Labour governments that followed Heath engaged in a protracted and politically sensitive programme to enhance the capabilities of the *Polaris* system.

The Pursuit of Anglo-French Cooperation and its Difficulties

Although the Anglo-American relationship had cooled under Harold Wilson, Heath envisaged a rather different strategic alignment with much greater emphasis on Europe. In terms of Britain's nuclear policies, Heath wanted to see Britain reclaim more room for manoeuvre in its foreign and defence policies, and a nuclear rapprochement with France suited his wider political and economic aspirations. However, the difficulties of trying to square the circle through trilateralism between Britain, France, and the US with the bilateral priorities of maintaining the strategic credibility of the British defence posture along with multilateral arrangements with NATO proved to be difficult issues for the Heath government to overcome. However well-intentioned and sincere Heath's wider European vision was, he was soon made aware just how closely bound the British nuclear programme had become with the United States and the difficulties that his proposals presented. This dependency was starkly indicated in a 1972 memorandum by the Ministry of Defence which revealed that, 'without US technical data and spares support, the UK [Polaris] force could cease to become effective in a matter of months'.[2]

The British nuclear programme was at least five years ahead of that of their French counterparts and the British had developed extensive experience of both warhead design and of producing a number of delivery methods.[3] These included stand-off missiles and free-fall bombs with variable yields, which would be of key interest to the French. It would save them considerable time and expenditure if a path of joint collaboration could be followed. Further assistance could be provided in terms of re-entry systems and penetration aids against Soviet anti-ballistic missiles (ABMs). However, due to the agreements with the United States, any bilateral arrangement with France would have to be fully endorsed by the Nixon administration. This was due to the fact that the British had 'no information of wholly and demonstrably British origin in this area'.[4] There was also a problem associated with British obligations under the Partial Test Ban Treaty (PTBT) of 1963, which meant that unless the French renounced atmospheric testing, there could be no collaboration. France showed no signs of wanting to do this.[5]

France wished to develop its own national programme and stood to gain from a nuclear rapprochement with the United Kingdom as they continued to develop and deploy both their tactical and strategic nuclear forces. As the British had learnt, sometimes by bitter experience, the resources needed to develop increasingly sophisticated nuclear weapons and associated delivery systems were considerable. A pooling of nuclear resources would have accelerated the French effort and served both Heath's purpose to dilute the political confines of the special relationship and maintain French interests in moving Europe away from over-reliance on the United States. France had left NATO's integrated military structure in 1966 because of what it saw as an over-reliance on US nuclear forces and the US nuclear guarantee. Paris had also expressed strong doubts concerning the reform of the NATO doctrine of 'Massive Retaliation' towards 'Flexible Response', a move strongly favoured by the Americans, the British, and the West Germans. The French government under both

Charles de Gaulle and his successor as president, Georges Pompidou, were equally concerned about the lack of consultation regarding nuclear release procedures and access to targetting information within NATO Europe.[6] The lack of a European finger on the nuclear trigger, despite the formation of NATO's Nuclear Planning Group (NPG) in 1967, was a constant concern for French policy-makers and a key reason behind their scepticism of NATO.

Despite the obstacles, during these early stages the French were keen on pressing home to the new government the advantages of joint cooperation in terms of the political unity of Europe. In November 1970, Michel Debré, the French minister of defence, met with Peter Carrington, the British Defence Secretary. At this meeting Debré, a powerful Gaullist, went to great lengths to try to convince Carrington how important the issue of nuclear collaboration was to the British application for EEC membership. Debré told his counterpart that: 'First everything pointed to closer Anglo-French cooperation; we were the only two nuclear powers; outside Europe, we were the only two countries with real interests and responsibilities'.[7] He continued: the 'key to European defence was Anglo-French cooperation. It was we who had to take the decisions on this and much depended on the degrees of political cooperation which we could achieve'.[8]

Heath showed himself to be prepared to pursue discussions with the French despite widespread scepticism and doubts from both the Foreign and Commonwealth Office (FCO) and the Ministry of Defence (MOD). Lord Cromer, the British ambassador to the US, felt that the British government stood to lose more than it would gain from failing to heed American sensitivities on the issue of Anglo-French nuclear cooperation. He warned that:

> A brief visit to the CIA or NSA alone, where the tip of the iceberg can be seen, has to be seen to be believed to give some feeling of the size of the American effort of which we share in. We are in practise receiving a great deal more valuable knowledge and information than the formal agreements could be interpreted as entitling us to... It would seem to me, however, imprudent to jeopardise these arrangements unless we are a great deal clearer on our own plans for an independent defence posture... we may end up by destroying credibility in what we have.[9]

This intelligence information included assessments of Soviet ABM defences and general intelligence on Soviet maritime capabilities (including anti-submarine warfare capabilities), with geodetic information also being passed to the UK which assisted the delivery accuracy of the UK's Polaris missiles.[10] The Foreign Office also pointed out that:

> While M. Debré is right in suggesting that delivery systems themselves are not covered by the McMahon Act, our existing Polaris missiles are of course purchased from the United States under the Polaris Sales Agreement of 1963. We could not

agree—without US approval—to any cooperation which might have to draw on Polaris related data.[11]

Sir Burke Trend joined those expressing caution when he pointed out that the extent of the collaboration between Britain and America was such that 'we have no warhead in design or service which does not incorporate some American information; and we could not therefore enter any worthwhile exchange, in the field of nuclear warhead design, without obtaining American consent'.[12]

The planned development of France's strategic forces was as much a political weapon as a strategic weapon. It was a signal of the French intention to guarantee her territorial integrity and independent freedom of action. Britain understood this viewpoint and was itself keen to ensure that Polaris was operationally independent. Although NATO remained the cornerstone of British defence policy, those supporting Heath's views believed that there were interests in common with France regarding nuclear independence. Following an Anglo-French meeting at High Wycombe, the centre of RAF Strike Command, it was argued that it had 'exactly achieved one of its main objects of helping to convince influential Frenchmen that we are masters in our own nuclear house'.[13] Major General Fraser, Assistant Chief of the Defence Staff (Policy), summed this feeling up when he stated that:

> Admiral Delahousse said to me on leaving 'You have done in one morning what I have been trying to do, vis-à-vis Paris for two years'. It was interesting that so great was the 'sales resistance' in this regard, that at question time General Pequignot's question was—'I understand that you have, in the last resort, national authority over the nuclear air forces, but am I right to conclude that doesn't apply to submarines?'. He was told—and I think at last believed—that he wasn't right'.[14]

The reasons Heath found it so difficult to alter the trajectory of the British nuclear policy begun by Macmillan and sustained by his successors was the high degree of dependency Britain now had on the United States in order to continue as a credible nuclear power without intolerable cost. When Harold Macmillan signed the Nassau Agreement between Britain and the United States in 1962 to purchase the Polaris missile system he was anticipating a relationship where both countries would be *interdependent*; however, far from Macmillan's concept of interdependency, from December 1962 there had instead evolved a high degree of *dependency*, in terms of both nuclear warheads and delivery systems. This placed restrictions on Britain's freedom of action in its nuclear weapons policy, with wider consequences for its foreign and defence policies. This was well understood by many of Heath's key advisers who remained sceptical of Anglo-French nuclear cooperation.

A meeting was planned for the end of July 1972 with Henry Kissinger, the US Secretary of State, in order to discover American feelings should there be a

British request to purchase the Poseidon missile, which was supported by the Royal Navy.[15] Prior to this meeting, Sir Burke Trend recommended that the prime minister, Chancellor of the Exchequer, and Secretary of State for Defence should be fully briefed on the available courses open to the government at this juncture.[16] As part of the background to these major decisions a key briefing paper was given by the Joint Intelligence Committee (JIC).[17]

Although the results of this assessment remain classified, it seems that detailed UK plans to target the Soviet Union were discussed. These plans were both in the context of joint targetting with the Americans ('deterrence in concert'), independent action ('independent deterrence'), and possibly deterrence in conjunction with the French.[18] In light of the available evidence, it appears that the Chiefs of Staff were able to maintain their preferred strategic targetting plan, with the 'Moscow Criterion' at its centre for the time being at least.[19] Zuckerman, who continued as Chief Scientific Advisor, remained critical of what he viewed as an overestimation of the need to improve Polaris against Soviet ABMs and indicated that the need to improve Polaris was based on the assumption that Britain might decide to conduct a nuclear strike against the Soviet Union without American participation. This proposition, he believed, was unlikely *in extremis*.[20] Nevertheless, his views were rejected and a decision was made late in the Heath government to opt for a UK-led Polaris improvement programme developed alongside the Americans—soon code-named *Chevaline*.[21] Faced with the realities of the situation, the prime minister accepted that, for the time being at least, there was no alternative to maintaining the close bilateral nuclear relationship with the United States. The sceptics of Anglo-French nuclear cooperation, such as Sir Burke Trend, had won the argument. Trend admitted that this further collaboration with the Americans:

> maintains and intensifies our dependence on the United States (and therefore reduces our chances of collaboration with the French) unless we are prepared simultaneously to maintain an independent technological effort of our own at vast expense... since we shall almost certainly be driven to accepting an increasing degree of United States assistance sooner or later, we might as well do so now, when we have an opportunity which might not recur under a different United States Administration. And the French, too, will find that, if they wish to stay in this league, they, like ourselves, will have to be prepared to accept United States help.[22]

Trend's considered view was also supported by the Chief of Defence Staff from 1971–3, Peter Hill-Norton, who noted that, although 'we should give ourselves the greatest room for manoeuvre and initiative in a fluid European situation... we should remain wholly dependent on American goodwill and facilities'.[23] Indeed, the scale of the dependency was such that Hill-Norton argued that the British would remain dependent on 'everything except the "front-end"—as we must with any option during the lifetime of the present SSBN force'.[24] With such advice it proved very difficult indeed for Heath to move Britain towards greater nuclear collaboration with France, despite Britain's accession to the European Economic Community during his period in office.

The Return of Labour and Chevaline

Following the General Election of November 1974, won by Labour under Harold Wilson, the Polaris Improvement Programme continued much as before—in secret and with little or no discussion among the full Cabinet of the new government.[25] This was done to avoid any potential embarrassment to the government and damaging splits in a party with a powerful unilateralist wing. If Tony Benn's account of this non-decision is accurate, Wilson told his colleagues that only 'a little bit of modernisation [was] going on'[26] to the tune of £24 million a year.[27] However, Wilson's official biographer, Philip Ziegler, comments that 'unless he (Benn) was both gullible and monstrously misinformed, he must have known that a great deal more than "a little bit of modernisation" was in question'.[28] Wilson himself knew full well the implications of modernization, even though he, like most politicians and civil servants, had only a limited understanding of the sophisticated technologies involved.[29]

Nevertheless, the Polaris Improvement Programme, now code-named Chevaline, may never have proceeded if swingeing cuts in Dennis Healey's 1975 budget had been applied to the ongoing Polaris Improvement Programme.[30] However, its very secrecy made it something of a sacred cow, and instead Chevaline was accommodated while the remaining defence budget was slashed. Perhaps more crucial were the deliberately nebulous statements which had been made by Wilson to the full Cabinet in November 1974 when, 'clearly expecting trouble', he requested endorsement for what amounted to no more than 'a minor modification to the existing system' which had already received 'unanimous endorsement' by the Defence and Overseas Policy Committee, even though they, like their Cabinet counterparts, were not in possession of the full facts.[31]

At a political level only an inner-Cabinet of four of Wilson's most trusted senior advisers—Foreign Secretary Jim Callaghan, Chancellor Dennis Healey, Home Secretary Roy Jenkins, and Secretary of Defence Roy Mason, overseeing executive nuclear policy decisions—had a comprehensive understanding of what was entailed and of the escalating costs involved, all of which were being kept studiously away from the Cabinet, the parliamentary party, and the Public Accounts Committee. This is hardly unprecedented in the history of British nuclear policy, but it does demonstrate the extent to which the secrecy surrounding Chevaline prevented a full and informed discussion of the programme outside of this inner-Cabinet committtee.[32] The Treasury, however, was now becoming increasingly concerned over the costs of Chevaline, which by 1975 had risen to an estimated £400 million. As a result, the entire project was submitted for a full review in September 1975 to identify whether full-scale development should proceed.[33] The secrecy surrounding the project was to continue over the following six years, inhibiting an informed discussion on the future direction of the project and allowing costs to escalate, even though the Treasury were concerned enough to only authorize expenditure in 3- and 6-monthly rolling cycles.

By November 1975 both the JIC and the Chiefs of Staff (COS) were pointing out to ministers that they believed that the current Polaris system was no longer fully effective at penetrating the improved Moscow ABM defences.[34] This had been considered a possibility since the early part of the 1960s, but by 1975, with improvements to Soviet ABM systems, this was now considered by the JIC, COS, and the nuclear weapons establishments on both sides of the Atlantic to be a strategic reality.[35] This realization prompted a fundamental reassessment of both the current targetting requirements centred on the 'Moscow Criterion' and of the British concept of independent nuclear deterrence. It was in this period that the JIC and COS as the 'primary keepers' of the prevailing strategic culture were to come under sustained political challenge.

Drawing on the findings of the substantial 1972 report by the JIC, and the Polaris Policy Committee meeting late in 1975 (both of which examined alternate nuclear targetting priorities), the Chief of the Defence Staff, Sir Michael Carver, suggested an option of targetting ten other cities west of the Ural Mountains, excluding Moscow entirely from the target list.[36] Carver believed that this 'would probably be regarded by the Russians as unacceptable damage'.[37] However, the CDS also felt that if the Soviets believed Britain was attacking undefended targets, then this would encourage them to extend the footprint of the current ABM defences. In this event Carver believed that removing the 'Moscow Criterion' from the centre of British independent nuclear targetting should be considered only 'a temporary expedient'.[38]

By March 1976 Carver informed Roy Mason, the Defence Secretary, that the independent nuclear targetting plan, known as the *National Retaliatory War Plan*, should be altered to one of two options. This was either to fire from the Atlantic to attack ten cities other than Moscow, or to head into the Mediterranean to launch at Moscow.[39] The plans were contingent upon 'prevailing circumstances'. These were not explicitly stated by Carver, but would probably have included the number of Polaris submarines available and the political climate during times of tension. In part, these changes were triggered by the political indecision and ongoing economic problems facing the country.

Britain's financial woes became much more acute in the latter half of the 1970s, and 1976 saw sterling devalued again while 'the country cheerfully continued to live beyond its means, and the outside world increasingly referred to "the English problem"'.[40] The 'sterling crisis precipitated a decision to relinquish virtually all overseas commitments by withdrawing entirely from Singapore, closing the Gan airbase in the Indian Ocean and withdrawing from the Simonstown Agreement with South Africa'. Overseas commitments with 'permanently stationed forces were thereafter effectively, with some minor exceptions, confined to Europe'.[41] With the defence of NATO now accorded increased priority, attention in some quarters turned to the future of Chevaline.

The Chevaline Programme, High-Level Politics, and Changes to Deterrence Criteria

The arguments for retargetting the UK strategic nuclear deterrent had a direct and sustained bearing on the Chevaline programme. With the costs having risen from the 1972 estimates of £235 million to an expected figure of £400 million by 1975, it was under serious threat of cancellation.[42] With the government involved in yet another major defence review (initiated in 1974), Chevaline was not only under intense pressure to succeed but also to justify its continued rationale.

Both of these factors were under renewed scrutiny because of the 1972 ABM Treaty and the 1974 protocol to the ABM Treaty (known as the 'Vladivostok Accords'). These agreements had limited Soviet ABMs to cover only the Soviet capital with a maximum of 100 missile launchers. In order to justify the maintenance of the 'Moscow Criterion', and with it the major argument for Chevaline, the Chiefs of Staff, backed by assessments of Soviet ABM capabilities from the Joint Intelligence Committee, began to mount a rearguard action to save Chevaline from cancellation.[43] The events that followed highlighted the continuing intergovernmental disputes at the decision-making level and also how *military* decision-makers can decisively affect *political* policy choices. As we will see, it also cast a shadow over the explicit non-partisanship of the civil service.

The COS, the MOD, and the JIC began this rearguard action by promoting the concept of the 'Moscow Criterion' to the prime minister, the Defence Secretary, and the Foreign Secretary. Pointedly, the Chief of Defence Staff wanted to exclude from the discussions on this issue the one remaining member of the executive Ministerial Committee on Nuclear Policy, Denis Healey, the Chancellor of the Exchequer (and former Defence Secretary).[44] Carver evidently felt that the alternative strategic plan of independent deterrence being suggested to Mason would leave Chevaline wide open to cancellation by the Chancellor. However, John Mayne, Mason's Private Under-Secretary, advised against this course of action. He counselled that to leave the Chancellor out of the equation concerning the retargetting of Polaris would be 'madness… inspite [sic] of the dangers'.[45]

Mayne suggested that Mason simply restate to Healey the argument for retaining Chevaline that was given back in September 1974. This was that cancellation would dilute both the deterrent effect on the Soviet Union whilst concomitantly damaging relations with the United States, who 'in past discussions stressed their wish to see Britain have a powerful deterrent capability'.[46] There does not seem to have been any further overt political discussion by Mason regarding targeting policy. Instead he chose to accept the advice of his Chiefs of Staff in regard to the 'Moscow Criterion'.

In line with the sentiments of the Chiefs, on 18 November 1975 Mayne produced for Mason a memorandum suggesting that until Chevaline was introduced into service, Polaris would be ineffective from the end of the year.[47] These discussions between senior members of the civil service and government regarding retargetting continued to gather political momentum. At a meeting between Sir John Hunt (Sir Burke Trend's successor as Cabinet Secretary), Secretary of State for Defence Mason, and CDS Sir Michael Carver, a little over a week later on 27 November, it was agreed that the Chancellor should *not* be told about the minute circulated from the Chiefs of Staff to the prime minister revising the COS criteria for strategic nuclear deterrence.[48] All three hoped that Healey could be kept away from the conclusions by the Chiefs of Staff, namely that deterrence could also be achieved if Polaris were retargetted to ten cities *excluding* Moscow.

This was further discussed prior to a meeting of the Public Expenditure Survey Committee due to take place on 5 December. There it was decided that if the prime minister wished to see the Chancellor informed of these conclusions, then a disclaimer would be issued by them that Healey did not 'need to know' about the retargetting options. At a subsequent high-level MOD meeting on 1 June 1976 it was further suggested that rather than targeting ten cities west of the Ural Mountains, five could be targeted, and this could also fulfil the criteria of deterrence. Mason again made the case for continuing to develop Chevaline, maintaining that it was essential to be able to continue to attack Moscow in the long-term. However, emphasizing the competitive nature of defence procurement policy—even in the highly prized nuclear field—in the climate of financial austerity brought about by the defence review, he felt it would be necessary to remind the prime minister of this need.[49]

At this meeting Sir Edward Ashmore, the Chief of the Naval Staff, reminded the group that what 'constituted a credible deterrent was political'.[50] Still, it is unclear why a total of five cities and not ten was now being considered an effective political deterrent. It is likely that targetting five cities and excluding Moscow from the target list would have led to further doubts placed against the case for retaining Chevaline. The Treasury had been absent from the meeting. They would very likely have seized on this option of relaxing the criteria for national deterrence to press the MOD to cancel the improvement programme and derail the 'critical momentum' that was building behind the retention of the Moscow Criterion and the need for Chevaline. Moreover, this would have reframed one of the key parameters of British nuclear weapons policy. It is likely that at least equal consideration would have been given to the reduced number of Soviet cities to be targeted by Polaris. With forty-four cities having been considered to be a 'credible deterrent' in 1958, and twenty cities in 1964, it is interesting that twelve years later ten cities, and then five, were considered to be acceptable for effective deterrence.[51] Perhaps more than anything this clearly indicates that the UK politico-military concept of 'minimum deterrence' was a moveable feast which rested in large measure on force levels and military capabilities, rather than being a hard rule based on certainty—a criterion which had been unsuccessfully challenged by Zuckerman in the 1960s.

Mason also expressed concerns that this review of the criteria for deterrence would be leaked.[52] A government leak threatened to bring out into the open the question of what constituted a politically acceptable minimum deterrent. This would cause further embarrassment to an administration battling industrial unrest and inflation in the domestic economy at the time. Two weeks later Mason informed James Callaghan, who had replaced Wilson as prime minister, of these retargetting recommendations with a view to informing the Foreign Secretary, Anthony Crosland, and Chancellor Healey.[53] Although it is not known for sure if this revision by the COS was accepted by the government, David Owen (Crosland's successor as Foreign Secretary in February 1977) suggests that there would have been no political reason not to accept this advice. He himself had no knowledge of these discussions when he became Foreign Secretary.[54]

To question the basis of a minimum national deterrent coupled with the risk of government leaks could have proved extremely damaging to the confidence of those involved with the Chevaline programme and would also have dented nuclear relations with the United States. It would also have given critics of the British nuclear programme, including those in the Labour Party with links to the Campaign for Nuclear Disarmament (CND), added ammunition to attack the foundations of the nuclear deterrent.

Still, it was argued that if Chevaline was cancelled, then the resources that were being provided would be freed up and could be reallocated to a successor system.[55] Under these terms of reference Mason suggested that any talk of successor systems 'should cease forthwith, at least for two years. Such talk would undermine Chevaline, and the possibility was politically out of the question'.[56] To assist with the rearguard action to preserve Chevaline, in June 1976 Mason agreed to approach Tony Crosland, whose term as Foreign Secretary lasted just ten months, armed with a full presentation team prior to recommending to the prime minister that Chevaline should be allowed to continue at 'full speed'.[57] This was duly granted.

With regard to these deliberations, in a 2011 BBC documentary Lord Healey commented angrily that the key civil servants at the time did not tell him, because he might have acted in a way that they did not like, and cancelled Chevaline.[58] He stated that it was 'disgraceful' that this was done, even on grounds of national security. When asked how he felt about the implication that even he, as Chancellor of the Exchequer and a former Defence Secretary, could not be trusted, he replied: 'Not be trusted to agree with them. Well, sod them!' Healey went further, claiming that: 'If civil servants conceal the most important facts about the decisions you have to take, they're betraying their country. It's a form of treason.'[59]

Whilst not going as far as invoking 'treason', Lord Owen was also critical of the role of the civil service in these deliberations, claiming:

> It's quite a disgraceful judgement because he [Healey] did have a need to know. I think Sir John Hunt [the Cabinet Secretary at the time] crossed the line and he should not have been party to the decision to freeze Denis Healey out... That was, I think, a reprehensible decision, and it should be made clear to future cabinet secretaries where the line is. And he crossed the line.[60]

The stakes were high. When asked if this could have brought down the government Healey answered 'Conceivably, I think so, yes.'[61] In regard to Chevaline, as David Owen informed Parliament in November 2000, during debates on the Freedom of Information Act:

> One of the major arguments used against cancellation was its effect on the capability of our nuclear deterrent. It was felt that if one came forward and announced that one was cancelling a programme on which one had spent £700 million and which had been started to improve the penetration of missiles, one would flag to everybody—and very visibly to the Soviet Union—that one's existing deterrent was not effective. Nobody argued more strongly against cancellation than the Ministry of Defence and the intelligence community. They argued powerfully that it was absurd to cancel the programme, having spent so much money on it.[62]

By the time the US-USSR SALT II negotiations had ended in 1979, 'Chevaline was running far behind schedule and even further above its planned costs'[63] and the COS were ordered to produce a report providing justification for the maintenance of the 'Moscow Criterion' on which strategic necessity

Chevaline's military utility was, to a large degree, based. This, Denis Healey claims, they failed to do. Instead 'they produced a recommendation in favour of it, without any serious argument except that to cancel Chevaline would damage our prestige in both Moscow and Washington'.[64] However, by now time was running out for Callaghan's government, and Chevaline would pass to the incoming administration of Margaret Thatcher following the Conservative victory in the May 1979 General Election.

Conclusion

The history of Chevaline, and its predecessors, reflects an important theme in the British nuclear experience—the continuation of the tradition of nuclear secrecy which had been established by the Attlee government in the 1940s. As we have seen, Parliament was only indirectly informed of the existence of an independent nuclear programme in 1948 and little information was revealed to the public about the atomic tests in 1952, the thermonuclear tests in 1957/58, or the close nuclear relationship with the United States which developed in the late 1950s and early 1960s. All of the key nuclear decisions were taken by a small number of very senior government ministers, meeting in informal ad hoc committees. These decisions had been kept secret from the main Cabinets of the day and the general public. This reflects an important part of what Peter Hennessey has described as the 'secret state'.[65]

In part, this secrecy was due to a deep-seated conviction by the political and defence establishment that nuclear matters are of such overwhelming importance to the security of the state that extraordinary measures are necessary to protect national secrets. In the case of Labour governments, there has also been a perceived need by the prime minister of the day to avoid criticisms from left-wing MPs and indeed from Cabinet ministers who might be expected to oppose new nuclear developments. Heath, Wilson, and Callaghan kept access to information about the Polaris Improvement Programme restricted to a small group of senior colleagues which for Wilson and Callaghan were also because of concerns that nuclear matters were a sensitive and highly controversial issue in Labour Party internal politics.

Another characteristic of the Polaris Improvement Programme was that it lasted for such a long period. Britain had begun its own research on anti-ballistic missile defences and offensive capabilities to deal with them in the 1950s. The recognition that a more focused research effort was needed to improve the Polaris system occurred just as it was deployed from 1967. It was not until 1982, however, that Chevaline began to be deployed. This delay was largely due to the fact that, although help was received from the United States, Britain had to resolve many of the very difficult technical problems (some of which were unique to the UK) largely on its own, which, in turn, helped sustain Anglo-American nuclear cooperation. In a scientific and technological sense there is no doubt that Chevaline was a major achievement. 'Hardening' and separating re-entry bodies over a larger area while in flight was particularly difficult to resolve. As the Soviet ABM system developed, Britain was faced with changing technological problems which required cutting-edge scientific work. This had to be done with limited financial resources, given the severe economic problems Britain faced throughout the 1970s. Technological uncertainty was also compounded by the political uncertainties associated with an evolving arms control agenda over which Britain had no control, and changes in government domestically, which led to inevitable delays and hesitation.

Given this long gestation, it is perhaps surprising that the Chevaline project was not cancelled at some point. There were certainly many opportunities for this to happen. Throughout the 1970s both Labour and Conservative governments (or at least select Cabinet ministers) were aware that costs were escalating rapidly and the Treasury expressed continuing concern from the mid-1970s onwards. Given the programme's long development time, cancellation could have occurred at several junctures (particularly during the 1976 defence review) and the Treasury consistently put pressure on the select few politicians who were key to sustaining the project to justify the rising costs. Despite this, the project continued to receive high-level political support and was never seriously at risk of cancellation. This seems to have been due to two main factors.

First, its retention (and that of Polaris itself) lies in the fact that the nuclear deterrent was accorded the highest priority by both the Conservatives and Labour (despite discordant views within the parties). Both the prime minister and the small team of senior Cabinet members who oversaw major decisions of nuclear policy accepted the views of their most trusted defence advisers, namely that the Moscow Criterion must remain central to Britain's strategy of last resort, an independent nuclear strike.[66] Having accepted this, it was only necessary to plan to achieve this with a high degree of certainty that Polaris warheads would be capable of penetrating to the target successfully. Given the deployment of ABM systems around Moscow, along with prospects for deployment of successor systems, Chevaline had to cope with any advances in ABM systems which the Soviets may deploy, within what Sir Michael Quinlan has called 'our predictive reach'.[67] Quinlan indicated some years later in the context of Polaris that the continued priority for attacking targets in and around Moscow:

> did not rest just on a narrow obsession with assailing the city itself, but reflected the fact that the characteristics of the Soviet ABM system meant that abandoning

the attempt to be seen as capable of defeating it would have entailed conceding effective sanctuary to a very large area around the city—its exact size and configuration depending on the precise azimuth and elevation of the incoming attack... in the order of tens of thousands of square miles.[68]

For Labour, given their public commitment not to purchase a successor system to Polaris, some sort of improvement programme was the only option if the Soviet Union developed an ABM system, designed to protect Moscow, which could defeat an unmodified UK Polaris force. For Edward Heath's Conservative government in the early 1970s, the political calculations were rather different.

The only replacement available was the US Poseidon system and Heath did not wish to highlight Britain's special strategic relationship with the Americans at a time that he was trying to gain access to the Common Market. Improving Polaris suited his political purpose as well as maintaining important British security interests. The second reason why cancellation was not considered, it would appear, was that having spent so much money on the project there was a belief by both Labour and Conservative governments that this money would be wasted if Chevaline was not seen through to completion. Just as importantly, it would be seen by the general public to have been wasted at a time of domestic financial austerity, and this would have adverse political consequences. Better to take the line of least resistance, keep the project quiet, and keep it going. If it could be completed satisfactorily, there would be distinct advantages to offset the costs. Britain would have retained its own credible deterrent, and the special nuclear relationship would have been preserved with British scientists making a contribution to high-level nuclear research of benefit to the US. Beneath the senior political, civilian, and military personnel lay a large-scale industrial programme which manufactured British nuclear warheads and their delivery systems. This was centred on the Atomic Weapons Research Establishment at Aldermaston and the Royal Aircraft Establishment at Farnborough. Both were important parts of the nuclear advocacy coalition that retained an interest in improving Polaris and in the subsequent debate about replacement.

7

The Polaris Replacement Debate under Labour

> *Ultimate deterrence is perceived to work, because no nuclear weapons state (NWS) can feel confident enough to act on a judgement that an adversary, seeing the painful destruction of all that he most valued, would withhold retaliation on account of some cool calculation of ethics or utility.*
>
> Duff-Mason Report, December 1978*

Apart from the debates over Chevaline, the final two years of James Callaghan's Labour government (1977–9) also saw it institute a series of detailed studies which examined the options for replacing *Polaris*. In doing so, the same small group of ministers who presided over the fate of *Chevaline* recognized that in view of Labour's manifesto commitment not to replace Polaris, a 'major row' would ensue in the party if these studies became known.[1] With its commitment to these studies, Callaghan and his inner-Cabinet imposed an extremely high level of secrecy on British nuclear weapons policy, especially with regards to the strategic deterrent, and deliberately excluded the full Cabinet from the policy-making process whilst actively minimizing parliamentary debate. This continued the element of strict secrecy which had characterized the British nuclear experience since the Second World War. At the same time, within the group of nuclear advocates there were important differences over nuclear operational issues.

In line with Hyman's thesis about the role of key political leaders in nuclear decision-making, it was the prime minister himself, James Callaghan, who appears to have been the first to raise the subject of Polaris replacement in a September 1977 memorandum to Fred Mulley, Mason's replacement as Defence Secretary. Both Callaghan and Mulley concurred that Polaris replacement was a 'politically sensitive matter'.[2] As this issue emerged, and with Chevaline still facing ministerial opposition, David Owen, the Foreign and Commonwealth Secretary, suggested a new study of the criteria for effective deterrence (centred on the 'Moscow Criterion') which had last been examined by the Joint Intelligence Committee (JIC) in 1972.[3] He felt that this would help to frame the debate over Chevaline and replacement options. However, a renewed study was not favoured by Mulley, who argued that the fundamental requirements of deterrence had not changed since 1972 and had already been reaffirmed in 1976.[4] Faced with this disagreement, the prime minister compromised by agreeing to a limited study which would update the 1972 JIC assessment.[5]

Owen's Foreign and Commonwealth Office Study

Owen now instructed his Private Office Policy Unit in the Foreign and Commonwealth Office (FCO) to examine the options for the replacement of Polaris in anticipation of this eventuality. David Owen was to become a key figure in the replacement debate that was to follow. Options for cruise missiles in the context of SALT II featured centrally in the paper that resulted, as did the need to support NATO and pay heed to the views of Britain's allies. It also detailed the parameters for British national targeting and the ability to inflict 'unacceptable damage' on the Soviet Union with ten cities, other than Moscow, used as a baseline for nuclear planning.

The system options they examined were manned aircraft delivering bombs or missiles, ballistic missiles (either ground-based or submarine-based), and cruise missile variants (air-launched, ground-launched, sea-launched, or submarine-based). Each option was critiqued in some depth. Aircraft were found to be vulnerable to a pre-emptive attack whilst facing a formidable array of anti-aircraft defences integrated to protect Soviet cities and other high-value politico-military targets. Land-based ballistic missiles would similarly be vulnerable to a pre-emptive strike, whilst the limited geographical areas of the UK able to base them effectively ruled this option out. The Soviet *Galosh* anti-ballistic missile (ABM) system which protected a 350 mile radius around Moscow was limited by the ABM Treaty and Vladivostok Accords, but could be extended to provide radar coverage and protection for up to 500 miles to include both Leningrad and Kiev.[6] This did not affect the destructive potential of a US nuclear strike as the defence could be saturated by sheer numbers of incoming missiles armed with a mix of multiple re-entry vehicles (MRVs) and multiple independently targetable re-entry vehicles (MIRVs), but it did affect the calculations of France and Britain, who had much smaller deterrent forces. The Galosh system was the primary consideration behind the Chevaline improvement to Polaris.

The paper noted that submarine-launched ballistic missiles (SLBMs) offered relative invulnerability given the difficulties Soviet anti-submarine warfare

(ASW) forces would have in locating and destroying any more than a single British SSBN with two of the four Polaris submarines on patrol 50–75 per cent of the time.⁷ Soviet ASW capabilities were not expected to advance to an extent whereby Britain's SSBNs would be excessively vulnerable, whilst improvements in reactor technology and refitting and repair could permit a successor force to operate two submarines as a Continuous-at-Sea-Deterrent (CASD). Cruise missiles, which became Owen's preferred option, were highly accurate with a Circular Error Probability (CEP) of 200ft. If detected on radar, their relatively slow subsonic speed and low altitude flight profile made them vulnerable to surface-to-air missiles and aircraft interception, but their radar cross-section could be reduced, or they could be fitted with electronic countermeasures similar to those on aircraft or be provided with a supersonic capability.

Ground-launched cruise missiles (GLCMs) would, however, be a controversial system for the UK, with noticeable base facilities which would be highly visible to the Soviet Union. They could not be expected to be moved around Britain on mobile launchers for safety and security reasons, and they might be restricted by SALT II or SALT III—the series of US–Soviet negotiations on nuclear arms control. Air-launched cruise missiles (ALCMs) faced related problems but were deemed worthy of further study. Sea-launched cruise missiles (SLCMs), however, were considered much more viable for UK needs, with submarines relatively invulnerable to Soviet ASW and existing SSN ('Hunter Killer') submarines able to be converted for their use. Designing suitable warheads for cruise missiles was not felt to be a major problem. An outright purchase from the United States was thought to be the best option, and some work on UK cruise missiles could be placed with British industry; a third option would be to engage in European collaboration. Owen's report, therefore, came out in favour of a force of four or five submarines armed with cruise missiles. It was estimated that this would be expensive, but it was believed to be a cheaper solution than a replacement SSBN/SLBM force.⁸

A follow-up meeting between Owen and FCO and MOD officials took place on 17 October 1977, during which Owen criticized the 'Moscow Criterion'. Many of the fundamental questions this posed for a replacement system were discussed. These were issues which would become a feature of replacement deliberations during the remainder of the Callaghan government and into the Thatcher administration. Those present at the meeting accepted that the military rationale for the nuclear deterrent had always been less clear-cut than the political case and that it was difficult to envisage Britain acting independently of NATO. However, it was felt that it was possible that a British force could be used to 'trigger' US forces and frustrate Soviet attempts to detach the United States nuclear commitment to Europe. It was also believed that it provided Britain and the rest of Western Europe with the capacity to deter Soviet political and economic pressures.

Although Owen believed in British possession of nuclear weapons and of the need for a renewal of the strategic deterrent, he felt that the 'Moscow Criterion' should not be an overriding consideration. Moreover, he had reached the conclusion that 'To insist that a British deterrent must be able to destroy Moscow, and must therefore compete in sophistication with the deterrent forces of the superpowers, was to accept a commitment to a never-ending roller coaster of technology and cost. He did not believe that this was feasible or desirable.'[9] For these reasons, Owen was firmly opposed to a next-generation SSBN/SLBM system and did not want studies for a like-for-like replacement for Polaris to take place. He felt that if studies were initiated the result would be a 'forgone conclusion' for the Ministry of Defence, especially if the 'Moscow Criterion' was retained. What he proposed was a thorough examination of cruise missiles as an alternative and to prolong the life of Polaris whilst being open-minded about renouncing Continuous-at-Sea-Deterrence in peacetime.[10]

'Restricted Group' Deliberations

The autumn of 1977 saw the Ministry of Defence begin to examine the Polaris replacement issue in detail, and at the same time Callaghan organized an inner-Cabinet subcommittee, through a small 'Restricted Group' of senior ministers headed by the prime minister, together with Owen, Mulley, and Healey.[11] Its remit was to explore more fully the issues involved. Due to the Labour Party's 1974 commitment not to seek to replace Polaris, Callaghan and this 'Restricted Group' had to tread carefully.

The Group were advised that by the late 1970s the issue of replacement would become acute. It was estimated that it would take around a decade to procure and develop a working system through to completion by the mid-1990s when Polaris would have to be withdrawn.[12] Although the possibility of studies for a successor system had now entered ministerial deliberations, there was scepticism from Owen and Healey that studies should be initiated at this time. Some members of the 'Restricted Group' were open-minded regarding the preservation of the 'Moscow Criterion' as the central plank of Britain's national nuclear targeting policy and how it affected the replacement question. Instead, they questioned whether attacking undefended areas of the Soviet Union would be sufficient criteria for deterrence.

There was not a wholesale rejection of the 'Moscow Criterion'. Members of the 'Restricted Group' accepted that abandoning it would potentially weaken the deterrent threat that Britain posed. There was also a recognition that Britain could be priced out of the market for a successor system, and they saw the 'Moscow Criterion' and successor systems as not necessarily linked issues. Whilst the 'Restricted Group' decided to continue with Chevaline, a proposal to launch a study on successor systems was questioned as being 'too early', with a decision not needed until 1980. Such a study meant to some members that 'an ineluctable process could be set in train which it would be difficult to control or conceal'.[13] For this reason David Owen again pressed for a thorough re-examination of the 'Moscow Criterion'—defined at this meeting as the capacity to destroy 40 per cent of the Moscow area—and the possibility of cruise missiles as a replacement deterrent over a like-for-like ballistic missile replacement.[14] This was accepted.

On 2 November 1977 Sir John Hunt convened a high-ranking group of civil service 'Mandarins' in his room in the Cabinet Office which would oversee the study focusing on updating the 'Moscow Criterion'. It included Sir Michael Palliser and Sir Antony Duff from the Foreign and Commonwealth Office, Sir Frank Cooper and Michael Quinlan from the Ministry of Defence, and Sir Clive Rose and Clive Whitmore (as Secretary) from the Cabinet Office.[15] They were initially tasked to examine not only the continuing validity of the 'Moscow Criterion', but also cruise missile options for the UK, and to produce a report on the timing of any successor decision. The aim was to report to a Steering Group on Nuclear Matters led by Sir John Hunt, which in turn would report directly to ministers.

They noted that their examination of the 'Moscow Criterion' would now need to be much deeper than the last major study of Britain's deterrence criteria carried out by the JIC in 1972.[16] This included a fundamental inquiry into the British philosophy of deterrence without the 'Moscow Criterion' at its centre. Hunt appeared to be pushing the political agenda, as he had over Chevaline the year before, noting that the last meeting of the 'Restricted Group' of ministers implied a move to stay in the nuclear field and, with a General Election on the horizon, urged Callaghan not to delay setting the studies in motion.[17] Hunt's reasoning was that 'it would be irresponsible for the government to remove an option from a successor government, whether Labour or Conservative, simply by refusing to allow studies without any political commitment... [and which] might otherwise be closed off by arms control measures' after the lifetime of the present Parliament.[18]

On 1 December 1977 the 'Restricted Group' met again to discuss the range of options before them, recognizing that the October 1974 Manifesto stated unequivocally: 'We have renounced any intention of moving towards a new generation of strategic nuclear weapons' and that 'no study should be put in hand which would be inconsistent with this commitment'.[19] Yet this is exactly what was now discussed, as Callaghan and his ministers set in train a study of the various options for a successor system.[20]

Ministerial Approval for Successor Studies and the Terms of Reference

With ministerial authorization having been granted, detailed studies could now be undertaken for a number of options for a successor system. These options included cruise missiles, *Trident*, or an indigenous Submarine-Launched Ballistic Missile (SLBM) programme capable of carrying multiple re-entry vehicles (MIRVs).[21] Callaghan indicated he wanted to inform the Cabinet about these studies, but Hunt cautioned against this course of action.[22] He warned that divulging matters that had hitherto been considered to be of the utmost secrecy, bearing on 'genuine issues of national security', had traditionally been conducted by a small inner-Cabinet of senior ministers. As 'the Russians have always set [this] as a prime espionage target', Hunt advised that bringing this before the full Cabinet was not a wise course of action.[23] He therefore sought to dissuade Callaghan from divulging these studies along with the discussions about the 'Moscow Criterion'.[24] Hunt suggested postponing informing the Cabinet and maintaining the 'need to know' rule until Callaghan had discussed this with the 'Restricted Group' but, in his words: 'This is not however to say that a *decision* should be taken behind the backs of the Cabinet'.[25]

Hunt also told Callaghan that this 'could create a political problem for you within the Labour Party with both those in favour and those against us staying in the nuclear game exploiting the situation for their own purposes. And what if some members of the Cabinet refused to agree that the studies should go ahead?'[26] Hunt went on to point out that Labour already faced difficulties over this issue and this would stir up trouble in the context of the next General Election Manifesto, although 'the Cabinet ought to be conditioned to this well before the Manifesto has to be drafted...but even so is the time ripe yet?'[27] Nothing further was said on the matter and Callaghan's tacit agreement with Hunt's advice on this course of inaction preserved the continuity of the discussion and decision-making process of nuclear weapons policy as established since 1945.[28]

It was agreed that five interrelated areas of study should be undertaken. These were: the philosophy of deterrence; NATO's concept of Alliance deterrence; the purposes a UK deterrent served; potential changes in the politico-strategic environment up to 2010; and finally the criteria for deterrence over the longer term.[29] These studies were to be undertaken by a group led by Sir Anthony Duff from the FCO and a group led by Professor Sir Ronald Mason, the Chief Scientific Adviser in the Ministry of Defence. Duff was asked to look at the deterrence criteria and the international implications of a replacement, while Mason's remit was to look at the technical options. Their deliberations were to last a year.

The Duff group recognized that they needed to avoid confusion about whether they were discussing strategic deterrence or nuclear deterrence more generally, with issues of 'tactical' or 'theatre' nuclear weapons being topical issues of discussion in the context of SALT II, 'grey area' systems, and NATO Theatre Nuclear Force (TNF) modernization (all of which were under active discussion both domestically and internationally). They accepted two fundamental propositions: first, that Britain would never attack a non-nuclear weapons state (NNWS) with nuclear weapons, and second, that 'first-use' was not a credible option for the British state as it would invite wholesale nuclear retaliation.

In terms of the 'second centre' of decision role that the British independent deterrent provided for NATO, it was noted that there might be circumstances stemming from an international crisis where the United States might refuse to use its nuclear weapons in support of NATO and that there could be a gradual decline in the US commitment to NATO. Although it was unclear whether a British deterrent could 'trigger' American re-coupling to NATO under these circumstances, it was felt that it nevertheless added a considerable measure of credibility of threat for the Alliance. It could also deter Soviet threats to British territory in a war between NATO and the Warsaw Pact and provide a further insurance policy if NATO collapsed.[30]

In a meeting on 15 March 1978, it was considered whether Continuous-at-Sea-Deterrence (CASD) was an essential requirement for a future British deterrent. Although they recognized that any platform must remain under positive political control, they assessed a Soviet 'bolt from the blue' (a surprise attack with little or no warning) as extremely unlikely, and that this might allow a future force to be brought to a state of readiness in conditions of rising political tensions. However, considerable doubts were raised regarding this posture as it could be interpreted by the Soviets as provocation. It could also weaken ministerial resolve as this became known to the general public as well as the Soviets. Moreover, it was recognized that an international crisis could last longer than the period over which the force was able to sustain a heightened state of readiness.

The prime minister was kept closely informed of the progress of the Duff-Mason teams, as was David Owen, who took a keen interest in the studies alongside the two other members of the 'Restricted Group', Denis Healey and Fred Mulley. Hunt informed Callaghan in July that: 'I think that the group which conducted the study has done good job on a difficult subject. They have recognised that this is an area where it is not possible to reach hard and fast conclusions and that in the end we can only make informed judgements.'[31]

The chief question in relation to timing was whether the Duff-Mason studies on deterrence, and their discussion of the 'Moscow Criteria' in particular, would impact upon the decision to proceed with Chevaline with the annual progress report due in July. This was crucial to the future of Chevaline, with Denis Healey inclined to cancel the project if the 'Moscow Criterion' was judged to be unnecessary. Chevaline could be 'trickle funded' in the meantime, which would keep the project going until a decision to proceed or cancel was made.[32]

Bryan Cartledge, the prime minister's Private Secretary for Overseas Affairs, simultaneously wrote to Callaghan explaining that 'these papers are not easy or short and you will wish to consider them at leisure'.[33] Callaghan evidently did not find it easy reading, telling Cartledge (who he knew well from his time as Foreign Secretary): This is a chilling paper (& should probably never be read without a countervailing paper on how the UK looks in the eyes of Soviet strategists!)'.[34] The prime minister was presented with a number of options for nuclear targetting in the study. These were:

1. Disruption of the main governmental organs of the Soviet state.
2. Breakdown level damage to a number of cities, including Moscow.
3. Breakdown level damage to significantly larger number of cities than under option 2, but without Moscow or any other city within anti-ballistic missile (ABM) coverage.
3b. Grave, but not necessarily breakdown level, damage to thirty major targets outside ABM coverage.[35]

Although he favoured leaving discussions until the autumn, his personal view was to 'go for options 2 or 3, if 1 is out of the question on expenditure/cost grounds. But we must carry others with us (i.e. Ministers). Meanwhile continue with the funding for Chevaline. Other Ministers (i.e. Defence, F+CS + Chancellor) can be told the *timetable*'.[36]

The 'Owen Criteria' and the Cruise Missile Option

As the Duff-Mason studies progressed, David Owen increasingly believed that there was an 'ineluctable process' towards Trident which he feared had now begun. In order to force a debate on the cruise missile option amongst the three other members of the 'Restricted Group', he ordered members of his Private Office Policy Unit, with assistance from the Cabinet Office and Solly Zuckerman, the former Chief Scientific Adviser, to produce a paper by which 'the four of us explored the Tomahawk cruise missile'.[37]

Leading on from this, Owen again questioned the 'Moscow Criterion', believing that the British concept of national deterrence was tied too closely to American ideas and should instead be more closely aligned to European (as distinct from NATO) rationalizations. He proposed instead that 'the ability to destroy, say, half a dozen major cities in the Soviet Union was perfectly adequate'.[38] Owen and his team offered a detailed critique of existing deterrence criteria.[39] The paper was broken up into three sections dealing with NATO doctrine and weapons systems, the case for a British nuclear deterrent and type of force required, and, lastly, the options for a replacement deterrent.

The British contributions to NATO's nuclear forces amounted to 5 per cent of NATO's stockpile, and it was assumed the Americans could make up this number if the UK dropped out of the nuclear field. However, it was known that the West German government valued the British deterrent both as a 'second centre' of decision-making and as a possible 'trigger' for US nuclear forces. The mainstay of Britain's strategic rationale for the deterrent was the defence of British territory should NATO collapse or the US nuclear guarantee become invalid and Britain needed to defend itself as it had in 1940 and the Battle of Britain. For this purpose Owen's paper recognized the need to be able to inflict major damage on civilian and industrial targets, but it was felt that the 'interpretation of "major damage" is debatable', as was the argument that it 'must include the capability for taking out the city of Moscow'.[40] They recognized that judgements of deterrence criteria were necessarily subjective, and they questioned whether the Russians would regard the potential destruction of other cities such as Minsk, Leningrad, or Kiev as worth the risk of attacking Britain with nuclear weapons.

In the wider context of the political weight attached internationally to the British nuclear programme, it was argued that this enabled Britain:

> to play a greater role in international affairs than its economic or conventional military strength would otherwise warrant; and that the renunciation by Britain of a nuclear status would in the long run seriously diminish our general influence on world affairs including for example, our retention of a permanent seat on the UN Security Council. It is also sometimes argued, in the contrary sense, that renunciation would constitute a catalyst to international arms control efforts, would be a major step in arresting the further horizontal proliferation of nuclear weapons and would invest the renouncing country with a very considerable moral authority which would increase its political influence. Experience shows that this political 'halo' effect might last for a year or so but would soon wear off.[41]

It was accepted that these political judgements were difficult to assess, but it was also felt that giving up nuclear weapons would enhance French prestige as the only remaining European nuclear power adding to their weight in the EEC and disturbing the West Germans.

The Duff-Mason Report and Replacement Options

On 9 December 1978 Callaghan noted that decisions about the future of the deterrent would depend on cost and relative independence, including the capacity to fire the missiles independently, and requested reports on US and Soviet strategic nuclear doctrine to be prepared to help frame the studies.[42] Duff-Mason were now asked to consider the following six areas:

 (i) The politico-military requirement.
 (ii) Criteria for deterrence.
 (iii) Operational and technical characteristics.
 (iv) International developments.
 (v) Options.
 (vi) Resources and comparative costs.

They began by arguing that deterrence required that a potential aggressor needed their opponent to believe in their capacity to inflict 'unacceptable damage' and the possibility that the deterrent would be used. NATO's triad of conventional, theatre, and strategic nuclear weapons were intended to deter Soviet aggression through a capacity to climb the 'escalation ladder', outweighing any possible gains they sought. Britain did not need to deter the Soviet Union at the level of the United States, as any gains through eliminating the United Kingdom were substantially lower. Whilst there was no guarantee that a UK government would launch a retaliatory attack on the Soviet Union following a massive nuclear attack on Britain, the Soviet Union should believe this was a probable or possible outcome of any aggression.

The Soviet Union was considered to be the only existential threat facing the United Kingdom in the next 30–40 years that the study team had used as a timeframe. It suggested that European links with the United States would continue, although there might be a decline in the US nuclear guarantee, with the British deterrent seen to assume four main roles:

 (i) *A numerical contribution to NATO's assigned nuclear forces.*

   It was argued that the UK contribution to NATO should not be overstated, but was significant.

 (ii) *A second centre of decision-making.*

   This was seen as the distinctive quality of the British contribution because it complicated the deterrent calculations of the Soviet Union, who had to take heed of the decision-making of a separate government to the United States. This was seen to guard against any decline in the US nuclear guarantee with the British deterrent, like France's, the nucleus of a distinct European nuclear capability which would dissuade West Germany from becoming a nuclear weapons state. Secondly, Britain could act independently of the US should the situation demand it.

(iii) *A capability for independent defence of national interests.*

It was felt that should collective security fail, the British deterrent provided for the ultimate option for national defence and counter politico-military pressures or to deter aggression, but a question remained with regard to whether this was a necessary or credible contingency.

(iv) *Political status and influence.*

It was argued that giving up Britain's status as a Nuclear Weapons State 'would be a momentous step in British history'. British nuclear weapons provided access to, and influence over, US thinking on defence and arms-control policies, enabling Britain to play a leading role in international arms control and non-proliferation negotiations. A decision to replace Polaris would, nevertheless, have a detrimental effect on non-proliferation efforts by Non-Nuclear Weapons States, who would see this as inconsistent with the government's declared arms control and non-proliferation aims.[43]

Although the costs of replacement would be high and detract from conventional weapons spending, it was seen as a unique capability not provided by Britain's European allies (France was omitted from this judgement).[44]

The study made a careful examination of the concept of deterrence for medium-sized nuclear powers in the timescale up to 2010 and the politico-military requirement itself. Their reasoning was as follows: potential aggressors (specifically the Soviet Union) could make objective assessments of the level of British capabilities (through public statements and intelligence gathering activities) as well as the politico-military resolve to use that capability. Echoing Clausewitz's 'remarkable trinity' of 'primordial violence, hatred and enmity', 'the play of chance and probability', and 'subordination, as an instrument of policy' in making these assessments, uncertainty played a significant part in weighing up the decision-making process to escalate hostilities and cross the nuclear threshold, but all three elements of the trinity were to reveal themselves explicitly as well as implicitly.[45]

With the Soviet Union achieving approximate strategic parity with the United States, Western thinking of the role played by strategic nuclear weapons had undergone modification. This had required the adoption in 1967 of a strategy of 'Flexible Response' by NATO and a 'ladder of escalation'. Strategic nuclear forces could only be effective:

if they form part of a chain of closely linked military capabilities, each of which must be strong enough to face an aggressor with a decision that he would need to pitch his action, initially or later, at a scale or level so severe as to risk progressively involving higher levels of Western capability right up to the strategic nuclear level.[46]

This view of a 'seamless robe of deterrence' was largely the product of the thinking of Michael Quinlan, who was a key member of the Duff-Mason group.[47]

It was argued that although the deterrent strategies of the superpowers could not be read across for medium-sized nuclear weapons states such as Britain and France, the level of 'unacceptable damage' they could inflict could never be ignored. Moreover, threats of nuclear war might bring in the superpowers, given the potential consequences and the effects on bipolarity. The scale of damage capable of being inflicted by a medium-sized nuclear power did not need to be on the scale of a superpower in order to deter nuclear war, but it was felt that it had to be a capability the Soviet Union could not be sure of neutralizing. There were two supporting factors that also needed to be taken into account: whether a British government would, in the most dire circumstances, seek to use its nuclear weapons independently of the United States, and whether the Soviet leadership believed it would? It was the second of these which the Duff-Mason study team judged to be the crucial deterrence criteria.

Although the British military capability was seen to act as a deterrent against all forms of military attack on British interests, the strategic nuclear deterrent was designed against the highest of all these threats—nuclear attack upon the United Kingdom. Deterrence of this order would be achieved by posing 'unacceptable damage' to the Soviet Union. But:

> If this threat failed to deter and if the Soviet Union had mounted massive nuclear strikes against our cities, the use of our strategic nuclear force would not ward off further damage, and indeed there might be little of value left undamaged. In these circumstances the actual use of our strategic nuclear force in retaliation against the Soviet Union would represent a reaction of rage and revenge. *If this ultimate stage were reached, there can be no certainty that a Government would take a deliberate decision to launch this act involving the killing of large numbers of enemy civilians but serving no rational purpose for their own country* (emphasis added).[48]

The important thing was that the Soviet leaders believed in British political resolve up to this point.[49] In terms of moral judgements, it was argued that deterrence was based on the belief that no nuclear weapons state (NWS) could feel sufficiently confident to attack an adversary in the hope that his opponent would not retaliate on grounds of ethics.[50]

The Report also looked at the politico-strategic environment up to 2010. They based their assumptions on the continuation of an adversarial relationship with the Soviet Union, that NATO would continue, and the US commitment to

European security would remain largely undiminished (although the US nuclear guarantee might not be valid in circumstances short of general war), and also that further political evolution of the EEC could lead West Germany to consider a nuclear capability for itself. It was further argued that if a decision was not made to renew the strategic deterrent, it would lead to a progressive abandonment of the British nuclear programme because there would be insufficient work for the UK's nuclear weapons establishments. Over the course of time Britain would cease to be a nuclear weapons state.

Duff-Mason argued that NATO as a whole valued the UK's nuclear contribution, including its deep-strike theatre capabilities provided through Polaris as well as the *Buccaneer* and *Vulcan* aircraft force. The national command and control of these forces provided for the 'second centre' of decision role for NATO and a bulwark against any reduction or loss of the American nuclear guarantee in circumstances short of general war. It complicated Soviet calculations of engaging in aggression against NATO with the concomitant risk of escalation, and additionally it meant that nuclear decision-making was not the sole preserve of US presidential decision-making. Britain's contribution to the Alliance was of particular importance because the French could not be relied upon to come to the aid of the Alliance. In terms of possible cooperation with France it was argued that:

> Anglo-French co-operation could have benefits for our relations with our European partners; but, compared with the US alternative, it would involve greater risks for NATO cohesion, and general political difficulties for the UK given French determination not to participate in nuclear arms control. US agreement would be required but the US attitude is uncertain. If in view of these problems a US option were preferred, there would be advantage, in terms of relations with the French, in seeking an agreement with the US which allowed the development of Anglo-French cooperation in the running of their strategic submarine force.[51]

On seeing the first two parts of the Duff-Mason Report on 11 December 1978, David Owen argued that the 'theoretical and practical aspects of the problem can[not] be considered in isolation from one another'.[52] He felt the report concentrated too heavily on strategic systems without dealing with the differences which were already apparent in public discussions of SALT II and NATO TNF modernization, which distinguished between 'strategic' and 'theatre' nuclear forces. More critically, he believed that the Report 'approaches the issue of deterrence from an excessively technical and numerical perspective, whereas I believe it should be viewed primarily in political terms' with 'deterrence judgements made by the super powers... no guide to our own requirements'.[53] He further added that there was no categorical judgement that could be determined for the level of 'unacceptable damage' that the Soviet leadership would consider worth destroying the United Kingdom for. It was also difficult for him to conceive of circumstances where the UK would be forced to act alone with the threshold of destructive capability unnecessarily high, adding: 'We have to assume that the Russian leadership will behave rationally, for if they do not we are doomed'.[54] Owen was unconvinced that the Soviet leadership 'would be willing to risk even a single major Soviet city for the limited prize of an attack on Britain alone. It is their assessment of our political resolve to *use* nuclear weapons which will deter them, rather than the precise degree of "severe structural damage" which they judge us capable of inflicting'.[55]

Meanwhile, on 15 December, Hunt delivered to Callaghan Part III of the Duff-Mason Report, which dealt with system options.[56] Hunt again expressed scepticism about lowering the deterrence criteria too far in terms of the level of damage required. He told Callaghan that collaboration with the US had to continue so long as Polaris remained in operational service.[57] A comprehensive background history was also provided which detailed the development of Anglo-American nuclear collaboration from inception up to the present, and the scale of the ties that had been entered into with the US through the 1958 Mutual Defence Agreement and 1963 Polaris Sales Agreement. Information on warhead designs had to be considered to be a joint arrangement and could not be passed to a third party (such as the French) without prior US agreement. Material and equipment for nuclear propulsion were similarly restricted, as was information on re-entry systems.

A wide range of options had been examined, with the options now narrowed down to ballistic missiles and cruise missiles. Due to the potential for pre-emptive attack all basing options other than submarines were ruled out, despite possible Soviet advancements in anti-submarine warfare (which carried an accepted risk). There were perceived to be operational drawbacks and cost penalties if a decision was made to try and procure the French M-4 (with this technology at least a generation behind the Americans), whilst the 6,500 mile range of Trident II D-5 was seen as unnecessary for UK needs and also came with support and cost disadvantages. Trident C-4, purchased from the Americans, with its 4,000 mile range and MIRV capability, was seen as the best option on technical and cost grounds, with an in-service date of 1994. There were also two fall-back options.

The first was the C-4 missile—minus MIRV, if agreement could not be reached for the sale of MIRV technology, although this option was uncertain on technical grounds (i.e. could C-4 be 'de-MIRVed'?). The second was to re-motor and modernize Britain's Polaris force using some Trident technology to provide an increased range of 3,000 miles. However, this would require an increased number of missiles on patrol to meet the damage criteria. Moreover, this would be a UK-unique solution and the experience of Chevaline meant this was to be avoided if at all possible. This was known as the 'Chevaline

The Polaris Replacement Debate

Imperative'.[58] A MIRVed Trident force would offer higher accuracy than the present Polaris force, providing the UK with the ability to attack separate targets with superior effectiveness against anti-ballistic missile defences. Moreover, the Royal Navy and AWRE had by now accumulated substantial experience of operating ballistic missiles and designing warheads alongside the US Navy and American nuclear laboratories.[59] This was their preferred option, if it could be afforded.

Following the Report, on 19 December 1979 Owen submitted a detailed critique of the 'Moscow Criterion'.[60] He declared his dissatisfaction with the ability to destroy at least ten major cities or inflict damage on thirty major targets as the minimum criterion for the British deterrent. Instead, Owen pushed for greater consideration of the cruise missile option as being effective, smaller, and cheaper than the other main options proposed in the Report. He took issue with Option 3a, with the 'breakdown' level damage specified at 50 per cent. If fewer cities were chosen, then the 300 cruise missiles which Duff-Mason argued (in Part III) would be necessary could be reduced, with extra allowance for aircraft attrition.[61] This critique was later known as 'thirty bangs in thirty places'.[62]

Owen also favoured keeping Polaris going for as long as possible, arguing that the next fifteen years 'are likely to bring important developments in the politico-military and arms control field, which could drastically alter the basis on which we currently assess our national deterrent requirement'.[63] Although there would be constraints in terms of the life of the missiles, with Polaris being decommissioned by the USN in the early 1980s, Owen questioned whether it might be possible for the UK to purchase their stockpile of missiles? He suggested to Callahan that if this was put to President Carter at the forthcoming four-power summit at Guadeloupe 'the answer would be yes, and you might, like Macmillan, get them at a bargain price' whilst sounding him out about Tomahawk.[64]

In response to this, Hunt made clear that the only stage that had been reached was whether the time was right to talk to the Americans to sound out what level of cooperation might be forthcoming and their costing of the various options. Subject to agreement, this could then be raised at the Guadeloupe Summit, which had been arranged for January 1979 to discuss a range of European nuclear issues between Carter, Callaghan, Schmidt, and Giscard, centred largely on TNF modernization and the fall-out from the 'neutron bomb' cancellation.[65] He also suggested that the arguments in Owen's paper might be taken up, but disparagingly he added, 'I have however myself considerable doubt about a bargain basement deterrent'.[66] Sounding like a fellow minister, as opposed to a non-partisan civil servant (albeit the most senior civil servant), he further added that although the case for the retention of a strategic deterrent needed to be carefully balanced, it also had to be credible 'both to ourselves and to our potential enemy. If it is not so credible, it would be better to do without it'.[67] Hunt concluded: 'This does not mean that it has to have the ability to destroy Moscow. Indeed I would not recommend going for Option 1 in the criteria study. It does, however, mean the assurance of creating other unacceptable damage'.[68]

Fred Mulley, the Defence Secretary, also sent Callaghan a note critiquing Owen's argument for the SSNs armed with cruise missiles to be considered as the platform for the strategic deterrent force. This reflected the MOD's unhappiness with Owen's suggestions because they believed they diminished the roles of the SSNs, 'which have other things to do besides hide'. Additionally, current patrol patterns were believed to be incompatible with strategic deterrent operations.[69]

The Duff-Mason Report was subsequently discussed at short notice by the 'Restricted Group' on the 21 December 1978 and again on 2 January 1979.[70] At the meeting on 21 December there was general consensus that Polaris should be replaced against the background of future uncertainty. It was felt that the continuity provided by the UK's retention of a strategic nuclear deterrent was a stabilizing factor in the international system, especially regarding Germany, whilst also acting as a balance to France, who otherwise would become Western Europe's sole remaining nuclear power. Furthermore, it was argued that: 'we could not rule out the possibility that within the timescale we had to consider we might find ourselves having to face alone Soviet political pressure or military threats. In this situation, a British deterrent would provide us with the basis for resistance'.[71]

At the 2 January meeting two courses of action were recommended. The first was to outline to Carter the general position faced by the government on the replacement question and to ask what the president was prepared to make available. The second was to make a specific request, but again without commitment. This could take the form of one of three options—a ballistic missile force, a hybrid force of ballistic and cruise missiles, or a force based solely on cruise missiles. There was consensus amongst the 'Restricted Group' that Guadeloupe represented an ideal opportunity to raise these issues with Carter in private discussions at a time when he might very well be sympathetic to the British position.[72]

Facing both domestic and international problems, the shared belief was that he required support from his European allies, and 'President Carter might well conclude that Britain was his best friend and staunchest ally on this issue'.[73] Owen remained steadfast in his support for the cruise missile option, but this was not a view which was accepted by the 'Restricted Group' as a whole, with Trident C-4 high on the list of preferred options. Callaghan summed up the discussion, noting that whilst they were not yet ready to take a decision even in principle, 'he himself favoured the Trident C4 option'. Nevertheless, there was agreement that he approach Carter at Guadeloupe.[74] If Carter showed willingness to be helpful he should run with this, and the prime minister intended to respond favourably if he gave positive indications that a request for C-4 would be greeted sympathetically. In doing so it was recognized that a major dispute within the Labour Party would probably ensue and a new manifesto commitment would have to be drafted.[75]

Callaghan's record of his famous 'walk on the beach' with Carter at the Guadeloupe Summit from the 4 January 1979 began with him waking Carter from a mid-afternoon nap in order 'to talk to him about something important'.[76] In the discussion that followed the prime minister raised the question of the possible purchase of Trident C4 from the United States. President Carter responded positively and indicated that he would be willing to sell the missile to Britain. The full record of Callaghan's discussion with Carter was subsequently communicated to his fellow ministers in the 'Restricted Group': Denis Healey, David Owen, and Fred Mulley.[77]

Callaghan, facing deep unpopularity over his handling of the 'Winter of Discontent' upon his return from sunnier climes, was pressed not to delay establishing contact with the Americans.[78] In February Sir Ronald Mason and Sir Clive Rose were sent to Washington to begin discussions, where they were joined by Defence Secretary Fred Mulley and the US Secretary of Defense, Harold Brown. However, time was now running out for Callaghan's government.[79] This decision on replacement, along with the management of Chevaline through to completion, would pass to the incoming administration of Margaret Thatcher following the Conservative victory in the General Election of 3 May 1979. To assist with deliberations regarding the successor system, Callaghan broke with government convention regarding the passing on of information from an outgoing opposition government and supplied Mrs Thatcher with a summary of his recent meeting with Jimmy Carter and his Polaris replacement file.[80] This was agreed after Hunt requested authority to show the record of the Guadeloupe meeting between Callaghan and Carter to Mrs Thatcher.[81] Callaghan wrote his firm opinion over the top of the document, stating unequivocally: 'The incoming Prime Minister should be briefed on the need for replacing Polaris (or otherwise—as she thinks!) & should decide to make her own approach to President Carter'.[82]

Conclusion

During the deliberations of the Duff and Mason groups, and the debates within the 'Restricted Group' of select ministers that followed, there were never any suggestions that Britain's nuclear deterrent should be abandoned. The four key ministers never doubted that they 'wanted Polaris replaced and that Britain should retain its independent nuclear deterrent'.[83] Nevertheless, despite the recommendations of the Duff-Mason Report and Callaghan's own preference, there were important disagreements between ministers about the targetting requirements of deterrence and the best option to replace Polaris. This reflected different beliefs about the requirements for effective deterrence. David Owen's critique of the 'Moscow Criterion' was the first sustained ministerial challenge to this targetting philosophy, a philosophy which had underpinned and justified procurement of state-of-the-art strategic deterrent systems since its inception in 1962. He was joined in this critique of existing nuclear doctrine by Denis Healey, who emphasized the political nature of the judgements made about the requirements of deterrence when he argued that:

> David Owen and I both felt that the Chevaline programme was too expensive. We didn't need to be able to hit Moscow. But again, I think, the thing slipped through, after this very perfunctory and almost meaningless paper by the Chief Scientist [if anything this was more related to Duff's part of the report]. This is not, after all, to do with technology; this is to do with how likely you think a certain contingency, how you think the other side will react to their knowledge that you have certain capabilities. That's what it's all about. It's nothing whatever to do with scientists or, with respect, with generals.[84]

The recommendation from the Duff-Mason Report, however, was that Trident C-4 was the best option for Britain and the 'Moscow Criterion' should remain the basis of British nuclear planning. This was accepted by the prime minister and supported by his Defence Secretary. The influence of Duff, Mason, and indeed Sir John Hunt was, arguably, considerable in shaping their views. The key decision nevertheless remained with the prime minister. Had Callaghan won the 1979 election, knowing that a request for Trident to the American president would be favourably received, he was prepared to pursue this option and face the inevitable difficulties from within his own party. As it was, he lost the election, and hence the formal decision on the replacement of Polaris was left to his successor, Margaret Thatcher and her incoming Conservative government.

8

The Adoption of Trident

> *In ethical terms, the issues surrounding nuclear weapons are difficult, if not agonising. But in the debate between those who judge it better to keep those terrible weapons so as to use them as a shield for peace, and those who judge it better to discard them in order to maintain peace by some new, untried and, I would suggest, historically improbable route, the arguments are, I would suggest, on the side of deterrence.*
>
> John Nott, March 1981[1]

Unlike her Labour predecessors, Margaret Thatcher and her new Conservative government appeared fully committed to the continuation of a British nuclear deterrent. In opposition Thatcher had been critical of Labour's policies concerning nuclear weapons. In office she was to be a strident advocate of both the strategic deterrent and of strengthening the bonds between Britain and the United States in foreign and defence policy.[2] When Thatcher won the May 1979 General Election the *Chevaline* modification to *Polaris* was nearing completion and a decision would soon be made to announce the programme. At the same time, a decision had to be made about the purchase of *Trident* missiles from the United States.

The Chevaline Announcement

Mrs Thatcher had long been a strong supporter of nuclear deterrence and this became very evident when she became prime minister. However, between 1979 and 1983 the strategic environment continued to alter with the growth of the nuclear forces of both superpowers and the perceived need for NATO Theatre Nuclear Force (TNF) modernization. How the government responded to the challenges of an increasingly tense superpower relationship was to be a source of great controversy both nationally and internationally, with public concerns evident from popular protests led by the Campaign for Nuclear

Disarmament (CND). These developments formed the backdrop to Mrs Thatcher's embrace of the nuclear deterrent and the eventual public announcement of Chevaline.

On 24 January 1980 the new Defence Secretary, Francis Pym, announced to the House of Commons:

> The strategic environment in which they operate [the four Polaris submarines] and the whole alliance operates is not static. Without breaching the provisions of the 1972 treaty on anti-ballistic missile defence, the Soviet Union has continued to upgrade its ABM capabilities, and we have needed to respond to that upgrading so that we can maintain the deterrent assurance of our force. The previous Conservative Government therefore pressed ahead with a programme of improvements to our Polaris missiles, which our immediate predecessors continued and sustained. The House will, I am sure, understand that I cannot go deep into detail, even to correct the widely mistaken assertions which have sometimes appeared in public, but I think the programme has now reached a stage where I can properly make public more information about it.
>
> The programme, which has the codename Chevaline, is a very major and complex development of the missile front end, involving also changes to the fire control systems. The result will not be a MIRVed system, but it includes advanced penetration aids and the ability to manoeuvre the payload in space. The programme has been funded and managed entirely by the United Kingdom with the full co-operation of the United States... It has been a vital improvement. I do not think the House will be surprised that it has also been costly. The programme's overall estimated cost totals about £1,000 million.[3]

With the words quoted above, the new Secretary of State for Defence revealed for the first time the existence of a project that had remained a closely guarded secret, even from many Cabinet members of four governments, since the late 1960s. At this time the Royal Navy was building towards outfitting and working up the weapons and safety systems of *HMS Renown*, in preparation for continuous operational patrols of a Chevaline-equipped submarine to begin in 1982.[4] With the status of Chevaline now largely resolved, Mrs Thatcher and her government could wholeheartedly move on to the question of replacement.

The experiences of operating Polaris and developing Chevaline, both of which were accomplished with the full support of the United States, had generated a great deal of politico-military momentum to continue cooperation on a successor system. It was believed that the costs of going it alone in an age of increasingly sophisticated and expensive delivery systems were too much for the country to bear without major cuts in conventional defence expenditure—a debate brought sharply into focus by the 1981 Nott defence review and 1982 Falklands Conflict.[5] As a result, the experiences of operating Polaris as both a survivable and credible nuclear deterrent alongside their

US allies came to heavily influence the available options when it came to the replacement question.

Initial Trident Discussions Amongst MISC 7

Shortly after Mrs Thatcher's election victory she held a meeting to debate the Duff-Mason Report which had now been circulated to an inner-Cabinet of ministers formed by her under the designation MISC 7 (Miscellaneous 7) in order to discuss the issues.[6] MISC 7, although a new committee, was not unique in either its composition or terms of reference. As we have seen, similar inner-Cabinet committees had been presided over by Clement Attlee, Harold Wilson, Edward Heath, and James Callaghan. It was anticipated by senior officials in the MOD that MISC 7 would rapidly make a decision on a successor system, with the likelihood of procuring Trident C-4 from the US. This meant opening prime minister-to-president discussions, as James Callaghan had recommended, with a further remit for official civil service contacts to begin.[7]

MISC 7 first met on Thursday 24 May 1979 at 5.00 pm in 10 Downing Street. It was led by the prime minister who, with her forceful personality and zeal, came to dominate MISC 7 and ministerial decision-making on the replacement decision. This first meeting (which also discussed SALT, the Comprehensive Test Ban Treaty, and nuclear release procedures) had before them the Duff-Mason Report. Mrs Thatcher noted that whilst the government was committed to a successor system, and that Duff-Mason had recommended C-4 as the preferred option, more information was needed on the costs and implications of the other options it had examined. This could only be obtained from the US, and it was proposed that a small team headed by Sir Clive Rose and Professor Sir Ronald Mason should be sent to Washington for discussions.[8]

Despite opinion within the Ministry of Defence firmly behind Trident C-4, MISC 7 noted in its first meeting that 'this would be a very expensive option and we would need to look very carefully at the possibility of going for something cheaper'.[9] MISC 7 further noted that 'It was essential therefore that the options should be examined and presented by officials without any implied Ministerial backing for the C4 so that all factors, including cost, could be taken into account when the decision was reached'.[10] Whilst it was noted that Cyrus Vance, the US Secretary of State, had been extremely forthcoming regarding American willingness to help, there was also the possibility of Anglo-French nuclear cooperation. However, although there were some political attractions in closer Anglo-French defence collaboration, it was argued that there was also a need to 'avoid anything which might damage our nuclear links with the Americans on which our present deterrent depended'—a view long held by defence officials.[11]

Sir Clive Rose, of the Cabinet Secretariat, took note that 'Ministers were genuinely anxious that no options should be foreclosed and that they should be in a position to make their decisions as between alternatives on the basis of a thorough rehearsal of the facts, including technical characteristics and cost.'[12] The visit of his team of civil servants to Washington in July 1979 was therefore intended to be a major contribution to a revised version of Part III of the Duff-Mason Report, which had covered system options.[13]

Rose felt that the two main options under consideration (Trident C-4 and cruise missiles) and the timescale for their delivery into service were reliant upon resolving the re-motoring problems the British were experiencing at this time with the Polaris-Chevaline system. Furthermore, with the industrial capacity for large, long-range missiles suitable for an SLBM having been abandoned following the cancellation of *Blue Streak* in 1960 and the withdrawal from the civilian European Launcher Development Organisation in 1968, the start-up costs, timescale, and technical considerations ruled out re-starting an indigenous large UK missile programme. Similarly, although an indigenous cruise missile capability was within the technical reach of the UK, it would entail a substantial effort with uncertainties over costs and timescale. Additionally, he recognized that 'we could make ourselves independent of the US for navigation and targeting data [but] only with great difficulty, if at all'.[14]

With these substantive issues in mind, seven main options for ballistic missiles and their front-ends were re-examined. These options were:

a. *Chevaline (Polaris A-3TK) MRV system.* Chevaline would require new equipment for existing designs, some of which was long out of production. It faced major disadvantages in long-term reliability and uncertain support costs. There would be a total loss of commonality with the US, with their remaining Polaris fleet being phased out by 1981. It had a limited range[15] and was vulnerable to Soviet ASW capabilities. However, no new warhead development would be required.

b. *An upgraded Polaris MRV system (A4).* This would be a specially developed system for UK needs which would share some commonality with the US Trident system. It would have an increased range over Polaris (up to 2,800 miles) with more reliable propulsion and control systems. The 'front end would be similar in concept to Chevaline' although a major redesign would be needed, but not necessarily a new warhead programme. The A4 had already undergone an initial conceptual design study, but at this point it was considered impossible to accurately say what the optimum characteristics would be in terms of performance trade-offs.

c. *The Poseidon MIRV system (C3).* This had various ranges depending on the warhead configuration (a maximum of 2,500–2,800 miles)[16] and would

The Adoption of Trident

have to be purchased 'second hand' as the US began to phase out their Poseidon force between 1988 and 1992. Although there would be some compatibility with existing British facilities, long-term system reliability and support costs were uncertain since the system would be unique to the UK throughout its service life as the US would be operating Trident. A new nuclear warhead programme would be needed and a series of nuclear tests to prove the warhead.

d. *The Trident I (C4) MIRV system.* Trident, it was believed, would form the major element of the US SLBM programme up to the year 2000. A UK warhead programme would be required but, if successful, the current UK test series might prove sufficient. This had a range of up to 5,800 miles.

e. *Trident C4, but without MIRV.* This would require a major redevelopment of the 'front end' by the UK and would have to be an MRV system with a reduced nuclear warhead and power accuracy. This would necessitate a high-risk development programme on at least the scale of Chevaline, with range reduced to 2,500 miles. Again, there would be trade-offs in performance characteristics, which were difficult to forecast and would depend on the extent to which the US insisted on de-MIRVing the system by removing the capability to manoeuvre in space.

f. *The Trident II (D5) system.* This was under early development in the US, with no decision yet taken on completion and deployment. It was a much larger missile than C-4, with a longer range and probable higher accuracy. The extra range was not considered essential for UK needs and higher costs than C-4 were likely. It too would require a new warhead programme [with a planned range of up to 6,500 miles].

g. *The French M4 system.* This was essentially an MRV with some capability, albeit well below US MIRV standards, for engaging spaced targets. Missile range was estimated at 2,200 miles, and a UK warhead programme would be needed. Scale and test requirements were uncertain.[17]

In the review it was believed that a fully developed UK MIRV system was 'virtually out of the question' because it would far exceed 'the complexity, cost and demands on scarce manpower resources of Chevaline'.[18] This limited UK options should the US decline to sell MIRV technology to the UK. As a result, the remaining options, it was felt, were 'inferior and far less certain' to either Trident C-4 or D-5.[19] With the new US D-5 missile being in excess of UK requirements, it was argued that 'Trident C-4 with MIRV has a clear advantage over the other US and French ballistic missiles... as a system in service with the US Navy it would bring great technical, operational and logistic advantages. There would [also] be no need to develop a UK "front-end", apart from the warheads'.[20]

MISC 7 and the Advice of Military Officials

Using the Duff-Mason Report as a basis for a decision regarding a successor system, Mrs Thatcher used the MISC 7 committee to debate these detailed options more fully and to formulate a way forward. With regard to system options, the final decision would depend on whether the US would provide Britain with MIRV technology. If this was not forthcoming, the fall-back options remained the C-4 with an MRV system or the A-4 option. Furthermore, if a fifth submarine was built this could be used to offset criticism from the US over the planned retirement of the *Vulcan* bombers (which were nuclear-capable and tasked both with NATO and national war plans). Mrs Thatcher felt that if C-4 was eventually chosen 'it would be necessary to press hard for access to MIRV technology'.[21]

At the committee Dwin Bramall, the Chief of the General Staff (CGS), also raised the question of affordability and expressed concerns about whether the costs of the strategic successor system could be accommodated without cuts in other areas of the defence programme. Bramall argued that 'To lower that threshold to finance a successor system would be a high price to pay and we should continue to argue for extra funding to avoid this'.[22] It is interesting to note that Bramall, a supporter of the British deterrent when in office, has since become one of a number of former ministers and defence officials who question the need for a twenty-first century replacement.[23]

At the time of the MISC 7 meetings, the Defence Policy Staff (DPS) produced a report reflecting the views of the Chiefs of Staff and the Ministry of Defence towards the replacement debate. They focused on three categories of the Duff-Mason report in order.[24]

1. The Politico-Military Requirement
2. Criteria for Deterrence
3. System Options and their Implications

The Politico-Military Requirement discussed the 'general concept of deterrence, the strategy of flexible response imposed on the Alliance by the establishment of strategic parity between the superpowers, and Soviet strategic philosophy with its emphasis on pre-emption, survival and war-winning'.[25] The DPS stated that in the Duff-Mason Report:

> [The] language is carefully muted and it attempts to avoid any trace of advocacy. In spite of this its message is clear: that possession of a credible strategic nuclear deterrent gives a most important and distinctive quality to the UK's defence, both as a nation and as a member of the NATO alliance.[26]

The DPS felt that the 'second-centre of decision' provided by British nuclear weapons was essential to the UK's position vis-à-vis NATO and the Warsaw

Pact by enhancing the political weight of the country through an independent nuclear capability. It also provided 'added coupling for the US strategic systems to the defence of Western Europe which gives the UK its special voice to the nuclear councils of the Alliance'.[27] This 'could work against a weakening of US resolve in crisis or war; and...could serve as a focus of European strength and cohesion in case of any long-term decline in the US guarantee'.[28]

In terms of the independence of the British nuclear deterrent, it was argued that without a strategic nuclear deterrent (capable of fulfilling the criteria of deterrence by inflicting unacceptable damage on the Soviet Union), 'the UK's threat to employ nuclear forces in a NATO context would ultimately be a bluff that the Soviet Union could call'.[29] Furthermore, in an extensive exposition of the British concept of independent nuclear deterrence so far declassified, the DPS stated that 'credibility resides partly in the material and organisational ability to mount an unacceptably damaging strike whatever the conditions, and partly in the will to do so'.[30] The DPS continued:

> These two factors support each other; and the combination of them must sufficiently impress the Soviet Union to ensure deterrence. We would add only that Soviet leaders now, and probably in the future, are realists...they will not be impressed—or deterred—by strategic systems that have a very low chance of inflicting unacceptable damage against the defensive measures of the day.[31]

France too, in their 1972 defence white paper (*Livre Blanc*), had also articulated that the purpose of their strategic nuclear force (*force de dissuasion*) was founded on the ability to inflict 'unacceptable damage' on the Soviet Union.[32]

As we saw earlier, the criterion for unacceptable damage in the Duff-Mason Report was set in the context of destroying the Soviet Union's capacity to compete with other superpowers in terms of industry and war-making potential. As noted in Chapter 7, this criterion was defined in four scenarios:

1. Disruption of the main governmental organs of the Soviet state.
2. Breakdown level damage to a number of cities, including Moscow.
3. Breakdown level damage to significantly larger number of cities than under option 2, but without Moscow or any other city within anti-ballistic missile (ABM) coverage.
3b. Grave, but not necessarily breakdown level, damage to thirty major targets outside ABM coverage.[33]

The Report had suggested that 'any one of the options would constitute an unacceptable level of damage'.[34]

The DPS, however, took exception to this as the 'least demanding of the options becomes the governing one' and 'in our view, the position is nothing like so simple'.[35] The DPS instead produced their own assessment of the damage deemed necessary to deter the Soviet Union. They argued that: 'There will be many circumstances, particularly in situations of advanced escalation, where UK strategic forces capable only of Option 3b ('30 bangs in 30 places' as it was called) would be insufficient to deter a Soviet strike aimed at, say, knocking the UK out of a war'.[36]

The DPS placed this view in an historical setting. With over 20 million casualties resulting from the Nazi invasion of the Soviet Union during World War Two and a similar number killed during the Stalinist purges between 1930 and 1950, 'this must give at least a measure of the threshold with which UK planning has to deal'.[37] In this context the assessment of the criteria for deterrence articulated by the DPS must be much larger than thirty cities, 'if a crude criteria of megadeaths is to apply'.[38] Instead of this, the DPS pressed for the retention of the 'Moscow Criterion' as the capital was still considered to be of the greatest importance in terms of population and in industrial and administrative terms. The loss of the Moscow area, they believed, would be a blow from which the Soviet Union would not recover. This would place them in a position of long-term inferiority with both the US and China.[39]

Part II of the Duff-Mason Report had dealt with the operation of future strategic systems. This indicated the terms of reference for 'independence'. This was defined as 'true independence of the capability, maintainable for at least one year if the support of a collaborative partner were withdrawn'.[40] It was felt at the technical working level that the Polaris force with the Chevaline front-end could continue for four or five years without further US help, and Trident for up to seven years.[41] This meant that if called upon, the deterrent could be fired independently without reference to either the United States or NATO. Second, there had to be high assurance that a future system would be invulnerable to a pre-emptive attack. Third, it was preferable for the system to be on a continuous state of readiness, and, last, that there was a 50 per cent probability that the 'full damage threatened would be achieved'.[42] Each of these three points from the Duff-Mason Report was accepted without comment by the Defence Policy Staff.[43]

As was seen in Chapter 7, the Duff-Mason Report eventually came to favour the Trident C-4 missile in a submarine platform, over cruise missiles. However, even at this early stage, it was recognized that if C-4 was chosen, its larger size meant that the increased propellant used in the missile posed problems for the facilities at Coulport (the Royal Naval Armament Depot near Faslane) due to explosive regulations at the facility overseen by the Ordnance Board. These concerns were kept strictly 'in-house', with an unspecified greenfield site within the UK being considered as a backup should the problems of expansion at Coulport not be overcome.[44] However, Richard Mottram, a senior official in the MOD, believed it 'most unlikely that we would ever get agreement to a new "greenfield" site in the UK' and that 'we must now look positively at all possible options short of this'.⁴⁵ Sir Frank Cooper, a key civil service figure in the defence field and 'one of Whitehall's most colourful and outspoken mandarins'⁴⁶ suggested that careful consideration should be given to storing at least some of the missiles (the number of which would depend on the number of submarines and patrol cycles) in the US.⁴⁷ The question of missile storage subsequently became part of a series of questions under examination by the Royal Navy.⁴⁸

The Trident Purchase

Following discussions in MISC 7, ministerial desire to reach agreement with the Americans was hampered by the American wish for this not to take place before the 12 December NATO meeting in Brussels to discuss Theatre Nuclear Force (TNF) modernization. This meeting was to result in what became known as the 'Dual Track' decision, which led to the deployment of ground-launched cruise missiles at Greenham Common. The issue of TNF and successor systems was judged to be an issue that needed to be tackled separately from the acquisition of Trident by Britain.⁴⁹ This was because the TNF modernization decision had caused a great deal of consternation throughout Europe.⁵⁰ Members of the Carter administration let the British know that a formal request would also be better delayed after the ratification of SALT II, which was the 'mainspring' of the Carter Presidency, without which, it was argued, it would 'be destroyed'.⁵¹

In October 1979 Thatcher and Carter had engaged in highly secret dialogues on Polaris replacement. It was at this point, as Mrs Thatcher recorded in her memoirs, that a Presidential Determination was received to 'supply us with whatever we needed', but she was asked to 'slow... our approach'.⁵² For the Thatcher government, however, delays resulting from the need to ratify SALT II could mean that the 'Russians could wreck the agreement' whilst exposing the British government to domestic pressures, due to widespread speculation on Polaris replacement now appearing on television and in the press.⁵³

Despite Carter's assurance, the decision to purchase Trident C-4 was still far from straightforward. How a Polaris replacement was to be funded remained a central and problematic issue. Sir Robert Armstrong, who as Cabinet Secretary formed part of the government's institutional memory on top secret issues such as this, reminded the prime minister ahead of the December 1979 meeting of MISC 7 that: 'This is a *key decision*, which will affect our most important means of defence over the next 40 years and thereby the basis of our international military posture, and will have major implications for the defence budget, and indeed for our public expenditure, for a least the next decade'.⁵⁴ Armstrong noted that the costs of the replacement would come out of the contingency reserves for the defence budget up to 1983–4, but neither MISC 7 nor the full Cabinet had been told of this. Whilst the case for public expenditure would have to be reopened for other fiscal reasons, the Chancellor 'would not make a fresh attack on the defence budget'.⁵⁵ However, the Defence Secretary would make a case to increase the overall defence budget after 1983/4, and this would be highly challenging for the government, who were in the midst of a recession. The existing defence effort was already under pressure from the US, who attached great importance to the UK's conventional forces as well as Polaris replacement.

Armstrong added that this set of issues could not be immediately resolved by MISC 7, with Polaris replacement viewed as 'our *top defence priority*' and the most important pillar of Britain's defence policy, with 'this pillar...the last to go'.⁵⁶ If this was the prevailing view, the Chancellor and the Defence Secretary could argue whether this should be paid for by 'new money or by cuts elsewhere in the defence programme or by a bit of both'.⁵⁷ Armstrong distilled the issues facing MISC 7 into six points:

(a) Do we retain our strategic deterrent?
(b) What should it be capable of doing?
(c) Which weapon should we choose?

   ...Other major issues—

(a) Number of boats
(b) Foreign policy factors
(c) Timing of announcement⁵⁸

As Geoffrey Howe, the Chancellor, had been absent from the first meeting of MISC 7 in May, Armstrong recommended that the decision to replace Polaris be reaffirmed with Pym, the Defence Secretary. The recommendation should be for C-4 and a four-boat force, at an estimated cost of £7 billion to be spread over twenty years.⁵⁹ Nevertheless, Howe remained concerned that the financial cost of a successor system would weigh heavily on deliberations. The Chancellor, who Mrs Thatcher 'was always irritated by...[with his] quiet, almost inaudible voice, his tendency to be long-winded and his slightly pudgy, soft bespectacled demeanour', was committed to tackle Britain's formidable economic troubles of 'inflation, industrial performance, and unemployment, in that order'.⁶⁰

Armstrong also reminded Mrs Thatcher that 'your Nuclear Release exercise in October pointed up the disadvantages of only having one boat on patrol', and that 'It is now generally recognised that the cancellation of the fifth Polaris boat in 1965 was *an expensive mistake*'.⁶¹ Armstrong thus emphasized the benefits of five boats against the Soviet ASW threat. He also pointed out

The Adoption of Trident

that C-4 'will keep us *totally dependent* on United States co-operation over a very long period... [but Britain had] full operational independence in a crisis'.[62] Support from successive US administrations and Congress would be needed to maintain C-4, with the UK not able to keep going for more than 6–12 months without US support. He cautioned that:

> We cannot foresee how Anglo-United States relations will develop over the next 40 years. It is impossible to be as confident of continuing support for a quarter of a century ahead in 1979 as it was in 1949. But they have not so far either let us down or used our dependence as a means of pressure. In any case we have no real alternative. Going it alone would be prohibitively expensive. This only leaves co-operation with the Americans or co-operation with the French.[63]

In terms of Anglo-French nuclear cooperation, Armstrong stated:

> In the light of your discussion with *President Giscard* on 19th November [during which Giscard had been told of the UK's intent to modernize and continue collaboration with the US[64]], our preference will come as no surprise to him. Our basic reason for not choosing the French alternative is that it would almost certainly give us a *less effective weapon at greater cost*. If we were convinced that we should base our long term decisions on the hypothesis that the American connection was likely to decline, and the French connection to become our *predominant international link*, then we should arguably go into partnership with the French.[65]

But he advised that:

> Politically and economically it would be a more evenly balanced partnership, but it would seriously worry the *Germans*. It would pose great problems with the Americans, on whom we remain dependent for keeping Polaris going through the 80s. And is France's *long term reliability* inherently greater than America's?[66]

Armstrong suggested that the prime minister recommend to MISC 7 a five-boat C-4 MIRVed force which should be put to President Carter as an extension of the 1963 Polaris Sales Agreement, with Cabinet being informed of the approach to the president.[67]

On 15 July 1980 the full Cabinet was informed of this decision.[68] However, there was little chance to debate the Trident purchase as later that day the Secretary of State for Defence, Francis Pym, announced the decision in the House of Commons.[69] Pym was not asked by Thatcher to say anything on the matter to the full Cabinet. As such, they had never been briefed on the detailed discussions which had taken place under strict secrecy.[70] Whilst the prime minister had brought the Trident decision to Cabinet there was never any suggestion that it was open to debate. John Nott, who was then Secretary of State for Trade and Industry, recounts in his memoirs how he was 'shocked that the Cabinet had neither been given any facts nor consulted on the issue'.[71] Nott, alone amongst the Cabinet, complained to Mrs Thatcher but to no avail, later adding 'No-one supported me, there was complete silence around the Cabinet table.'[72]

Pym (the Secretary of State for Defence) set out the government's reasons for the decision in July 1980 and in the simultaneous White Paper—Defence Open Government Document 80/23 (DOGD 80/23).[73] The document set out the British concept of deterrence and, in passing, set out the case for Chevaline and Trident. It was argued that: 'Successive United Kingdom Governments have always declined to make public their nuclear targeting policy and plans, or to define precisely what minimum level of destructive capability they judged necessary for deterrence.' It continued: 'The Government however thinks it right now to make clear that their concept of deterrence is concerned essentially with posing a potential threat *to key aspects of Soviet state power*'.[74] The wording was particularly important as it was an attempt to mark a shift in British strategic nuclear targetting policy away from population centres and towards selective use against strictly military targets. As such, it was designed to be a significant departure from previous targeting policy based on the 'Moscow criterion'. However, as critics argued, attacks on 'key aspects of Soviet State power' would still have involved huge civilian casualties (see Appendix 6). With the NATO 'Dual Track' decision high on the political agenda, although the document was a move in the direction of public education and government openness, it still left major concerns in the minds of many, particularly on the left, regarding the role of nuclear weapons in keeping the peace. During this time there was significant growth in the Campaign for Nuclear Disarmament (CND) from a membership of 5,000 in 1979 to 100,000 in 1985, along with the highly active peace camps at Greenham Common established in the early 1980s.[75]

With a storm of anti-nuclear sentiment brewing in the country, a full parliamentary debate finally took place on 3 March 1981, during which Sir John Nott, the new Defence Secretary, made his position clear, observing that:

> The Secretary of State for Defence, for good or ill, has occasion to learn more, and to think more than most people, about nuclear weapons—and I can tell the House that I view them with total horror. No one should for a moment contemplate what happened at Hiroshima and Nagasaki with any milder feelings. It is therefore right that the Christian conscience should be engaged in thinking about these problems.
>
> ... To engage the emotions—as the promoters of CND know very well—is an easy task. The showing of the film 'The War Game' in a village hall in the evening in the presence of young families has a predictable outcome. To argue the choices before us so as to engage the intellect is a much harder task. But for those who take the view that the concept of nuclear deterrence is morally tenable, so long as we lack a better and surer way of avoiding the horrors of war, there is, I believe, wide support.

John Nott then went out of his way to argue that British nuclear forces were necessary because of the threat still presented by the Soviet Union.

> It is not an option for any Western Government to transport us all back to some pre-nuclear paradise. Nor is it an option, alas, to transform the Soviet Union into something other than what it is. We need have no quarrel whatever with the people of the Soviet Union... But we are not dealing with the Russian people, and the military power that confronts us is not wielded and directed by the Russian people. It is in the hands of rulers whose history and patrimony is that of Lenin and Stalin and the deeds they wrought; of rulers whose system has no more democratic safeguards now than it had in the bloodiest parts of that history, not so very long ago. We have to deal with the leaders of a closed totalitarian State of hostile ideology, huge military power, and a proven willingness to use that power without scruple when it thinks it can safely get away with it. They are capable of using—and, in my view, would use—nuclear weapons as a source of blackmail were we ever to give them such a chance... [although] I am keenly aware that there is at the moment a widespread concern about nuclear war—a concern perhaps more consciously felt than for several years past... Trident is a proven system, of great power, firmly in service with the United States. In short, if we are to stay in the strategic nuclear business at all, the case for Trident as the most cost-effective way of doing so is overwhelming. We have to face the cold fact that credible strategic nuclear capability for the 1990s and beyond does not come cheaper than this. If we are not prepared to afford Trident we had better get out of the business altogether.

Nott also pointedly argued that Labour in Office had been involved in serious discussions about the future of the deterrent:

> It is all very well... to criticise us for not having had a debate here earlier on Trident. Five whole years passed while we were in Opposition and there was never a debate in the House on Chevaline, because no one, outside a small circle—of which the right hon. Member for Devonport [David Owen] was one—was even told about the project.[76]

With the Conservatives having a healthy majority in Parliament and with little backbench discord from their own ranks, the Commons, as expected, endorsed 'the Government's decision to maintain a strategic nuclear deterrent and the choice of the Trident missile system as the successor to the Polaris force' by 316 votes to 248.

Thatcher, Trident D-5, and the Reagan Administration, 1981–1988

In January 1981 Ronald Reagan was inaugurated as the fortieth president of the United States, replacing Jimmy Carter. His administration promised to face down the perceived Soviet threat from a position of strength. They looked to accomplish this through a thorough modernization of their military forces, both conventional and nuclear, along with a much less flexible stance on arms control than Carter had demonstrated, backed by tough diplomatic and political action and strong rhetoric in public and private.[77] This modernization process was to have direct and lasting implications for the upgrade of Britain's strategic deterrent with the government of Mrs Thatcher, who was to form a powerful personal bond with the Reagan administration and its policies, committed to the purchase of Trident C-4 from the United States. With force modernization a centrepiece of renewed American efforts to deal with what they (and many in the West) saw as a mounting Soviet threat, there was a growing belief in Whitehall that Britain would be encouraged to abandon C-4 in favour of the Trident II D-5 with its enhanced capabilities.

On 24 August 1981 Casper Weinberger, President Reagan's Defense Secretary, informed the British government in writing that the president had directed him to formally offer the Trident D-5 missile to Britain.[78] The Chiefs of Staff immediately supported the purchase of D-5. With the US now moving ahead with the programme, seeing the benefits of commonality with the Americans—including potential cost savings and the use of US support facilities—they argued that a prudent choice for the D-5 would provide 'a robust insurance against future Soviet developments'.[79] John Nott, Pym's replacement as Defence Secretary, also made the point to MISC 7 that:

> To decide not to proceed with Trident (D-5) would be in effect to opt out of the nuclear business. It is also probably inevitable that within our lifetime other smaller nations will acquire a nuclear capability. In the eyes of our allies, and of our enemies, we would seem quite a different nation (and the Conservative Party quite a different party). Colleagues will recognise that this is an issue of tremendous national importance.[80]

Once again we see the importance of nuclear weapons in Britain's perceived national identity (as well as that of the Conservative Party).

The Cabinet Secretary, Robert Armstrong, also noted that during the last meeting of MISC 7 some ministers had argued that NATO's doctrine of 'Flexible Response' might no longer be sustainable due to the Soviet Union improving its nuclear capability at all levels. This was combined with a perception that US decoupling from Europe was seen to be increasing due to various European doubts regarding the deployment of GLCMs and *Pershing II*—a result of the 'Dual Track' decision. Armstrong also made the point that a decision not to proceed with a replacement system would place immediate doubts against Polaris, meaning that the UK nuclear research and development capacity would wither away with a concomitant impact upon nuclear relations with the Americans enabled by the 1958 MDA. He further noted that:

The Adoption of Trident

The Chiefs of Staff are conditioned to staying in the game, and I do not think that they have really contemplated the implications of coming out of it. The political as well as the military implications of coming out are so tremendous that your colleagues are likely to conclude that we should stay in. If they do you will want to establish that a British deterrent must be clearly effective; and that its independence is crucial. We are not of course logistically independent as the French are (at a terrible [financial] price); but if the Americans ever cut off their support our force would remain viable for a time (considerably longer with Trident than with Polaris) and would at least have the option of sustaining it with a crash programme of our own thereafter. Our operational independence is complete.[81]

The remaining factors relating to D-5 were well rehearsed and centred on the need for relative invulnerability of the platform to permit an assured second-strike capability upon which effective deterrence depended. Armstrong argued that there were four options:

(a) stay with C-4;
(b) stay with C-4 initially, but build a large enough submarine to enable D-5 to be fitted later;
(c) go for D-5 and four boats;
(d) go for D-5, but build only three boats.

Of these, he argued:

if (a) we will have no friends; and (d) we will be generally be seen as militarily unreliable, since there would be no margin for accidents. So I think the real argument will end up as (b) versus (c) with (b) being championed as politically safer while (c) is defended as both cheaper and easier to negotiate.[82]

The final reason was seen as the most important. It was argued that there was no certainty that NATO would continue to exist as a cohesive security organization over the next twenty to thirty years, and there were even doubts about whether the US commitment to the defence of Europe would last. However: 'Unfortunately, this argument could not be used in public. It would also be important to avoid suggesting that British reliance on American help undermined the independence of the deterrent.'[83]

The government were satisfied that operational independence was sufficient and the added reliability of D-5 meant that US logistical support would be required less frequently. This meant that if support was withdrawn by a future US administration, the government of the day would have time to provide for this contingency. It was also argued that although some of Britain's allies would prefer to see the UK's conventional forces bolstered at the expense of its nuclear capability, the general consensus was that the independent UK strategic deterrent was politically valued by the United States and by NATO. Domestically, the opposition parties were seen as 'ambivalent' towards nuclear weapons. Whilst opposing Trident, they were 'not uniformly opposed to British nuclear weapons and if they came to office might conclude that there were objective reasons for upholding a decision to acquire a D5 force, as the Labour Party had done in the case of the Polaris force in 1964'.[84] Labour had after all made a strong case to the public prior to the 1964 General Election that the deterrent was neither independent nor would it deter, and it could be cancelled. Despite this, upon entering government they stuck with Polaris by portraying it as 'past the point of no return', when it could indeed have been cancelled at little financial cost.[85] In effect, Labour had traditionally conceived of national security in much the same way as the Conservatives when in government, despite what they said in opposition.[86]

The issues were discussed in Cabinet in January 1982. The briefing received 'general support' from Cabinet with 'appreciation' for the full ministerial briefing that had been offered (and in all but one case taken up) on 21 January.[87] Of the briefing itself, Nott noted in his autobiography that:

> [after] persuading a somewhat reluctant Margaret Thatcher ... and [obtaining the] permission of the Americans ... we explained to the Cabinet how much we knew about Soviet nuclear, biological and chemical capabilities, where their command and control bunkers were situated, and how the development of anti-ballistic missile defences bore down on the requirements for a credible deterrent. This was an era where the extent of satellite photography and electronic and signals intelligence was not much known to those outside a small circle ... My colleagues were fascinated; but the Chancellor had come from a good lunch and slept during the briefing.[88]

Importantly, it was made clear during the Cabinet discussion that there would be no cost penalties should a future government choose to cancel the programme. With a General Election due the following year, and with Labour having adopted a policy of unilateral nuclear disarmament under the leadership of Michael Foot, 'the government could not be accused of pre-empting the issue'.[89] Reflecting traditional Anglo-French rivalries, it was also stated that 'internationally it would have been unthinkable to leave France as the only effective nuclear power in Western Europe', and if support was ever renounced by the United States 'the success of the Chevaline programme suggested Britain would not be technologically unable to replace it on a national basis'.[90] Mrs Thatcher summed up the discussion, noting that a formal reconfirmation of the Trident II (D-5) agreement would be put to the Cabinet on 11 March, ahead of the public announcement and publication of a further Open Government Document explaining the decision.[91]

The announcement by Nott took place in the House of Commons on the afternoon of 11 March 1982.[92] By July 1982, however, a further decision was needed on whether to expand facilities at Loch Long in Scotland or to proceed with the favoured option of using US facilities at Kings Bay in Georgia on America's east coast. The US had found no problems with this arrangement provided that the warheads were mated and de-mated in the UK. The advancement in missile technology meant that the D-5 could remain on board the submarine for up to ten years before refurbishment (considerably longer than Polaris). All the vital control, guidance, and electronic packages could be exchanged either at sea or in harbour without offloading any missiles. The common pool of missiles at Kings Bay meant that the Service Life Evaluation (SLE) of the missiles could be conducted jointly, which obviated the need for much of Coulport's work.[93] This could help alleviate the 'strong and vociferous [anti-nuclear] opposition' from what Nott described as the 'lunatic fringe' and elsewhere.[94]

The only reservation the government expressed with regard to using Kings Bay was the perception of a reduction in British independence. However, the radically increased length of time between the replacement or refurbishment of D-5 compared with Polaris actually increased national independence in the event that US support was cut off (although the UK would still depend on the US to supply and repair individual components—stocks and spares of which could be stored in the UK). Moreover, two to three stocks of missiles would be held onboard the submarines themselves, depending on the SSBN refit cycle. For these reasons Nott recommended proceeding with proposals for the use of Kings Bay and to plan for early public announcement pending agreement from MISC 7.[95]

A public announcement was immediately agreed by Mrs Thatcher and was made on 9 September.[96] The formal diplomatic agreement for the sale of D-5 to the UK was finalized on 19 October 1982. As with the 1980 understanding, the 1982 Trident D-5 agreement used the Polaris Sales Agreement as the framework within the ambit of the American Foreign Military Sales Programme.[97] The government later decided, after a great deal of discussion within the Ministry of Defence, that the best option was an elongated version of the *Trafalgar* class of nuclear-powered hunter killer submarine that was smaller than the American *Ohio* class.[98]

When the decision to purchase the more potent Trident D-5 was made public, a year before American Cruise missiles began to be deployed in the UK, debate had become polarized. The Labour Party (with unilateral nuclear disarmament as a manifesto commitment) and the Campaign for Nuclear Disarmament now stood on one side whilst the Conservatives stood on the other. With election victory in June 1983, Mrs Thatcher could perhaps justifiably claim to have carried the country with her on the nuclear issue.[99] The Trident Agreement was a potent political issue in the General Election, and mixed with the 'Dual Track' decision to bring nuclear weapons once more into the forefront of public consciousness.

For the first time, there was clear water between the two parties on the nuclear issue. Throughout the election campaign Mrs Thatcher had stuck to the decision to purchase D-5 despite opposition to nuclear weapons raging 'inside and outside Parliament until the issue was decided finally by the electorate'.[100] By now there was deep concern that Britain was being tied inexorably into American foreign and defence policy.[101] This concern was not aided by the terms of the Trident purchase, but there would have been no cost penalties if the Conservatives had lost the 1983 General Election and a decision had been made to cancel the programme. It remains a matter of conjecture whether or not a Labour government would have cancelled the Trident programme if they had returned to power in the 1980s with either Michael Foot or Neil Kinnock as leader. It is certainly possible that many on the right wing of the party, including grandees such as Denis Healey, would have opposed such a move.[102] The ending of the post-war political consensus on the nuclear issue was to be only temporary, and it returned again under Neil Kinnock in 1989 and continued during John Smith and Tony Blair's leadership of the Labour Party.

Conclusion

Given the Duff-Mason studies undertaken by the previous Labour government, there are clear signs that Trident would also have been chosen by the Callaghan government had they stayed in office.[103] This points to the inherent continuity between UK governments on nuclear weapons issues. As with the Callaghan government, the Duff-Mason Report critically informed the deliberations of the new Conservative government of Margaret Thatcher regarding a successor to Polaris, and the experiences of Chevaline helped to reinforce this decision.

The Trident purchase also held out the possibility of contributing to a more flexible counter-force nuclear posture. Writing shortly before his death, Michael Quinlan—a key figure in the development of British nuclear weapons policy—argued that the reference to 'Soviet state power' related to the Trident agreement in a Defence Open Government Document in 1980 was 'deliberately chosen—partly with ethical concerns in mind—to convey that, while cities could not be guaranteed immunity, the UK approach to deterrent threat and operational planning in the Trident era would not rest on crude counter-city or counter-population concepts'.[104]

This was an important change, though it went largely unrecognized by the public at the time. Whether it would have made a significant difference in terms of civilian casualties in the event of the nuclear force being used is unlikely.

Despite notable concerns over costs, Trident II D-5 came to be embraced rapidly by both the Conservative government of Margaret Thatcher and by senior figures in the Royal Navy. Support for the D-5, however, was not universal.[105] As Colin McInnes recounted in his appraisal of the decision to purchase Trident II: 'Despite strong Ministry of Defence support for the D5 ... certain members of the government were hesitant'.[106] McInnes puts this down to 'Popular criticism, the breakdown in the all-party consensus on nuclear weapons, the increased cost, and the change in timescale (making it more vulnerable to cancellation after the next general election)'.[107] Senior members of the Ministry of Defence also harboured reservations regarding D-5, including Dwin Bramall and Michael Carver, two members of the powerful Chiefs of Staff Committee.[108] Their concerns rested on grounds of cost and the impact upon conventional capabilities. They also felt that D-5 was 'very high risk' and provided too much insurance for a second strike by the UK. However, the stark choice put to MISC 7 was whether to continue having an effective strategic deterrent or to get out of the nuclear deterrent business altogether. There remained some dissent in Cabinet—primarily from Francis Pym and Peter Carrington, both former Defence Secretaries—about the excessive capabilities of Trident D-5 for Britain's needs. However, in line with Jacques Hymans' argument about the key role of the main political leader in nuclear decision-making, Mrs Thatcher remained firmly committed to retaining and updating Britain's nuclear capability. She did, in private, have some reservations about actually using the nuclear force in a crisis. In a conversation with Sir Rodric Braithwaite about whether she could have pressed the button if deterrence failed, she told him: 'I want grandchildren too'.[109] Nevertheless, on Trident she remained steadfast, as she did on the other big nuclear issues towards the end of the Cold War period.

9

NATO Modernization Plans, SDI, and the End of the Cold War

> *[T]o be successful with a policy of deterrence it is necessary to deter each and every level... we have to have sufficient power through our allies to deter at the strategic level and sufficient power among ourselves to deter at the theatre nuclear force level... the latest weapons, such as the SS20s, are already being provided to the Warsaw Pact. We have no modern reply... we must have the modernization of the theatre nuclear forces... we are always prepared to negotiate on disarmament.*
>
> Margaret Thatcher, 27 November 1979[1]

Apart from the *Trident* decisions, during the period from 1979 to 1990 the Thatcher government faced a series of difficult nuclear issues associated with the modernization of Intermediate Range Nuclear Forces (INF), Short Range Nuclear Forces (SNF), and the American Strategic Defense Initiative (SDI). These issues produced major debates in Britain (and the rest of Western Europe) and, in the case of SDI, differences of view between Britain and the United States. Following Mrs Thatcher's departure from Office in 1990, her successor, John Major, faced new challenges to Britain's nuclear policies as the Cold War came to an end. The Major government also had serious concerns about the potential use of chemical and biological weapons in the Gulf War of 1990–1 and what Britain's response might be if such weapons were used.

The Modernization of Intermediate Range Nuclear Forces (INF)

Following the Soviet development of SS-20 missiles targeted on Western Europe, there was a great debate in the West about what was seen as the declining credibility of the Flexible Response strategy. This led to a decision in December 1979 to modernize NATO's Theatre Nuclear Forces with ground-launched cruise missiles (GLCMs) and *Pershing II* missiles to fill what was believed to be 'a deterrent gap'. In April 1981 a Memorandum of Understanding (MOU) was drafted, covering the logistics of GLCMs to be based in Britain.[2] During internal debates, many of which were designed to answer parliamentary questions regarding growing public concerns about the GLCMs, it was noted by officials that the government were satisfied with the existing 'joint decision' arrangements for the use of US nuclear forces based in Britain. It was recognized that the cost for 'dual key' mechanisms would run to 'several hundred million pounds and over 1000 Service personnel'.[3] There was, however, an awareness that the modernization of INF capabilities could help to relaunch the kind of CND campaign which had been so popular in the late 1950s.

In November 1982, at a meeting of MISC 7 (Mrs Thatcher's inner-Cabinet committee dealing exclusively with nuclear weapons), John Nott admitted that the government had underestimated public opposition to the deployment of cruise missiles, with opinion polls showing that, although there was support for an independent deterrent, there was less support for a 'cruise missile force which was not under British control', and this could undermine support for the independent deterrent ahead of the election.[4] As a result, Mrs Thatcher decided that a request should be made to the US for British servicemen to be trained to operate the missiles and launchers. It was thought that training British personnel could act as a hedge against a future political requirement for a 'dual key' arrangement resulting from public and parliamentary pressure.[5]

With deployment scheduled to take place by the end of 1983, the wisdom of the government's position came under sustained scrutiny. In April 1983 Dafydd Wigley, an Opposition politician from Plaid Cymru, tabled a motion in Parliament for a referendum on cruise missiles. Michael Heseltine, who had succeeded John Nott as Defence Secretary, argued for the rejection of this motion on the grounds that the Soviet Union had

> sought to avoid genuine [arms control] negotiations by a series of offers designed to appear conciliatory while preserving their military superiority... [hoping] that CND, and similar movements in the other Western countries, will force a reversal of the INF modernisation decision, without involving the Soviet Union in any substantive arms reductions.[6]

It turned out that basing GLCMs in the UK was to prove difficult to sell to a vocal minority of the British public, and this led to a succession of anti-nuclear protests, mirroring those taking place across Europe. These were centred upon the proposed sites of the UK's cruise missile bases at RAF Greenham Common and RAF Molesworth.[7] Despite the protests, the Conservative government stuck to its decision to station cruise missiles in the UK.[8] On 1 May 1983, two months after Reagan publically proclaimed the Soviet Union to be an 'Evil Empire' and the announcement of the Strategic Defense Initiative (SDI), an agreement was reached between President Reagan and Prime Minister Thatcher on command and control for the UK-based GLCMs.[9] This was an extension of the Truman–Churchill Agreement for consulting on nuclear use if time permitted, alongside the Murphy-Dean Understanding for nuclear firing. This resulted in the warheads and launchers arriving in Britain in November 1983 (five months after the General Election which returned Mrs Thatcher's government to power for a second term).[10] This was the culmination of over six years of study within NATO over what form TNF modernization should take in what was termed the 'Second Cold War'. It was felt by Mrs Thatcher that if the deployment of cruise and Pershing II did not go ahead, then it might lead to the de-coupling of the US security guarantees to Western Europe. There was still discord in Europe—notably in West Germany—with regard to deployment, but both the Reagan administration and the Thatcher government believed that 'a strong defence posture [was] ...an absolute prerequisite for any constructive relationship with the USSR and therefore deterrence [was]...the condition for détente'.[11]

The deployment of GLCMs and Pershing II was seen by Mrs Thatcher and her Conservative government as enhancing deterrence through nuclear 'equipoise' at all levels of the nuclear 'escalation ladder' while at the same time enabling negotiations on arms control with the Soviet Union to take place from a position of strength. Michael Heseltine was charged with 'winning' the public relations battle.[12] It was believed that these new weapons provided NATO with options to respond to Warsaw Pact incursions (or nuclear strikes) at 'sub-strategic' levels, which could then be used to help bring about war-termination through selective nuclear use, without resorting to counter-value (population) targeting.[13] However, the 'dual track' decision of 1979, linking deployment with arms control negotiations, became strongly associated in public minds with the development of the Soviet SS-20 mobile MIRVed missile (a view encouraged by NATO members),[14] rather than the claimed war-termination mission of the missiles or their broader role in NATO strategy.[15]

The 'dual track' decision became the subject of extensive popular discussion in the UK. It was proposed that NATO would not deploy cruise and Pershing missiles provided that the Soviet Union reversed its deployment of the SS-20—the so-called 'zero option'. Opponents, however, focused their attention on the need for a unilateral decision not to deploy any intermediate nuclear forces. Despite large-scale protests, neither the rejuvenated 'peace movement', with CND in its vanguard, nor the Labour Party managed to achieve a majority public acceptance of their views.[16] In the United Kingdom, with defence and disarmament a major theme of the 1983 General Election, Mrs Thatcher's Conservative government was returned with an increased majority.[17]

As Mrs Thatcher recounts: 'The timing of deployment was bound to be a sensitive matter... with demonstrations stretching police resources'.[18] One of the concerns of opponents was that the GLCMs might have a first strike potential. This was rebutted by the government on the grounds that relatively small numbers would be deployed. It was also argued that the slow flight times of the missiles meant that the Soviet Union would have ample time to launch a counter-strike.[19] Another concern was the growing number of SS-20s deployed by the Soviets at a time when there was little progress being made on the 'zero option' at the Conference on Disarmament in Geneva. This became a difficult issue for the British government, with the Americans continuing to negotiate bilaterally with the Soviet Union on issues that affected UK security interests and those of NATO. Anglo-American relations also became strained over the US invasion of Grenada (a Commonwealth member) in October 1983 and the president's proposals for SDI.[20]

Differences over SDI and Reykjavik

Following Gorbachev's emergence as Soviet leader in March 1985, a summit meeting was held at Geneva against the backcloth of continuing superpower arms-control talks and a general easing of political tension. Prior to his accession, Thatcher had publicly stated:

> I like Mr Gorbachev. We can do business together. We both believe in our own political systems. He firmly believes in his; I firmly believe in mine. We are never going to change one another. So that is not in doubt, but we have two great interests in common: that we should both do everything we can to see that war never starts again, and therefore we go into the disarmament talks determined to make them succeed.[21]

At the same time, a significant disagreement took place between Reagan and Thatcher over the American president's apparent commitment to the ultimate goal of eliminating nuclear weapons. The Strategic Defence Initiative, labelled 'Star Wars' by the media, was also a complex and problematic issue for Britain. Heseltine asked the question: 'What if the Soviet Union succeeded in developing such a system in turn, which might then neutralise the British and French independent deterrents?'[22] This was also Mrs Thatcher's fear.

Thatcher's government was also concerned about the lack of consultation with the UK and the stated aim of President Reagan of eliminating all ballistic missiles within a decade, which was seen as adding to the opposition Labour Party's stance on unilateral nuclear disarmament. This was an issue which was to become centre stage in the 1987 General Election. In a pre-election interview Mrs Thatcher publicly restated her views on the retention of Trident and nuclear deterrence, and with it provided a clear exposition of British national identity which harked back to memories of the Second World War and traditional British political and military policies. Thatcher stated her belief that if Labour won the election:

> the damage done to NATO, the damage done to liberty because Britain has always stood for liberty, the damage done to Britain's defences, would be so deep, so fundamental that they [the Chiefs of Staff] could no longer be responsible for carrying the burden of defence...that is a fundamental part of the way of life in which I believe...Britain isn't just another country. We wouldn't have grown to an empire if we were just another European country of the size and strength that we were. It was Britain that stood when everyone else surrendered and if Britain pulls out of that commitment, it is as if one of the pillars of the temple had collapsed. Because we are one of the pillars of freedom. And hitherto everyone, including past Labour Prime Ministers, have known that Britain would stand and Britain had a nuclear weapon.[23]

These strongly-held beliefs about nuclear deterrence, as held by the prime minister, were particularly evident after the Reykjavik superpower summit in October 1986, which broke down largely because the US negotiating team refused to abandon research into SDI.[24] As Sir Bryan Cartledge, the British ambassador to the Soviet Union at this time, noted:

> There was a definite worry about how far Reagan was going to go, and whether he was a reliable ally. I don't mean reliable in the sense of letting us down or anything, but whether he was, whether he was behaving entirely rationally would be a better way of putting it. I think those worries receded the more contact Margaret Thatcher had with him. I think she usually came back from her meetings with him reassured that he knew where he was going and it wasn't over the edge. But initially, both with the Evil Empire speech and with the SDI there was concern in London that he was going to go much further in the direction of confrontation than any American President had gone before, and a sense that we were dealing with a new phenomenon really, which might require a great deal of hard work to keep in check, or to help to keep in check, because obviously we couldn't do it all by ourselves. As I say, personal contact between Margaret Thatcher and Reagan which worked very well right, more or less until the end, she felt that things were under control so the worry didn't get any worse.[25]

However, at Reykjavik in October 1986, Reagan proposed an agreement which would eliminate all strategic nuclear forces (bombers, long-range cruise missiles, and ballistic missiles) within five years and strategic ballistic missiles within ten years. Gorbachev counter-proposed the elimination of all strategic forces by the end of that ten-year period. Although the Soviets agreed not to seek further inclusion of the British and French deterrents from future INF negotiations (a vital precondition for the Thatcher government), Mrs Thatcher greeted the Reykjavik negotiations 'as if there had been an earthquake beneath my feet'.[26]

Thatcher, who by this stage of her premiership had a firm grip of British defence and foreign policy, was a committed believer in the need for nuclear weapons to ensure that deterrence continued to bring stable peace between East and West. She believed that Reagan's proposal 'would... have effectively killed off the Trident missile, forcing us to acquire a different system if we were to keep an independent nuclear deterrent' and she was intensely relieved when this proposal failed because the US 'steadfastly refused to abandon SDI research'.[27] She remained concerned, however, that these proposals would be resurrected at future negotiations and was disquieted by the INF 'zero option' because in her view the GLCMs and Pershing II were needed to deter a Soviet conventional attack—with NATO conventional forces long assumed to be outmatched by those of the Warsaw Pact.

This led her to request a meeting with President Reagan at Camp David early in 1987. Before the meeting, however, she requested a full briefing from the Chiefs of Staff (COS) on the full implications of the Reagan proposal. She was informed that in some US quarters it was believed that NATO would not be undermined if ballistic missiles were jointly withdrawn, with the GLCMs, Pershing II, and nuclear artillery providing 'an even better deterrent'.[28] The COS doubted this view, however, and argued that GLCM and the nuclear bombers would remain vulnerable to Soviet defences. They believed that such forces were increasingly vulnerable to pre-emptive attack, thus weakening deterrence and making NATO's strategy of 'Flexible Response' unviable. In February 1987 she visited Washington for discussions on these issues with the Reagan administration, and extracted a commitment at Camp David that the US were not seeking to renege on the supply of Trident to Britain and would continue to modernize its own strategic forces. After all her concerns, Mrs Thatcher recorded 'I had reason to be well pleased'.[29]

Prior to a visit to Moscow at the end of March, she continued to publicly state her belief that peace could only be achieved through 'realism and strength' and reiterated these points in face-to-face meetings with the Soviet leadership.[30] She was told that the Soviet Union desired arms control agreements to reduce their military budget (which was bankrupting their economy) and that the failure of the 'zero, zero' option at the Reykjavik summit was being laid at her door. She defended her position robustly in private discussions, and then on Soviet state television, by arguing that the Soviet Union wished to see the de-nuclearization of Europe, 'leaving the USSR with a preponderance of conventional and chemical weapons'.[31] Gorbachev, in a private conversation with her, had also argued that the Soviets would 'match' SDI. Mrs Thatcher reflected on her return that it had been the 'most important foreign visit I had made'.[32]

In July 1987 Mrs Thatcher again visited Washington to offer her political support for Reagan, who was in the midst of the 'Irangate' scandal.[33] This was designed largely to discuss the Intermediate Range Nuclear Forces Treaty (INF) which was due to be signed that December. It was an issue that she had mixed feelings about, especially the 'zero option'. Thatcher wanted to see the withdrawal of the SS-20, which had precipitated the deployment of cruise and Pershing II, but it was also seen by her as heralding a possible 'decoupling' of US nuclear forces from Western Europe and removing a critical rung in the 'escalation ladder'. She thought that such forces were important in deterring a possible conventional attack by superior Warsaw Pact forces, and believed that this would fuel possible West German neutrality and raise doubts about NATO's 'Flexible Response' strategy. Thatcher recorded in her memoirs that: 'It was this question—the avoidance of another "zero" on Short-Range Nuclear Forces (SNF)—which was to divide the alliance so seriously in 1988-9'.[34]

Divisions Over Short Range Nuclear Forces

One way of dealing with this problem was for the US to allocate Submarine Launched Cruise Missiles (SLCMs) and additional *F-111* aircraft to NATO, alongside a Follow-On to Lance missile (FOTL) for use in Europe and a new tactical nuclear missile. These would replace existing free-fall bombs, such as the UK's *WE-177* carried on *Tornado* aircraft, which would thereby reduce West German pressures for early discussion of SNF reductions. Mrs Thatcher also wanted to retain older Pershing IAs for a few years until the end of their operating life and not include them in an INF Agreement. She again met with Gorbachev at RAF Brize Norton on his way to sign the INF Treaty in December 1987. She recognized that 'Britain's own security interests were closely bound up with the US-Soviet arms negotiations' and had direct implications for the future of Britain's Trident force.[35] At this meeting, although she did not want to be seen as a 'broker' between the US and the USSR, she questioned him on INF and the START negotiations and restated her belief in nuclear weapons as the best method of ensuring peace—a position Gorbachev saw as a choice between sitting 'on a powder keg rather than an easy chair'.[36]

Despite Thatcher's doubts, the bilateral INF Treaty was subsequently signed and a further superpower summit on Strategic Arms Reduction Talks (START) was arranged for the first half of 1988, alongside a Soviet announcement that they would withdraw from Afghanistan in May. At a NATO heads of government meeting in Brussels in March divisions emerged between some of the European members of the Alliance and the United States. The communiqué which was issued at the end of the meeting was at odds with the arguments being used by Reagan and Gorbachev on eliminating nuclear capabilities:

> By maintaining credible deterrence the Alliance has secured peace in Europe for nearly forty years. Conventional defences alone cannot ensure this; therefore, for the foreseeable future there is no alternative to the Alliance strategy for the prevention of war. This is a strategy of deterrence based upon an appropriate mix of adequate and effective nuclear and conventional forces which will continue to be kept up to date where necessary.[37]

Immediately after the summit Mrs Thatcher indicated to Reagan, ahead of his next meeting with Gorbachev in Moscow in May 1988, that although this had demonstrated 'unity' between Britain and the US and NATO, she regretted that the West Germans had not agreed to tie negotiations on SNF into an agreement on the need for conventional parity and a ban on chemical weapons. Reagan agreed that NATO should not go down this road unless agreement in these other areas of arms control were reached. Although START negotiations were underway, they were likely to be complex and might not be achieved over the short term. Indeed, he concluded in London on his return from Moscow, SDI remained non-negotiable and SLCMs would not be included in START.[38]

Reagan's two terms as president were about to come to an end and the British would now have to work with his former vice president, George Bush, who was elected in November 1988. The role of SNF was to continue to divide NATO. For some members, their contribution to Alliance defence and deterrence could well increase in importance as the INF Treaty was implemented, with NATO still facing superior conventional forces. Other members were less concerned about the modernization of SNF. These deliberations disturbed both British and West German governments, with Helmut Kohl, the German Chancellor, arguing for a more comprehensive series of arms control agreements. These were discussed by both governments at the December 1988 Rhodes European Council meeting.

Mrs Thatcher records in her memoirs that, as 1988 ended, she still saw a clear military threat emanating from the Soviet Union. In a further meeting with Gorbachev in London in April 1989 she restated the need for modernization of SNF, including FOTL, and bluntly raised the issue that the Soviets had not declared the full quantities and types of chemical weapons they held. However, the Kohl government, much to Thatcher's dismay, were now softening their position on SNF modernization as part of a 'comprehensive package'. They backtracked on the joint statement made about SNF at the Anglo-German summit in Frankfurt between 20–21 February 1989. This movement towards what was known as a 'third zero' option was strongly opposed by Mrs Thatcher, who told Kohl that Britain's intelligence sources were indicating what 'the Soviet Union's real views and intentions' were and that NATO forces were now at an 'irreducible minimum' to enable the 'Flexible Response' strategy to be effective.[39]

Thatcher and the British government now began to find themselves isolated on these issues ahead of the Brussels Summit of NATO'S fortieth anniversary in 1989, with the Bush administration also placing SNF modernization on the negotiating table. They now also linked SNF to the Conventional Forces in Europe (CFE) discussions taking place in Vienna, which were examining substantial cuts in this area within an accelerated timeframe. In a speech in Mainz in May President Bush also spoke of the West Germans as 'partners in leadership', which further irritated Thatcher.

That summer the collapse of communism in Central and Eastern Europe heralded the beginning of the end of the Cold War and *military* debates over arms control would, in large measure, be overtaken by *political* events. In the Soviet Union the Communist Party gradually ceded totalitarian control over the state and subsequently moved towards the adoption of a multi-party system in 1991. This led to free elections and the accession of Boris Yeltsin as Russian president. Mrs Thatcher found it difficult to adjust to these changing political circumstances and the end to bipolarity between East and West.[40] At the same time, she was increasingly at odds with members of her own Cabinet over a range of issues, including her style of leadership. In November 1990 this led to a coup against her by her Cabinet colleagues and her replacement with John Major. While her leadership at home eventually brought about her fall from office, some have argued that her leadership abroad, especially her strong anti-Soviet stance alongside President Reagan, was one of the culminating factors which ended the Cold War. Charles Powell, Mrs Thatcher's Private Secretary, has argued that the implementation of the 'dual track' decision was 'the single most important step in bringing the Cold War to an end, probably, alongside the SDI... and seeing it through to the end was a long process'. In this, Mrs Thatcher played a key role.[41]

The End of the Cold War and the Major Years

Mrs Thatcher's successor, John Major, was to face his first big test as prime minister when Saddam Hussein's Iraq invaded neighbouring Kuwait on 2 August 1990, with international focus now shifting away from events in Europe for a time. One of the most intriguing aspects of the first Gulf War was the impact the conflict had on Britain's deterrent posture outside of the Soviet/Russian context. This is highlighted in Major's memoirs and in an accompanying BBC television documentary, 'The Major Years'. Having been fully briefed by Sir Percy Cradock, the chairman of the Joint Intelligence Committee, on the potency of the Republican Guard in Iraq, Major argues that the conflict brought a nagging worry:

> would Saddam Hussein dare to use chemical or biological weapons on the battlefield? General Colin Powell, Chairman of the US Joint Chiefs of Staff, had told me his 'greatest fear' was that Saddam would be stupid enough to use such weapons. We dare not rule out the use—even prior to the conflict—of chemical weapons as an instrument of terror in population centres in the UK, the US or any of the countries forming part of the allied force. It was the first time we had ever faced such a threat, and it underlined the vulnerability of Western societies. We knew the Iraqis had sophisticated biological and chemical weapons, but we *thought* they had no warheads capable of carrying them, and that they had not mastered airburst technology.[42]

Major added:

> We made it clear that we would not tolerate any Iraqi use of chemical or biological weapons, whether against troops or as a weapon of terror against unprotected civilian populations. So did the US. In private, Saddam Hussein received as unmistakable warning about the immediate and catastrophic consequences for Iraq of any such attacks on civilians. I hoped he would take notice, but was not confident. I knew that if he did use these diabolical weapons, we would have to escalate our response to bring the war to a speedy and conclusive end before too many of our troops were exposed to them.[43]

In the BBC interview Major revealed that Saddam Hussein 'was given an unmistakable message that the response would be dramatic if he chose to use that sort of weapon in the conflict to come. He was told diplomatically precisely the scale of response there would be but I don't wish to enlarge on that'.[44] He pointed out that the Americans 'were still rocking' from the departure of Mrs Thatcher; furthermore, he had no experience of a venture of this kind, and he barely knew President Bush. Prior to the conflict he invited the Archbishop of Canterbury, Robert Runcie, and Cardinal Basil Hume to the Cabinet Room to seek their support, but 'both churchmen recognised that a military strike was becoming inevitable, and they were fearful of escalation and a large loss of life'.[45] Major, who felt their religious backing was important, added 'This was a valid fear, since Iraq had claimed publicly to have a 'secret weapon' capable of inflicting hundreds of thousands of casualties on allied troops...we thought this was a bluff, but couldn't be sure'.[46] When Scud missiles were launched by Iraq against Israel, alarm bells started ringing. Their warheads contained only conventional explosives, however, and this remained the case for the rest of the war. The prime minister recounts that knocking them out was a key task given to Special Forces and the RAF, with chemical and biological weapons sites targeted alongside the Scud launch sites (identified through shared intelligence with the Americans) by dual-capable Tornado GRIs.[47] How Britain and the United States would have responded had Saddam Hussein used chemical weapons remains unclear. The nature of the 'dramatic' response was never spelled out.

Rapid victory followed and a ceasefire was announced on 28 February 1991. However, Saddam Hussein remained in power, and although some were urging the allies to invade Iraq and topple Hussein, this was not part of the terms of the UN resolutions which had authorized the use of force. As Major remarked: 'We would have won the war and lost the peace'.[48] These were issues that would return twelve years later in the second Gulf War.

The End of the Cold and British Nuclear Procedures and Capabilities

Following this, and with the end of the Soviet Union and the Cold War, some attention was given to procedures relating to Britain's nuclear forces. In the new, radically different international environment, the system of nuclear retaliation procedures with 'nuclear deputies' was allowed to lapse (to be reinstituted after the attacks of 9/11).[49] Despite the changes taking place, Major still had all the responsibilities for dealing with Britain's nuclear capabilities. In the first few days of his premiership he drafted his 'letters of last resort', which would be placed in the locked safes of Britain's four *Polaris* submarines. When doing so he retired to the seclusion of his weekend home, the Finings, in his constituency of Huntingdon, writing them out by hand and passing them, sealed, to the Cabinet Secretary. He described this as 'a most chilling introduction to the responsibilities of his premiership'.[50] He would be the first prime minister to write these for the post-Cold War world and the new *Vanguard* class of Trident carrying submarines—the first of which was launched in March 1992. Sir Robin Butler, the Cabinet Secretary, recalls that:

> There has to be a provision for what happens if the government has been destroyed by a nuclear strike and somebody has then got to say, 'Well, we have our missiles on submarines out under the seas, and what should the commanders of those submarines do?'... So that falls on the Prime Minister to make, and... send those instructions... And only one person, who is the initiator of them, knows what the orders are—and that is the Prime Minister... they're likely to be handwritten... but the Prime Minister has to do it personally... it's a very sobering decision for anybody to have to make because it has to be made at a time of peace and it faces a Prime Minister immediately they come to power.[51]

When asked by Peter Hennessy how the two prime ministers he served—John Major and Tony Blair—reacted to this, Butler pointed out 'They reacted as you'd expect any human being to react—soberly; shocked if they hadn't realized before that this was one of the things that they would have to do at the start of their administration. So I would say it was a shock and a sobering one'. 'For both of them?'. 'For anybody'.[52]

As the Soviet Union disintegrated in December 1991 Major was left to wonder 'what would follow it?...Nor did we know who would control the huge nuclear arsenal that had held the world in a Cold War for decades'.[53] This was an issue which vexed Western leaders, especially the problems posed by the former Soviet republics, who now had their own nuclear weapons. This was eventually resolved when they decided to 'return' them to Russia. At the same time President Bush began the Presidential Nuclear Initiatives programme, which saw the removal of vast numbers of tactical weapons from western and central Europe.[54]

In many ways, the primary purpose of the British strategic deterrent had now diminished and, as Major hinted, greater efforts would now be placed on reductions in Britain's nuclear capabilities—which had been designed largely to deter a dragon now slain. British policy was now increasingly focused on non-proliferation and counter-proliferation efforts. Despite the end of the Cold War, however, the 'future uncertainty' argument retained its saliency as a core justification for the retention of Britain's strategic deterrent. The 1992 Conservative election manifesto claimed that increasingly threats were coming from outside Europe, and 'many more countries are acquiring large stocks of modern arms' including nuclear, biological, and chemical weapons. As a result, 'Britain must be able to respond to any unexpected danger'.[55]

In an anarchic international system, and with the stability and certainty of Cold War bipolarity now at an end, the Major government felt it prudent to continue with Trident. There were also practical reasons for this. As Michael Quinlan argued: 'The capital investment in the Trident force was well-advanced by 1989, and nearing full commitment by the time the Soviet Union broke up.'[56] He also noted that:

> Purely in weight of strike potential the United Kingdom could have been content with less than Trident could offer, even in the eight-RV C.4 version originally chosen (let alone the twelve-RV D.5 version to which the United Kingdom switched in early 1982, when it had become clear that the United States was committed to proceed with its acquisition and deployment). Both the original choice and the switch were driven in large measure by the long-term financial and logistic benefits of commonality with the United States.[57]

Although Trident had long been planned to enter operational service by 1994, continuing worries over the policies of the new Russian Federation and the completion of its second generation anti-ballistic missile system brought about the earlier than planned retirement of the Polaris force and the deployment of Trident.[58] A briefing ahead of the 1992 General Election stated:

> Estimates of the future force levels of the successor states to the Soviet Union remain highly uncertain. The former Union armed forces are shrinking and fragmenting; Republics are setting up their own forces. The CIS [Commonwealth of Independent States] may survive in some form, but it appears unlikely to have a long-term future as a coherent military organisation. Even so Russia is by far the largest military power in Europe and will remain so. Other Republics, notably Ukraine, may also inherit or obtain sizeable arsenals.

In terms of 'future uncertainty', one of the hallmarks for the retention of a nuclear capability, it also added:

> The risk has gone of the kind of East-West conflict that threatened us in the past but allowance needs to be made for uncertainty over developments in the former Soviet Union...Beyond Europe, risks from the proliferation of weapons of mass destruction are increasing against a background of instability. The threat posed by terrorism remains...To meet these risks and challenges, the UK plays a full part in the various European security fora: particularly NATO and WEU. Military forces are likely to play an increasing role in political stabilisation, preventive diplomacy, crisis management, humanitarian aid and peacekeeping and we can expect to become involved in UN tasks and multinational, ad hoc coalitions.[59]

It also noted that, should the US withdraw logistical support for Trident (or Polaris), the force would still remain operational for 'several months at the very least', and the four Vanguard class submarines were due to enter operational service in 1994, 1995, and 1998, armed with up to twelve warheads in sixteen missiles. The four Polaris submarines were now beginning the process of decommissioning, with *HMS Revenge* the first in 1992. The UK's 'sub-strategic' nuclear artillery and *Lance* missiles (using US warheads) were removed from service in the autumn of 1991 as part of a NATO-wide decision, with Britain's maritime patrol aircraft also losing their nuclear role in February 1992. US nuclear depth bombs (NDBs) were due for removal from RAF St Mawgan in Cornwall over the summer of 1992. This left the WE-177 family of gravity bombs in the non-strategic stockpile capable for deployment on Royal Navy *Sea Harriers* and RAF Tornados and *Buccaneers* and could be used as NDBs on RN *Sea King* and *Lynx* helicopters (with all WE-177s all now stored ashore). The Buccaneers were due to be phased out by April 1994, with Tornados taking over their role (including four squadrons in Germany).[60]

The end of Cold War hostilities later brought further substantial changes to Britain's non-strategic nuclear forces. As John Simpson recalls:

the UK ceased to participate actively in the NATO arrangements under which it had access to US nuclear warheads; it removed the WE177A gravity and depth bombs from its naval vessels; withdrew from service its WE177B 450-kt gravity bombs; and withdrew without replacement its remaining WE177A and C gravity bombs by 2007.[61]

In addition, in 1992 'NATO strategy was changed by relegating the nuclear weapons assigned to SACEUR to a "last resort" capability'.[62] Simpson also records that the period from 1993 to 1995 witnessed a series of exchanges between British and French governments on nuclear aspects of European defence and NATO issues, with the UK seeing a 'residual threat from the Russian Federation [that] required the continuation of the UK deterrent force in its assigned NATO role'.[63]

Conclusion

The end of the Cold War, it is argued by many, was the result of the strength of the West, as personified by the 'special relationship' between Ronald Reagan and Margaret Thatcher. According to this view, they shared common views about facing down the Soviet Union from a position of strength, both military and political, with Western economies effectively bankrupting the Soviet economy through military expenditure. However, there was also discord between them and within NATO over the INF Treaty and the 'zero options' proposals. As Richard Aldous argues: 'This was an issue that transcended military considerations. It raised questions about political resolve and symbolism, intra-alliance solidarity, and the extent to which NATO policy could be directed by domestic public opinion ... It was a debate that cut to the heart of the Atlantic Alliance'.[64] Mrs Thatcher and her ministers were deeply sceptical about SDI and its implications for Trident missiles recently bought from the United States.[65] President Reagan's ideas about a nuclear-free world also caused alarm in London, particularly because they threatened the purchase of the Trident D-5 missile from the US.

Britain remained firmly committed to retaining nuclear weapons. As Michael Heseltine noted: 'We were the only European members of the NATO alliance wholly committed, wholly nuclear. The French weren't part of the integrated structure of NATO, the Germans weren't nuclear. So I don't think anyone could argue that we weren't the lead partner in the NATO alliance'.[66] Heseltine was one of the chief candidates for the office of prime minister in November 1990 when Mrs Thatcher was forced to resign following a Cabinet rebellion against her policies and leadership style. However, the position passed to John Major, who had to deal with the collapse of the Soviet

Union a year later and the ending of the Cold War, and who would go on to win the 1992 General Election. He was prime minister when the first of Britain's new Trident-carrying submarines, *HMS Vanguard*, was launched in March 1992, with the first test firing of its MIRVed missiles in May 1994 and the first operational deterrent patrol in early 1995. Vanguard was followed by *HMS Victorious* in September 1993 and *HMS Vigilant* in October 1995. The final submarine, *HMS Vengeance*, was launched in October 1998—a little under eighteen months after the General Election of 1997 that saw Tony Blair's 'New' Labour elected in a landslide victory. It would not be long before debates about Britain's nuclear capabilities began again.

10

Trident Replacement/Renewal: From 'New Labour' to the Coalition Government

> [T]he nuclear threat has not gone away. In terms of uncertainty and potential risk it has, if anything increased.
>
> David Cameron, April 2013[1]

During the period from 1997 to the present, both Labour and Conservative prime ministers continued to support the retention of Britain's nuclear capability. Nevertheless, tensions existed between different beliefs about how best to achieve international security in a world of uncertainty and challenge. During the Blair and Brown administrations tensions existed between policies designed to maintain a nuclear deterrent posture and the perceived need for Britain to contribute to arms control initiatives, especially in relation to the growing dangers of nuclear proliferation. During the Cameron Coalition government from 2010–15, Conservatives and Liberal Democrats had different views about *Trident* renewal/replacement and the requirements of effective deterrence, especially given the austerity caused by the 2008 financial crisis. Traditional concerns about the impact of spending scarce resources on nuclear weapons for Britain's conventional forces also resurfaced during the period.

Nuclear Policy Under 'New Labour'

Tony Blair's 'New Labour' government had a radical political programme, including a desire to pursue an 'ethical' foreign policy, backed by a landslide parliamentary majority when it entered office in May 1997.[2] In terms of the nuclear deterrent it was unclear whether there would be an equally radical change, but the Blair government—with George Robertson as Defence Secretary, Robin Cook as Foreign and Commonwealth Secretary, and Gordon

Brown as Chancellor—did commit themselves to a major Strategic Defence Review (SDR), which they began almost immediately.[3] Despite Russia beginning to stabilize under President Yeltsin, a major series of events took place during Blair's administration which challenged British foreign and defence policy, including its 'ethical' dimension, in quite fundamental ways.

In 1998, as part of the Strategic Defence Review (SDR), it was decided to operate only forty-eight warheads (all in the kiloton range) on board each Trident SSBN rather than the ninety-six the Conservative government had planned, and to put it on 'several days readiness' to fire. Coupled with this, it was also decided to de-target the Trident force (although plans remained for their employment). It has also been suggested that rather than take its full complement of sixteen missiles on normal deterrent patrols, only twelve were loaded, armed with five warheads or fewer apiece.[4] In line with longstanding public declarations, the 1998 SDR stated:

> Britain's Trident force provides an operationally independent strategic and sub-strategic nuclear capability in support of NATO's strategy of war prevention and as the ultimate guarantee of our national security. In current circumstances, nuclear forces continue to make a unique contribution to ensuring stability and preventing crisis escalation. They also help guard against any possible re-emergence of a strategic scale threat to our security.[5]

Additionally, the UK/US Trident force remained the only one committed to NATO, and Britain's is the only European nuclear force assigned to the Alliance due to the fact that France continued to operate its nuclear forces on a national basis only. (Under President Sarkozy, however, it did agree to rejoin NATO's integrated military structure, which it left in 1966 but did not include its nuclear deterrent as part of this agreement. This was a decision reconfirmed by Sarkozy's successor, President Hollande.)[6]

One of the striking things about the SDR was the balance the government was trying to achieve between reinforcing its commitment to the Non-Proliferation Treaty (NPT), while at the same time justifying the continuing determination to retain Britain's nuclear deterrent. The Strategic Defence Review (SDR) argued that:

> Britain has repeatedly made it clear that we will not use nuclear weapons against a non-nuclear weapon state not in material breach of its nuclear non-proliferation obligations, unless it attacks us, our allies or a state to which we have a security commitment, in association or alliance with a nuclear weapon state. Britain has also undertaken to seek immediate UN Security Council action to assist any non-nuclear-weapon state party to the Non-Proliferation Treaty that is attacked or threatened with nuclear weapons.[7]

At the same time it stated that:

> Britain's Trident force provides an operationally independent strategic and substrategic nuclear capability in support of NATO's strategy of war prevention and as the ultimate guarantee of our national security. In current circumstances, nuclear forces continue to make a unique contribution to ensuring stability and preventing crisis escalation. They also help guard against any possible re-emergence of a strategic scale threat to our security.[8]

Alongside this posture there were discreet alterations made to Britain's declaratory policy concerning potential nuclear use. These had a direct bearing on NATO and on the concept of 'extended deterrence' provided by the UK and the US. The SDR noted, for example, that Britain's rationale for its nuclear forces was based in part on a potential strategic attack on NATO, although at the same time it counselled:

> No threat on this scale is in prospect. It would, however, be unwise to conclude that one could never reappear but the conventional forces needed to threaten such an attack would take many years to create. This Mission therefore provides for longer term insurance through a credible nuclear deterrent...The Strategic Defence Review has conducted a rigorous re-examination of our deterrence requirements. This does not depend on the size of other nation's arsenals but on the minimum necessary to deter any threat to our vital interests. We have concluded that we can safely make further significant reductions from Cold War levels, both in the number of weapons and in our day-to-day operating posture.[9]

The result of the SDR was that Britain abandoned the *WE-177* air-launched gravity-bomb, leaving Trident as the UK's sole nuclear weapons system operating as a 'minimum deterrent'. As a result of the more stable international security environment, the Blair government revised the criteria for 'minimum deterrence', thus enabling Trident's submarine loading to be decreased to forty-eight warheads.[10] There was also a frank admission, as part of a conscious effort for increased transparency in British nuclear weapons policy, that:

> nuclear deterrence remains a controversial and complex issue because of the terrible consequences of any use of nuclear weapons. There are no easy answers here...We and NATO have radically reduced our reliance on nuclear weapons, but in present conditions nuclear deterrence still has an important contribution to make in insuring against the re-emergence of major strategic military threats, in preventing nuclear coercion, and in preserving peace and stability in Europe.[11]

Despite the reduction of nuclear capabilities, tensions between government non-proliferation policies and continuing support for the nuclear deterrent clearly existed. In March 2002 Geoff Hoon, then the Secretary of State for Defence, told a Defence Select Committee hearing regarding ballistic missile defence that:

> There are clearly some states who would be deterred by the fact that the United Kingdom possesses nuclear weapons and has the willingness and ability to use them in appropriate circumstances. States of concern, I would be much less confident about... [but they] can be absolutely confident that in the right conditions we would be willing to use our nuclear weapons. What I cannot be absolutely confident about is whether that would be sufficient to deter them from using a weapon of mass destruction in the first place.[12]

As the late Lord Tim Garden, spokesman for the Liberal Democratic Party in the House of Lords, suggested 'Students of nuclear policy took this as a major change in UK thinking. We were now apparently contemplating the potential use of nuclear weapons against an enemy using chemical [and by implication biological] weapons. This could run counter to our negative security assurances'.[13] The circumstances of these negative security assurances, as outlined above, are that:

> The United Kingdom will not use nuclear weapons against non-nuclear-weapon States Parties to the Treaty on the Non-Proliferation of Nuclear Weapons except in the case of an invasion or any other attack on the United Kingdom, its dependent territories, its armed forces or other troops, its allies or on a State towards which it has a security commitment, carried out or sustained by such a non-nuclear-weapon State in association or alliance with a nuclear-weapon State. In giving this assurance the United Kingdom emphasises the need not only for universal adherence to, but also for compliance with, the Treaty on the Non-Proliferation of Nuclear Weapons [NPT]. In this context... Her Majesty's Government does not regard its assurance as applicable if any beneficiary is in material breach of its own non-proliferation obligations...[14]

Both non- and counter-proliferation activities (the former aimed at reducing nuclear stockpiles, the latter at rolling back nuclear stockpiles and activities) centred on the NPT had become a growing aspect of British nuclear weapons policy during the post-Cold War era.[15] This had been reflected in a gradual shift in emphasis from 'hard power', through military capabilities, towards a set of 'soft' power activities, such as economic sanctions and diplomacy. As George Robertson stated shortly before his departure as NATO Secretary General in 2004, 'military means are only one instrument in the armoury. Maybe even the least important of those elements that are needed... Diplomatic pressure, economic pressure, communications pressure is going to have to be deployed.'[16] 'Soft' security issues were thus accorded increasing priority.

However, it is also clear that 'hard' power through military force continued to be utilized where 'soft' power had failed to prove effective, most notably in Afghanistan where Britain had been a staunch ally of the US since 2001 and in the invasion of Iraq in 2003.[17] In the latter case it was the prospect of WMD able to be used in forty-five minutes that precipitated the controversial invasion and the policy of regime change that led to the capture and death of Saddam Hussein and many other key figures.[18] Whether the US or UK would have used nuclear weapons if WMD had been used against the invading forces is a moot point. It is now known that Iraq had abandoned its WMD programmes (and therefore did not have an active nuclear weapons programme) in the aftermath of the first Gulf War in the early 1990s and that Western intelligence was flawed.[19] The experience of the second Gulf War also heavily influenced security calculations regarding Iran's putative nuclear weapons programme under President Ahmadinejad and the use of chemical weapons in Syria.[20]

Trident Renewal/Replacement

Against this background of 'hard' power and the return to the use of state-based conflict, by 2006 Tony Blair was being told by the Ministry of Defence that the question of whether to replace Trident was now an issue that required addressing. He informed Parliament in December 2006 that:

> The current Vanguard submarines have a service life of 25 years. The first boat should leave service in 2017. We can extend that for five years. In 2022, that extension will be concluded and in 2024 the second boat will also end its extended service life. By this time, we will only have two Vanguard submarines. This will be insufficient to guarantee continuous patrolling. The best evidence we have is that it will take us 17 years to design, build and deploy a new submarine. Working back from 2024, that means we have to take this decision in 2007. Of course, all these timelines are estimates, but they conform to the experience of other countries with submarine deterrents as well as our own.[21]

He noted that the Trident II D-5 missiles would not need replacing until around 2042 due to the US Trident D-5 'Life Extension Programme', and he confirmed that a formal Exchange of Letters with President George W. Bush had taken place (similar to that used for the original Trident purchases in 1980 and 1982). This would enable Britain to participate in any new US missile programme after this date. In commending a replacement deterrent to Parliament Blair was conscious that 'Britain has had an independent nuclear deterrent for the last half century. In that time the world has changed dramatically, not least in the collapse of the Soviet Union, the original context in which the deterrent was acquired.'[22]

In taking this decision (whilst prepared to examine the possibility of moving to three SSBNs rather than four, which had been the force size since the Wilson government in the 1960s), Blair repeated a series of arguments for retention which have become common themes in British nuclear weapons policy. These reflected a core belief in the deterrent power of nuclear weapons.

They were needed because of 'future uncertainty' associated with the nuclear programmes of North Korea and Iran and other 'rogue states' who sponsored terrorism. He argued that Britain was not prepared to unilaterally disarm in these circumstances and that nuclear weapons remained an 'insurance policy' for the British state. In making this case Blair emphasized 'the risk of giving up something that has been one of the mainstays of our security since the War'. This was not a judgement he was prepared to make. He summed up his view that: 'In the early 21st century, the world may have changed beyond recognition, since the decision taken by the Attlee Government over half a century ago. But it is precisely because we could not have recognised then, the world we live in now, that it would not be wise to predict the unpredictable in the times to come'.[23] In his 2010 memoirs, however, Blair candidly admitted that he hesitated over the decision to renew Trident but 'I thought giving it up too big a downgrading of our status as a nation, and in an uncertain world, too big a risk for our defence'. He added: 'The expense is huge, and the utility in a post-Cold War world is less in terms of deterrence, and non-existent in terms of military use... and frankly inconceivable that we would use our nuclear deterrent alone, without the US'. Gordon Brown, who would replace him as prime minister in June 2007, was 'similarly torn'.[24]

The simultaneous White Paper issued by the government in December 2006 to explain the Trident renewal decision further announced that the explosive yield of the warheads was being reduced to 'considerably below that of the standard warhead': the operational warhead stockpile was being reduced to less than 160—the smallest of the declared NWS.[25]

In the White Paper the government indicated its intention to replace Trident. It identified 'Five enduring principles' that underpinned its decision:

1. To deter nuclear attack and prevent nuclear blackmail and acts of aggression that cannot be accomplished by other means.
2. A 'minimum' deterrent in line with the 1998 SDR and changes in the global security environment leading to the reduction of the number of operationally available warheads from less than 200 to fewer than 160.
3. A continuing policy of strategic ambiguity regarding potential employment including the potential for first use.
4. The assignment of Trident to NATO in support of collective security for the Euro-Atlantic area. This in turn forms part of the Alliance's overall strategy and the nuclear guarantee afforded by the British commitment.
5. A 'second centre' of nuclear decision within the NATO alliance. Potential adversaries might be prepared to 'gamble' that neither the US or France would retaliate to an attack on the UK or upon its allies. Britain could therefore act alone 'where supreme national interests are at stake'.[26]

The announcement caused dismay to many of the government's own supporters who wished to get rid of nuclear weapons and led to criticism from a number of quarters. Rebecca Johnson, the founder of the Acronym Institute which promotes nuclear non-proliferation and disarmament, argued that:[27]

> The White Paper [in which the British government set out its case for Trident replacement] appears to be stuck in a time warp. It is a mishmash of cold war platitudes and scaremongering about new and unknown threats. Even where the reader may share the government's concerns about some of the identified threats, the White Paper disappoints with its dearth of evidence or argument to back up its assumptions and conclusions that perpetuating reliance on nuclear weapons is the only (or right) response for Britain to be able to deter or address such threats.
>
> In keeping with its style of presenting assertions as if they were self-evident facts, the White Paper reduces realistic and compelling arguments about the positive role Britain could have in devaluing nuclear weapons and creating the conditions to facilitate global disarmament to parodies. It sets up and then dismisses such parodies and a variety of straw arguments, but does not seriously engage with the fundamental questions relating to common security, deterrence or reducing nuclear dangers. Nuclear and conventional weapons are juxtaposed as if these were the only defence tools available.[28]

Faced with these criticisms, members of the government emphasized the defensive and narrowly defined role of the British nuclear deterrent. In a speech at Kings College London in January 2007, the Secretary of State for Defence, Des Browne, stated that:

> [Nuclear weapons] should not be used for anything other than deterring extreme threats to our national security. The UK has in fact never sought to use our nuclear weapons as a means of provoking or coercing others. We will never do so. Nor are our weapons intended or designed for military use during conflict. Indeed, we have deliberately chosen to stop using the term 'sub-strategic Trident', applied previously to a possible limited use of our weapons. I would like to take this opportunity to reaffirm that the UK would only consider using nuclear weapons in the most extreme situations of self-defence.[29]

Remarks made by Lord Drayson, Parliamentary Under-Secretary for State in the Ministry of Defence, during debates in the House of Lords also emphasized the deterrent role of nuclear weapons. Drayson argued that 'we have deliberatively discontinued the use of the term sub-strategic, in the sense that it had been used previously to apply to a possible, limited use of our nuclear weapons'.[30] Balancing support for non-proliferation policies and at the same time outlining the desire to replace Trident, however, was not an easy task. This was made even more difficult by an international debate at the time about the growing dangers of nuclear proliferation and the need for more radical policies by Western governments to reduce the saliency of nuclear weapons.

The Government of Gordon Brown and the Continuing Dilemma

In June 2007 Tony Blair resigned and Gordon Brown took over as prime minister. Like Blair, Brown was firmly committed to retaining a British nuclear force, but he also supported efforts to prevent further nuclear proliferation. In January 2007 an article appeared in the *Wall Street Journal* authored by four elder statesmen of American politics: George Shultz, William Perry, Henry Kissinger, and Sam Nunn. These influential figures called for 'a world free of nuclear weapons', arguing that the world was very different in the post-Cold War Era when:

> Nuclear weapons were essential to maintaining international security during the Cold War because they were a means of deterrence. The end of the Cold War made the doctrine of mutual Soviet-American deterrence obsolete. Deterrence continues to be a relevant consideration for many states with regard to threats from other states. But reliance on nuclear weapons for this purpose is becoming increasingly hazardous and decreasingly effective...Apart from the terrorist threat, unless urgent new actions are taken, the US soon will be compelled to enter a new nuclear era that will be more precarious, psychologically disorienting, and economically even more costly than was Cold War deterrence. It is far from certain that we can successfully replicate the old Soviet-American 'mutually assured destruction' with an increasing number of potential nuclear enemies world-wide without dramatically increasing the risk that nuclear weapons will be used...Reassertion of the vision of a world free of nuclear weapons and practical measures toward achieving that goal would be, and would be perceived as, a bold initiative consistent with America's moral heritage. The effort could have a profoundly positive impact on the security of future generations.[31]

This article was supported by four former British Foreign and Defence Secretaries (Michael Rifkind, David Owen, George Robertson, and Douglas Hurd) in an article in *The Times* on 30 June 2008. They also argued for a new initiative by the government to make greater progress on multilateral arms control and disarmament. They argued that, in their view, 'the ultimate aspiration should be to have a world free of nuclear weapons'. They accepted that this would be difficult and would take time, but they saw it as an achievable objective. The fact that these senior US and UK figures, who had traditionally supported (and indeed helped to formulate) the nuclear policies of their respective governments, gave their views added weight. Significantly, the 'zero option' was also championed by President Obama in a later speech in Prague in April 2009. The president argued that 'in a strange turn of history the threat of global nuclear war has gone down, but the risk of nuclear attack has gone up' as the threat of nuclear proliferation has increased. And so, he stated 'clearly and with conviction America's commitment to seek peace and security in a world without nuclear weapons ...we must not ignore the voices who tell us that the world cannot change'.[32]

These sentiments, at both the domestic and the global levels, appeared to galvanize 'New Labour' policy with Margaret Beckett, the Foreign Secretary, arguing at the Carnegie Centre in Washington, that:

> What we need is both vision—a scenario for a world free of nuclear weapons. And action—progressive steps to reduce warhead numbers and to limit the role of nuclear weapons in security policy. These two strands are separate but they are mutually reinforcing. Both are necessary, both at the moment too weak.[33]

Beckett tried to balance support for both nuclear disarmament and Britain's nuclear deterrent:[34]

> in taking the decision to retain our ability to have nuclear weapons, the UK government was very clear about four things. First that we would be open and frank both with our own citizens and with our international partners about what we were doing and why. Second that we would be very clear and up front that when the political conditions existed, we would give up our remaining nuclear weapons. Third that we were not enhancing our nuclear capability in any way and would continue to act strictly in accordance with our NPT obligations. And fourth that we would reduce our stock of operationally available warheads by a further 20 per cent—to the very minimum we considered viable to maintain an independent nuclear deterrent.[35]

Alongside these national measures, government policy was also to support the ratification of the Comprehensive Test Ban Treaty, to promote Confidence and Security Building Measures with increased transparency, and to support the NPT through concerted diplomacy alongside the other members of the P5 (the US, Russian Federation, China, and France). Despite these modifications of policy, however, the Labour government continued to believe that a British nuclear force was needed as a hedge against future uncertainty. The 2007 Defence White Paper reflected the government's belief that 'in a global environment still with so much uncertainty and potential danger now was not the time to decide to abandon entirely a capability which the United Kingdom had possessed for half a century'.[36]

Following Beckett's speech in February 2008, the Defence Secretary, Des Browne, also sought to try to balance the twin objectives of supporting nonproliferation and continuing support for a British nuclear capability in a speech at the Conference for Disarmament in Geneva. In his speech he expressed British support for the new bilateral Strategic Arms Reduction Treaty which was signed in April 2010 by the US and Russia. At the same time he announced that the 20 per cent reduction in the operational UK nuclear stockpile would leave 'fewer than 160' warheads and that the Atomic Weapons Establishments (AWE) would be partially reconfigured for nuclear forensics tasks to establish Britain as a 'disarmament laboratory'.[37]

The prime minister also wanted to play a role on the world stage, supporting measures designed to deal with the growing problem of nuclear proliferation associated with North Korea and Iran. Gordon Brown reasserted Britain's 'Great Power' responsibilities in a speech in London in March 2009, stating that 'as we approach the 2010 Review Conference I want us to renew and refresh for our times the grand global bargain, the covenant of hope between nations at the heart of the Non-Proliferation Treaty'. He added:

> it is a bargain under which we reaffirm the rights and responsibilities for those countries which forego nuclear weapons. But it is also a bargain under which there are tough responsibilities to be discharged by nuclear weapon states, for as successor states we cannot expect to successfully exercise moral and political leadership in preventing the proliferation of nuclear weapons if we ourselves do not demonstrate leadership on the question of disarmament of our weapons.[38]

This demonstration of 'Great Power' responsibility does not mean that the intentions were not sincere.[39] One initiative, leading on from the idea of Britain as a 'disarmament laboratory', was a P5 conference on 'Confidence Measures Towards Nuclear Disarmament' in September 2009, which discussed, among other issues, confidence-building measures, nuclear doctrines, and strategic stability.[40]

In addition, in February 2009 the Foreign and Commonwealth Office published a report entitled 'Lifting the Nuclear Shadow: Creating the Conditions for Abolishing Nuclear Weapons', in which it indicated there were some 'powerful arguments for reducing the role of nuclear weapons solely to deterring the use of nuclear weapons by others' and that, in general, it was important to reduce the saliency of nuclear weapons in national security policies.[41] The argument for retaining a British nuclear capability was now made in very broad terms:

> It related in essence to the unsettled and still-anarchic character of the international environment; to the continued intention of the United Kingdom to be a major load-bearing actor in it, and to have the confidence to accept responsibilities and risks accordingly; to the impossibility of predicting dangers far enough ahead for it to be acceptable to defer provision against them until they had become evident; and to the effective finality of any decision to withdraw from the possession of a nuclear armoury.[42]

That July the Cabinet Office published a 52-page command paper titled 'The Road to 2010', which again emphasized that government policy remained the eventual abolition of all nuclear weapons through multilateral disarmament.

The 'Road to 2010' stressed that the 'first pillar of the Nuclear Non-Proliferation Treaty (NPT) framework—preventing further proliferation... [should be] strengthened' and the conditions for nuclear disarmament also needed to be tackled.[43] These conditions were not specified, and it also asserted that the 'minimum deterrent' that Trident represented was intended to guard against a possible future where a nuclear threat emerged against the UK. This bolstered both national and collective security through the ongoing nuclear commitment to NATO. It further asserted that: 'The UK has shown global leadership across the three pillars of the NPT [non-proliferation, nuclear disarmament and access to civil nuclear energy] and has generated significant momentum leading up to the NPT Review Conference, notably through the Prime Minister's speech in March 2009'.[44] During that speech at Lancaster House Brown stated that 'as soon as it becomes useful for our arsenal to be included in a broader negotiation, Britain stands ready to participate and to act'.[45] For some this appeared to open up the possibility of unilateral nuclear disarmament, placed on the table as part of multilateral nuclear disarmament negotiations towards the end goal of a 'nuclear weapons free world'.[46]

Brown also publicly restated that the government was still looking into the possibility of moving from four boats down to three if this was technically feasible. He told the UN in September 2009 that he had requested 'our National Security Committee to report to me on the potential future reduction of our nuclear weapon submarines from four to three'.[47] According to a leaked dispatch to US officials from senior officials in the Cabinet Office, this 'caught many in the MoD, FCO and Cabinet Office by surprise', with

> Julian Miller, the deputy head of the foreign and defence policy secretariat at the Cabinet Office, assur[ing]...the political minister counsellor [in Washington on] September 24 that HMG would consult with the US regarding future developments concerning the Trident deterrent to assure there would be 'no daylight' between the US and UK.[48]

As the role of the prime minister has been, and remains, crucial in forming nuclear weapons policy, this was an atypical schism between senior civil servants and the prime minister, albeit one that was not intended to become public at the time. This nevertheless showed that tensions remained between supporting the non-proliferation agenda and going ahead with the renewal or replacement of Trident.

The Conservative–Liberal Democrat Coalition

In May 2010 a new Conservative–Liberal Democrat Coalition government led by David Cameron came to office. Immediately, a Strategic Defence and Security Review (SDSR) was undertaken and its findings were published in October 2010.[49] The SDSR recognized that there was no existent direct threat to the UK, but that proliferation concerns remained and the future strategic and security environment was uncertain. Moreover, the UK strategic deterrent played an important role in the collective security role enabled by NATO. Whilst it remained the case that Britain would only consider the use of nuclear weapons in extreme circumstances, any possible use was left ambiguous—including possible use against threats from chemical and biological attack by states (the other two elements of the 'WMD' triptych).[50]

However, doubts were soon expressed regarding the cost of replacing Trident against both the background of the 2008 economic crash and against the changing security environment and the lack of credibility of a nuclear response against a range of future threats. As Lord King, the Conservative Defence Secretary under John Major and an adviser to David Cameron when he was Leader of the Opposition, claimed: 'I think in the current world we live in, top table credibility comes from availability to help in peace-keeping, in conflict resolution and having armed forces that can exist, co-ordinate and co-operate in the new high-tech, highly sophisticated systems'.[51] Michael Portillo, another former Conservative Defence Secretary, in May 2011 described Trident replacement as 'nonsense' and 'a waste of money' undertaken purely for 'prestige' reasons.[52] These views, however, were not shared by the Cameron government.

As part of delivering 'value for money' the SDSR also announced that a decision on a replacement warhead would be deferred (under the previous Labour government there had been discussion of a new Reliable Replacement Warhead)[53] and costs for replacement missile compartments would also be reduced. In addition the coalition now planned on extending the life of the four Vanguard class SSBNs—though it was unclear how this would be accomplished, with the last Labour government having been informed by technical advice from the MOD that this was not feasible and could carry safety risks.[54] This life extension programme (alongside a US–UK Trident D-5 Life Extension Programme) meant that the second investment round need now not be made until 2016; described as the 'Main Gate' decision.[55] Contemporaneously, Anglo-French nuclear initiatives could again be explored as part of the 2010 Lancaster House Treaty and the Teutates projects.[56]

The SDSR also led to four practical reductions to be phased in over the following few years. There would now be no more than forty warheads per submarine (from the previous limit of forty-eight), leading to a reduction in the 'operationally available' warhead stockpile from less than 160 to no more than 120 and an overall stockpile of no more than 180 by the mid-2020s. This was combined with fewer missiles on deterrent patrols: now no more than eight. Replacement warheads were now not required until at least the late 2030s, and the current Vanguard class would not now need replacing until the late 2020s and early 2030s; with the first of the new class of SSBN estimated for delivery in 2028 with possible completion by 2035.[57] This new class would half the current number of missile tubes to eight and have a common US UK design for the centre missile compartment.[58]

In April–May 2010 a NPT Review Conference took place, providing the prime minister with an opportunity to show leadership through the P5 alongside new US President Barack Obama. As John Simpson states, the resultant 'disarmament plan of action contained several commitments with strong links to UK policies'.[59] This included 'diminishing' the role and significance of nuclear weapons in all military and security concepts, doctrines and policies' (Action 5c); discussing policies that could 'prevent the use of nuclear weapons and eventually lead to their elimination' (Action 5d); and considering 'reducing the operational status of nuclear weapons systems' (Action 5e).[60] These multilateral action plans were followed up in further meetings of the P5 in Paris in June 2011, Washington in 2012, Geneva in April 2013, and at a meeting of the G8 earlier that month.[61]

As with the Labour prime ministers before him, however, David Cameron continued to support the case for an upgraded British nuclear deterrent. In April 2013 he offered his rationale for seeking to replace Trident when he stated:

> I know there are some people who disagree with our nuclear deterrent and don't want us to renew it. There are those who say that we don't need it any more, because the Cold War has ended. There are those who say we can't afford Trident any more, so we either need to find a viable cheaper option, or rely on the United States to protect us. And there are those who say that we should just get rid of our nuclear weapons entirely, in the hope that it would encourage others to do the same. I recognise these are sincerely held views. But as Prime Minister, with ultimate responsibility for the nation's security, I profoundly disagree with them.[62]

He cited the risk of proliferation through states such as North Korea and Iran and that, for national security protection against such threats, the 5–6 per cent of the defence budget it would cost was 'a price which I, and all my predecessors since Clement Attlee, have felt is worth paying to keep this country safe'.[63] Cameron discounted 'Trident Lite' solutions as a false economy with no credible alternatives to an SSBN-based force and—again echoing the Duff-Mason Report—leaving British security in the hands of the United States, or a situation like 1940, was not a gamble he was prepared to take.[64]

This was not a view shared by their Liberal Democrat coalition partners (particularly senior figures such as Nick Clegg and Danny Alexander)[65] and resulted in a Trident Alternatives Review, published in July 2013 as an unclassified study by the Cabinet Office supported by other departments, particularly the Ministry of Defence and FCO.[66] Its terms of reference were an examination of:

- credible alternatives to a submarine-based deterrent
- credible submarine-based alternatives to the current proposal, for example modified Astute class submarines using cruise missiles
- alternative nuclear postures, that is non-Continuous-at-Sea-deterrence which could maintain credibility.

The review looked towards the strategic environment up to 2060, with one of the clear changes from the Cold War being a movement away from a deterrent posture of 'assured destruction' or 'unacceptable damage' to one of 'unacceptable loss'. This was defined as 'the ability to inflict a level of damage that a potential aggressor would judge outweighed any benefit they might gain by a particular course of action' and the resolve to use this capability.[67] This bears remarkable similarity to the deterrence criteria detailed in the Duff-Mason Report although, unlike during the Cold War, no potential nuclear adversary was defined.[68] Instead, it outlined five 'generic' deterrent postures:

a) *Continuous deterrence.* A continuous deterrent presence capable of causing the required level of damage and sustained for the life of the system, representing as close as each system can get to an assured second strike capability. For non-ballistic missile systems, limitations in range mean that this could only be focused against a specific adversary.

b) *Focused deterrence.* This posture would be maintained for a specific period and focused against a specific adversary, although for ballistic missile systems their inherent range would also enable near-global deterrence. At all other times, the system would adopt a reduced readiness level.

c) *Sustained deterrence.* Deployment of some deterrent capability would be maintained, but not necessarily close to a potential missile launch point. Deployment would be covert (submarines), ambiguous (ship), or dispersed (aircraft) to make it difficult for a potential adversary to predict when they might be within reach of the system.

d) *Responsive deterrence.* As for 'Sustained deterrence', but gaps between deployments would be permitted. The frequency and length of deployment would be irregular so that a potential adversary cannot predict when and for how long a gap in deployment might occur.

e) *Preserved deterrence.* This posture would only be adopted at low readiness. No deterrent platforms would be regularly deployed but the UK would maintain the ability to deploy if the context changed. The platforms might be deployed without nuclear weapons for training purposes and could conduct conventional duties as long as they could be made available for deterrent duties if required.[69]

Trident Replacement/Renewal

It recognized that AWE was optimized for the MIRVed warheads carried by Trident and there would be logistical difficulties in producing a warhead for a different platform whilst maintaining Trident for the remainder of its service life. A new warhead could not be produced before 2040—prior to the end of the service life of the current Vanguard class SSBNs. The system options they eventually looked at are detailed in Figure 10.1:

Platform	Delivery Vehicle	Warhead Design
Large Aircraft	Stealthy Cruise Missile	Cruise missile warhead
Fast Jet	Stealthy Cruise Missile	Cruise missile warhead
Supersonic Cruise Missile	Cruise missile warhead	
Free-fall bomb	UK bomb	
Surface Ship	Stealthy Cruise Missile	Cruise missile warhead
SSN(Horizontal launch)	Stealthy Cruise Missile	Low radiation cruise missile warhead
SSN(Vertical launch)	Stealthy Cruise Missile	Cruise missile warhead
SSBN	Trident D5 ballistic missile	UK Trident
Silo	Trident D5 ballistic missile	UK Trident

Figure 10.1 Trident Alternatives Review

Among the alternative delivery platforms examined was the fifth generation *F-35 Lightening II Joint Strike Fighter*, as well as hypersonic cruise and glide vehicles and options such as silo-based missiles (long ago ruled out as impracticable). It recognized that a 'surge' capacity or dual-use platform was problematic and that a reduction from a four- to a three-boat SSBN force could leave a gap in Continuous-at-Sea-Deterrence (CASD). The Liberal-Democrats, however, were not averse to ending this posture.[70] It was also argued that alternative launch platforms carried command and control problems as launch or patrol areas would be different to SSBN forces. Aside from cost factors, which were as uncertain as they are for a like-for-like replacement system, there remained the question of whether the industrial and scientific base in the UK for SSN and SSBNs could be maintained with a movement to an alternative platform. There was also some doubt over whether a reduction or renunciation of Britain's strategic deterrent posture would have a positive effect on multilateral non- and counter-proliferation efforts—the so-called 'halo effect'.[71]

David Cameron, however, restated to defence contractors in Glasgow in April 2013 two of the longstanding rationales for the Conservative belief in a like-for-like replacement—'future uncertainty' and 'insurance against nuclear blackmail'. Cameron specified: 'The world we live in is very uncertain, very dangerous: there are nuclear states and one cannot be sure of how they will develop...We cannot be sure on issues of nuclear proliferation, and to me having that nuclear deterrent is quite simply the best insurance policy that you can have, that you will never be subject to nuclear blackmail'.[72] For Cameron it was important for Britain to support non-proliferation initiatives, but nuclear proliferation remained a problem for British security that required the continuation of a nuclear deterrent capability. In December 2013 the government therefore issued contracts to BAE Systems for the design of a new class of SSBNs designed to be among the stealthiest in the world, with some £650m already spent on successor designs.[73]

Differences of ideas and beliefs about nuclear weapons within both parties and within the coalition, however, led to the postponement of the decision to replace the Trident submarines until after the 2015 General Election. Despite the disagreements, both parties favour the continuation of a British nuclear deterrent.[74] Indeed, none of the three main political parties advocate unilateral nuclear disarmament, and are instead debating the form rather than the function of the nuclear deterrent. The 'Deterrent Habit of Mind' in an uncertain world remains central to the government's thinking, but what form that deterrent should take in the future remains the subject of ongoing debate.[75] This is not the case for the Scottish Nationalist Party, which argued that it would remove Trident from its base at Faslane near Glasgow if it won the referendum for Scottish independence in September 2014.[76]

One thing is clear: if Britain does (as seem likely) continue as a Nuclear Weapons State (NWS), it is also likely to continue nuclear weapons cooperation with the United States. The Mutual Defence Agreement of 1958 continues to be used as a two-way exchange process for nuclear weapons designs between Britain and the United States[77] and the 1963 Polaris Sales Agreement continued to provide for cooperation on delivery platforms (specifically SSBNs). A March 2013 discussion involving Sir Jeremy Greenstock, Lord David Hannay, Sir Richard Mottram, and Lord Gus O'Donnell (all former senior civil servants) noted that maintaining 'the status quo has enormous weight in politics'.[78] They also argued that it was not Britain's role as a NWS that provided the UK with a distinctive role in international affairs (including a seat on the UNSC), but a range of both 'hard' power factors (such as conventional military strength and collective security arrangements) and 'soft' power (economic vitality and diplomacy), with the core argument now whether to retain CASD.[79]

Belief in the importance of 'hard' power, however, reflected in the need to retain a fully effective deterrent, was very much at the heart of the views of MOD officials. In November 2013 the MOD, as a central part of the nuclear advocacy coalition, emphasized the need for Britain to retain a credible deterrent force:

> The first duty of the Government is to defend the interests and citizens of the United Kingdom. Our nuclear deterrent exists to prevent, at the extreme, any threat to our national existence, or nuclear blackmail from a nuclear-armed state against the UK homeland or our vital interests. We hope never to use nuclear weapons, but, to deliver deterrent effect under all foreseeable circumstances, our ability to do so must be credible and assured at all times; and this depends on there being no doubt in the mind of a potential adversary about our ability and determination to employ our nuclear weapons if necessary.[80]

As such there was a strong conviction amongst officials that it would be necessary to extend the service life of the Trident system to around 2042, continuing its close collaboration with the United States. Events in Eastern Ukraine in 2014, with Russia under President Putin, suspected of destabilising the country through direct military intervention and breaching the principal of national sovereignty and respect for international law also concentrated minds in terms of NATO's collective conventional capabilities and ultimately its nuclear guarantees. Simultaneously, the rise of Islamic State militants in Syria and Western Iraq (ISIS/ISIL) also added to the 'future uncertainty' argument. Both cases also raise valid questions regarding the deterrent value of nuclear weapons and the stabilising role they play in the international system in two very different but major international events.

Conclusion

Traditionally, when faced with the disarmament/deterrence dilemma, British prime ministers have consistently decided in favour of deterrence. This was particularly true of the Attlee government in the late 1940s when faced with attempts to achieve international control of atomic weapons at a time when key decisions had to be made over whether to develop an independent national nuclear capability. It was also true in the mid- to late 1950s when the Macmillan government was being pressed to join a moratorium on nuclear testing at a time when it was developing a thermonuclear weapons capability to match that of the United States and the Soviet Union. It only joined the ban when its testing programme was complete. Similarly, it joined the Partial Test Ban Treaty in 1963, which banned tests in the atmosphere, but continued to test underground. It also signed the Non-Proliferation Treaty in 1968 which, under Article VI, committed the nuclear powers to strive for nuclear disarmament, but provided no timescale for this to be achieved. Britain also remained reluctant to see their deterrent included in the superpower SALT, START, and SORT negotiations from the 1970s through to the end of the Cold War and beyond.

It would be wrong, however, to conclude from this that British governments have been cynical about disarmament and arms control measures. They have often played an important part in promoting arms control initiatives, as

Macmillan did with the Partial Test Ban Treaty and the Blair, Brown, and Cameron governments did with significant unilateral reductions in Britain's nuclear capability. In the case of the Blair and Brown governments, John Simpson has argued that the possession of its nuclear deterrent capability has contributed to its role in support of nuclear non-proliferation:

> Through the UK's initiatives in 2007–09, made possible by its status as both an NPT nuclear weapons state and a depositary state, the country has been able to play a central role in creating an informal P5 multi-focused framework to progress disarmament and other objectives identified in the 2010 action plans. The UK's nuclear weapons status has therefore made it a major player in the global nuclear disarmament debate. The UK can also claim that its deterrent capacity has played a major role in nuclear non-proliferation through its contribution to the NATO nuclear umbrella over its non-nuclear weapons states.[81]

The Labour Foreign Secretary, Margaret Beckett, also argued in her Carnegie Centre speech in 2007 that the search for nuclear disarmament must continue to be an important goal even if it was not achieved in her lifetime:

> there is a danger in familiarity with something so terrible. If we allow our efforts on disarmament to slacken, if we allow ourselves to take the non-proliferation consensus for granted, the nuclear shadow that hangs over us all will lengthen and it will deepen. It may, one day, blot out the light for good. So my commitment to the vision of a world free of nuclear weapons is undimmed. And though we in this room may never reach the end of that road, we can take the first steps down it. For any generation, that would be a noble calling. For ours, it is a duty.[82]

The belief in a largely anarchic world in which trust was in short supply, however, remained the general dominant view of the Blair and Brown Labour governments, as it did with the Conservative–Liberal Democrat Coalition that followed. The Liberal Democrats continued to have doubts about whether a capability as sophisticated as Trident was necessary, but they nevertheless supported the views of the nuclear lobby that in an uncertain world Britain should retain its own nuclear force. At the same time, however, governments on both the left and the right have continued to see value in contributing to a rules-based international system in which there might be limited possibilities for building greater trust in international relations through step-by-step measures and small unilateral measures.[83] No government, however, has been prepared to make the 'leap of faith' that Prime Minister Attlee recommended to the American president, Harry Truman, in 1945. Until a substantial degree of trust between nations has been achieved, British governments continue to believe that nuclear weapons have a critical role to play in national security.

As well as the continuing tensions over disarmament, arms control, and deterrence, recent years have also seen a resurgence of another traditional debate over the balance between conventional and nuclear forces, and which provides a better capability for dealing with the changing nature of conflict in the twenty-first century. From within the defence establishment, Sir Henry Tizard argued in the late 1940s that spending on nuclear weapons took resources away from more important conventional forces needed for the air defence of Britain. In more recent years, former senior defence officials have also argued that nuclear weapons are not relevant in a world dominated by civil conflicts and terrorism. Field Marshal Lord Brammall—a former Chief of the Defence Staff, and one of Britain's most illustrious soldiers—argued in December 2013 that Britain should not be spending £20 billion on a replacement for Trident. In his words: 'it doesn't deter. We don't need it, we can't afford it. Look at 9/11. The US nuclear deterrent didn't deter it, and they didn't use it, they couldn't have'.[84] Instead he argued that Britain had to develop those capabilities, especially in the Army, that could deal with unexpected events.

The balance between conventional defence and the cost of the nuclear deterrent has also been a source of heated debate from other senior defence officials, including those who support the need for some form of continuing nuclear deterrent.[85] Cuts in conventional forces led Vice-Admiral Sir Jeremy Blackham, a former Deputy Chief of the Defence Staff, to note in August 2013 that:

> the nuclear deterrent is not a substitute for conventional capabilities. The credibility of flexible response depends upon deferring any decision to use nuclear weapons until the very existence of the nation is at stake... If the conventional means at our disposal are weak, the point of transition to nuclear use may be lowered to levels at which the risk of nuclear obliteration is self-evidently disproportionate to the issue at stake. At that point, it is likely that deterrence through the threat of nuclear use becomes incredible and can be so perceived by an opponent—a bluff waiting to be called. Thus, through conventional weakness, the nuclear deterrent is compromised, whether it is a rogue state or a major power that is involved. To be credible, the nuclear deterrent must be underpinned by strong conventional deterrence. [With the SDSR creating] some highly significant capability gaps [which] together with depleted equipment numbers and reduced manpower, have unbalanced our force structure, and for which no solutions are yet fully identified, let alone funded.[86]

Blackham warned that the effect of the SDSR on Trident replacement 'is likely to pose a far more severe challenge to the shrinking UK defence industry than did either Polaris or Trident', and 'without new money, the risks to the remaining conventional programme appear to be considerable. Conventional force levels are again at risk and so therefore is the credibility both of the nuclear deterrent and of deterrence more generally.'[87]

Significantly, a similar set of arguments were put forward by General Sir Nicholas Houghton, the serving Chief of Defence Staff, in December 2013 when he identified the international security situation as containing 'uncertainty; instability; the advent of threats which are more diverse, less existential and less symmetric than hitherto; and, fourthly, the increasing mutuality of nations and the interdependence of the world in general'. He continued: 'countries such as our own...derive their relative power and prosperity from the maintenance of a stable world and an international rules based order, are confronted by the twin challenges of change and instability'. Houghton also remarked that:

> Defence will need real growth in the next parliament if the reality of the force structure set out in the last SDSR is to be realised.... Unattended our current course leads to a strategically incoherent force structure: exquisite equipment, but insufficient resources to man that equipment or train on it. This is what the Americans call the spectre of the hollow-force. We are not there yet; but across Defence I would identify the Royal Navy as being perilously close to its critical mass in man-power terms.... Defence has for many years, certainly since the successful end of the cold war, and in strong international company within Europe, been managing the decline of military hard power. Defence funding has been reducing and we have enjoyed reduced manoeuvre room in how we spend Defence's money...If the United Kingdom wants to stay in the Premier League of smart power then it must invest in Armed Forces that can generate hard power capability that is credible in respect of conventional coercion and deterrence. Increasingly we have spent it on large capital equipment programmes often with an eye on supporting the United Kingdom's Defence industrial base.[88]

Houghton drew on the wider national defence context in mapping British defence priorities and national and international identity drawn from the military ability and political willingness to project 'hard' power.[89]

Yet is should also be borne in mind that within the reduced defence budget the UK is building two large aircraft carriers, of a size comparable with the US *Nimitz* class and the French carrier the *Charles de Gaulle*. They are being equipped with the fifth generation VSTOL F-35B Lightning II Joint Strike Fighter purchased from the US. Part of their importance is that it provides Britain with a potential global reach capability in support of foreign and defence policy, even with only a single carrier operational at any one time. It also provides interoperability with the United States Navy, but not with the French who are flying *Rafale*, which is incompatible with the two *Queen Elizabeth* class carriers.

Still, similar concerns to Houghton's have been expressed by other commentators. In the context of mapping out the priorities of the British armed forces to the strategic deterrent Malcolm Chalmers points out that:

> The stability of the strategic SSBN force is in stark contrast to the rest of the UK's front line. The number of regular British Army personnel fell from 167,000 in 1975 to 104,000 in 2012, and is now due to fall to 82,000. Between 1975 and 2012, the number of major surface combatants in the Royal Navy has been reduced from seventy-seven to twenty-two, and the number of fast jet squadrons from forty-one

to eight. The fleet of attack submarines, which consisted of twenty-eight vessels in 1975, has now been cut to seven, the minimum level necessary to generate concurrent carrier and SSBN protection. While the SSBN force has remained almost unchanged in scale, therefore, it has become a proportionately larger part of the UK's force structure over the decades since its introduction.[90]

This view was taken up by Robert Gates, the former US Secretary of Defense, in January 2014. Gates argued that the cuts in Britain's conventional forces, especially in the naval field, meant that Britain no longer had a 'full spectrum' capability and this was jeopardizing the traditional close military ties between Britain and the United States. The implication was that this was putting at risk the UK's traditional 'special relationship' identity.[91]

Given the ongoing need for financial restraint, the opportunity costs associated with Trident replacement seem likely to continue. However, faced with the choice of abandoning or downsizing the deterrent and transferring these resources to conventional defence, a 2013 YouGov opinion poll found that 35 per cent would support replacing Trident with a less powerful or expensive system, 26 per cent with another equally powerful system, whilst 24 per cent supported unilateral nuclear disarmament.[92] Despite the support for replacing Trident with a less sophisticated deterrent, the poll showed that, overall, 61 per cent of the public still favoured the retention of a nuclear force. This support, together with the consensus between the main political parties regarding the need for some form of replacement, suggests that the British nuclear experience will continue well into the future, unless there is a dramatic change in the beliefs of the key decision-makers, members of the powerful nuclear lobby, and the general public.[93] Nuclear disarmament would also require a significant change in the prevailing British national identity. Indeed that national identity was reconfirmed by Scotland who voted in September 2014 to remain part of a United Kingdom for the foreseeable future. As a result contingency planning for separation, including rebasing Trident from Faslane, now will not be required.

Conclusion

The doctrine of nuclear deterrence is not an eternal verity but is largely based on a belief system.

K. Berry et al[1]

No one can demonstrate to the satisfaction of all concerned that his theories about how present and future weapons can be used to prevent or win wars are the predictions that reality could and will prove correct.

W. Schilling[2]

As we suggested in the Introduction, traditional approaches to the motivations behind the development of nuclear weapons tend to argue that in an anarchic international environment states seek such weapons in order to enhance their security and prestige. Prestige is seen as a key element of the search for security, rather than an end in itself. Implicit in these approaches is a kind of technological determinism which suggests that once a state has the necessary scientific and technological infrastructure, it will go on to develop such weapons. In some respects the British experience seems to confirm such approaches. Britain first decided to try to develop atomic weapons at a time of existential threat during the Second World War. Then, in 1947, as the Cold War gathered momentum, the decision was taken to develop an independent atomic capability following the ending of the wartime collaboration with the United States which had produced the first nuclear weapons used against Japan. Britain had the basic scientific, engineering, and technological base to suggest that it could develop such weapons successfully, and it decided to go ahead. According to this view, as Michael Quinlan has argued, 'it is hard to imagine that Britain...would have done otherwise'.[3] Realist approaches also help to explain why Britain decided to develop thermonuclear weapons in the mid- to late 1950s and why it was decided to purchase *Polaris* and *Trident* missiles from the United States during the Cold War. They may also help to explain why Britain has retained nuclear weapons into the post-Cold war period, given the uncertainties and dangers of the age. This book has tried to argue, however, that, although such approaches have some merit, they are somewhat limited in their explanatory power, and that much more can be gleaned from looking at the beliefs, culture, and identity factors which lay at the heart of the British nuclear experience from the Second World War until today.

In the immediate aftermath of the War, there was a strong belief within the new Labour government of Clement Attlee that everything had changed with the development of atomic weapons. Traditional ideas of war 'were completely out of date'. The sort of thing that had been considered 'a Utopian dream in the past' had now become 'the essential condition of the survival of civilization and possibly of life on the planet'.[4] It was now important for Britain, the US, and the Soviet Union to create a 'New World Order', beginning with the international control of atomic energy. This belief, however, soon gave way to a recognition that a new form of great power politics was underway and that the ability to deter an attack through the development of atomic weapons was the most likely—and, indeed, the 'only'—way of ensuring British security. This produced a new 'deterrence habit of mind'. There was no certainty that this would work. It was 'in a strict sense speculative'.[5] The propositions about the achievement of nuclear weapons for deterrence that were adopted at the highest levels of government could not look for rigorous evidentiary proof, 'since such propositions are essentially about alternative history—about what would or might have happened had matters been other than they were'.[6] Thus, as Berry and Schilling have argued, nuclear deterrence has been part of a belief system that could not be proved or indeed disproved.[7]

Both geography and history reinforced this nuclear belief system.[8] As an island nation and maritime power, Britain had traditionally felt reasonably secure. With the strategic bombing campaign and V1/V2 attacks of the Second World War and the advent of atomic weapons, Britain was now highly vulnerable to destruction should a new war break out. This produced a security mindset in which nuclear deterrence became deeply entrenched much sooner than in the United States with its different geography and history. For Britain the most advanced weapon systems of the day had traditionally brought security and status, especially during its period of colonial pre-eminence. Continuing this aspect of traditional strategic culture, atomic and thermonuclear weapons, and the means to deliver them, were believed by governments on both the left and the right (sometimes in different ways) during the Cold War to be a vital part of the nation's foreign and defence policies.

Initially, the possession of atomic weapons was believed to be a critical ingredient of Britain's Great Power status and ability to influence the United States. Status and prestige were seen to reinforce security, but they were also important in their own right, particularly to secure influence in Washington and also as an essential basis for Britain's membership of the Security Council of the United Nations and her role in the world more generally. As time went on, as Andrew Pierre has argued, they were increasingly seen by governments as an important means of disguising Britain's decline and bolstering Britain's influence in the world. As such, they became an essential part of the evolving national identity.[9] Leaders such as Attlee, Churchill, Wilson, Heath, and Thatcher had somewhat different conceptions of Britain's national identity, but in each case nuclear weapons had a role to play in their ideas of the UK's position in the world.

The relationship between nuclear weapons, political identity, and policy-making is an interesting one, and one that this study has attempted to consider in some detail. It has been argued that there are a number of dimensions of the British political-military establishment's national self-identity that relate to nuclear weapons. First, there is the argument that nuclear weapons underpin Britain's core identity as a major 'pivotal' power with a responsibility for the upkeep of the current international order and a duty to intervene with military force in conflicts that threaten peace and stability. In this sense, leaders have believed that Britain is a 'force for good' in the international system and nuclear weapons reinforce an interventionist foreign policy that supports universal values of peace and freedom and the Rule of Law. Second, this argument suggests that the possession of nuclear weapons is 'perceived to be part of what enables Britain to maintain political credibility in Washington, gain access to the highest levels of policy-making to support the "special relationship", and keep America engaged in the world'.[10] This 'special relationship identity' has been at the heart of British foreign and defence policy from the Second World War onwards and nuclear weapons have been one of the central elements of this identity. And, third, it is argued that Britain has attempted to construct a regional self-identity as a responsible and leading defender of Western Europe. With French withdrawal from the military structure of NATO in 1966, British nuclear weapons were viewed as being held 'in trust' for Europe, just in case the Soviet Union perceived that the US might be reluctant to defend Europe. This was reflected in the 'Second Centre' justification for British nuclear forces put forward at various times by British governments.

As we noted in the Introduction, Jacques Hymans has suggested that the 'National Identity Conception' of the key political leaders is of crucial importance in decisions relating to nuclear weapons. This study supports Hymans' thesis. One of the main reasons why Britain has remained a nuclear power from the Second World War until today is that all prime ministers have believed that nuclear weapons have a vital utility. There have been some differences in their views about nuclear weapons, with Wilson playing down the 'independence' of the nuclear deterrent and Heath seriously considering

Conclusion

nuclear collaboration with the French, but all have supported the need for a sophisticated nuclear capability. However, this study has also shown that while the beliefs of individual leaders are of major importance, British experience suggests that other individuals and groups have also played an important role in nuclear decision-making. High-level decisions relating to the acquisition of atomic and thermonuclear weapons were taken by small ad hoc groups of ministers and not by prime ministers on their own. GEN 75, GEN 163, and MISC 7 are important examples of this. Many other decisions, often of an operational nature, were also taken by other groups and committees, such as the Chiefs of Staff Committee, the Joint Technical Warfare Committee, and the Defence Policy Staff. We have also tried to show that some individual officials, because of their expertise and position, have also played a very significant role in influencing and determining policy in certain directions. These include scientists such William Penney and William Cook, and officials such as Sir Michael Quinlan, Sir Robert Armstrong, Sir Burke Trend, and Sir John Hunt.

This study has shown that one of the reasons for the *entrenchment* of the priority given to nuclear weapons since 1945 has been the role of a powerful nuclear advocacy coalition, containing different individuals and groups, such as those mentioned above, who, over time, have successfully influenced the debate within government in support of developing and retaining a British nuclear capability. It would be wrong, however, to suggest that no differences have occurred within this group of nuclear supporters. As the study has shown, there have been constant and significant differences over such things as the priority to be given to nuclear weapons within overall defence policy, especially in terms of the balance between conventional and nuclear capabilities; over whether deterrence is better served through a counter-force or a counter-city strategy; over the number of Soviet cities that needed to be targeted for effective deterrence; over whether nuclear weapons had a practical use in warfare; and over whether a nuclear war could be kept limited. As an illustration of this, Solly Zuckerman argued, in his book *Nuclear Illusion and Reality*, that between 1957 and 1982 five of the seven officers who held the post of Chief of the Defence Staff in the British military hierarchy made statements after they retired which were critical of official British and NATO nuclear policy.[11] Different beliefs about the utility and role of nuclear weapons clearly existed within the nuclear advocacy coalition, even though these were not often apparent to the general public outside government.

The fact that differences of view and belief within the political-military establishment were kept out of the public gaze highlights an important characteristic of the British nuclear experience—that of secrecy. Decisions were invariably made by small groups, often with other members of the Cabinet unaware of what had been decided, let alone the general public. This was justified in terms of vital national security, but it was also often due to domestic party political considerations. At times, there were some within the Cabinet and the governing party who held very different views and beliefs about nuclear deterrence, as well as the dangers of proliferation and disarmament, to those of the prime minister and like-minded supporters.

Many of those outside government who have opposed the nuclear deterrent policy have done so on ethical grounds, reflecting very different moral beliefs to those of the nuclear advocates. However, there have also been some ethical differences within the nuclear advocacy coalition itself. In general, three ethical positions on nuclear weapons have existed, especially in the debates of the late 1950s and early 1960s, and those of the 1980s. First, there have been those who have argued that, by their nature, nuclear weapons are immoral. According to this view there is a moral imperative 'always and unconditionally' to renounce the possession of such weapons 'regardless of circumstances and consequences', because they undermine the principles of 'discrimination' and 'proportionality' which are at the heart of the Just War Tradition. The second position is that while possession of nuclear weapons might be morally acceptable as a means of preventing war, the *use* of such weapons must always be morally wrong because of the dangers of escalation. And, third, it has been argued that some use of nuclear weapons, in ways and on a scale the prospects of which could provide effective deterrence, might in extreme circumstances be morally tolerable. In many ways all three stances pose ethical dilemmas, depending upon one's ethical beliefs.

The first, absolutist, position, raises the very real problem for ethical opponents that a state that renounces nuclear weapons might be faced with an opponent that refuses to give them up and then uses them to impose its will upon the non-nuclear state. The second, it has been argued, fundamentally undermines the belief, shared by many strategists, that deterrence and use cannot be separated, if the credibility of deterrence is to be preserved. And the third, opponents contend, poses the danger that even the limited use of nuclear weapons is likely to escalate out of control, with cataclysmic consequences, regardless of a government's intention.

For much of the Cold War the government opted for a fairly crude version of the third position. Nuclear weapons were believed to be the best means to deter war and preserve British freedoms and could therefore be justified in moral terms. Looking back, even some of those officials who supported the ethical case for nuclear deterrence have argued that 'some of the contingency plans formulated for their potential use on a massive scale would have been morally intolerable to execute in any circumstances whatever'.[12] According to this view, the deliberate targeting of Soviet cities and the threat to deliberately kill millions of non-combatants, which characterized British nuclear targeting plans for many years, must be regarded as alien to any interpretation of the Just War Tradition.

In 1980, however, when the government decided to acquire Trident missiles, it published a document which said that the nuclear deterrent force would target 'key aspects of Soviet state power'.[13] These words were deliberately chosen to indicate that the UK no longer wished to threaten a 'crude counter-city strike against Moscow and other Soviet cities as part of its national deterrent doctrine'. This change in doctrine was the work of Michael Quinlan, who has been described as 'the leading civilian thinker within the British government on defence policy, a key architect of British and NATO nuclear doctrine and strategy during the Cold War, and one of the most brilliant and influential nuclear thinkers of his time'.[14] Quinlan was a senior civil servant and a Catholic, with a strong interest in ethical issues. These moral beliefs shaped his approach to nuclear weapons and helped directly shape British nuclear policy in the 1980s and 1990s (and indirectly beyond that). Quinlan believed that nuclear weapons were important both for war prevention and, if deterrence failed, for war termination. He rejected interpretations of the Just War Tradition that contended either that nuclear weapons themselves were inherently immoral or that their use was necessarily immoral (even if there was an ethical justification for deterrence). In his private correspondence (including with some fellow Catholic thinkers) he went out of his way to argue that in the nuclear age the most important moral objective was to rule out war between the major powers. He accepted that if deterrence broke down and that 'the awful moment of decision ever came, the right moral and prudential decision in a particular situation might be not to use them, whatever the provocation'.[15] But he also believed that it could be morally legitimate to use them in certain circumstances in order to persuade an opponent that it had crossed a red line and ought to pull back. Deterrence without a convincing plan to use nuclear weapons, he believed, lacked credibility. The targets, however, had to be carefully chosen. To *deliberately* target non-combatants was ethically unacceptable. It was this belief that led to the change in British policy in 1980.

This shift in doctrine, however, was very controversial. For some observers it was merely 'window dressing'. Many of the targets of British nuclear weapons were close to major Soviet cities and it was therefore inevitable that there would be very significant non-combatant casualties should British missiles be fired against 'key aspects of Soviet state power'.[16] Quinlan accepted that this would be the case, but argued that unintended civilian deaths could be morally acceptable according to the principle of 'double effect'. In a letter to the distinguished Quaker Sydney Bailey in 1981, he explained the idea of 'double effect' in the following way:

> I do regard it as wrong (I think without qualification) to make non-combatants (leaving aside the problems of defining the term) the deliberative object of attack,

in the sense of attack whose point is, and whose success depends upon, their killing. I believe however that their killing can be accepted if it is the incidental effect of attack directed to other and legitimate ends, provided that the incidental effect is both kept to the minimum feasible and not disproportionate to the legitimate effect sought.[17]

Quinlan accepted that this was 'a hard argument to sustain—it is at full stretch'.[18] Nevertheless, he held to his strong moral conviction because it was 'less difficult' and, in his view, morally superior to the other ethical alternatives. At the time there were many who fundamentally disagreed with him. The point here is not who was right and who was wrong, but rather to highlight the kind of moral beliefs that have helped to shape British nuclear policy.

It is perhaps of interest that, although he did not change his position significantly in retirement, he was increasingly aware of the difficulties his ethical position posed. In his book, *Thinking about Nuclear Weapons: Principles, Problems, Prospects* (written just before he died) he accepted that:

> it cannot be right to acquiesce uncritically, for the rest of human history, in a system that maintains peace between potential adversaries partly by the threat of colossal disaster. Any serious moral stance must recognise a duty, alongside that of striving to reduce the costs and risks of nuclear armouries and maximising their war-prevention benefits so long as they continue to exist, to work towards a world in which security can be maintained without incurring at all the burdens which they entail.[19]

Quinlan also accepted that strategic planning in the past had often 'slipped into over-elaboration and over-insurance, insufficiently recognizing...the robustness which the huge reality of nuclear weapons conferred upon war prevention even without extreme refinement'[20] (see Appendix 3). This criticism reflects another important feature of the British nuclear experience relating to the significance of the constant debates over the requirements of deterrence which have taken place. In 1947 it was argued that Britain needed 1,000 atomic bombs. This figure was based on the rather simplistic idea that because it was likely that twenty-five Soviet bombs would knock Britain out of a future war, and the Soviet Union was forty times bigger than Britain, the stockpile needed was thus forty times twenty-five, making 1,000. In 1958 it was believed that the ability to destroy 44 cities in the Soviet Union was necessary for deterrence. By 1964 this had been reduced to twenty cities. By 1972 planning was based on ten cities, and by 1976 the number of cities to be targeted could be as low as five. During the 1970s there was also an ongoing debate about whether or not it was essential for deterrence to target Moscow (the so-called Moscow Criterion). By 1980, as we have seen, the deliberate targetting of Soviet cities was dropped in favour of targeting 'Soviet State Power'. Therefore, what was believed to be required for 'minimum deterrence' during the Cold War constantly changed, often as a result of changing economic circumstances and what could be afforded at the time. As Sir Edward Ashmore told a meeting of the Ministry of Defence in June 1976, 'what constituted a credible deterrent was political'.[21] During the post-Cold War period, as well, 'minimum deterrence' has remained the basis of British nuclear doctrine, but the requirements for that policy have changed. Britain's stockpile of nuclear weapons was reduced from 200 to 160, and then down to 120. Also, the number of nuclear warheads deployed in each Trident submarine has been reduced from forty-eight to forty, and it is envisaged that the new class of submarines being planned will have eight missile tubes rather than the current sixteen. Again, political judgement, often dictated by economic factors rather than military strategic logic, has invariably been at the heart of British nuclear planning, especially regarding the requirements of 'minimum deterrence'.

Indeed, Lord Owen argues that:

> Minimum deterrence is about deterring nuclear strikes against us in Britain. It is not about beating Russia in a military confrontation in which America has backed off. If deterrence has failed, i.e. we have been attacked by nuclear weapons... If our threat has failed then a response is not automatic, and very few, if any, Prime Ministers would ever contemplate, in reality, nuclear retaliation. Retaliation is not allowed for under the UN Charter. Defence of a vital interest is. It is essential to ensure that people understand that there is no automaticity in UK deterrence. It is a free-standing decision whether to retaliate. Much depends on how much damage has already been done and whether you are dealing with a futile gesture. I have never seen what Prime Ministers write to a Commander of a submarine but I am pretty sure I know what Jim Callaghan wrote and it was effectively if there has been a nuclear strike on the UK you are to make contact with our most important friend and ally, the US, and put yourself under the command and control of the US President and eventually any such UK, Commonwealth (Canada and Australia) government that can establish itself outside the UK.[22]

Apart from the dilemmas associated with the ethical beliefs attached to the possession of nuclear weapons and the policies relating to the requirements of nuclear deterrence, Andrew Pierre has argued that the British nuclear experience has also been characterized by four main paradoxes. These relate to nuclear proliferation, independence versus interdependence, alliance relationships, and the frontiers of science and technology. On the question of nuclear proliferation, he argues that although the UK was the first amongst the nuclear powers to have a serious debate about giving up nuclear weapons, 'paradoxically Britain probably did far more harm than good for the cause of non-proliferation'.[23] This argument is based on the fact that Britain held a unique position as the first second-ranking nation in the post-war international system to acquire a nuclear capability. And by its rhetoric and actions,

British political leaders effectively encouraged other nations to follow suit. Pierre identifies the justifications given in France (and further afield) for developing a nuclear force: 'Nuclearism', he argued, 'is a contagious disease'.[24] Echoing P.M.S. Blackett, in his view the period from 1948 to 1952 was a critical period for limiting the nuclear club. With the Cold War gathering momentum, Britain gave up on international control and highlighted its security, as well as status and political influence, as reasons for developing its atomic capability.

Pierre has a case. Whether other countries would have followed the British lead had the UK decided not to go ahead with developing atomic weapons is not clear. As he says, 'we will never know to what extent Britain started this type of nuclear reaction'.[25] The late 1940s and early 1950s, however, were a critical time and similar arguments were subsequently used by other states to justify their own nuclear programmes. At one stage the Chiefs of Staff argued that Britain had an inalienable right to nuclear weapons. If this was true of Britain, then it was perhaps not surprising that other states would feel the same. Paradoxically, Britain was to play a leading role in the negotiations to try to limit proliferation in the 1960s and beyond, but often the position of continuing to maintain its nuclear capabilities (like that of the other nuclear weapon states) while trying to prevent others from developing similar capabilities was seen as self-serving by many non-nuclear states who also believed that their security and status would be enhanced by developing nuclear weapons. British beliefs were shared by a number of other states with nuclear aspirations.

There has undoubtedly been tension between policies supporting non-proliferation and policies supporting nuclear deterrence. The position that respective governments have taken is that nuclear proliferation is largely outside its control and, in a world in which the spread of nuclear weapons (and other weapons of mass destruction) is likely to take place, its responsibility is to provide for national security, and that nuclear deterrence is the best way to do that.

A second paradox identified by Pierre was Britain's attempt to preserve both independence and interdependence in nuclear matters. Following both the 1958 MDA and the 1962 Nassau Agreement, governments argued that Britain could achieve the benefits of technological interdependence through a close nuclear partnership with the United States whilst at the same time retaining an independent nuclear deterrent. Political leaders also supported nuclear integration in NATO, but insisted on independence of action should circumstances dictate it. Pierre argues that one of the lessons of the British experience is that 'nations that become dependent on another state's strategic technology do lose some of their perceived political independence'.[26] In his view, claims of both independence and interdependence led to 'illogicalities' in the operational requirements of the nuclear force and in its operational doctrine. Target plans were integrated with those of the US Strategic Air Command, and British forces depended on a range of US capabilities, including early-warning and intelligence assets, and later various launching and fire control systems, communications equipment, and high-stress steels for submarine hulls. As a result, Pierre argues that Britain 'undoubtedly lost a measure of her strategic independence'.[27]

Although it is true that Britain has lost 'a measure of her strategic independence' as a result of its close nuclear partnership with the United States, it is perhaps going too far to argue that this has led to 'illogicalities' in the operational requirements of its nuclear force. Polaris and Trident missiles were, and remain, allocated to, and normally targeted by, NATO's Supreme Allied Commander, Europe (SACEUR), as part of his General Strike Plan. However, the missiles can be redirected relatively easily to targets in the National Retaliatory War Plan should the government believe that is necessary in the 'national interest'. It is true that, given the closeness of the operational relationship with the US, over time, it would become increasingly difficult for Britain to fire its missiles independently should the US end the nuclear partnership with the UK. Nevertheless, it does retain the ability to fire its missiles independently -if deemed essential in certain circumstances. Should the United States hold back when faced with the nuclear decision amid the heat and fear of war, while still remaining politically committed to Britain (and European security), Britain would have what is sometimes called 'Mark 1 independence'. This is the basis of what became known as the 'Second-Centre Role' for British nuclear forces. According to the 1980 Defence Open Government Document published in 1980:

> If Britain is to meet effectively the deterrent purpose of providing a second centre of decision-making within the Alliance, our force has to be visibly capable of posing a massive threat on its own. A force which could strike tellingly only if the United States also did so—which plainly relied, for example, on US assent to its use, or on attenuation or distraction of Soviet defences by United States forces— would not achieve the purpose. We need to convince Soviet leaders that even if they thought that at some critical point as a conflict developed the US would hold back, the British force could still inflict a blow so destructive that the penalty for aggression would have proved too high.[28]

Whether Soviet leaders themselves ever concerned themselves with this 'Second-Centre Role' remains very difficult to know. Equally, it is impossible to know if British leaders faced with such a situation would actually have launched its missiles. But that is the basis of the 'deterrence belief'. It does seem likely, however, that the UK did (and still does) retain that capability, even if 'Mark 2 independence', postulating US estrangement from Britain and Europe, almost certainly lacks credibility. Nevertheless, there is a sense in which there is no necessary contradiction between 'independence' and 'interdependence'.

Pierre's third paradox concerns issues of identity. He claims that Britain's role as a nuclear power and the 'special' nuclear partnership with the United States 'may have been injurious to her long term interests to the extent that it encouraged Britain to feel that it could avoid Europe'. In Pierre's words:

> Self-identity as the second nuclear power in the West, and a self-image of continuing worldwide responsibilities encouraged Britain to refuse to join the Schuman Plan in 1950, to refrain from supporting the abortive European Defence Community in 1954, to hold back from the European Economic Community in its early and formative years and to reject beforehand the possibility of eventually permitting an MLF/ANF scheme to transform itself into a European nuclear force.[29]

In some respects, given that Pierre was writing in 1972, this paradox has been relatively less important since Britain has been a member of the European Union (EU). Britain has often seen itself as a bridge between Europe and the United States and at times has embraced greater European defence cooperation. Nevertheless, something of the paradox still remains. Britain has clung on to its close nuclear partnership with the US and has often been a rather reluctant member of the EU. This has resulted in a rather schizophrenic quality to British foreign and defence policy, with nuclear weapons held on behalf of Europe and, at the same time, reinforcing the self-identity of the UK as a major 'pivotal' power outside Europe with a particular responsibility to help preserve the international order.

Pierre's fourth paradox focuses on Britain's attempts to be at the 'frontier' of science and technology. He argues that Britain became the victim of her own success in science and technology. Because of her traditional position of leadership in these fields there was a strong belief for some time after the Second World War that the UK could go on competing with the two superpowers. As Britain's economic prosperity declined, however, the result was that it faced constant problems in the procurement field, especially in relation to the means of delivering nuclear weapons. These solutions highlighted the nation's scientific and technological dependence (as well as decline).

Clearly, Pierre has a point. These procurement difficulties can be seen with the problems Britain faced with the V-Bomber force, the cancellations of *Blue Streak*, *TSR2*, and *Skybolt*, as well as the Polaris Improvement Programme and *Chevaline*. It was increasingly clear that Britain could not easily develop an indigenous nuclear delivery system which would allow her to retain a credible deterrent force. As good as many features of her scientific and technological base remained, Britain did not have the economic resources—or, indeed, the political will—to compete in the nuclear field with the United States and the

Soviet Union. Britain's solution, as we have seen, was to seek interdependence with the United States, unlike the other nuclear powers, such as France and China, who sought a more indigenous route. There were cost and technological advantages to this solution, but there were also costs that governments of both political parties were prepared to incur.

Apart from these paradoxes, one of the primary questions which follows from the main themes developed in this book is whether it might be possible for Britain to break away from its traditional approach to nuclear weapons and seek a non-nuclear future? For this to happen, as we argue in Chapter 10, there would have to be a fundamental change in the kind of beliefs, culture, and identity issues which have embedded nuclear weapons at the centre of British foreign and defence policy since the Second World War. As Ritchie has argued, 'if Britain is to relinquish nuclear weapons these powerful... conceptions and the causal relationships and interests they generate will have to be transformed and the meanings assigned to British nuclear weapons reconceptualised'.[30] Given that the beliefs, culture, and identity issues associated with nuclear weapons have become entrenched, this will not be easy. Much of the literature on strategic culture, for example, focuses on the continuity of state behaviour. In his work on the subject, Jack Snyder talked about 'semi-permanent elite beliefs, attitudes and behaviour patterns socialized into a distinctive mode of thought'.[31] Harry Eckstein has also argued that culture creates 'past learning outcomes that become sedimented in the collective consciousness and are relatively resilient to change'.[32]

There are those, however, who disagree with this view. Colin Gray has argued that 'culture is learned, not genetically inherited. So it can be changed.'[33] This is very much the position of Constructivist writers on international relations and international security. Those who argue that such a change is conceivable focus on 'the acceptance and institutionalisation by the policy elite of a non-nuclear British identity', which will help bring about changes in Britain's role in the world as well as in its relationship with the United States and Europe.[34] The key question is: what would have to change in order for a prime minister and policy elite that has consistently believed that nuclear weapons have utility, to reverse this belief and move in a non-nuclear direction? It could perhaps occur as a result of the shock of a significant nuclear accident;[35] the election of a charismatic prime minister committed to a non-nuclear future for Britain; the emergence of a powerful non-nuclear advocacy coalition supported by public opinion; or perhaps a gradual resolution of the world's major conflicts and a growing serious international commitment to nuclear disarmament. None of these things can be ruled out, but for the time being, at least, the beliefs, culture, and identity issues which have led Britain to develop and retain a nuclear capability for nearly seventy years remain firmly in place.[36]

The fact that nuclear deterrence is not 'an eternal verity' but a belief system, does not, of course, mean that it is necessarily wrong or mistaken. It does, however, suggest that there are a number of different judgements about how best to achieve both national and international security. It also suggests that we should be sceptical of those who claim to know the 'truth' and who speak with great certainty, assurance, and apparent authority about the continuing need for nuclear deterrence or for particular requirements of a nuclear deterrent policy. The least we should expect is an open and honest debate about the utility and dangers of nuclear weapons and a willingness to listen seriously to those who hold different beliefs to our own on this vitally important subject.

APPENDIX 1
British Nuclear Weapons, 1945–present

Weapon	Kiloton/Megaton	Type	Method of Delivery	Years Deployed
Blue Danube	Kiloton	Gravity Bomb	Air Delivered	1953–1961
Violet Club (Interim Megaton Weapon)	Megaton Range (boosted fission)	Gravity Bomb	Air Delivered	1958–1959
Yellow Sun Mk. 1	Megaton	Gravity Bomb	Air Delivered	1961–1969
Red Beard	Kiloton	Gravity Bomb	Air Delivered	1961–1971
Red Beard Mk. 2	Kiloton	Gravity Bomb	Air Delivered	1960–1971
Yellow Sun Mk. 2	Megaton	Gravity Bomb	Air Delivered	1959–1963
Blue Steel	Megaton	Stand-off missile	Air Delivered	1963–1969
WE-177B	High Yield Kiloton	Gravity Bomb	Air Delivered	1966–1998
WE-177A	Kiloton	Gravity Bomb/NDB	Air Delivered	1969–1992
Polaris A-3T	Megaton	SLBM	Submarine Launched	1968–1994
WE-177C	High Yield Kiloton	Gravity Bomb	Air Delivered	1974–1998
Polaris-Chevaline A3TK	Megaton	SLBM	Submarine Launched	1982–1994
Trident D-5	Megaton	SLBM	Submarine Launched	1994–present

APPENDIX 2

US Nuclear Weapons supplied to the UK, 1945–present

Weapon	Kiloton/ Megaton	Type	Method of Delivery	Years Deployed
Thor	Megaton	Intermediate Range Ballistic Missile	Ground Launched	1959–1963
Corporal*	Kiloton	Battlefield Missile	Ground Launched	1960–1965
Honest John*	Kiloton	Battlefield Missile	Ground Launched	1960–1977
6' Howitzer*	Kiloton	Battlefield Gun	Ground Launched	1960–1992
8' Howitzer*	Kiloton	Battlefield Gun	Ground Launched	1960–1992
MK 101 'Lulu'**	Kiloton	Nuclear Depth Bomb	Surface Ship Launched	1965–1971
Lance***	Kiloton	Battlefield Missile	Ground Launched	1976–1993
Gryphon****	Megaton	Ground Launched Cruise Missile	Ground Launched	1983–1988

* Supplied Under Project E.
** Supplied Under Project N.
*** Supplied under similar arrangements to Project E and N whereby US nuclear warheads were used for British-operated equipement.
**** Operated under a revison to the Murphy-Dean Agreement of 1958.

APPENDIX 3

Strategic Strike Planning by Bomber Command, 1962

The strategic target policy for Bomber Command is set out in COS (57) 224 which for the case of purely national, *unilateral*, action states:

'If the UK should be forced to take unilateral retaliation against the USSR, the target policy of Bomber Command should be to attack the Soviet centres of administration and population. This is the most effective target system for our limited forces'.

1. Plans for the employment of the Medium Bomber Force against this target system are drawn up by Bomber Command. Actual targets are selected according to operational considerations from a priority list, provided by the Air Ministry. Successive plans have changed only in tactics and in variation of the number of cities to be attacked as dictated by developing offensive and defensive capabilities. The current plan provides for attacks on 15 cities. (Thor does not, of course, figure in this plan).

2. Dealing with *joint UK/US planning*, COS (57) 224, states:-

'In the event of co-ordinated action with the USAF, the target policy for Bomber Command should be determined solely by considerations of timing, tactics, aircraft performance and weapon availability, subject to the proviso that the *combined strike plan* should include targets which must be hit in the first strike if the war is to be finished quickly and the damage done to the UK and Western Europe kept as low as possible.'

3. In considering the application of this directive for *co-ordinated* planning it is most important to take full cognisance of the massive weight of strike resources now available for the '*combined* strike' referred to in the latter part of the Chiefs of Staff directive, quoted in the immediately preceding paragraph.

4. In this context, the current co-ordinated Plan, effective from 1 August, 1962, provides for attacks by MBF aircraft and/or Thor missiles on:-

16—Cities, as centres of administration and population (and, of course, of control).
44—'Offensive Capability' Targets i.e. airfields.
10—'Defensive Capability' Targets, e.g. air defence control centres.
28—IRBM's (Selection of these targets is by mutual agreement between Bomber Command and Strategic Air Command and there can be no suggestion of US authorities arbitrarily imposing targets upon the UK strike force. They have been selected to provide the best operational tactical plan).

5. The targets included in current planning fall well within the target systems authorised by the Chiefs of Staff.

6. There has, however, been some change of emphasis between the Bomber Command part in the previous and current co-ordinated plans. The MBF and Thor in the previous plans were directed primarily against cities—48 cities, 6 air defence targets and 3 L.R.A.F. bases. In isolation this could be interpreted as a significant change in the direction of counter-force strategy. However, the co-ordinated plan for all-out retaliation covers the targets previously allotted to Bomber Command. This plan is therefore fully compatible with the Strategic Target Policy which was formulated against the background of the use of massive retaliation and on the assumptions that the Western Powers would not take the initiative and that we would counter actual Soviet aggression.

7. At the same time we know that the Americans have other plans about which we have not been consulted specifically and we are aware that the agreed Bomber Command participation in co-ordinated action would be compatible with all these.

8. There has, however, been no direct suggestion of pre-emptive action in the joint preparation of plans by Bomber Command and SAC. This line has been confirmed in recent discussions between the Ministry of Defence and Mr McNamara.

9. It is none-the-less prudent to have alternate plans; the decision on implementation being clearly a matter for political judgement at the time. Furthermore, should there be disagreement between ourselves and the Americans in the event it would still be possible to direct the Medium Bomber Force to concentrate on centres of administration and population, as in the case of unilateral action, at the same time as the Americans attacked alternative target systems.

10. The co-ordinated plan is re-written once a year, the next revision being due in July, 1963. If there is any change in emphasis which could conflict with the existing COS policy I will, of course, let you know.

Source: TNA, AIR 8/2201, ACAS (ops) to PS VCAS, 5 October 1962.

APPENDIX 4
Nuclear Targetting (1972)

a. It must be capable of inflicting on Soviet Russia a level of damage which Soviet leaders would regard as unacceptable as the price for an aggression on the United Kingdom or her European allies. This level was defined in 1962 as the equivalent of the destruction of the five largest Russian cities. Although we have no reason to doubt the continuing validity of this criterion, we consider that it would now be timely to obtain comment on certain specific points.

b. Our assessment of the likely development of the Soviet defences (taking into account such limitations as may arise from a SAL agreement) leads us to conclude that we shall be unable to maintain this criterion in full unless our strategic nuclear force has the ability to penetrate to and strike certain targets within the Soviet defensive system, by whatever means,and that whatever the development of Soviet defences, this ability to penetrate must ensure for us an ability to strike what the Soviets themselves must regard as crucially worthy of defence. It thus becomes the principal criterion of effectiveness in considering the level of threat we should pose.

Source: TNA, DEFE 13/752, Annex A, COS 45/72, 25 April 1972.

APPENDIX 5

Secret
United States/United Kingdom Agreements in the Military Nuclear Field

1. Since 1958, the United Kingdom nuclear defence programme has been based on the United States/United Kingdom Agreement for Co-operation on the Uses of Atomic Energy for Mutual Defence Purposes (the 1958 Defence Agreement) which provides for exchanges of information, equipment and special nuclear materials. Classified information exchanged under this Agreement has been concerned with all aspects of weapons design, development and production. There have also been extensive transfers of materials and equipment in support of both our nuclear weapons and nuclear propulsion programme. Under the Agreement also certain United States facilities are made available for United Kingdom use, notably the underground nuclear testing facilities in Nevada.

2. We obtained the Polaris weapons system, less the nuclear warheads, from the United States under the 1963 Polaris Sales Agreement and we continue to rely upon this Agreement for the maintenance of the missiles and fire control systems. The Polaris submarines themselves are, however, independent of American support except for the supply until 1980 of enriched uranium for their reactors. Under contracts already agreed we rely, again until 1980, on supplies of other special nuclear materials for our nuclear warhead programme, but thereafter we aim to be self-sufficient in these materials. Our basic nuclear warhead technology is our own, but it is heavily reinforced by information exchanges with the United States under the 1958 Defence Agreement.

3. For the present and foreseeable future, the continuation of the 1958 and 1963 Agreements is of vital importance to us. Our reliance on the Americans will in certain respects be reduced after 1980, but, until much nearer the end of the life of the present Polaris force, we shall need the support provided under the 1963 Agreement. The 1958 Agreement will continue to be essential to us in the event of a CTBT being concluded. Further ahead it is not yet possible to forecast. Our future requirements will depend on what decision is taken about a successor to the Polaris force and on the nature of the system selected. One of our principal aims in relation to the SALT II negotiations has

been to ensure that, to the maximum possible extent, no options for future bilateral co-operation are closed by the terms of any provisions in the United States/Soviet Agreement. This point is covered in the separate brief on SALT.

SECRET

Source: TNA, PREM 19/14, Sir John Hunt to *Prime Minister The Future of the Deterrent*, 4 May 1979.

APPENDIX 6

DASB/B397/81
Brief for the Chief of the Air Staff, 1981

Committee: Presentation of SofS on Strategic Nuclear Targetting
No. & Date of Meeting: Monday 26 October 1981 at 10.30
Material for brief provided by: VCAS
Subject and Paper No: **British Strategic Nuclear Targetting Policy**

1. Following the presentation on British Strategic Nuclear Targetting to your Committee, CDS suggested to SofS a further comprehensive presentation on the principal target options. SofS accepted this recommendation and thus a presentation will be the main item at your meeting on Monday.

2. You will recall that the earlier presentation was very useful and comprehensive. Both the presentation and discussion confirmed that Moscow was the core of the UK deterrent posture. The debate centred around the availability of additional assets accruing from C4 and D5, their use for additional targeting options and the political utility of these wider options.

3. When the minutes of your meeting were published and a draft submission prepared, it became apparent that the agreed line was open to slightly different interpretations in respect of the launch of additional missiles against additional targets.

4. In clearing the submission the main issue of contention was reference to 'a single target list'. Implicit in the reference was CNS's contention that the employment of a single list ie Moscow plus, involved a 'one-button-push', simultaneously to release all the assets. A further issue was an AFD proposal to incorporate reference to the prospective but in extremis use of the Tornado in a strategic role.

5. CDS considered that the revised submission still did not meet the requirements adequately to represent the consensus of opinion of your Committee and therefore circulated his own re-draft. This re-draft still incorporated reference to 'a single target list'. Following AFD representations the word 'single' was deleted from the final submission.

6. You will note that reference to the Tornado was not incorporated. Doubtless you will wish to make reference to the Tornado's strategic capability in the critical situation of a UK nuclear confrontation with the Soviet Union. Indeed you may

wish to emphasise that it would be an ideal weapon system to demonstrate resolve against military targets.

7. On the main issues, you may wish to confirm that Moscow must remain our core criterion and that we should preserve assets to meet the requirement. With the improved accuracy of the new systems we should plan to attack specific key areas rather than built up areas as a whole. Additional assets should be targeted in accordance with an agreed priority list. Release of weapons to targets should not irrevocably be linked to a single push-of-a button: options must be made available. Finally, the impression we give to the Soviet Union is vitally important and therefore it could degrade our deterrent posture if any lesser options were made public.

(R.A. Miller)
Group Captain
DASB

23rd October 1981

UK Eyes A
Top Secret

Source: AIR 8/2846, DASB/B397/81 Brief for the Chief of the Air Staff, 23 October 1981.

APPENDIX 7

Top Secret
Annex C
Anglo-American Understandings on Nuclear Release Procedures: President–Prime Minister Correspondence

1. The most recent reaffirmation of the personal understandings between President and Prime Minister about consultation on the use of nuclear weapons was given in the exchange of letters on 27 February 1981 between President Reagan and Mrs Thatcher. The full texts of their letters, together with the Memorandum of Understanding to which they refer, are attached as appendices.

2. The original version of the Memorandum of Understanding was enclosed with a letter of 6 February 1961 from President Kennedy to Mr Macmillan summarising the various understandings in existence at that time. Since then it has been the practise for the Prime Minister of the day to seek reaffirmation of the Memorandum whenever the office of President or Prime Minister has changed hands. Thus, its reaffirmation was sought by Sir Alec Douglas-Home from President Johnson on 20 December 1963, and given by the President on 28 February 1964. It was sought again by Mr Wilson on 8 December 1964 and was given the same day by President Johnson, and again in 1969 after President Nixon assumed office. It was sought by Mr Heath from President Nixon on 7 April 1971, and was given by the President on 4 May 1971. It was sought again by Mr Wilson on 16 December 1974 and given by President Ford on 9 January 1975. On 30 July 1976 Mr Callaghan sought a reaffirmation from President Ford which was given on 1 September 1976. Mr Callaghan exchanged letters of reaffirmation with President Carter on 4 March 1977. Mrs Thatcher did so on 25 June 1979.

3. The Memorandum was amended in 1965 by an exchange of letters between the Prime Minister and President Johnson to provide for joint decision prior to the release of United States nuclear depth bombs stored in the United Kingdom for use in emergency by United States and British maritime aircraft assigned to SACLANT.

4. Redacted under Section 3(4) of the Public Records Act.

5. Further amendments to the Memorandum were made necessary following Mr Heath's agreement, in a letter of 7 April 1971 to President Nixon, to the use of Holy Loch by United States Poseidon submarines on the same basis as their Polaris sister ships. In his letter of 4 May 1971 to Mr Heath, President Nixon confirmed that the Understandings in the Memorandum would apply with respect to Poseidon submarines 'In the same manner and to the same extent as with respect to Polaris submarines'.

6. A further amendment to the memorandum was made in the 1975 exchange of letters between President Ford and Mr Wilson. This amendment removed a possible ambiguity in earlier versions of the memorandum by specifying that all United States forces operating from land bases in the United Kingdom or in United Kingdom territorial waters are covered by the requirement for a joint decision by the Prime Minister and the President.

7. A further amendment to the memorandum was made in the 1977 exchange of letters between President Carter and Mr Callaghan. This amendment reflected more accurately the present position regarding nuclear weapons for Royal Air Force aircraft. Finally at the time of the 1981 reaffirmation between Mr Reagan and Mrs Thatcher, it was agreed by means of side letters from Sir Robert Armstrong to Mr MacFarlane that the arrangements for joint decision would apply to the cruise missiles to be based in this country. This was subsequently reflected in the Wright-Eagleburger agreement, signed on 17 May 1983.

Source: TNA, CAB 196/124-1, Robert Armstrong to *Prime Minister Nuclear Release Procedures and Related Matters*, Strictly for the Personal Information and Use of the Prime Minister *Warning: This paper is to be seen only by CLARET indoctrinated personnel*, Annex C. Anglo-American Understandings on Nuclear Release Procedures: President-Prime Minister Correspondence, June 1983.

APPENDIX 8

Main Committees Dealing with Nuclear Weapons Issues in the 1940s and 1950s

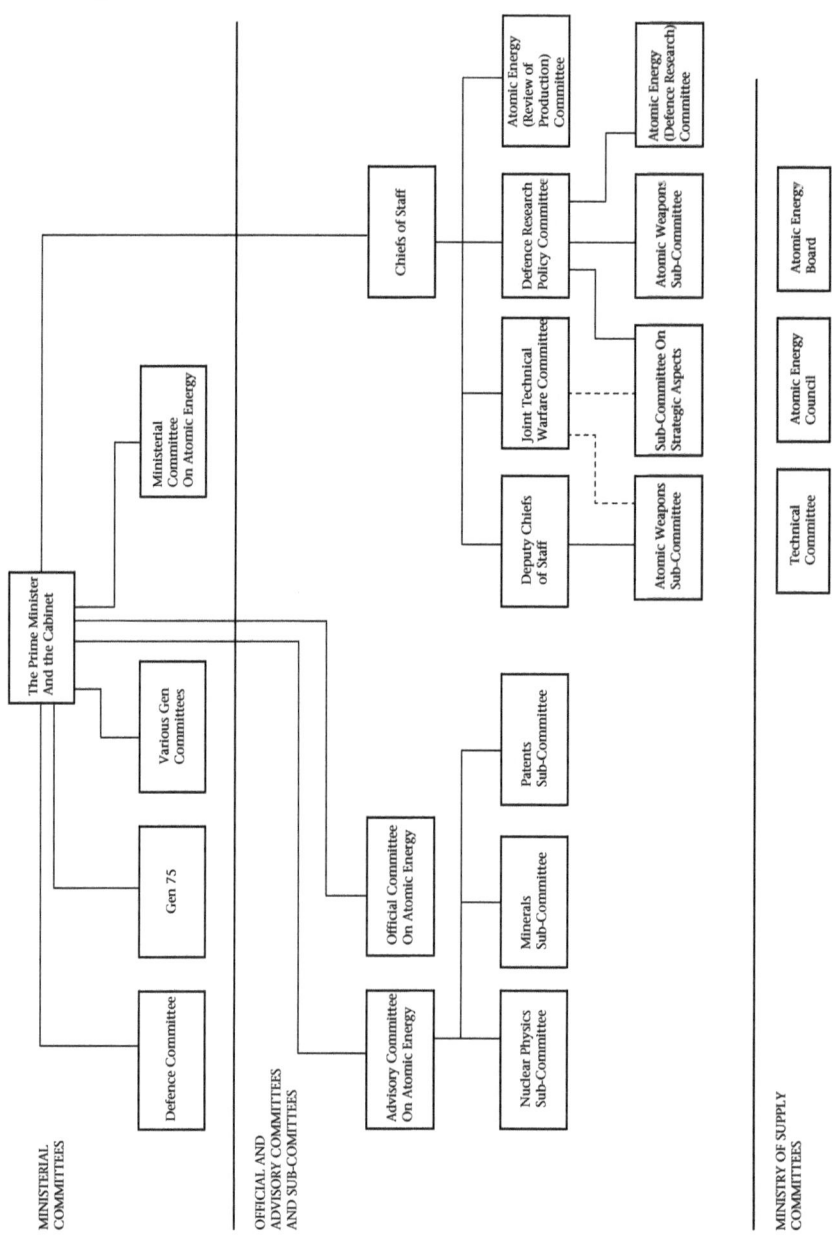

Appendices

1. *Gen 75*. A small group of Cabinet Ministers who met between August 1945 and December 1946 to discuss atomic weapons.
2. *Gen Committees*. Consisting of a small number of again with a small number of Cabinet Ministers who met between 1947 and 1952. Later known as *Misc Committees*.
3. *Defence Research Policy Committee*. This Committee was set up in January 1947 to advise Ministers and the Chiefs of Staff on scientific policy in the defence field.
4. *Joint Technical Warfare Committee* advised COS on the strategic aspects of atomic energy.
5. *Atomic Energy (Defence Research) Committee*. Set up in January 1948 to advise the Defence Research Policy Committee on the links between defence research programmes and atomic energy defence research.
6. *Atomic Energy Review (Review of Production) Committee*. Set up in January 1948 to report to the COS on the scale of atomic energy production with respect to defence requirements.
7. *Advisory Committee on Atomic Energy* (sometimes known as the Anderson Committee after its Chairman). It met between September 1945 and December 1947 to advise the government on the development of atomic energy for both civil and military programmes and international aspects of atomic energy.
8. *Official Committee on Atomic Energy*. This Committee met between August 1947 and September 1957 and was responsible for considering issues relating to atomic energy which required discussions between various government departments.
9. *Atomic Weapons Sub-Committee*. This was set up in 1945 to report to the Deputy COS on use of atomic Energy in the development of weapons. It became a *Defence Research Policy Committee Sub-Committee* in 1947.
10. *Technical Committee*. This Committee met between March 1946 and March 1956 under the auspices of the Ministry of Supply to advise on the atomic energy project. It contained many eminent scientists and engineers.
11. *Atomic Energy Council*. The Council met between March 1946 and October 1951 again as part of the Ministry of Supply oversight of atomic energy.
12. *Atomic Energy Board*. This Board replaced the *Atomic Energy Council* in October 1951.

The diagram and notes are based on a diagram contained in Margaret Gowing's book *Independence and Deterrence: Britain and Atomic Energy 1945–1952, Volume 1: Policy Making*, (London: Macmillan, 1974), pp. 58–9.

Endnotes

Introduction

1. Address by General George Lee Butler, (formerly Commander-in-Chief, US Strategic Air Command), at the National Press Club, 2 February 1998.
2. These include Lorna Arnold, *Britain and the H-Bomb* (Basingstoke: Palgrave, 2001); Brian Cathcart, *The Test of Greatness: Britain's Struggle for the Atom Bomb* (London: John Murray, 1994); John Baylis, *Ambiguity and Deterrence: British Nuclear Strategy 1945–1964* (Oxford: Oxford University Press, 1995); Ian Clark, *Nuclear Diplomacy and the Special Relationship: Britain's Deterrent and America 1957–1962* (Oxford: Clarendon Press, 1994); Ian Clark and Nicholas J. Wheeler, *The British Origins of Nuclear Strategy 1945–55* (Oxford: Clarendon Press, 1989); Lawrence Freedman, *Britain and Nuclear Weapons* (London: Macmillan, 1980); Margaret Gowing, *Britain and Atomic Energy 1939–45* (London: Macmillan, 1964); Margaret Gowing (assisted by Lorna Arnold), *Independence and Deterrence: Britain and Atomic Energy 1945–52* (2 Vols, London: Macmillan, 1974); A.J.R. Groom, *British Thinking about Nuclear Weapons* (London: Pinter, 1974); Peter Malone, *The British Nuclear Deterrent: A History* (London: Croom Helm, 1984); Richard Moore, *Nuclear Illusion, Nuclear Reality: Britain, the United States and Nuclear Weapons, 1958–64* (Basingstoke: Palgrave, 2010); Martin Navias, *Nuclear Weapons and British Strategic Planning 1955–58* (Oxford: Clarendon Press, 1991); Andrew Pierre, *Nuclear Politics: The British Experience with an Independent Strategic Force 1939–1970* (London: Oxford University Press, 1972); Richard N. Rosecrance, *Defense of the Realm: British Strategy in the Nuclear Epoch* (New York: Columbia University Press, 1968); John Simpson, *The Independent Nuclear State: The United States, Britain and the Military Atom* (London: Macmillan, 1983); Kristan Stoddart, *Losing an Empire and Finding a Role: Britain, the USA, NATO and Nuclear Weapons, 1964–70* (London: Palgrave, 2012). *The Sword and Shield: Britain, America, NATO, and Nuclear Weapons, 1970–1976* (Basingstoke: Palgrave, 2014) and *Facing Down the Soviet Union: Britain, the USA, NATO and Nuclear Weapons, 1976–1983* (Basingstoke: Palgrave, 2014).
3. See Judith Goldstein and Robert Keohane (eds), *Ideas and Foreign Policy* (Ithaca: Cornell University Press, 1993). For a detailed outline of constructivist theory, see Nicholas Onuf, *World of our Making* (South Carolina: University of South Carolina, 1989); Alexander Wendt, *Social Theory of International Politics* (Cambridge: Cambridge University Press, 1999); and J. Checkel, 'The Constructivist Turn in International Relations Theory', *World Politics* 50:2 (January 1998). Buzan and Hansen draw a distinction between 'Conventional Constructivism' and 'Critical Constructivism'. They argue that 'Conventional Constructivism' locates itself

Endnotes

within 'traditional, narrow definition of security studies', in which the task is to take the 'hard case' of national, military, state-centric security, but to explain it through the role of ideas and beliefs rather than material factors. It is distinguished from 'Critical Constructivism', which analyses 'discourses and the linkages between the historical and discursive constitution of identities on the one hand and security policies on the other'. See Barry Buzan and Lene Hansen, *The Evolution of International Security Studies* (Cambridge: Cambridge University Press, 2009), pp. 192–200. See also P. J. Katzenstein (ed.), *The Culture of National Security: Norms and Identity in World Politics* (New York: Columbia University Press, 1996), and William J. Long and Suzette T. Grillot, 'Ideas, Beliefs and Nuclear Policies: The Cases of South Africa and Ukraine', *The Nonproliferation Review*, Spring 2000, and <http://cns.miis.edu/npr/pdfs/long71.pdf>.
4. Ole R. Holsti, *The Belief System and National Images: John Foster Dulles and the Soviet Union* (Stanford: Stanford University Press, 1962). For a critical discussion of 'belief systems' and 'belief clusters' see Beatrice Heuser *Nuclear Mentalities? Strategies and Belief Systems in Britain, France and the FRG* (London: Macmillan, 1998).
5. R. Lane, *Political Man* (New York: The Free Press, 1972), p. 161.
6. See J. Vogler, 'Perspectives on the Foreign Policy System: Psychological Approaches', in Michael Clarke and Brian White (eds), *Understanding Foreign Policy: The Foreign Policy Systems Approach* (London: Edward Elgar, 1989).
7. Steve Smith and Martin Hollis, 'Roles and Reasons in Foreign Policy Decision Making', *British Journal of Political Science*, 16/3 (1986), pp. 269–86.
8. Alexander George, 'The Causal Nexus between Cognitive Beliefs and Decision-Making: The "Operational Code" Belief System', in L. Falkowski (ed.), *Psychological Models in International Politics* (Boulder, Col.: Westview Press, 1979), pp. 95–104.
9. Robert Jervis, *The Illogic of American Nuclear Strategy* (Ithaca: Cornell University Press, 1984).
10. Michael Quinlan, *Thinking about Nuclear Weapons: Principles, Problems, Prospects* (Oxford: Oxford University Press, 2009), pp. 13–14. Michael Quinlan had a long and distinguished career in the Civil Service. He was an administrative generalist in the Air Ministry in the 1950s, dealing with issues related to the V-Bomber force. From 1962 to 1965 he was Private Secretary to successive holders of the post of Chief of the Air Staff and from 1968 to 1970 he was a member of the Defence Policy Staff which worked on NATO nuclear policy. From 1970 to 1973 he was Defence Counsellor in the UK delegation to NATO. After a spell away from the MOD he returned in 1977 to the post of Policy Director dealing with NATO and national nuclear weapon policy. From 1981 to 1988 once again he was out of the nuclear field but remained involved in the key debates of the period, and in 1988 he returned as Permanent Under-Secretary of State in the MOD, the senior non-political civilian appointment. He remained in this position until 1992 when he retired. Even then he remained an important figure in high-level debates about nuclear strategy.
11. Quinlan, *Thinking about Nuclear Weapons*.
12. Nicholas J. Wheeler, 'The Roles Played by the British Chiefs of Staff Committee in the Evolution of Britain's Nuclear Weapons Planning and Policy Making, 1945–55' (PhD thesis, University of Southampton, 1988), pp. 411–12.

13. P. Sabatier, 'An Advocacy Coalition Framework of Policy Change and the Role of Policy Oriented Learning Therein', *Policy Sciences*, 2 (1988).
14. Martin Ceadel, *Thinking about Peace and War* (Oxford: Oxford University Press, 1989), pp. 72–3.
15. William Walker, *A Perpetual Menace: Nuclear Weapons and International Order* (London: Routledge, 2012).
16. T. Geiger and R.D. Hansen, 'The Role of Information on Decision-Making in Foreign Aid', in R.A. Bauer and K.J. Gergen (eds), *The Study of Policy Formation* (New York: The Free Press, 1968).
17. Jack Snyder, *The Soviet Strategic Culture: Implications for Limited Nuclear Operations* (Santa Monica, Calif.: RAND, R-2154-AF, September 1977).
18. Jack Snyder, 'The Concept of Strategic Culture: Caveat Emptor', in C.G. Jacobsen (ed.), *Strategic Power: USA/USSR* (Basingstoke: Macmillan, 1990).
19. Ken Booth, 'The Concept of Strategic Culture Affirmed', in C.G. Jacobsen, K. Booth, and D.R. Jones, *Strategic Power: USA/USSR* (London: Macmillan, 1990), p. 121.
20. Jeannie L. Johnson, Kerry M. Kartchner, and Jeffrey A. Larsen (eds), *Strategic Culture and Weapons of Mass Destruction: Culturally Based Insights into Comparative National Security Policymaking* (Basingstoke: Palgrave, 2009). For a discussion of the relationship between military culture and strategic culture, see Alastair Finlan, *Contemporary Military Culture and Strategic Studies: US and UK Armed Forces in the 21st Century* (Abingdon: Routledge, 2013).
21. Colin S. Gray, 'Strategic Culture as Context: The First Generation of Theory Strikes Back', *International Studies*, Vol. 25, (January 1999), p. 58.
22. David G. Haglund, 'What Good is Strategic Culture', *International Journal* (Summer 2004).
23. 'Cognition' is usually defined as an act or experience of knowing or acquiring knowledge.
24. Haglund, 'What Good is Strategic Culture', p. 502.
25. Richard Ned Lebow, *A Cultural Theory of International Relations* (Cambridge: Cambridge University Press, 2008).
26. Lebow, *A Cultural Theory of International Relations*, p. 24.
27. Lebow, *A Cultural Theory of International Relations*, p. 562.
28. See Alexander Wendt, *Social Theory of International Politics* (Cambridge: Cambridge University Press, 1999) and 'Collective Identity Formation and the International State', *American Political Science Review* 88:2, June 1994.
29. Jacques E.C. Hymans, *The Psychology of Nuclear Proliferation: Identity, Emotions and Foreign Policy* (Cambridge: Cambridge University Press, 2006).
30. Hymans, *Psychology of Nuclear Proliferation*, p. 1.
31. Michael MccGwire, 'Comfort Blanket or Weapon of War: what is Trident for?', *International Affairs*, 82:4 (June 2006), p. 644.
32. Nick Ritchie, *Trident and British Identity: Letting Go of Nuclear Weapons* (Bradford Disarmament Research Centre Paper, 2008).
33. Ritchie, *Trident and British Identity*, p. 5. For a detailed discussion of the scientific developments leading up to the Frisch-Peierls Memorandum and subsequent developments by the scientists supporting the Maud Committee see M. Gowing, *Britain and Atomic Energy*, 1939–1945 (London: Macmillan, 1964), pp. 3–89.
34. Pierre, *Nuclear Politics*, p. 303.

Endnotes

35. Scott D. Sagan 'Why Do States Build Nuclear Weapons? Three Models in Search of a Bomb', *International Security*, Vol. 21, No. 3, (Winter 1996–7).
36. Robert Jervis, 'The Symbolic Nature of Nuclear Politics', in R. Jervis, *The Meaning of the Nuclear Revolution* (Ithaca, NY: Cornell University Press, 1989).
37. The six scientists were G.P Thomson, Mark Oliphant, P.M.S. Blackett, James Chadwick, P.B. Moon, and J.D. Cockcroft. 'Maud' was a codename designed to obscure the work of the Committee. For the origins of this name, see L. Arnold and M. Smith, *Britain, Australia and the Bomb: The Nuclear Test and their Aftermath* (London: Palgrave, 2006), p. 293. The title was the result of a mistaken understanding of correspondence between Niels Bohr and Otto Frisch. This source also has a very good explanation of the importance of the Frisch-Peierls Memorandum, produced in the spring of 1940, which first explained the method needed to separate uranium-235 and the possibility of producing an atomic weapon.
38. Their estimate was that the material for the first bomb could be ready by 1943.
39. See Gowing, *Independence and Deterrence*, pp. 2–4.
40. <http://www.atomicarchive.com>.
41. The Maud Report was shown to Vannevar Bush, the primary military research adviser to President Roosevelt and James Conant, the new head of the National Defense Research Committee in the US. It was they who initiated the further studies which led to the Manhattan Project.
42. Arnold and Smith, *Britain, Australia and the Bomb*, p. 3. For a detailed discussion of British involvement in the Manhattan Project and the wide ranging Anglo-Canadian atomic collaboration during the Second World War see M. Gowing, *Britain and Atomic Energy 1939–1945* (London: Macmillan, 1964).
43. Arnold and Smith, *Britain, Australia and the Bomb*, p. 3.
44. Graham Farmelo, *Churchill's Bomb: A Hidden History of Science, War and Politics* (London: Faber, 2014).
45. Arnold and Smith, *Britain, Australia and the Bomb*, p. 3.
46. Quoted in *The Telegraph*, 2 October 2011. See Jeremy Paxman, *Empire: What Ruling the World Did to the British* (London: Viking, 2011). Paxman also argues that one of the legacies of Empire was a sense of superiority.
47. Quinlan, *Thinking about Nuclear Weapons*, p. 115.

Chapter 1

* Hennessey, Peter, *Cabinet's and the Bomb*. (Oxford: Oxford University Press, 2007).
** Hennessey, Peter, *Cabinet's and the Bomb*. (Oxford: Oxford University Press, 2007).
1. See TNA, AIR 41/87; Humphrey Wynn, *The RAF Strategic Nuclear Deterrent Forces: Their Origins, Roles and Deployment 1946–1969: A Documentary History* (London: Her Majesty's Stationary Office, 1994).
2. TNA, ADM 1/117259, Director of Plans, 2 Sept. 1945.
3. TNA, ADM 1/117259, ACNS (W), 15 Aug. 1945.
4. Rear Admiral H. G. Thursfield, 'The Lessons of the War', *Brassey's Annual* (London, 1946).
5. P. M. S. Blackett, 'Atomic Energy: An Immediate Policy for Great Britain'. Memorandum reproduced in Gowing, *Independence and Deterrence*, i. pp. 194–206. See also

P. M. S. Blackett, *Fear, War and the Bomb: Military and Political Consequences of Atomic Energy* (New York: McGraw-Hill, 1949).
6. Andrew Pierre, *Nuclear Politics*, pp. 72–3.
7. TNA, AIR 75/119, Slessor Papers, XIVA, 'Comments on Tizard Report', AMP (Slessor) to VCAS, 16 Jul. 1945.
8. Quoted in TNA, AIR 41/87, 'The RAF Strategic Nuclear Deterrent Forces', p. 8.
9. 'Letter from Mr Attlee to President Truman, 25 September 1945'. Reproduced in Gowing, *Independence and Deterrence*, i. pp. 78–81.
10. 'Letter from Mr Attlee to President Truman, 25 September', pp. 78–81.
11. 'Letter from Mr Attlee to President Truman, 25 September'.
12. Hansard, H. C. Deb., vol. 416, cols. 601–8, 22 Nov. 1945.
13. For a discussion of the distinction between 'idealist' and 'realist' thinking, see E. H. Carr, *The Twenty Years Crisis* (Basingstoke: Macmillan, 1981).
14. TNA, CAB 130/3, Gen 75/1.
15. 'Letter from Mr Attlee to President Truman', in Gowing, *Independence and Deterrence*, i. pp. 78–81.
16. TNA, CAB 130/2, Gen 75, 4th mtg., 11 Oct. 1945. Gen 75 consisted of a small group of trusted Cabinet ministers which was formed on an ad hoc basis to discuss atomic weapons. See Gowing, *Independence and Deterrence*, i. p. 21.
17. Gowing, *Independence and Deterrence*, i. p. 67.
18. TNA, PREM 8/111, Tube Alloys file 11, Ancam 420, 18 Sept. 1945.
19. TNA, CAB 128/2. CM(45)51, Confidential Annex.
20. Gowing, *Independence and Deterrence*, i. p. 67.
21. TNA, CAB 104/285, Drafts on File 59, pt. 1.
22. TNA, CAB 130/3, Gen 75/1.
23. Gowing, *Independence and Deterrence*, i. p. 72.
24. Gowing, *Independence and Deterrence*, i. p. 67.
25. 'Washington Declaration, 15 November 1945', Gowing, *Independence and Deterrence*, i. pp. 82–4.
26. Gowing, *Independence and Deterrence*, i. pp. 82–4.
27. 'The "Groves-Anderson" Memorandum, 16 November 1945'; See Gowing, *Independence and Deterrence*, i. pp. 85–6.
28. Gowing, *Independence and Deterrence*, i. p. 77.
29. Quoted in TNA, AIR 41/87, 'The RAF Strategic Deterrent Forces', p. 9.
30. Quoted in TNA, AIR 41/87, 'The RAF Strategic Deterrent Forces', p. 9.
31. TNA, AIR 41/87, 'The RAF Strategic Deterrent Forces', p. 1.
32. Sir Henry Tizard was a chemist by training who, before the war, had been Rector of Imperial College. In the war he chaired the Aeronautical Research Committee and led the development of radar and other major defence projects. He was also involved in the 'Tube Alloys' project which lead to the work on the atomic bomb. After the war he remained a senior scientific administrator in the defence establishment.
33. TNA, AIR 41/87, pp. 1–2.
34. TNA, AIR, 41/87, p. 2.
35. TNA, ADM 1/117259, 'Effect of the Atomic Bomb on Warfare', DNOR, 4 Sept. 1945.
36. TNA, ADM 1/117259, 'Influence of Atomic Bomb on War', Appendix to Admiral (Submarines). Letter no. SM.0311/383 dated 4 Sept. 1945.

Endnotes

37. TNA, PREM 8/116, 'Hollis to Prime Minister', 10 Oct. 1945.
38. TNA, AIR 20/7063, 'The RAF in 1956'. Report by the Future Planning Staff, 6 Feb. 1947.
39. TNA, CAB 82/26, DCOS (AWC) (46), 1, 30 Jan. 1946.
40. TNA, CAB, 82/26.
41. TNA, DEFE 4/3, COS (47) 57th mtg., 23 Apr. 1947.
42. TNA, DEFE 4/3.
43. Bernard Brodie, *The Absolute Weapon* (New York: Harcourt Brace, 1946). Quoted in Lawrence Freedman, *The Evolution of Nuclear Strategy* (London: Macmillan, 1981), p. 144 (our emphasis).
44. Ian Clark and Nicholas J. Wheeler, *The British Origins of Nuclear Strategy*, p. 47.
45. TNA, AIR 41/87, 'The RAF Strategic Nuclear Deterrent Forces', p. 17.
46. TNA, PREM 8/115, Jacob to Attlee, 12 Nov. 1945.
47. TNA, PREM 8/115.
48. Gowing, *Independence and Deterrence*, i. p. 188.
49. TNA, AIR 41/87, 'The RAF Strategic Nuclear Deterrent Forces,' p. 8.
50. TNA, AIR 41/87, p. 18 (author's emphasis).
51. Gowing, *Independence and Deterrence*, i. p. 183.
52. Gowing, *Independence and Deterrence*, i. p. 184.
53. Quoted in Brian Cathcart, *Test of Greatness*, p. 21.
54. Cathcart, *Test of Greatness*, p. 25.
55. Hansard H. C. Deb., Vol. 437, col. 1965 (16 May 1947).
56. Gowing, *Independence and Deterrence*, i. p. 28.
57. Gowing, *Independence and Deterrence*, i. p. 45.
58. Gowing, *Independence and Deterrence*, i. p. 34.
59. Quoted in Nigel Hamilton, *Monty: The Field Marshal 1944–1976* (London: Hamish Hamilton, 1986), p. 645.
60. TNA, CAB 81/95, PHP, (44) 27 (O), 9 Nov. 1944.
61. TNA, CAB 66/53, WP (44) 409, 25 Jul. 1944.
62. The 'security dilemma' reflects the problem of one state building up its defence forces because of fear of the military forces of another state, only to thereby cause that state to further build up its own forces. The developments of both states may be defensive, but they perceive each other's actions as offensive.
63. TNA, FO 371/50912, 'Stock-taking After V-E Day', 11 Jul. 1945.
64. TNA, FO 371/55581, 2 Apr. 1946.
65. TNA, FO 371/67579, 21 and 29 May 1947.
66. TNA, COS (47) 102 (O), 'Overall Strategic Plan, May 1947' and DO (47) 44. The plan is retained by the Cabinet Office but is reproduced in John Baylis, *The Diplomacy of Pragmatism: Britain and the Formation of NATO 1942–49* (Basingstoke: Macmillan, 1993), pp. 134–49. See CAB 131/2, DO (46) 47, 2 Apr. 1946 and CAB 133/86 PMM (46) 1, 20 Apr. 1946.
67. TNA, CAB 131/2, DO (46) 47, 2 Apr. 1946.
68. TNA, CAB 21/2086, DO (46) 10th. Mtg., 5 Apr. 1946 and CAB 21/2086, COS (46) 108th mtg., 12 Jul. 1946.
69. TNA, CAB 21/2086, DO (46) 10th mtg., 5 Apr. 1946.
70. Clark and Wheeler, *The British Origins of Nuclear Strategy*, pp. 91–111.

Endnotes

71. Apart from the research establishment at Harwell, the Atomic Weapons Research Establishment, Aldermaston, was responsible for the assembly of atomic bombs; a uranium metal factory had been set up at Springfields, a plutonium production pile had been built at Windscale, and work on the design of bombs was carried out at Fort Halstead.
72. Quoted in Gowing, *Independence and Deterrence*, pp. 78—81.
73. Tanya Ogilvie-White, *On Nuclear Deterrence: The Correspondence of Sir Michael Quinlan*, (Abingdon: Routledge, 2011), p. 49.
74. TNA, CAB 128/9, CM (47) 13, 28 Jan. 1947.

Chapter 2

1. *Nuclear Politics* (London: Oxford University Press, 1972), p. 87.
2. See Ian Clark and Nicholas J. Wheeler, *British Origins of Nuclear Strategy 1945–1955* (Oxford: Clarendon, 1989), (note 1), Ch. 3.
3. TNA, PREM 8/116, p. 130, Gen. Sir Leslie Hollis to PM (Attlee), 10 Oct. 1945.
4. The 1947 Overall Strategic Plan was first published in John Lewis, *Changing Direction: British Military Planning for Post-war Strategic Defence, 1942–1947* (London: Sherwood Press, 1988). It is also reproduced in John Baylis, *The Diplomacy of Pragmatism: Britain and the Formation of NATO, 1942–1949* (London: Macmillan, 1993). See TNA, DO(47)44, May 1947. Hereafter references will be to 1947 OSP.
5. See TNA, PREM 8/117, ACAE(45)11, FO Memo on international background to atomic energy. 11 Sept. 1945; CAB 134/6, ACAE(45) 2nd, 20 Sept. 1945; DEFE 4/1, COS(47) 1st, Confidential Annex, 'Imperial Defence College—General Policy', 1 Jan. 1947; CAB 84/79, JP(46)36 (Final), 27 Feb. 1946; CAB 131/2, DO(46)47. 'Strategic Position of the British Commonwealth', 2 April 1946; and CAB 130/2, GEN 75/7th, 1 Nov. 1945. See also Clark and Wheeler (note 1), pp. 21–2 and pp. 71–2.
6. 1947, OSP, para. 29.
7. TNA, CAB 131/9, DO(50)45, Report by the Chiefs of Staff on 'Defence Policy and Global Strategy', 7 June 1950. Hereafter referred to as 1950 GSP.
8. 1950, GSP, paras 13(c) and 58.
9. See Gowing, *Independence and Deterrence*, i, (note 2), p. 232.
10. 1950, GSP, para. 18.
11. See Clark and Wheeler, *British Origins of Nuclear Strategy*, p. 156, and Richard N. Rosecrance, *Defense of the Realm: British Strategy in the Nuclear Epoch* (New York and London: Columbia University Press, 1968), p. 162.
12. See Clark and Wheeler, *British Origins of Nuclear Strategy*, p. 162; Gowing, *Independence and Deterrence*, i. p. 413; and Rosecrance, *Defense of the Realm*, p. 158.
13. See Eric J. Grove, *Vanguard to Trident: British Naval Policy Since World War Two* (London: Bodley Head, 1987), p. 82. This followed the precedent set in 1950, when the COS met at Bracknell during their defence review. See Sir John Slessor, *The Central Blue: Recollections and Reflections* (London: Cassell, 1956), p. 436.
14. Grove, *Vanguard to Trident*, p. 83, and Rosecrance, *Defense of the Realm*, (note 1), pp. 164 and 171.
15. Anthony Seldon has argued that the significance of the 1952 Paper has been exaggerated: see Anthony Seldon, *Churchill's Indian Summer: The Conservative*

Endnotes

Government, 1951–5 (London: Hodder & Stoughton, 1981), p. 332. Its importance is accepted, but its innovatory nature is challenged, by Clark and Wheeler (*British Origins of Nuclear Strategy*, (note 1), p. 170). On the other hand it is regarded as a 'classic' by Andrew Pierre (*Nuclear Politics*, p. 87), borrowing the words of C.J.V. Murphy, 'A New Strategy for NATO', *Fortune* (Jan. 1953), p. 80.

16. Andrew Pierre, *Nuclear Politics*, p. 87, and Clark and Wheeler, *British Origins of Nuclear Strategy*, (note 1), p. 170.
17. Andrew Pierre, *Nuclear Politics*, p. 87.
18. See Alastair Buchan, 'Their Bomb and Ours', *Encounter* 12/1 (1959), p. 16; A.J.R. Groom, *British Thinking About Nuclear Weapon* (London: Pinter, 1974), p. 58; Samuel P. Huntington, *The Common Defence* (New York: Columbia University Press, 1961), p. 118; Pierre, *Nuclear Politics*, pp. 87–8; Rosecrance, *Defense of the Realm*, p. 171; Sir John Slessor, *The Great Deterrent* (London: Cassell, 1957), p. 304.
19. TNA, CAB 131./12. D(52)26, 'Defence Policy and Global Strategy', report by the Chiefs of Staff, 17 June 1952, para. 1. Hereafter references will be to the 1952 GSP.
20. See the documents of the Post-Hostilities Planning Staff, discussed in John Baylis, *The Diplomacy of Pragmatism: Britain and the Formation of NATO, 1942–49*, (Basingstoke: Macmillan, 1993), (note 12), pp. 20–30.
21. 1947, OSP, para. 13.
22. 1952, GSP, front page.
23. 1952, GSP, para. 1.
24. 1952, GSP, para. 6.
25. 1952, GSP, para. 7.
26. 1952, GSP, para. 9.
27. 1952, GSP, para. 10.
28. 1952, GSP, para. 14.
29. 1952, GSP, paras 72 and 123–4.
30. See PRO CAB I29/49, 'The Report of the Temporary Council Committee of the North Atlantic Council', 19 Feb. 1952.
31. The text of NSC68 is published in T.H. Etzold and J. Lewis Gaddis (eds), *Containment: Documents on American Policy and Strategy, 1945–1950* (NY: Columbia UP, 1978), pp. 385–442.
32. 1952, GSP, para. 16.
33. 1952, GSP, paras 15 and 17.
34. 1952, GSP, para. 72.
35. 1952, GSP, front page.
36. 1952, GSP, para. 2; see also 1950, GSP, para. 4.
37. 1950, GSP, para. 37.
38. 1952, GSP, paras 2 and 23.
39. See US National Archives (USNA), SG 13/10: Intelligence Guidance for North Atlantic Regional Planning, 27 Dec. 1949, P&O 381 Europe S (Section 111)(case 41), P&OTS 1949–1950 Files, RG319.
40. 1950, GSP, para. 11; see also 1952, GSP, para. 22.
41. 1952, GSP, paras 19–20.
42. 1952, GSP, para. 7.

43. 1952, GSP, para. 26.
44. 1952, GSP, para. 26.
45. See Robert Wampler, *Ambiguous Legacy: The United States, Great Britain and the Foundations of NATO Strategy, 1948–1957* (Harvard University PhD, 1991), note 9, pp. 324–56.
46. 1952, GSP, paras 26 and 36.
47. 1952, GSP, para. 37.
48. 1952, GSP, para. 36.
49. For a detailed analysis of Anglo-American discussions over the 1952 Paper and Alliance strategy, see Robert Wampler, *Ambiguous Legacy*, pp. 293–370.
50. 1952, GSP, para. 60.
51. 1952, GSP, para. 44.
52. See Lt.-Gen. Foulkes, 'Notes on Discussion with General Bradley', 15 Sept. 1952. USNA, RG2, Series 18. Vol. 223, File 1-60-1, CPA. 5.
53. 1952, GSP, para. 37.
54. 1952, GSP, para. 38.
55. 1952, GSP, para. 38.
56. 1952, GSP, para. 71(e).
57. 1950, GSP, paras 6 and 13(b).
58. 1952, GSP, para. 96.
59. 1952, GSP, para. 92.
60. See Alan Macmillan, 'British Atomic Strategy 1945–52' in John Baylis and Alan Macmillan (eds), *The Foundations of British Nuclear Strategy, 1945–1960*. International Politics Research Paper No.12, (Dept. of International Politics, University College of Wales, Aberystwyth, in association with the Nuclear History Program, 1992), pp. 42–5; and Clark and Wheeler, *The British Origins of Nuclear Strategy*, note 1, Ch. 4.
61. See Macmillan, *Riding the Storm*, pp. 51–2.
62. 1952, GSP, para. 96.
63. 1952, GSP, para. 101.
64. 1952, GSP, para. 92.
65. 1952, GSP, para. 94.
66. Fuchs was a theoretical physicist who was convicted of supplying nuclear information to the Soviet Union in 1950. He had worked on the Manhattan Project in the Second World War and had worked on both the atomic and hydrogen projects after the war.
67. Margaret Gowing questions whether the Fuchs betrayal was decisive in the failure to reach an agreement. See Gowing, *Independence and Deterrence*, i, note 2, p. 442.
68. 1952, GSP, para. 41; see also and compare with 1950, GSP, paras 16–17.
69. 1952, GSP, para. 41.
70. 1952, GSP, paras 7(1) and 42.
71. TNA, COS(52)361, Note to the Secretary, Chiefs of Staff 'Report on Defence Policy and Global Strategy', 15 July 1952, which is available in DEFE 5/40.
72. It is interesting to note that in 1995 the government remained even more sensitive about releasing information on chemical and bacteriological warfare than information on the use of atomic weapons.
73. 1952, GSP, paras 26–7 and 29.
74. 1952, GSP, para. 32.

Endnotes

75. See, for example Clark and Wheeler, *British Origins of Nuclear Strategy*, note 1, pp. 171–3; Grove, *Vanguard to Trident*, note 3, p. 85; and Rosecrance, *Defense of the Realm*, note 1, pp. 161–2.
76. It is interesting that the 1954 Defence White Paper mentions the possibility of a second phase of war in which 'hostilities would decline in intensity, though perhaps less so at sea than elsewhere'. It thus reiterates the language of the 1952 GSP. However, while the White Paper goes on to argue that 'a period of broken-backed warfare would follow', the 1952 GSP does not. The phrase 'broken-backed warfare' appears only once and in a wholly different context. If the Alliance could strengthen its defences in its southern area, the Chiefs hoped, then any Soviet action against Iran and Iraq 'would be a more disorganised, "broken-backed" invasion than anything we have hitherto envisaged'. Some writers may have assumed that the 1954 White Paper took its reference to 'broken-backed warfare' from the 1952 GSP. See Cmd. 9075, Statement on Defence 1954, para. 13, and the 1952 GSP, paras 33 and 58.
77. 1952, GSP, para. 31.
78. 1952, GSP, para. 32.
79. 1952, GSP, para. 33.
80. 1952, GSP, para. 33.
81. 1952, GSP, para. 32.
82. 1952, GSP, para. 33.
83. 1952, GSP, para 33.
84. 1952, GSP, para. 33 and 1950, GSP, para. 9.
85. 1952, GSP, paras 106–7.
86. 1952, GSP, para. 39.
87. 1952, GSP, para. 34.
88. See, for example Philip Darby, *British Defence Policy East of Suez, 1947–1968*, (Oxford: Oxford University Press, 1973), note 11, p. 47; C.J. Murphy, 'A New Strategy for NATO', note 5, p. 81; and Pierre, *Nuclear Politics*, note 5, p. 87. Rosecrance, in *Defense of the Realm*, however, gives more stress to conventional forces: pp. 168–9.
89. 1952, GSP, para. 40.
90. 1952, GSP, paras 77 and 103.
91. 1952, GSP, paras 93, 101, 103, 133–4, and 139(u).
92. 1952, GSP, paras 111–3.
93. 1952, GSP, paras 77 and 139(w).
94. 1952, GSP, section X1V and para. 77.
95. 1950, GSP, para. 22.
96. In particular Philip Darby, *British Defence Policy East of Suez*, note 11, p. 47, stresses this point. See also Rosecrance, *Defense of the Realm*, note 1, p. 162.
97. 1952, GSP, para. 11.
98. 1952, GSP, para. 71(j).
99. 1952, GSP, para. 18.
100. See Richard E. Osgood, *NATO: The Entangling Alliance* (Chicago and London: University of Chicago Press, 1962), pp. 84–98.
101. Stalin's Note of 10 March 1952 is in TNA, PREM 11/1684. See Saki Dockrill, *Britain's Policy for West German Rearmament 1950–1955* (Cambridge: Cambridge University Press, 1991), p. 121.

Endnotes

102. Dockrill, *Britain's Policy for West German Rearmament*, pp. 121–3.
103. 1952, GSP, para. 49.
104. 1952, GSP, para. 50.
105. 1952, GSP, para. 51.
106. 1952, GSP, para. 52.
107. 1952, GSP, paras 22, 26, and 69.
108. 1952, GSP, paras 69–70.
109. 1952, GSP, para. 70.
110. See Osgood, *NATO: The Entangling Alliance*, (note 106), pp. 257–8.
111. 1952, GSP, paras 43–4; see also 1950, GSP, para. 8.
112. 1952, GSP, paras 64–6.
113. 1952, GSP, paras 54–8 and 78–85. The Middle East had in the 1947 Overall Strategic Plan been assigned much greater importance than Western Europe, but by the time of the 1950 review it was Western Europe which was accorded greater importance. See the 1947, OSP, paras 36, 43 and 47; and the 1950, GSP, paras 22 and 44.
114. 1952, GSP, paras 22, 59–63, 86–91, and 139(x) and (y).
115. 1952, GSP, para. 60.
116. 1952, GSP, paras 86 and 89.
117. 1952 GSP, para. 139(cc).
118. 1952, GSP, para. 140.
119. TNA, CAB 1.28/25, CC(S2) 94th, Conclusions, 7 Nov. 1952.
120. On the 1957 Defence White Paper, see Martin Navias, *Nuclear Weapons and British Strategic Planning, 1955–1958* (Oxford: Clarendon, 1991), Ch. 5.
121. Rosecrance, *Defense of the Realm*, note 1, p. 168.
122. See TNA, DEFE 7/677. No. 822 Saving, Telegram from Sir Oliver Franks to the Foreign Office, 1 Aug. 1952.
123. C.J. Murphy's links with the US Air Force are noted by Samuel Wells in 'The Origins of Massive Retaliation', *Political Science Quarterly* 96/1 (Spring 1981), p. 43, note 23.
124. The differences between the 1952 GSP and the 'New Look' are noted by Clark and Wheeler, *The British Origins of Nuclear Strategy*, note 1, pp. 178–82.
125. See Wampler, *Ambiguous Legacy*, pp. 24–70.

Chapter 3

* Quoted in Margaret Gowing, 'Independence and Deterrence', Vol. 2, p. 500 (London: Macmillan, 1974) and by Brian Cathcart, 'Test of Greatness', p. 273 (London: John Murray, 1994).
** Speech given to the American Chamber of Commerce, London 1958. Reported in *The Times*, 14 November 1958.
1. James Chadwick and John Cockcroft had worked at the Cavendish Laboratory in Cambridge with Ernest Rutherford, who had split the atom in 1917. See Graham Farmilo, *Churchill's Bomb*, and Brian Cathcart, *Test of Greatness*, p. 16. Cathcart's book provides an excellent, detailed analysis of the scientific and engineering teams that worked on the bomb.
2. Cathcart, *Test of Greatness*, p. 20.

Endnotes

3. Cathcart, *Test of Greatness*, pp. 7–8.
4. Cathcart, *Test of Greatness*, pp. 46–7.
5. See Gowing, *Independence and Deterrence*. See also Lorna Arnold, *A Very Special Relationship: British Atomic Weapons Trials in Australia* (London: HMSO, 1987).
6. The Herod Committee was set up in 1948 to consider all matters relating to the introduction of atomic weapons into the RAF. This was followed by the Salome Committee in 1953, which dealt with the technical and supply aspects of the introduction of atomic weapons into the RAF.
7. TNA, AIR 41/87. The official history by Humphrey Wynn refers to two weapons having been delivered by the end of November.
8. TNA, AIR 41/87.
9. TNA, AIR, 41/87. See also TNA, DEFE 4/70, 12 May 1954.
10. TNA, AIR, 41/87. See also TNA, DEFE 4/70, 12 May 1954.
11. TNA, AIR 41/87.
12. TNA, DEFE 4/70, Note by First Sea Lord, 12 May 1954.
13. This involved a Japanese fishing boat being contaminated with nuclear fallout from an American hydrogen bomb test on the Biki Atoll in the Marshall Islands on 1 March 1954, causing widespread protests.
14. See A.J.R. Groom, *British Thinking about Nuclear Weapons* (London: Pinter, 1974).
15. PRO CAB 128/27, CC 48 (54), 7 July 1954. The issue was discussed in Cabinet on 7, 8, and 26 July.
16. Nigel Birch expressed the view that the decision to develop thermonuclear weapons might encourage nuclear proliferation, but this was rejected by other members of the Cabinet. TNA, CAB 128/27, CC48(54), 8 July 1954.
17. TNA, CAB, 128/27.
18. TNA, CAB, 128/27.
19. Quoted in Robert S. Norris, Andrew W. Burrows, and Richard W. Fieldhouse, *British, French and Chinese Nuclear Weapons*, p. 44.
20. Correspondence and discussions with Bryan Taylor (who worked on the H-Bomb at Aldermaston between 1955 and 1958 in the Mathematical Physics Division), Ken Allen (the Senior Superintendent of the Nuclear Research Division), and Lorna Arnold (the Official Historian at the United Kingdom Atomic Energy Authority). See also Sir William Cook, 'Obituary', *The Times*, 19 Sept. 1987. Three-stage devices were apparently designed and built 'at a later stage'. Letter from Bryan Taylor, 7 June 1994: 'Tom' was 'a modified RED BEARD made up of 12 kg of U.235 and 3 kg of plutonium'; 'Dick' comprised of 20 kg of U.235 and between 200 and 260 kg of U238, all of which was packed in a lithium 6 compound. Both 'Tom' and 'Dick' were surrounded by 'a 1 inch outer shell containing 4,400 lb of lead and bismuth'. A further outside case weighing 1,000 lb was made of a special alloy. According to declassified documents, 'the modified RED BEARD functions normally and the heat passes through to "Dick" warming it up to supercriticality. Meanwhile, neutrons are retarded by the lithium compound until the U235 is at the correct temperature. Neutrons are then released and bombard the supercritical U238/U235 giving, in theory, a perfect fusion.' TNA, AIR 2/13726, Operation 'GRAPPLE'. Details of

Endnotes

Megaton Warheads and Order of Firing, 18 Jan. 1957. For information about the different test devices see Lorna Arnold, *Britain and the H-Bomb*.

21. Scientists at AWRE at the time are sceptical of J.C. Ward's claim that he conceived the idea of radiation implosion quite independently. Private Correspondence.
22. TNA, AIR 41/87, 'The RAF Strategic Nuclear Deterrent Force'.
23. Operation Mosaic took place at Monte Bello between May and June 1956 and involved two detonations. Operation Buffalo took place at Maralinga between July and November 1956 and was the first trial to include an air drop of the Blue Danube Bomb. See also Group Captain Kenneth Hubbard and Michael Simmons, *Operation Grapple: Testing Britain's First H-Bomb* (London: Ian Allan, 1985), and Wilfred Oulton, *Christmas Island Cracker: An Account of the Planning and Execution of the British Thermonuclear Bomb Tests 1957* (London: Harmsworth Publishing, 1987).
24. Hansard, col.1382, 7 June 1956.
25. TNA AIR 41/87, 'The RAF Strategic Nuclear Deterrent Force'.
26. TNA, AIR, 41/87. See also TNA, DEFE 7/901.
27. *Yellow Sun* was the first deployed 'true' British thermonuclear device, entering service in 1958.
28. TNA, AIR, 41/87.
29. TNA, DEFE 7/902, 903, and 904. See also Oulton, *The Christmas Island Cracker*. Professor K.W. Allen has confirmed that the tests in the summer of 1957 were disappointing because the yield was much less than the 1 megaton that had been hoped for. However, he goes on to argue that 'they could also be regarded as a very significant success for the weapons engineers and the RAF -an air drop which worked perfectly first time'. Letter to one of the authors, 27 June 1994.
30. TNA, DEFE, 7/902.
31. TNA, DEFE, 7/902, 903, and 904.
32. TNA, DEFE, 7/902. Bryan Taylor told one of the authors that 'it is rather profligate to use many kgs of valuable U235 to make a single MT fission weapon when the same material would be sufficient for (the triggers of) many thermonuclear weapons. In that respect the choice of a fission design for the Interim weapon must have been something of a disappointment.' Letter, 20 June 1994.
33. R. McKie, 'The UK Gatecrashed the Superpower Club', *The Observer*, 6 Feb. 1994.
34. Norris, Burrows, and Fieldhouse, *British, French and Chinese Nuclear Forces*.
35. TNA, AIR, 41/87, 'The RAF Strategic Nuclear Deterrent'.
36. TNA, AIR, 41/87.
37. Quarterly Progress report to the Joint Committee on Atomic Energy: Part III Weapons. US Atomic Energy Commission (July–September 1958). It is also possible that an informal interchange between scientists had provided insights into the nuclear programmes of both countries despite the McMahon Act. According to Penney and his fellow scientist Macklen, 'the United States in the autumn of 1957 approached the United Kingdom with an invitation to explain the position which had been reached in the technology and design of British nuclear weapons, with a half-promise that if the position was technically good, collaboration in nuclear weapons might be resumed in areas where both sides had a stated interest. A presentation was made and favourably received': Penney and Macklen, 'William

Endnotes

Richard Joseph Cook', Biographical Memoirs of Fellows Of the Royal Society (London: The Royal Society, 1988), pp. 49–52.

38. Quarterly Progress Report to the Joint Committee on Atomic Energy.
39. Quarterly Progress Report. See TNA, DEFE 7/902, 903, and 904.
40. There was also a series of kiloton tests at Maralinga between September and October 1957 codenamed *Operation Antler*. The Grapple 'X' test was 1.8 mt, Grapple 'Y' was 3 mt, and Grapple 'Z' involved a series of tests with yields of 24 kt, 1 mt, 0.8 mt, and 25 kt. National Radiological Protection Board (NRPB) 266, ICRF, Second Report, Dec. 1993.
41. Opinions are divided about the impact of the IBM 704. Lorna Arnold told one of the authors that she believed it was 'of significance'. Bryan Taylor, however, is more doubtful. The latter told one of the authors that 'the IBM 704 was indeed a major addition to AWRE resources, but I doubt whether there was time between its commissioning and the Grapple 'X', 'Y', 'Z' tests for it to have played a decisive role'(letters to one of the authors, 17 May 1994 and 20 June 1994). K.W. Allen has indicated that the Grapple 'X' and 'Y' tests were more concerned with principles than computations (letter to one of the authors, 27 June 1994).
42. Letter to one of the authors from K.W. Allen, 27 June 1994.
43. TNA, AIR 41/87, 'The RAF Strategic Nuclear Deterrent'.
44. *The Times*, 14 November 1958.
45. Hansard, H.C. Deb. 549, col. 1091–2 (28 February 1956).
46. See Macmillan, *Riding the Storm*, Ch. 10.
47. Data from the files of the British Institute of Public Opinion.
48. Pierre, *Nuclear Politics*, p. 313.
49. Nigel Birch, Parliamentary Secretary to the Minister of Defence Harold Macmillan, did send a confidential Paper to Macmillan and Selwyn Lloyd, the Foreign Secretary, in 1954 setting out the arguments against the development of British thermonuclear weapons on the grounds that it would complicate disarmament efforts and encourage proliferation, but, as Andrew Pierre has argued, it did not receive 'adequate intellectual attention', *Nuclear Politics*, p. 313.

Chapter 4

1. Macmillan, *Riding the Storm*, p. 323 (London: Macmillan/Palgrave, 1971). Copyright © Harold Macmillan, 1971. By permission of Oxford University Press.
2. Ritchie, *Trident and British Identity*, p. 8.
3. This study supports some of the revisionist accounts of the Eisenhower administration. See R.H. Immermann, 'Confessions of an Eisenhower Revisionist: An Agonizing Reappraisal', *Diplomatic History* 14 (Summer 1990): pp. 319–42; S.G. Rabe, 'Eisenhower Revisionism', *Diplomatic History*, 17 (Winter 1993): pp. 97–115; C.J. Pach Jr and E. Richardson, *The Presidency of Dwight D. Eisenhower* (Lawrence: University Press of Kansas, 1991); and F. Greenstein, *The Hidden-Hand Presidency: Eisenhower as Leader* (New York: Basic Books, 1982).
4. Macmillan, *Riding the Storm*, p. 323.
5. For a study of the Anglo-American nuclear relationship during the Second World War, see Gowing, *Britain and Atomic Energy, 1939–1945*.

6. For a discussion of the British decision to develop nuclear weapons, see Gowing, *Independence and Deterrence*.
7. The exception was in the field of intelligence, which involved areas of nuclear cooperation.
8. Under the agreement the United States was to receive all the supplies of raw materials from the Belgian Congo for two years and would receive up to 2,547 tons of the British stockpile if the amount received from the Belgian Congo was not enough. As far as information exchanges were concerned, the United States and Britain agreed to cooperate in nine areas. These included topics for immediate declassification, health and safety, radioisotopes, fundamental nuclear and extra-nuclear properties, detection of a distant nuclear explosion, design of natural uranium reactors, and general research experience with named low-power reactors. See Gowing, *Independence and Deterrence*, pp. 248–9.
9. See John Baylis, *Anglo-American Defence Relations, 1939–1984* (London, Macmillan, 1984), p. 41.
10. See Simon Duke, *US Defence Bases in the United Kingdom: A Matter for Joint Decision?* (London: Macmillan, 1987), and John Baylis, 'American Bases in Britain: "The Truman–Attlee Understandings"', *The World Today*, Aug.–Sept. 1986.
11. See Macmillan, *Riding the Storm*, pp. 315–16. Some American officials argued that the Soviet test in August 1953 was not a true thermonuclear test. As a result it is often argued that the first real Russian H-bomb test did not take place until November 1956 (*Joe 19*). It seems likely, however, that 1953 was a true thermonuclear weapon test, but that the device was not the same type that the Americans were testing.
12. For a detailed discussion of Project E and Anglo-American cooperation in the mid-1950s, see Stephen Twigge and Len Scott, *Planning Armageddon: Britain, the United States and Command and Control of Western Nuclear Forces 1945–1964* (Reading: Harwood Academic Publishers); John Baylis, *Ambiguity and Deterrence*; and Richard Moore, *Nuclear Illusion and Nuclear Reality*.
13. See Timothy Botti, *The Long Wait: The Forging of the Anglo-American Nuclear Alliance, 1945–1958* (New York: Greenwood Press, 1987).
14. Memorandum for chairman JCS, Washington, 22 March 1956; CCS 381 (Military Strategy and Posture), RG 218, Chairman's File, Admiral Radford, 1953–1957, Modern Military Branch, National Archives II, College Park, Maryland.
15. In January 1956 Attorney General Herbert Brownell ruled that the administration could legally negotiate to transmit nuclear submarine propulsion information to the British. *Hearings before Subcommittee*, JCAE, 1958, 85th Cong., 2d sess, 1958, 516–19; Timothy Botti, *The Long Wait*, p. 160; John Simpson, *The Independent Nuclear State* (Basingstoke: Macmillan, 1986), p. 117.
16. *Hearings before Subcommittee*, JCAE, 1958, pp. 513–19.
17. UK Parliament, 554 H.C. Deb., 58, 554, 1406.
18. Jan Melissen has argued that during this period 'British negotiators were forced to swallow one deception after another'. *The Struggle for Nuclear Partnership: Britain, the United States and the making of an Ambiguous Alliance 1952–59* (Groningen: Styx, 1993), p. 9.

Endnotes

19. *Hearings before Subcommittee*, JCAE, 1958, pp. 513–19.
20. To make matters worse, the president had to go into the Walter Reed Hospital in Bethesda, Maryland, on 8 June for an emergency operation for ileitis.
21. Botti, *The Long Wait*, p. 164.
22. See John Baylis, 'The Development of Britain's Thermonuclear Capability 1954–61: Myth or Reality?', *Contemporary Record* 8 (September 1994). By far the best account of the 'Grapple' Tests is contained in Lorna Arnold, *Britain and the H-Bomb*.
23. TNA, FO 371/126682, AU 1051/26, Washington tel. to Foreign Office, 1 January 1957.
24. Botti, *The Long Wait*, pp. 171–5. See also an excellent article by Jan Melissen, 'The Restoration of the Nuclear Alliance: Great Britain and Atomic Negotiations with the United States, 1957-58', *Contemporary Record* 6 (Summer 1992).
25. Eden's Government fell on 9 January 1957, and on 22 January President Eisenhower directed the US Embassy in London to invite the new prime minister, Harold Macmillan, to a conference on 22–24 March in either Washington or Bermuda. See Macmillan, *Riding the Storm*, pp. 240–2.
26. TNA, FO 371/126707, AU 11913/1. Logan to Forward, 23 January 1957. See also TNA, FO 371/126683, AU 1051/28G. Sandys' telegram to Macmillan and Lloyd, 28 January 1957.
27. USNA, Dulles calls Radford, 17 June 1957, *Minutes of Telephone Conversations of John Foster Dulles and Christian Herter, 1953–1961* (Frederick, MD, 1980), reel 6, 216–17; M.H. Armacost, *The Politics of Weapons Innovation: Thor-Jupiter Controversy* (New York: Columbia University Press, 1969), pp. 183–5; *Defence: Outline of Future Policy* (London: Her Majesty's Stationery Office, 1957), Cmnd. No. 124; M. Navias, *Nuclear Weapons and British Strategic Planning*, p. 138.
28. *Hearings before Subcommittee on Agreements for Co-operation, JCAE, Amending the Atomic Energy Act of 1954: Exchange of Military Information and Material with Allies*, 85th Cong., 2d sess., 1958, pp. 513–14. In a secret annex the two leaders also agreed to prior consultations on testing initiatives and a common policy toward French nuclear ambitions. See Lewis L. Strauss, *Men and Decisions* (London: Doubleday, 1962), pp. 369–74.
29. Contrary to the view of Jan Melissen, Norman Dombey, and Eric Grove, Britain did explode a thermonuclear device in the Grapple test. Both 'Short Granite' and 'Purple Granite', detonated on 15 May and 19 June, respectively, were thermonuclear devices. The yields of 0.3 megatons and 0.2 megatons were disappointing, but these were only the first tests, and others were scheduled in November (Grapple X) to improve the yield. See Melissen, *The Struggle for Nuclear Partnership*, p/35; Norman Dombey and Eric Grove, 'Britain's Thermonuclear Bluff', *London Review of Books* 14 (22 October 1992), pp. 8–10; John Baylis, 'The Development of Britain's Thermonuclear Capability', *Contemporary Record*, Vol. 8, (Summer 1994); Botti, *The Long Wait*, p. 187; and Arnold, *Britain and the H-Bomb*, chap. 14.
30. 570 H. C. Deb 5s., pp. 567–9, 575–6, and 1035–9.
31. Macmillan, *Riding the Storm*, pp. 301–4; Dulles call to Strauss, 17 June 1957, *Telephone Conversations of John Foster Dulles and Christian Herter, 1953–1961*, reel 6, 220.

32. Stassen had acted on his own initiative without the knowledge of the president or Dulles. See memorandum for Dulles by Eisenhower, 4 June 1957, Eisenhower's Papers as President/Ann Whitman File (AWF) Dulles-Herter series, Box 7, Dwight D. Eisenhower Library, Abilene, Kansas; and Macmillan, *Riding the Storm*, pp. 301–4.
33. Ian Clark and David Angell, 'Britain, the United States and the Control of Nuclear Weapons: The Diplomacy of the Thor Deployment, 1957-1958', *Diplomacy and Statecraft* 2 (November 1991); Botti, *The Long Wait*, pp. 194–5.
34. M.H. Armacost, *The Politics of Weapons Innovation*, pp. 58–9.
35. See Melissen, *The Struggle for Nuclear Partnership*, pp. 63–92.
36. J.R. Killian, *Sputnik, Scientists, and Eisenhower: A Memoir of the First Special Assistant to the President for Science and Technology* (Cambridge, MA: MIT Press, 1977), p. 7.
37. TNA, PREM 11/2554, Washington tel. to Foreign Office, 7 October 1957.
38. TNA, PREM 11/2554, Foreign Office telegram to United Kingdom Embassy in Washington, 10 October 1957. See also Macmillan, *Riding the Storm*, pp. 315–16. Shortly after Macmillan wrote to Eisenhower, a major fire broke out in the nuclear reactor at Windscale. Macmillan's diary reveals that he played down the dangers of the fire because he feared that 'complete disclosure of the nuclear disaster might have alerted Congress and jeopardized his historic chance to secure atomic secrets from the United States'. Melissen, *The Struggle for Nuclear Partnership*, p. 45; Alastair Horne, *Harold Macmillan, Vol. 2, 1957–1986* (London: Macmillan, 1989), pp. 53–5.
39. USNA, Dulles' call to Merchant, 17 October 1957, *Telephone Conversations of John Foster Dulles and Christian Herter, 1953–1961*, reel 6, 722.
40. Macmillan, *Riding the Storm*, pp. 320–3.
41. Memorandum of conversation, Macmillan Talks, by Dulles, 24 October 1957, AWF, International Series, box 20; Melissen, *The Struggle for Nuclear Partnership*, p. 44; Botti, *The Long Wait*, pp. 201–2. Eight technical subcommittees were set up covering the following areas: nuclear materials exchange; nuclear warheads; nuclear propulsion; delivery systems; biological warfare, chemical warfare, and radiological defence; defence against ballistic missiles; aircraft and aeroengines; and electron tubes and infrared. At their Washington meeting, Macmillan and Eisenhower decided to adopt a neutral position on French attempts to develop nuclear weapons. This was a delicate issue, especially with the French seeking British, as well as Italian and West German, cooperation. The Anglo-American position was 'neither to assist nor to actively hinder the French programme'.
42. Memorandum for the president by Dulles, 21 October 1957; AWF, Dulles-Herter Series, box 7, folder Dulles Oct. 1957 (1).
43. Melissen, *The Struggle for Nuclear Partnership*, p. 12. For a discussion of the broader alliance context of Anglo-American negotiations, see Beatrice Heuser, *NATO, Britain, France and the FRG Nuclear Strategies and Forces for Europe, 1949–2000* (Basingstoke: Macmillan, 1997).
44. See Marc Trachtenberg, *A Constructed Peace: The Making of a European Settlement, 1945–1963*, (Princeton: Princeton University Press, 1999). For a discussion of plans for Franco-Italian-German (FIG) nuclear cooperation, see Melissen, *The Struggle for Nuclear Partnership*, pp. 149–50.

Endnotes

45. It appears that the US representatives at the Washington conference were making policy 'on the hoof'. The meeting to clarify what information should be given to the British took place on 25 October. USNA, Dulles calls to Quarles and Strauss, both 25 October 1957, *Telephone Conversations of John Foster Dulles and Christian Herter, 1953–1961*, reel 6, 674–5; Melissen, *The Struggle for Nuclear Partnership*, p. 45. When Eisenhower met Macmillan on 24 October, he told him that 'there were a few, about four, applications of such high secrecy that very few people in his own government knew about them and he did not think these could be the subject of joint pooling unless and until we were satisfied that the Soviets themselves knew about them. He said he thought there were about two of these the Soviets knew about now, which reduced to only about two the data which would continue to be restricted.' Memorandum of conversation, 24 October 1958, Papers of John Foster Dulles, General Correspondence and Memoranda, box 1.
46. Botti, *The Long Wait*, p. 203.
47. TNA, PREM 11/2554. Telegram by Powell to Hood, 11 November 1957, PREM 11/2554; telegram by Hood to Powell, 15 November 1957. See also Melissen, *The Struggle for Nuclear Partnership*, p. 45, and Botti, *The Long Wait*, p. 206. The best account of the US–UK Technical talks is contained in Arnold, *Britain and the H-Bomb*, chap. 14.
48. *New York Times*, 2 June 1957. During Rickover's visit of 27–30 May, the United States hoped to persuade the British to discuss the technology of their Calder Hall reactor and other developments in the commercial nuclear power field. The British, however, continued to demand that US companies using the technology should pay royalties to the government.
49. R.G. Hewlett and F. Duncan, *Nuclear Navy, 1946–1962* (Chicago: University of Chicago Press, 1974); *Hearings before Subcommittee, JCAE, 1958*, p. 164.
50. These difficulties had included attempts by American officials to link the deployment of Thor missiles in Britain with NATO plans (agreed in December 1957) for an IRBM under SACEUR's control. The British remained determined to retain a bilateral agreement, but they were prepared to accept a vague commitment to link the missiles to Article 5 of the North Atlantic Treaty. For a discussion of the alliance discussion to the negotiations, see Melissen, *The Struggle for Nuclear Partnership*, p. 45.
51. USNA, Dulles calls to Quarles, 4 November 1957, *Telephone Conversations of John Foster Dulles and Christian Herter*, reel 6, 223. The United States eventually deployed seven squadrons of Thor and Jupiter IRBMs in a number of NATO countries, including Britain, Italy, and Turkey. Despite criticisms by the Chief of the Air Staff in Britain that the missiles were 'highly vulnerable', the government accepted the agreement because of its political symbolism. See Ian Clark, *Nuclear Diplomacy and the Special Relationship: Britain's Deterrent and America, 1957–1962* (Oxford: Oxford University Press, 1994), pp. 53–4; and S.J. Ball, *The Bomber in British Strategy: Doctrine, Strategy and Britain's World Role, 1945–1960* (Boulder, Co: Westview Press, 1995).
52. USNA, Strauss to Eisenhower, 19 December 1957, enclosure: Interim Report to the President and the Prime Minister from Strauss, Quarles, Plowden, and Powell, AWF, Administration Series, box 4, folder AEC 1957(1).

53. The Soviet government had just completed a series of tests, and Britain still had a number of important tests planned in April, August, and September.
54. Duncan Campbell, *The Unsinkable Aircraft Carrier: American Military Power in Britain* (London: Michael Joseph, 1984), pp. 55–7.
55. This involved the Ballistic Missile Early Warning System (BMEWS) and the Missile Defence Alarm System (MIDAS).
56. Denis Healey (for the Labour Opposition) quoted in the House of Commons a statement made by Dulles on 19 November 1957 in which he said that there was 'no question of a veto on the use of [American] nuclear weapons being exercised by other countries. No government could legally cast a veto against a decision of another government taken for its own defense.' 578 H.C.Deb. 5s.,1152–4; 579 H.C. Deb. 5s., pp. 212–17 and 371–3.
57. Macmillan, *Riding the Storm*, pp. 474–5; Botti, *The Long Wait*, p. 223.
58. When Macmillan visited Washington on 7 June 1958, he once again raised the issue of the use of American bases in Britain. As a result, a new agreement was initiated by the prime minister and the president that replaced 'the loose arrangement made by Attlee and Churchill'. See Macmillan, *Riding the Storm*, p. 494.
59. By this stage the president had convinced the chairman of the JCAE, Senator Carl Durham (D-NC), of the need to cooperate more effectively in the nuclear field with US allies.
60. *Hearings before the Subcommittee on Agreements for Cooperation, JCAE, Amending the Atomic Energy Act of 1954—Exchange of Military Information and Materials with Allies,* 85th Cong., 2d sess., 1958, 102 (emphasis added). See also R.W. Dyke and F.X. Gannon, *Chet Hollifield: Master Legislator and Nuclear Statesman* (Washington: University Press of America, 1996).
61. The Calder Hall reactors were primarily for producing military plutonium, but they were also dual-purpose reactors that, as a by-product, would generate electricity for the national grid. They would also serve as prototypes for the civil nuclear power stations Britain planned to build.
62. The US position was undermined by splits between the different agencies involved in the negotiations. The DOD in particular was opposed to introducing a 'civilian consideration' into an essentially military agreement. *Hearings before Subcommittee, JCAE, 1958*, pp. 501–3.
63. Public Law 479, 85th Cong. 68 Stat. 176.
64. *Agreement between Government of the United Kingdom of Great Britain and Northern Ireland and Government of United States of America for Co-operation on Uses of Atomic Energy for Mutual Defense Purposes*, Washington, 3 July 1958, US Department of State, *United States Treaties and Other International Agreements* 9 (Washington, 1959), p. 1028.
65. *Amendment to 1958 Atomic Energy Agreement*, Washington, 2 May 1959, US Department of State, *United States Treaties and Other International Agreements*, 10:1274.
66. Botti, *The Long Wait*, p. 248 (emphasis added).
67. TNA, FO 371/135551, ZE 120/87G, Telegram from Foreign Office to Washington, 20 August 1958.
68. *Outline of Information to be Initially Exchanged with the UK*, undated, White House Office, Office of the Staff Secretary, (OSS) Subject Series, Alphabetical Subseries,

Endnotes

box 5, DDEL. The report suggested that the following kinds of information should not be revealed to the British at that stage: information concerning the use of the two-stage principle, propagation burning, radiation flow, or any other information concerning the TN secondary or unique case design, information concerning the internal design revealing general or specific dimensions or configurations of the nuclear components (of the Mk. 15/39 weapon), and information about the fission-fusion ratio of nuclear efficiencies.

69. USNA, Conference with the President, 20 August 1958, White House Office, OSS, Subject Series, Alphabetical Subseries, box 4.
70. USNA, Memorandum of conversation between the President and Dr Libby, 21 August 1958, White House Office, OSS, Subject Series, Alphabetical Subseries, box 4. Initially, Libby was not inclined to share information with other states (including Britain), but in 1953 he took charge of Project Sunshine, designed to evaluate the global effects of nuclear testing. During this exercise it became clear to American officials that the United States should enlist the British in this evaluation. Libby appears to have become more sympathetic to the British during the implementation of Project Sunshine.
71. USNA, Telegram from Herter to embassy in London, Presidential Handling, 20 August 1958, International Series, box 21, folder Macmillan-President 6/1/58-9/30/58(4), DDEL; memorandum of conference with the President on 21 August 1958 by Goodpaster, 23 August 1958, White House Office, OSS, Subject Series, Alphabetical Subseries, box 3, folder AEC Vol. 11 (4) (August–September 1958).
72. The two documents were *United States Nuclear Weapons Systems Data (for Initial Information Exchange with the United Kingdom) Compiled by the Division of Military Application of the AEC*, Reference Symbol, 7720(13), and *US-UK Agreement on the Use of Atomic Energy for Mutual Defence—Information Transmitted by the UK Representatives Compiled by Atomic Weapons Research Establishment*, Reference CWD/4309. The US delegation of thirteen included: Major General Herbert Loper, Assistant to the Secretary of Defense for Atomic Energy; Brigadier General Alfred Starbird, Director of Military Application, Atomic Energy Commission; Dr Norris Bradbury, Director of Los Alamos Laboratory; Dr James McRae, President of the Sandia Corporation; and Dr Willard Libby, AEC Commissioner. The UK delegation of eight included Sir William Penney, member of the Atomic Energy Authority; Sir William Cook, member of the Atomic Energy Authority; Mr Edward Newley, Chief of Weapons Development, Atomic Energy Research Establishment, Aldermaston; and Sir Frederick Brundrett, Scientific Adviser to the Ministry of Defence.
73. The UK gave the Americans information about the following designs: Green Grass, Flagpole, the Pendant, and Burgee devices, a 6-inch gun shell; a 1,350-pound warhead; and a 2,200-pound device. White House Office, OSS, Subject Series, Alphabetical subseries, box 5.
74. AEC Quarterly Progress Report to the JCAE, Part III—Weapons, July–September 1958, DOE/NOO, Progress Reports on Selected Programs, no. 73760, cited in Norris et al., *British, French and Chinese Nuclear Weapons*, p. 48. See also letter to the president, 26 September 1958, White House Office, OSS, Subject Series, Alphabetical Subseries, box 4. For a very useful analysis of these meetings, see Melissen, *The*

Struggle for Nuclear Partnership, pp. 51–4. On 6 September Eisenhower authorized that fabrication prints and material specifications be furnished to the United Kingdom. AEC Quarterly Progress Report to the JAEC, Part III—Weapons, January–March 1959.

75. Macmillan, *Riding the Storm*, p. 565. The United States, however, also recognized some weaknesses in the British programme. According to an American account of the Washington meeting: 'The British apparently do not have an appreciation that plutonium produced from uranium subjected to higher burn-up in their reactors is usable in weapons. This knowledge would be of great significance to their civilian power programs. In addition, they have apparently not exerted major effort toward making their weapons one-point safe.' AEC, Quarterly Progress Report to the JCAE, Part III—Weapons, July–September 1958, 14.
76. USNA, Program Status Report to the JCAE, Part III—Weapons, 13 December 1958, no. 73756. See 'Record of the Second Meeting of the Technical Experts Held Pursuant to Section 11 of the Technical Annex to the Agreement between the Government of the United States of America and the government of the United Kingdom of Great Britain and Northern Ireland For Cooperation on the Uses of Atomic Energy for Mutual Defense Purposes', White House Office, OSS, Subject Series, Alphabetical Subseries, box 5.
77. TNA, FO 371/135506, ZE 13/74, Telegram from Washington to Foreign Office, 25 September 1958.
78. Record of the Second Meeting of the Technical Experts, White House Office, OSS, Subject Series, Alphabetical Subseries, box 5.
79. This information was obtained from Arnold, *Britain and the H-Bomb*, pp. 203–17.
80. Arnold, *Britain and the H-Bomb*, and Record of the Second Meeting of Experts.
81. Record of the Second Meeting of Experts. Discussions took place on a range of technical, scientific, and engineering issues, including weapon electronics, uranium and plutonium fabrication, high explosives, tritium, beryllium, solid fission materials, plastics, rubber and adhesives, engineering, and weapons assembly. See R. Norris et al., *British, French, and Chinese Nuclear Weapons*, p. 49.
82. Norris et al., *British, French, and Chinese Nuclear Weapons*, p. 52. See Program Status Report to the JCAE, Part III—Weapons, 31 December 1958.
83. Quarterly Progress Report to the JCAE, Part III—Weapons, January–March 1959, April–June 1959, no. 73764; Quarterly Progress Report to the JCAE, Part III—Weapons, July–September 1959, no. 73766; Progress Report on Selected Programs to the JCAE, Part III—Weapons, May 1960, no. 73768, cited in Norris et al., *British, French and Chinese Nuclear Weapons*, p. 49.
84. See Arnold, *Britain and the H-Bomb*.
85. See Norris et al., *British, French and Chinese Nuclear Weapons*, p. 49.
86. The Polaris warhead was the ET-317. AEC, Progress Report on Selected Programs to the JCAE, May 1960, Part III—Weapons, 15, suggests the W47 was used, while Peter Jones has argued that a WE177 warhead was used. See P.G.E.F. Jones, 'Overview of History of U.S. Strategic Weapons', in *The History of the UK Strategic Deterrent*, Proceedings of the Royal Aeronautical Society (London, 1999).
87. Norris et al., *British, French and Chinese Nuclear Weapons*, p. 49. Other topics discussed included hydrodynamics and shock relations for problems with spherical

and cylindrical symmetry, cross-sections, radiochemistry, atomic demolition munitions, warhead hardening, asymmetric detonations, terrorist nuclear threat response, nuclear weapons accidents, and nuclear waste management.
88. See Richard Ullman, 'The Covert French Connection', *Foreign Policy* 75 (Summer 1989), pp. 3–33.
89. The full title is *Agreement between the Government of the United Kingdom and Northern Ireland and the Government of the United States of America for Co-operation on the Uses of Atomic Energy for Mutual Defence Purposes*. The claim that the agreement is 'one of the most remarkable' ever reached between two sovereign states is based on the range and depth of nuclear collaboration that developed between the two states. The MDA remains at the heart of the Anglo-American nuclear relationship at the present time. For information about the renewal negotiations in 2014 see *The Guardian*, 13 June 2014.
90. David Reynolds, 'A "Special Relationship"? America, Britain, and International Order since the Second World War', *International Affairs*, 62 (Winter 1985–6), pp. 1–20.
91. Pierre, *Nuclear Politics*; G.M. Dillon, *Dependence and Deterrence: Success and Civility in the Anglo-American Special Nuclear Relationship, 1962–1982* (London: Gower, 1983).
92. George Ball, *The Discipline of Power* (London: Bodley Head, 1968), p. 102. For a discussion of the problems caused by the Anglo-American nuclear partnership for alliance cohesion, see Melissen, *The Struggle for Nuclear Partnership*, pp. 109–14.
93. Pierre, *Nuclear Politics*, p. 316. Whether nuclear proliferation was encouraged and alliance cohesion undermined as a result of the 1958 act remains very difficult to prove one way or the other.
94. Trachtenberg, *A Constructed Peace*.
95. Ball, *The Discipline of Power*.
96. Eric Schlosser *Command and Control* (London: Allen Lane, 2013). See also *The Guardian*, 'Nuclear weapons: An accident waiting to happen', 13 October 2013.
97. See <www.atomicarchive.com>, accessed 17 January 2014.
98. The terms of the 'Murphy-Dean Agreement' of 7 June 1958 confirmed the basic understanding that the use of bases in the UK by American forces would be a matter of joint decision by the two governments. The Murphy Dean Agreement is mentioned in a number of documents. See TNA, CAB 21/4061 and AIR 8/2201; see also Macmillan, *Riding the Storm*, p. 494.Trachtenberg argues that the dual-key arrangements were in fact a deliberate fiction devised largely to convince Congress that there was effective control over American nuclear weapons.
99. Statement by Mr Frederick Jandrey, Deputy Assistant Secretary for European Affairs, *American Foreign Policy Foreign Documents, 1958, Western Europe* (Department of State Publications, 7522, 1962), p. 647.
100. Macmillan, *Riding the Storm*, p. 323.
101. Ritchie, *Trident and British Identity*, p. 1.

Chapter 5

1. Taken from national archives. TNA, PREM 11/4229. The PM's Talks with President Kennedy and Mr Diefenbaker in the Bahamas, 18–22 December 1962.

Endnotes

2. Jan Melissen, 'The Thor Saga: Anglo-American Nuclear Relations, US IRBM Development and Deployment in Britain, 1955–1959', *The Journal of Strategic Studies*, vol. 15, no. 2 (June 1992) pp. 172–207. See also Clark, *Nuclear Diplomacy and the Special Relationship*, Ch.1.
3. TNA, AVIA 92/25, History of Blue Streak, April 1960.
4. For an outline of the breakdown of atomic collaboration, see, for example, Pierre, *Nuclear Politics*, pp. 112–20, and for the period between the passing of the McMahon Act and the resumption of nuclear exchanges, see, for example, S. J. Ball, 'Military nuclear relations between the United States and Great Britain under the terms of the McMahon Act, 1946–1958', *The Historical Journal*, Vol. 38 (June 1995), pp. 439–54.
5. The Royal Aircraft Establishment (RAE) at Farnborough began work on MRBM programmes in the latter half of 1953 and both de Havilland and English Electric produced proposals for contracts which were issued in 1955. Woomera, the Australian missile testing range set up by the British government in 1947, was also preparing to launch missiles of a 700 or 800nm range. Furthermore, RAE 'made full use of V2 documentation gained at the end of the war and had German engineers who knew of the future lines their German teams had been thinking along'. Private correspondence, October 2002.
6. The decision to cancel Blue Streak was based in no small measure on the wide ranging study conducted for the government by Sir Richard Powell and the Future Policy Report (1960) which was prepared to assess future defence needs. The Minister of Defence accepted the concerns contained in the Powell Report and decided to cancel Blue Streak, which 'has no military value', and cease development of a revised version of Blue Steel whilst trying to elicit from the Americans 'whether they would be prepared to sell us, without strings, their airborne ballistic missile W.S.138 (or Skybolt)'. TNA, PREM 11/2945, Meeting on Defence Policy, 19 February 1960.
7. See, for example, R. Turnill, 'The Legacy of Sputnik', *The Daily Telegraph*, 27 September 1997 and Nicholas Hill, *Vertical Empire* (Coventry: Imperial College Press, 2002).
8. See Richard Moore, 'Bad Strategy and Bomber Dreams: A New View of the Blue Streak Cancellation', *Contemporary British History*, Vol. 27, 2, (2013). The RAF had rather unrealistic dreams of developing a new high-performance manned bomber to replace the V-Bomber force. Moore argues that this was rather more important than cost or technological obsolescence.
9. It must be mentioned that 'The size of the RV [re-entry vehicle] was large by later standards, but also the Soviet radars envisaged had far less power. The real issue is that Blue Streak could have benefited from the ongoing reduction in warhead sizes and by going to MIRV. However there were some issues not fully understood or even [sic] unsuspected that were found later by Chevaline.' Private correspondence, October 2002.
10. Harold Macmillan, *Pointing the Way* (Basingstoke: Macmillan, 1972), pp. 253–5.
11. TNA, PREM 11/2945, Prime Minister's Discussion on Deterrence Policy, 20 February 1960.

Endnotes

12. Although the term 'cruise missile' had not been invented then.
13. This point is well covered by the Chief Scientific Advisor to the British government, Sir Solly Zuckerman: Solly Zuckerman, *Monkeys, Men and Missiles*, pp. 239–41.
14. P.J. Roman, 'Strategic Bombers over the Missile Horizon, 1957–1963', *Journal of Strategic Studies*, Vol. 18, 1 (January 1995), pp. 198–236.
15. TNA, PREM 11/3716, Ormsby-Gore to Foreign Office, 8 November 1962; PREM 11/3716, FO to Paris (Samuel from Wright), 9 December 1962; TNA, PREM 11/3716, Zuckerman to Ministry of Defence, 9 December 1962; TNA, PREM 11/3716, de Zulueta to Ormsby-Gore, 11 December 1962.
16. Baylis, *Ambiguity and Deterrence*, pp. 241–358.
17. The design of the Resolution class SSBN largely followed the design of the UK's Valiant class, the RN's first nuclear-powered submarines, with a reactor section grafted onto the US-designed missile compartment, which had been largely manufactured by the UK, building a new forward section to house both the forward torpedo tubes and sonar equipment; Grove, *Vanguard to Trident*, p. 242.
18. The A-3 was a significant step forward from the A-2, with a vastly greater maximum range and the capacity to house three warheads as opposed to the single warhead of the A-2. Equally important was that only the A-3 was guaranteed to be supported by the USN and government defence contractors during the expected lifespan of the UK Polaris force. Private source; see also John Pike, Federation of Atomic Scientists (henceforth FAS.org), Nuclear Weapons Page, USA, <http://www.fas.org/nuke/guide/usa/slbm/a-3.htm>, accessed 5 October 2002.
19. The MLF was to consist of twenty-five destroyers, each armed with six Polaris missiles under the control of SACEUR in NATO.
20. Clark, *Nuclear Diplomacy*, p. 374.
21. Alastair Horne, *Macmillan Vol. 2* (Basingstoke: Macmillan, 1989), p. 442.
22. A. Brooks, *V-Force: The History of Britain's Airborne Deterrent* (London: Janes, 1982), p. 123.
23. Pierre, *Nuclear Politics*, p. 231.
24. For a comprehensive list and valuable synopsis of US nuclear facilities, see The Brookings Institute, The US Nuclear Weapons Cost Study Project website, US Nuclear Weapons Research, Development, Testing, and Production, and Naval Nuclear Propulsion Facilities, <http://www.brook.edu/dybdocroot/fp/projects/nucwcost/sites.htm>, accessed 3 June 2002.
25. The Joint Working Groups (JOWOGs) had first been set up as part of the 1958 MDA, along with the Joint Atomic Energy Information Group (JAEIG) which provided a mechanism for passing information along with regular 'Stocktakes' or 'Reviews' which ensured that everyone employed in each specialist area worked to mutual advantage. Confidential correspondence, October 2002. Although the MDA was published as a government Command Paper the substance of the agreement remained hidden in a series of classified annexes. The same was also true for the 1959 US/UK agreement relating to nuclear materials and the specific terms of the 'barter exchanges' under the MDA. TNA, PREM 13/3129, S. Zuckerman to Prime Minister, 16 December 1964.

26. Now Lockheed Martin. As with the UK effort, a large number of both government and private contractors played a part.
27. Harold Macmillan, *At the End of the Day 1961–1963* (Basingstoke: Macmillan, 1973), p. 335.
28. G.M. Dillon, *Dependence and Deterrence: Success and Civility in the Anglo-American Special Nuclear Relationship 1962–1982* (Aldershot: Gower, 1983).
29. Similar conservative assessments of the destructive potential of American nuclear forces are to be found amongst the US defence intelligence and military community. This, it has been argued, is a feature of an organizational (or bureaucratic) frame of mind through its definition and solving of problems. William Burr, 'The Nixon Administration, the "Horror Strategy" and the Search for Limited Nuclear Options, 1969–1972', *Journal of Cold War Studies*, Vol. 7, No. 3 (Summer 2005), p. 47; and Lynn Eden, *Whole World on Fire: Organizations, Knowledge and Nuclear Weapons Devastation* (Ithaca: Cornell University Press, 2003).
30. TNA, DEFE 13/752, Annex A to COS 45/72, 25 April 1972.
31. TNA, DEFE 13/752.
32. For the amount of damage required, see Baylis, *Ambiguity and Deterrence*, pp. 220–362.
33. Confidential correspondence, 7 April 2006.
34. Private correspondence with Sir Michael Quinlan, 23 October 2002.
35. John Baylis, 'British Nuclear Doctrine: The "Moscow Criterion" and the Polaris Improvement Programme', *Journal of Contemporary British History*, Vol. 19, No. 1 (Spring 2005), pp. 53–65.
36. See, for example, Clark and Wheeler, *British Origins of Nuclear Strategy*, pp. 43–90 and 210–29, and Baylis, *Ambiguity and Deterrence*, pp. 359–89.
37. TNA, WO 216/934, VCIGS to Festing, 26 September 1958.
38. See Baylis, *Ambiguity and Deterrence*, Ch. 10.
39. *The Times*, 22 May 1963.
40. Quoted in Pierre, *Nuclear Politics*, p. 256.
41. *Let's Go with Labour for the New Britain*, The Labour Party's Manifesto for the 1964 General Election (London: Transport House, 1964).
42. See Pierre, *Nuclear Politics*, pp. 276–83.
43. Pierre, *Nuclear Politics*.
44. For detailed information, see Kristan Stoddart, *Losing an Empire and Finding a Role: Britain, the USA, NATO and Nuclear Weapons 1964–70* (Basingstoke: Palgrave Macmillan, 2012), pp. 16, 19–20, 22–6, 34–5, 54, 60–70, 76–7, 85, 120–1, 167, 170–1, 197, 231, 239, 247, 259, and 270.
45. TNA, CAB 164/713, P. Rogers to Frank Cooper *Deployment of Polaris Submarines*, 11 November 1966, and *The Times*, 17 February 1966. John Young, 'Killing the MLF?', *Diplomacy and Statecraft*, Vol. 14, June 2003, pp. 295–324.
46. 704 H.C. Deb. Col.592–600 (17 December 1964).
47. Quinlan, *Thinking about Nuclear Weapons*, p. 36.
48. Quinlan, *Thinking about Nuclear Weapons*, p. 37.
49. Quinlan, *Thinking about Nuclear Weapons*, p. 39.
50. Quinlan, *Thinking about Nuclear Weapons*, p. 38.

Endnotes

51. Philip Ziegler, *Wilson: The Authorised Life of Lord Wilson of Rievaulx* (London: Weidenfeld & Nicolson, 1993), pp. 208–9.
52. Quoted in Peter Hennessy, *Muddling Through: Power, Politics and the Quality of Government in Postwar Britain* (London: Indigo, 1997), p. 116.
53. Denis Healey, *The Time of My Life* (London: Penguin, 1990), p. 302.
54. 'Recollections of a Secretary of State for Defence', *Journal of the Royal Air Force Historical Society*, Vol. 31 (2004), p. 12.
55. TNA, DEFE 13/350, P.S. to S. of S. *The Case for 5 S.S.B.N.s*, 19 October 1964.
56. TNA, DEFE, 13/50. On JIGSAW studies, see files within the class, TNA, DEFE 19/91 and Richard Moore, 'A JIGSAW Puzzle for Operations Researchers: British Global War Studies, 1954–1962', *Journal of Strategic Studies*, Vol. 20, No. 2 (June 1997), pp. 75–91.
57. On strategic culture see, for example, Alastair I. Johnston, 'Thinking about Strategic Culture', *International Security*, Vol. 19, No. 4 (Spring 1995), pp. 32–64; and Colin S. Gray, 'Strategic Culture as Context: The First Generation of Theory Strikes Back', *Review of International Studies*, Vol. 25, No. 1 (Jan. 1999), pp. 49–69.
58. Richard Baker, *Dry Ginger: The biography of Admiral of the Fleet Sir Michael Le Fanu* (London: W.H. Allen, 1977), p. 1.
59. For a reflection of this, see Steve Smith and Martin Hollis, 'Roles and Reasons in Foreign Policy Decision Making', *The British Journal of Political Science*, Vol. 16, No. 3 (1986), pp. 269–86.
60. TNA, DEFE 13/350, *Annex A TO COS 75/66 NATO Targeting of the Polaris Force*, 22 June 1966.
61. TNA, DEFE 13/350.
62. TNA, DEFE 11/437, G. Leitch D.U.S. (Pol.) to Secretary of State, 19 July 1967.
63. TNA, DEFE 11/437, DWH to *PRIME MINISTER*, 3 August 1967.
64. TNA, DEFE, 11/437.
65. TNA, DEFE 11/437, G. Leitch D.U.S. (Pol.) to Secretary of State, 19 July 1967.
66. Steven Twigge and Len Scott, *Planning Armageddon: Britain, the United States and the Command and Control of Western Nuclear Forces, 1945–1964* (Amsterdam: Harewood, 2000), pp. 321–2.
67. TNA, DEFE 11/437, DWH to *Prime Minister Annex A Draft Memorandum to SACEUR Assignment of Polaris Missiles*, 3 August 1967.
68. TNA, DEFE 11/437, DWH to *Prime Minister Annex B Draft Memorandum to SACLANT Assignment of Polaris Submarines*, 3 August 1967.
69. Although patrol in the North Atlantic was always favoured, if they were not assigned in this way the Polaris submarines would have to patrol in the Mediterranean as this was the only area under SACEUR's control for which deployment was suitable. Whilst the Baltic Sea was also under the remit of SACEUR this was 'not suitable for Polaris operations'. TNA, DEFE 11/437, DWH to *Prime Minister*, 3 August 1967.
70. TNA, DEFE, 11/437.
71. TNA, DEFE 13/548, *Guide for Duty Commanders On Polaris Operations*, 2 July 1968. They did, however, exploit the contours in the ocean to evade Soviet hunter killer submarines although towards the end of their service life, when the nuclear

reactor life was limited, at least once a submarine 'sat' on the bottom of the ocean and did not move for a patrol. Confidential correspondence, 6 April 2006.
72. TNA, DEFE 11/437, DWH to *Prime Minister Annex B Draft Memorandum to SACLANT Assignment of Polaris Submarines*, 3 August 1967.
73. TNA, DEFE 11/437, DWH to *Prime Minister*, 3 August 1967.
74. From the evidence released so far it is not possible to tell what happened during Brown's visit.
75. TNA, DEFE 11/437, DWH to *Prime Minister*, 3 August 1967. His minute was then sent for discussion to the Ministerial Committee on Nuclear Policy. TNA, DEFE 11/437, Derek Andrews to P.D. Nairne, 7 August 1967.
76. Confidential correspondence, 6 April 2006.
77. TNA, DEFE 11/437, DWH to *Prime Minister*, 3 August 1967.
78. Lawrence Freedman, *US Intelligence and the Soviet Strategic Threat* (Basingstoke: Macmillan, 1977); and John Prados, *The Soviet Estimate: US Intelligence Analysis and Russian Military Strength* (New York: Dial Press, 1982).
79. *The Times*, 22 February 1966.
80. For further discussion on the Healey-Schroeder Report and the PPGs, see Beatrice Heuser, 'European Defence before and after the "turn of the tide"', *Review of International Studies*, Vol. 19, No. 3 (October, 1993), pp. 409–19.
81. TNA, DEFE 13/547, DWH to *PUS Political Control of Polaris Force*, 16 August 1967.
82. TNA, DEFE 13/547, Draft letter from PS/Secretary of State to Michael Halls, No. 10, 15 September 1967. Nothing is presently known about the composition of this committee, and although there are listings of their deliberations in The National Archives, Kew, they are withheld under Section 3(4) of the Public Records Act.
83. TNA, DEFE 13/547, E. Broadbent to Michael Halls, 29 September 1967.
84. TNA, PREM 13/2571, DWH to *Prime Minister Polaris—Command and Control of Firing Orders*, 21 March 1967.
85. Between March 1967 and June 1968 a backup communications system for Polaris was initiated in Whitehall at 'the second Polaris HQ'. TNA, PREM 13/2571, *Final Version Procedure for routine daily tests from No. 10 Downing Street of the closed circuit television link with Polaris HQ*, 11 June 1968.
86. Although not stated, this would probably have included the prime minister's designated deputies in the chain of command. Moreover, as Sir Frank Cooper, who was Deputy Secretary (Policy) in the Ministry of Defence at this time, said in an interview with Peter Hennessy given in 2000, 'the key word is "authorised". The Prime Minister can only authorize... the use of nuclear weapons... he cannot give an order. The only legitimate orders can be given by commissioned officers of Her Majesty's forces.' Cooper continued: 'this distinction between authorisation and the power to give orders is a very important one... this is where you are into the Royal Prerogative basically'. This means that 'members are servants of the crown, not mere instruments of ministers'. Peter Hennessy, *The Secret State: Whitehall and the Cold War* (London: Penguin, 2002), pp. 183–4.
87. TNA, PREM 13/2571, DWH to *Prime Minister Polaris—Command and Control of Firing Orders*, 21 March 1967.
88. TNA, PREM 13/2571, A.N. Halls to *Sir Burke Trend*, 23 March 1967.

Endnotes

89. TNA, PREM 13/2571, Burke Trend to Mr Halls, 6 April 1967.
90. TNA, PREM 13/2571, HW to *Secretary of State for Defence*, 10 April 1967. Discussions also ensued to ensure that no one could imitate the prime minister. See, for example, TNA, PREM 13/2571, P.J. Hudson to A.N. Halls, 16 September 1969.
91. TNA, PREM 13/2571, M. Hodges to A.N. Halls, 6 September 1967. Hodges, a Royal Navy captain, was (amongst other things) the Communications Advisor to No. 10. TNA, PREM 13/2571, Michael Halls to E. Broadbent, 15 September 1967.
92. TNA, PREM 13/2571, M. Hodges to A.N. Halls, 6 September 1967.
93. TNA, PREM 13/2571, Ewan Broadbent to A.N. Halls, 10 September 1967.
94. TNA, PREM 13/2571, J.O.H. Burrough to A.N. Halls, 24 January 1968. However, Burrough felt that a drill twice daily 'fills me with some misgivings', as did the prospect of these to take place in the early evenings as the Cabinet Office remained busy. He suggested they should take place at 8.45am and again at 2.00pm, with a review of these arrangements after three months. TNA, PREM 13/2571, Michael Halls to J.O.H. Burrough, 26 January 1968.
95. TNA, PREM 13/2571, J.O.H. Burrough to A.N. Halls, 24 January 1968.
96. TNA, PREM 13/2571, John Burrough to A.N. Halls, 2 May 1968. The 'two man rule' did not apply to the tests. TNA, PREM 13/2571, J.H. Burrough No.87/3/7A, 14 May 1968.
97. TNA, PREM 13/2571, J.H. Burrough No.87/3/7A, 14 May 1968.
98. TNA, PREM 13/2571, *Note for the Record*, 29 June 1968.
99. TNA, PREM 13/2571.
100. A similar conundrum would also have faced the US president: Burr, 'The Nixon Administration, the "Horror Strategy"', p. 46.
101. TNA, DEFE 13/548, *Guide for Duty Commanders on Polaris Operations*, 2 July 1968.
102. TNA, DEFE 13/548.
103. Hennessy, *The Secret State*, pp. 171–93. See also Twigge and Scott, *Planning Armageddon*, pp. 12, 83–5, 88, 202, 210–12, and 321.
104. Hennessy, *The Secret State*, p. 186.
105. Hansard, *Fifth Series, Vol. LXV, 1914*, pp. 1809ff.
106. Peter Hennessy, *The Secret State: Preparing for the Worst 1945–2010* (London: Penguin, 2010), pp. 310–59.
107. Private correspondence with Sir Michael Quinlan, 23 October 2002.
108. TNA, DEFE 44/115, *Appendix 1 to Annex A to COS 1181/8/2/66 The Soviet Anti-Ballistic Missile Programme Outline Intelligence Report Covering Inception to September 1965;* TNA, CAB 168/27, EF/D/01059, Robert Press to Sir Solly Zuckerman ABM/PENAIDS, 23 July 1970.
109. Zuckerman, *Monkeys, Men and Missiles*, p. 392.
110. For a somewhat different view of the role of AWRE in the Polaris Improvement Programme, see Graham Spinardi, 'Aldermaston and British Nuclear Weapons Development: Testing the "Zuckerman thesis"', *Social Studies of Science*, Vol. 27, No. 4 (August, 1997), pp. 547–82.

Endnotes

111. Zuckerman, *Monkeys, Men and Missiles*, p. 392.
112. Zuckerman, *Monkeys, Men and Missiles*, p. 393.
113. Zuckerman, *Monkeys, Men and Missiles*, p. 393.
114. TNA, PREM 13/2493, Technical Discussion with the Americans on Polaris hardening—M.J.V. Bell to A.M. Palliser, 19 February 1969.
115. Frank Panton, 'Polaris Improvements and the Chevaline System 1967–1975/6', *Prospero, Proceedings from the British Rocketry Oral History Conferences at Charterhouse*, No. 1 (Spring 2004), pp. 110–11.
116. This was merely confirming the government's position, which had been laid out by Solly Zuckerman at a 1965 nuclear 'Stocktake' meeting. This had also been confirmed by Healey to Robert McNamara in April 1967, and repeated in the House of Commons on 13 June 1967. Private correspondence with Richard Moore, 9 April 2006.
117. Zuckerman, *Monkeys, Men and Missiles*, p. 405. It has also been pointed out to one of the authors by several senior officials on more than one occasion that Zuckerman remained within the Cabinet Office until the early 1980s, when he was 'made to retire'.
118. TNA, CAB 165/600, Burke Trend to *Prime Minister*, 1 December 1967.
119. TNA, CAB 165/600, *Prime Minister British Nuclear Weapons Policy* (PN(67)6 and PN (67)7), 1 December 1967.
120. TNA, CAB 165/600, Burke Trend to *Prime Minister*, 1 December 1967; and TNA, CAB 165/600, *Prime Minister British Nuclear Weapons Policy* (PN(67)6 and PN(67)7), 1 December 1967.
121. TNA, CAB 165/600, Burke Trend to *Prime Minister*, 4 January 1968.
122. TNA, DEFE 13/770, V.H.B. Macklen DCA(PN) to DUS(P), 6 May 1970.
123. TNA, CAB 168/277, S.Z. to *Sir Burke Trend*, March 1970. Zuckerman presumably meant AWRE and the MOD by 'the boys'.
124. See Chapter 1.

Chapter 6

1. 'Denis Healey, 'The Bomb, the Chancellor and Britain's Nuclear Secrets', BBC Radio 4 documentary 2011, <http://www.bbc.co.uk/programmes/b00zdj01#synopsis>, accessed 26 July 2011.
2. TNA, PREM 15/1359, *Strategic Nuclear Options* (Memorandum by the Ministry of Defence) *Annex E Collaborative Options—LTWP Sub-Group Report*, 2 November 1972.
3. This view is based on extensive conversations held over a number of years with several officials at different levels of the British nuclear effort and represents their considered view.
4. TNA, PREM 15/1359, *Strategic Nuclear Options* (Memorandum by the Ministry of Defence) *Annex E Collaborative Options—LTWP Sub-Group Report*, 2 November 1972.
5. TNA, PREM 15/1359.
6. Heuser, *NATO, Britain, France and the FRG*, pp. 93–123.

Endnotes

7. TNA, FCO 41/764, *Annex to PMVOM(W)(70)26 Extract from Record of Conversation between Lord Carrington and M. Debré on 20 November*, 10 December 1970.
8. TNA, FCO 41/764.
9. TNA, FCO 41/764.
10. TNA, DEFE 13/752, Ministry of Defence *UK Strategic Nuclear Force—Short Term Working Party Report*, 3 June 1971.
11. TNA, DEFE 13/752.
12. TNA, DEFE 13/752.
13. TNA, DEFE 13/752.
14. TNA, DEFE 13/752.
15. TNA, PREM 15/1359, Ref. A03540 Burke Trend to *Prime Minister Nuclear Deterrent*, 16 February 1973.
16. TNA, PREM 15/1359, *Prime Minister Future of the Nuclear Deterrent*, 27 June 1972.
17. TNA, PREM 15/1359, J.H. Petit to Lord Bridges, 7 August 1972.
18. This report into the Effectiveness of the UK Nuclear Deterrent by the JIC has been retained under Section 3(4) of the Public Records Act. TNA, PREM 15/1359, JIC(A) (72)30, 7 August 1972.
19. John Baylis and Kristan Stoddart, 'Chevaline: Britain's Hidden Nuclear Programme, 1967–1982', *Journal of Strategic Studies*, Vol. 26, No. 4 (December 2003), pp. 141–2.
20. TNA, PREM 15/1359, S. Zuckerman to Prime Minister, 17 July 1970.
21. TNA, PREM 15/2038, W.F. Mumford to The Lord Bridges, 21 December 1973.
22. TNA, PREM 15/1360, Burke Trend to *Prime Minister The Nuclear Deterrent: Polaris Improvements*, 13 July 1973.
23. TNA, DEFE 13/1038, CDS to *S of S Polaris Improvements*, 22 June 1973.
24. TNA, DEFE 13/1038.
25. This is not unusual in specific discussions concerning the British nuclear deterrent.
26. Philip Ziegler, *Wilson: The Authorised Life of Lord Wilson of Rievaulx* (London: Weidenfeld 1993) p. 460.
27. Tony Benn, *Against the Tide: Diaries 1973–1976* (London: Arrow 1990) pp. 267–8.
28. Ziegler, *Wilson* (note 72) p. 460.
29. Confidential correspondence, October 2002.
30. The codename was chosen after Kevin Tebbit of the Ministry of Defence rang up London Zoo and asked for the name of an animal like an antelope. He was given the name 'Chevaline'.
31. Grove, *Vanguard to Trident* (note 5) p. 358.
32. Perhaps though this lack of a full and open discussion in Cabinet is as much an indicator of Wilson's fears over a government split as it is of his selective marshalling of the facts surrounding Chevaline.
33. Records Management, Operational Selection Policy OSP11, *Nuclear Weapons Policy 1967–1998*, 2 February 2003.
34. TNA, DEFE 13/1039, *Meeting British National Criteria for Strategic Deterrence*, 10 November 1975.
35. TNA, DEFE 13/1039.
36. For the 1972 assessment for nuclear deterrence, see TNA, DEFE 5/192/45, *The Rationale for the United Kingdom Strategic Deterrent Force*, 25 April 1972.

37. TNA, DEFE 13/1039, *Meeting British National Criteria for Strategic Deterrence*, 10 November 1975.
38. TNA, DEFE 13/1039.
39. TNA, DEFE 13/1039, *Chief of the Defence Staff to Secretary of State Soviet ABM Cover*, 31 March 1976.
40. Walter Laqueur, *Europe in Our Time* (New York: Viking 1992) pp. 466–8.
41. United Kingdom Parliament Page, <www.parliament.the-stationery-office.co.uk/pa/cm199798/cmselect/cmdfence/138/13804.htm>, accessed on 11 November 2002.
42. Denis Healey, the Chancellor of the Exchequer regarded it 'as one of my mistakes as Chancellor not to get Chevaline cancelled': Healey, *The Time of My Life*, p. 313. Healey reiterated this view in a 2011 interview for the BBC: BBC 'Document' website, 'The Bomb, the Chancellor and Britain's Nuclear Secrets', <www.bbc.co.uk/programmes/b00zdj01>, accessed 26 July 2011.
43. This reflected a move away from the alternative 'temporary' targeting option suggested earlier by Carver which focused on Soviet cities other than Moscow.
44. TNA, DEFE 13/1039, J.F. Mayne to *Secretary of State Top Secret UK Eyes A Atomic Artificer*, 18 November 1975.
45. TNA, DEFE 13/1039.
46. TNA, DEFE 13/1039, *Top Secret UK Eyes A* MO 18/1/1 *Prime Minister Polaris Improvements*, 18 September 1975. Mayne, as Private Under-Secretary to Mason, was not primarily responsible for policy advice.
47. TNA, DEFE 13/1039, J.F. Mayne to *Secretary of State Top Secret UK Eyes A Atomic Artificer*, 18 November 1975.
48. TNA, DEFE 13/1039, *Top Secret UK Eyes A* MO 18/1/1 *Note for the Record Meeting British National Criteria for Strategic Deterrence*, 27 November 1975.
49. Present at the meeting were Roy Mason (Secretary of State for Defence), Bill Rodgers (Minister of State for Defence), Sir Michael Carver (Chief of the Defence Staff), Sir Frank Cooper (Permanent Under-Secretary of State at the MOD), Professor Hermann Bondi (Chief Scientific Advisor in the MOD), E.C. Cornford (Procurement Executive), Sir Edward Ashmore (Chief of the Naval Staff), A.P. Hockaday (Deputy Under-Secretary of State, Policy), Victor Macklen (Chief Advisor, Projects and Nuclear), and John Mayne (Private Secretary to Secretary of State for Defence). TNA, DEFE 13/1039, *Note for the Record of a Meeting in the Defence Secretary's Office held on Thursday 27th May at 2.30pm*, 1 June 1976.
50. TNA, DEFE 13/1039.
51. TNA, DEFE 13/350, P.S. to S. of S. *The Case for 5 S.S.B.N.s*, 19 October 1964.
52. TNA, DEFE 13/1039, *Note for the Record of a Meeting in the Defence Secretary's Office held on Thursday 27th May at 2.30PM*, 1 June 1976.
53. TNA, DEFE 13/1039, RM to *Prime Minister*, 11 June 1976.
54. Private correspondence with Lord Owen, March 2006. See also the transcript of 'The Chevaline Experience and the First Trident Decision, 1967–1980', Witness Seminar held at Charterhouse School, Surrey, UK, 13 April 2007, conducted by the Mountbatten Centre for International Studies and the Centre for Contemporary British History.

Endnotes

55. TNA, DEFE 13/1039, *Note for the Record of a Meeting in the Defence Secretary's Office held on Thursday 27th May at 2.30PM*, 1 June 1976.
56. TNA, DEFE 13/1039.
57. TNA, DEFE 13/1039.
58. BBC 'Document' website, 'The Bomb, the Chancellor and Britain's Nuclear Secrets', <www.bbc.co.uk/programmes/b00zdj01#synopsis>, accessed 26 July 2011.
59. BBC 'Document' website.
60. BBC 'Document' website.
61. BBC 'Document' website.
62. Hansard, House of Commons Debates, <http://www.parliament.the-stationery-office.co.uk/pa/cm199798/cmselect/cmdefence/138/13804.htm>, accessed 11 November 2002.
63. Healey, *The Time of My Life*, p. 456.
64. Healey, *The Time of my Life*, p. 456.
65. Peter Hennessy, *The Secret State: Whitehall and The Cold War* (London: Penguin 2002).
66. Heuser, *NATO, Britain, France and the FRG*, pp. 74–92.
67. Private correspondence with Sir Michael Quinlan, 23 October 2002.
68. Private correspondence with Sir Michael Quinlan, 15 August 2006.

Chapter 7

* Taken from national archives, TNA, PREM 16/1977, *Factors Relating to Further Consideration of the Future of the United Kingdom Strategic Deterrent Part I: The Politico-Military Requirement Summary of Report*, December 1978.
1. TNA, PREM 16/1564, Conclusions of a Ministerial Meeting held at No. 10 Downing Street at 09.45 am, Friday 28 October 1977.
2. TNA, PREM 16/1564, F.M. to *Prime Minister Chevaline*, 19 September 1977.
3. TNA, PREM 16/1564, E.A.J. Fergusson to Bryan Cartledge *Chevaline*, 23 September 1977.
4. TNA, PREM 16/1564, R.L.L Facer to B G Cartledge *Chevaline*, 29 September 1977.
5. TNA, PREM 16/1564, Clive Rose to Mr *Cartledge* c Sir John Hunt *Chevaline*, 30 September 1977.
6. On the Galosh system and its importance to British strategic nuclear targeting, see Kristan Stoddart, 'The Wilson Government and British Responses to ABMs, 1964–1970', *Journal of Contemporary British History*, Vol. 23, No. 1 (March 2009), pp. 1–33 and K. Stoddart, 'Maintaining the Moscow Criterion: British Strategic Nuclear Targeting, 1974–1979', *Journal of Strategic Studies*, Vol. 31, No. 6 (December 2008), pp. 897–924.
7. This was based on the area of sea room they could operate in and was complicated once the SSBNs moved into deep water.
8. W.J.A. Wilberforce to Mr Moberly PS/PUS Private Secretary, 22 September 1977. Reproduced in Owen, *Nuclear Papers*, pp. 75–96. Many of these issues regarding cruise were subsequently examined in detail by the Nuclear Matters Working Party detailed below. TNA, DEFE 68/405, NMWP(78)11 Ministry of Defence

Working Party on Nuclear Matters Cruise Missile Options for a UK Strategic Deterrent Note by the Secretary, 21 June 1978.
9. Summary Record of a Meeting on Military Nuclear Issues in the Secretary of State's Office at 10.15 am on Monday 17 October 1977. Reproduced in David Owen, *Nuclear Papers*, pp. 97–103.
10. Summary Record of a Meeting on Military Nuclear Issues in the Secretary of State's Office at 10.15 am on Monday 17 October 1977. Reproduced in Owen, *Nuclear Papers*, pp. 97–103. In doing so he rejected the number of seventeen additional SSNs put forward by Ian Smart in his recent Chatham House study. Ian Smart, 'British foreign policy to 1985: The future of the British nuclear deterrent: technical, economic and strategic issues', *Royal Institute of International Affairs*, (1977).
11. This was a highly secret committee that even lacked the Gen number normally assigned to Labour government subcommittee.
12. TNA, PREM 16/1564, John Hunt to *Prime Minister Military Nuclear Issues*, 25 October 1977.
13. TNA, PREM 16/1564, Conclusions of a Ministerial Meeting, 10 Downing Street, 09.45 am, 28 October 1977.
14. TNA, PREM 16/1564.
15. TNA, DEFE 68/405, Nuclear Matters Note of a meeting held in Sir John Hunt's Room, Cabinet Office, on Wednesday, 2 November 1977 at 5.30 pm, 2 November 1977.
16. Kristan Stoddart, *The Sword and the Shield Britain, America, NATO and Nuclear Weapons, 1970–1976* (Basingstoke, Palgrave 2014).
17. TNA, PREM 16/1564, John Hunt to *Prime Minister Nuclear Defence Policy*, 29 November 1977.
18. TNA, PREM 16/1564, Cabinet Nuclear Defence Policy Note of a Meeting held at 10 Downing Street on Thursday 1 December 1977 at 10.00 am, 6 December 1977.
19. TNA, PREM 16/1564.
20. TNA, PREM 16/1564.
21. TNA, DEFE 25/325, *Terms of Reference for a Study of Factors Relating to Further Consideration of the Future of the United Kingdom Nuclear Deterrent*, undated 1978.
22. TNA, PREM 16/1564, John Hunt to *Mr. Cartledge Top Secret and Personal*, 9 December 1977.
23. TNA, PREM 16/1564, John Hunt to *Prime Minister Nuclear Studies*, 13 December 1977.
24. TNA, PREM 16/1564.
25. TNA, PREM 16/1564.
26. TNA, PREM 16/1564.
27. TNA, PREM 16/1564.
28. Hennessy, *The Secret State*, pp. 52–9; Peter Hennessy, *The Prime Minister: The Office and its Holders Since 1945* (London: Penguin, 2000), pp. 389–90.
29. TNA, DEFE 68/405, *Criteria for Deterrence* Note of a Meeting held in Sir Antony Duff's room, Foreign and Commonwealth Office, on Wednesday 4 January 1978 at 11.00 am, 5 January 1978.

Endnotes

30. TNA, DEFE 68/405, *Criteria for Deterrence* Note of a meeting held in Sir Antony Duff's Room, Foreign and Commonwealth Office on Thursday 23 February 1978 at 3.00 pm, 23 February 1978.
31. TNA, PREM 16/1977, John Hunt to *Prime Minister Criteria for Deterrence*, 13 July 1979.
32. This also had a bearing upon decisions regarding Labour's 1974 Manifesto commitment. TNA, PREM 16/1977, John Hunt to *Prime Minister Criteria for Deterrence*, 13 July 1979.
33. TNA, PREM 16/1977, BGC to *Prime Minister The UK Deterrent*, 20 July 1978.
34. TNA, PREM 16/1977.
35. TNA, DEFE 25/335, *The Future of the UK Nuclear Deterrent*, 13 August 1979.
36. TNA, PREM 16/1977, BGC to *Prime Minister The UK Deterrent*, 4 August 1978.
37. Owen, *Time to Declare*, p. 381, and Hennessy, *Muddling Through: Power, Politics and the Quality of Government in Postwar Britain*, p. 124.
38. TNA, PREM 16/1977, David Owen to *Prime Minister Nuclear Weapons Policy*, 31 July 1978.
39. TNA, PREM 16/1977.
40. TNA, PREM 16/1977.
41. TNA, PREM 16/1977, David Owen to *Prime Minister Nuclear Weapons Policy*, 31 July 1978. A similar series of judgements were arrived at in December. G.G.H. Walden to B.G. Cartledge, 12 December 1978. Reproduced in Owen, *Nuclear Papers*, pp. 151–7.
42. France was added soon after. TNA, PREM 16/1977, John Hunt to *Prime Minister Future of the British Deterrent*, 7 December 1978. Callaghan's request was handwritten on Hunt's note.
43. TNA, PREM 16/1977, *Factors Relating to Further Consideration of the Future of the United Kingdom Strategic Deterrent Part I: The Politico-Military Requirement Summary of Report*, December 1978.
44. TNA, PREM 16/1977.
45. Carl von Clausewitz, *On War*, translated by Michael Howard and Peter Paret, abridged, with an introduction and notes by Beatrice Heuser (Oxford: Oxford University Press, 2007), esp. pp. xxvii–xxxii and 30–1. See also Beatrice Heuser, *Reading Clausewitz* (London: Pimlico, 2002).
46. TNA, PREM 16/1977, *Factors Relating to Further Consideration of the Future of the United Kingdom Strategic Deterrent Part I: The Politico-Military Requirement Summary of Report*, December 1978.
47. See, for example, the fine tribute paid by Sir Richard Mottram in his obituary in *The Guardian*, 2 March 2009. Quinlan's views of the 'seamless robe of deterrence' and TNF modernization can also be found in Tanya Ogilvie-White, *On Nuclear Deterrence: The Correspondence of Sir Michael Quinlan*, pp. 167–259.
48. TNA, PREM 16/1977, *Factors Relating to Further Consideration of the Future of the United Kingdom Strategic Deterrent Part I: The Politico-Military Requirement Summary of Report*, December 1978.
49. See, for example, Hennessy, *The Secret State*, pp. 78–80.

Endnotes

50. TNA, PREM 16/1977, *Factors Relating to Further Consideration of the Future of the United Kingdom Strategic Deterrent Part I: The Politico-Military Requirement Summary of Report*, December 1978.
51. TNA, DEFE 24/2122, *The Study of Factors Related to Further Consideration of the Future of the UK Nuclear Deterrent Summary of Part III on System Options and their Implications*, undated 1979.
52. TNA, PREM 16/1977, David Owen to *Prime Minister Future of the British Deterrent*, 11 December 1978.
53. TNA, PREM 16/1977.
54. TNA, PREM 16/1977.
55. TNA, PREM 16/1977.
56. This meant that after the two December meetings of the 'Restricted Group', more work was required to refine the studies 'which were very quickly drafted'. TNA, DEFE, pp. 25–335, *SCDS(B)1 to PSO/CDS Call on S of S to Discuss Nuclear Matters Working Party (NMWP) 12 December 1978*, 12 December 1978.
57. TNA, PREM 16/1977, John Hunt to *Prime Minister Future of the British Deterrent*, 15 December 1979.
58. Peter Malone, *The British Nuclear Deterrent* (London: Croom Helm, 1984), p. 114.
59. TNA, DEFE 24/2122, Duff Mason Report on factors relating to the further consideration of the future of the UK nuclear deterrent Part III System Options, December 1978.
60. An early copy of this paper had been provided to Callaghan the week before. TNA, PREM 16/1977, G.G.H. Walden to B.G. Cartledge, 12 December 1978.
61. TNA, PREM 16//1978, David Owen to *Prime Minister Future of the British Deterrent*, 19 December 1978.
62. TNA, DEFE 25/335, *Chiefs of Staff Committee Meeting Tuesday 21 August 1979 at 1045 Item 1 Nuclear Matters The Future of the UK Nuclear Deterrent Commentary on the Duff/Mason Report*, 17 August 1979. Quoted in Owen, *Nuclear Papers*, p. 22.
63. TNA, PREM 16/1978, David Owen to *Prime Minister Future of the British Deterrent*, 19 December 1978.
64. TNA, PREM 16/1978.
65. Owen, *Time to Declare*, p. 380.
66. TNA, PREM 16/1978, John Hunt to *Prime Minister Future of the British Deterrent*, 20 December 1978. Owen, *Time to Declare*, p. 381.
67. TNA, PREM 16/1978, John Hunt to *Prime Minister Future of the British Deterrent*, 20 December 1978.
68. TNA, PREM 16/1978.
69. TNA, PREM 16/1978, FM to *Prime Minister Future of the British Deterrent*, 20 December 1978.
70. Owen, *Time to Declare*, p. 381.
71. TNA, PREM 16/1978, Cabinet Nuclear Defence Policy Note of a Meeting held at 10 Downing Street on Thursday 21 December 1978 at 9.45 am, 22 December 1978.
72. TNA, PREM 16/1978.
73. TNA, PREM 16/1978.
74. TNA, PREM 16/1978.

Endnotes

75. TNA, PREM 16/1978.
76. TNA, PREM 16/1978, *Prime Minister's Conversation with President Carter: 3.30 p.m., 5 January, at Guadeloupe*, 5 January 1979; K.O. Morgan, *Callaghan: A Life* (Oxford: Oxford University Press, 1997), p. 620; Callaghan, *Time and Chance*, pp. 554–7.
77. TNA, PREM 16/1978, LR to The Prime Minister *Personal Chancellor of the Exchequer Nuclear Defence Policy*, 17 January 1979.
78. His return from Guadeloupe was a public relations disaster. As recounted in the tabloid newspaper the *Daily Mail*: 'Widespread national strikes had brought the Labour government to its knees. Rubbish was piling up in the streets and walk-outs by gravediggers in Liverpool and Manchester had even left bodies unburied. So on January 17, 1979, Mr Callaghan decided he needed to declare a state of emergency. The announcement would be made at 3.30pm the next day, he decided. But he was talked out of it by his Cabinet, who feared it would inflame the situation. The Prime Minister had already rejected calls to declare a state of emergency on January 4. A week later he infamously told journalists that suggestions of "mounting chaos" were an exaggeration. His remarks were paraphrased the next day under the headline "Crisis, What Crisis?"—words which helped condemn Labour to defeat at the next election.' 'Winter of Discontent led Callaghan to brink of calling in the Army, 30-year papers reveal', *Daily Mail*, 30 December 2009.
79. TNA, PREM 16/1978, Jim Callaghan The Prime Minister *Secret for the President's Eyes Only*, 27 March 1979.
80. Hennessy, *Muddling Through*, pp. 126–7, and private correspondence with Lord Owen, March 2006.
81. TNA, PREM 16/1978, John Hunt to *Mr. Cartledge Nuclear Matters*, 27 March 1979.
82. TNA, PREM 16/1978. On Callaghan's reasons for passing this information on, see Hennessy, *The Secret State*, pp. 317–18.
83. Owen, *Time to Declare*, p. 382.
84. Quoted in Hennessy, *Muddling Through*, p. 124.

Chapter 8

1. House of Commons debate on 3 March 1981. Available at <http://www.theyworkforyou.com/debates/?id=1981-03-03a.137.0#g219.2>, accessed 8 August 2013.
2. Bill Jackson and Dwin Bramall, *The Chiefs: The Story of the United Kingdom Chiefs of Staff* (London: Brassey's, 1992), pp. 386–400.
3. Hansard, House of Commons Debates, <http://hansard.millbanksystems.com/commons/1980/jan/24/nuclear-weapons>, accessed 9 March 2014.
4. TNA, DEFE 25/335, *CNS* to Secretary of State, 15 June 1979.
5. The Nott Defence Review was aimed at concentrating the rising costs of the British defence effort on the nuclear and conventional forces allocated to NATO. The Nott Review hit the Navy's conventional capability hardest, and even after the pivotal role the surface fleet played during the victorious Falkland's War of 1982 many of the cuts stayed. This was despite concerted public criticism from senior figures of the Royal Navy that the government was jeopardizing the country's war-fighting

potential. Andrew Dorman, 'John Nott and the Royal Navy: the 1981 Defence Review Revisited', *Contemporary British History*, Vol. 15, No. 2 (Summer 2001), pp. 98–120; Andrew Dorman, 'VIEWPOINT—The Nott Review: Dispelling the Myths?', *Defence Studies*, Vol. 1, No. 3 (Spring 2001), pp. 113–21; and Andrew Dorman, Michael Kandiah, and Gillian Staerck, 'The Nott Review Witness Seminar', Centre for Contemporary British History, 20 June 2001.

6. On the style of Cabinet government, see Peter Hennessy's majestic *Whitehall* (London: Fontana, 1990), pp. 307–18; Hennessy, *The Prime Minister: The Office and its Holders Since 1945* pp. 400–1, 410, and 427–8; see also Lawrence Freedman, *Britain and Nuclear Weapons* (Basingstoke: Macmillan, 1980), p. 62.
7. TNA, DEFE 24/2122, M.E. Quinlan DUS(P) to CSA *Nuclear Matters*, 10 May 1979.
8. TNA, CAB 130/1109, MISC 7(79) 1st Meeting Cabinet Nuclear Defence Policy, 24 May 1979.
9. TNA, CAB 130/1109.
10. TNA, CAB 130/1109.
11. It was also noted that there might be West German objections to Anglo-French collaboration as it might undermine US commitments to Europe and a brief requested on the issue of collaboration. TNA, CAB 130/1109, MISC 7(79) 1st Meeting Cabinet Nuclear Defence Policy, 24 May 1979. The second meeting of MISC 7 dealt with the future supply of HEU through 'Project Destiny' and whether the US would supply it or whether the UK would need to develop Capenhurst for this purpose. This had potential non-proliferation concerns and 'could weaken the posture we were at present adopting towards Pakistan's nuclear aspirations'. TNA, CAB 130/1109, MISC 7(79) 2nd Meeting Cabinet Nuclear Defence Policy, 10 July 1979.
12. Although it was mistakenly written as MISC 1 in the document. TNA, DEFE 24/2122, Clive Rose to Ron Mason, 13 June 1979.
13. TNA, DEFE 24/2122, Clive Rose to Ron Mason, 13 June 1979.
14. TNA, DEFE 68/406, *Future of the UK Nuclear Deterrent Part III—System Options*, August 1979.
15. TNA, CAB 196/123, R.L.L. Facer to *Mr Goodall Briefs for a Labour/Alliance Administration*, 6 June 1983.
16. Ranges redacted in the original reference but stated later in Duff-Mason.
17. TNA, DEFE 68/406, *Future of the UK Nuclear Deterrent Part III—System Options*, August 1979.
18. TNA, DEFE 68/406.
19. TNA, DEFE 68/406.
20. TNA, DEFE 68/406.
21. TNA, CAB 130/1109, MISC 7(79) 3rd Meeting Cabinet Nuclear Defence Policy, 19 September 1979.
22. TNA, DEFE 68/406, *Confidential Annex to COS 22nd Meeting, held on Tuesday 21st August 1979 at 10.45am*, 21 August 1979.
23. Top Level Group of UK Parliamentarians for Multilateral Nuclear Disarmament & Non Proliferation, <http://toplevelgroup.org/about-2/biographies/>, accessed

Endnotes

10 August 2013; and Edwin Bramall, 'The case for keeping Trident is political, not military', *The Independent*, 8 August 2013.
24. Although it has been suggested by one senior official at the technical working level that the Duff-Mason criteria for deterrence had existed since 1960. Confidential correspondence, 6 April 2006.
25. TNA, DEFE 25/335, *The Future of the UK Nuclear Deterrent*, 13 August 1979.
26. TNA, DEFE 25/335.
27. TNA, DEFE 25/335.
28. TNA, DEFE 25/335.
29. It was also noted in a handwritten addition beneath that 'This capability also represents our insurance should collective security arrangements fail.' This was ticked in the margin as 'Accepted', possibly by Francis Pym for whom the digest was intended. TNA, DEFE 25/335, *The Future of the UK Nuclear Deterrent*, 13 August 1979.
30. TNA, DEFE 25/335, *The Future of the UK Nuclear Deterrent*, 13 August 1979.
31. TNA, DEFE 25/335.
32. Livre Blanc sur la Défence de 1972 (Paris: Ministre de la Défence, 1972). The intellectual foundations for this nuclear posture can be found in (General) Lucien Poirier, 'Quelques problèms actuels de la strategie nucleáire francaise', *Défence Nationale* (December 1979), pp. 43–62, and further expanded in Lucien Poirier, *Essais de stratégie théorique*, Institut de stratégie comparée (Paris: F.E.D.N. 1982).
33. Poirier, 'Quelques problems'.
34. Poirier, 'Quelques problems'.
35. Poirier, 'Quelques problems'.
36. Poirier, 'Quelques problems'.
37. Poirier, 'Quelques problems'.
38. Poirier, 'Quelques problems'.
39. Poirier, 'Quelques problems'.
40. Poirier, 'Quelques problems'.
41. Confidential correspondence, 6 April 2006.
42. TNA, DEFE 25/335, *The Future of the UK Nuclear Deterrent*, 13 August 1979.
43. TNA, DEFE 25/335.
44. TNA, DEFE 24/2122, M.E. Quinlan to *VCNS Coulport and Successor Systems*, 11 July 1979.
45. TNA, DEFE 24/2122, R.C. Mottram *PS/PUS* to *Sec/VCNS Coulport and Successor Systems*, 13 July 1979.
46. Sir Frank Cooper, *The Telegraph*, 30 January 2002.
47. TNA, DEFE 24/2122, R.C. Mottram *PS/PUS* to *Sec/VCNS Coulport and Successor Systems*, 13 July 1979.
48. TNA, DEFE 24/2122, VCNS to DUS(P) *Coulport and Successor Systems*, 16 July 1979.
49. TNA, DEFE 24/2122, J.N.H. Blelioch to *DUS(P)*, 6 August 1979.
50. Heather Wilson, 'Anglo-American relations after the INF Treaty', in Michael Clarke and Rod Hague (eds), *European Defence Co-operation* (Manchester: Manchester University Press, 1990), pp. 94–7; and Lawrence Freedman, *Britain and Nuclear Weapons*, pp. 119–26. See also Chapter 7.

Endnotes

51. TNA, PREM 19/159, R.L. Wade-Gery to *Sir Robert Armstrong Polaris Replacement: Dr Aaron's Call*, 30 November 1979.
52. Margaret Thatcher, *The Downing Street Years* (London: Harper Collins, 1993), p. 245; and TNA, PREM 19/159, Robert Armstrong to *Prime Minister Future of the Strategic Deterrent* (MISC 7), 4 December 1979.
53. This increased the risk of government leaks, with Mrs Thatcher asked to consider whether the MISC 7 decision should only be revealed to Cabinet 'just before you are ready to make an announcement'. TNA, PREM 19/159, Robert Armstrong to *Prime Minister Future of the Strategic Deterrent* (MISC 7), 4 December 1979.
54. TNA, PREM 19/159, Robert Armstrong to *Prime Minister Future of the Strategic Deterrent* (MISC 7), 4 December 1979.
55. TNA, PREM 19/159.
56. TNA, PREM 19/159.
57. TNA, PREM 19/159.
58. TNA, PREM 19/159.
59. TNA, PREM 19/159.
60. Charles Moore, *Margaret Thatcher: The Authorized Biography, Volume One: Not For Turning* (London: Allen Lane, 2013), pp. 353 and 455–81. This is a view Geoffrey Howe himself disputed in a conversation with one of the authors.
61. TNA, PREM 19/159, Robert Armstrong to *Prime Minister Future of the Strategic Deterrent* (MISC 7), 4 December 1979.
62. TNA, PREM 19/159.
63. TNA, PREM 19/159.
64. TNA, PREM 19/159, R L Wade-Gery to *Sir Robert Armstrong Polaris Replacement: Dr Aaron's Call*, 30 November 1979.
65. TNA, PREM 19/159, Robert Armstrong to *Prime Minister Future of the Strategic Deterrent* (MISC 7), 4 December 1979.
66. TNA, PREM 19/159.
67. TNA, PREM 19/159.
68. Peter Hennessy, *Cabinet*, p. 155. TNA, CAB 126/68/6, *Cabinet* Conclusions of a Meeting of the Cabinet held at 10 Downing Street on Thursday 17 July 1980 at 10.30am, 17 July 1980.
69. This slightly earlier than planned public announcement was forced on the government as Richard Birt, a journalist, was about to break the story in America for the *New York Times*. Hennessy, *Cabinet*, p. 155. TNA, D.J. Wright to J.F. Halliday *British Strategic Nuclear Force*, 15 July 1980. As the government brought the decision forward, Birt's story was usurped and did not appear.
70. TNA, PREM 19/417, Robert Armstrong to *Prime Minister Cabinet: Parliamentary Affairs*, 16 July 1980.
71. John Nott, *Here Today, Gone Tomorrow: Recollections of an Errant Politician* (London: Politico's, 2002), p. 216.
72. Transcript of the 'Cabinets and the Bomb' Workshop held at the British Academy in 2007, <http://www.britac.ac.uk/pubs/review/perspectives/0703cabinetsandbomb-2.cfm>, accessed 14 August 2013.

Endnotes

73. The Future United Kingdom Strategic Nuclear Deterrent Force, *Defence Open Government Document 80/23, Ministry of Defence*, July 1980.
74. The Future of the United Kingdom Strategic Nuclear Deterrent Force (emphasis added).
75. David Reynolds, *Britannia Overruled: British Policy and World Power in the 20th Century* (London: Longman, 1991), pp. 260–1.
76. Nott's speech and the full debate that followed can be found here: <www.theyworkforyou.com/debates/?id=1981-03-03a.137.0#g219.2>, accessed 8 August 2013.
77. See, for example, Paul Kengor, *The Crusader: Ronald Reagan and the Fall of Communism* (New York: Regan Books, 2006) and John Patrick Diggins, *Ronald Reagan: Fate, Freedom, and the Making of History* (New York: W.W. Norton & Company, 2007). The presidential National Security Decision Directive (NSDD) authorizing this modernization can be found at <http://www.reagan.utexas.edu/archives/reference/Scanned%20NSDDS/NSDD12.pdf>, accessed 14 July 2013.
78. TNA, PREM 19/417, Caspar Weinberger to Her Excellency Margaret Thatcher, 24 August 1981.
79. TNA, AIR 8/2846, D C G Brook Air Cdre PSO/CDS to *Secretary of State The Future of the UK Strategic Nuclear Deterrent*, 16 October 1981.
80. TNA, CAB 130/1160, MISC 7(81)1 Cabinet Nuclear Defence Policy United Kingdom Strategic Deterrent Memorandum by the Secretary of State for Defence Appendix 2, 17 November 1981.
81. TNA, PREM 19/694, Robert Armstrong to *Prime Minister The United Kingdom Strategic Deterrent* MISC 7(81)1, 11 January 1982.
82. TNA, PREM 19/694.
83. TNA, CAB 130/1182, Cabinet Nuclear Defence Policy Most Confidential Record to MISC 7(82) 1st Meeting, Tuesday, 12 January 1982, 18 January 1982.
84. TNA, CAB 130/1182.
85. Kristan Stoddart, *Losing an Empire and Finding a Role*, pp. 18–27.
86. An interesting examination of Labour's nuclear weapons policies during the 1980s can be found in Scott, 'Selling or Selling Out', pp. 115–37.
87. TNA, CAB 128/75, *Cabinet* Most Confidential Record to CC(82) 8th Conclusions, 4 March 1982.
88. In his defence Howe, the Chancellor, as a member of MISC 7 would have heard the briefing before. Nott, *Here Today, Gone Tomorrow*, p. 217.
89. TNA, CAB 128/75, *Cabinet* Most Confidential Record to CC(82) 8th Conclusions, 4 March 1982.
90. TNA, CAB 128/75.
91. TNA, CAB 128/75.
92. HC Deb 11 March 1982 Vol. 19 cc975–86, available from <http://hansard.millbanksystems.com/commons/1982/mar/11/trident-missile-programme>, accessed 24 February 2013.
93. TNA, CAB 130/1182, MISC 7(82) 4 Cabinet Nuclear Defence Policy United Kingdom Strategic Deterrent: *Annex A Effect of Missile Processing on the Independence of the UK Deterrent*, 19 July 1982.
94. TNA, CAB 130/1182.

Endnotes

95. TNA, CAB 130/1182.
96. TNA, PREM 19/695, John Coles to Richard Mottram *United Kingdom Strategic Deterrent: Missile Processing*, 9 September 1982.
97. TNA, FO/93/8/466, Sir Oliver Wright to George Shultz, 19 October 1982.
98. For a fuller discussion of the submarine basing options, see Colin McInnes, *Trident: The Only Option* (London: Brassey's, 1986), pp. 20–2.
99. Jackson and Bramall, *The Chiefs*, p. 392.
100. Jackson and Bramall, *The Chiefs*, p. 392.
101. Reynolds, *Britannia Overruled*, pp. 276–7.
102. Reynolds, *Britannia Overruled*, pp. 276–7.
103. Hennessy, *Muddling Through:* p. 127.
104. Quinlan, *Thinking About Nuclear Weapons*, p. 126.
105. Private interview with Sir John Nott, 3 May 2006.
106. McInnes, *Trident: The Only Option*, p. 24.
107. McInnes, *Trident: The Only Option*, p. 24.
108. Although the latter had retired he remained a powerful politico-military figure.
109. Rodric Braithwaite, *Across the Moscow River: The World Turned Upside Down* (New Haven CT: Yale University Press, 2002), p. 52.

Chapter 9

1. Hansard HC [974/1100-06] Speech given 27 November 1979. Available at <http://www.margaretthatcher.org/document/104179>, accessed 2 May 2014.
2. TNA, FCO 46/2769, R.J. Harding (Head of DS8) *MOU on GLCM Basing in the UK*, 14 April 1981.
3. TNA, FCO 46/2769, J.M. Legge (Head of DS17) to *APS/S of S*, 8 April 1981. The dual-key arrangement meant that the British and the US officials had separate keys, both of which were needed to fire the missile. The system was designed to ensure that neither could launch the missile without the authority of the other.
4. TNA, CAB 130/1182, Most Confidential Record to MISC 7(82) 4th Meeting, 12 November 1982.
5. TNA, CAB 130/1182, MISC 7(82) 4th Meeting, 12 November 1982.
6. Document provided to the author through a Freedom of Information Act (FOIA) request, henceforward FOIA, but lacking a file number. Michael Heseltine to the Rt Hon John Biffen MP, 11 April 1983. His remit was 'to take on the peace protest movements, and to secure the deployment of cruise missiles'. Private interview with Lord Heseltine, January 2012.
7. Beatrice Heuser and Kristan Stoddart, 'Großbritannien zwischen Doppelbeschluss und Anti-Kernwaffen-Protestbewegungen', in P. Gassert, T. Geiger, and H. Wentker (eds) *Zweiter Kalter Krieg und Friedensbewegung: Der NATO-Doppelbeschluss in deutsch-deutscher und internationaler Perspekive* (Munich: Oldenbourg, 2011), pp. 305–24.
8. Beatrice Heuser, *Britain, NATO, France and the FRG: Nuclear Strategies and Forces for Europe, 1949–2000* (Basingstoke: Macmillan, 1997), pp. 56–7.
9. In March 1983 the US president described the Soviet Union as an 'Evil Empire' because of its human rights record and control over Eastern Europe. He also

proposed a ground-based and space-based system for defence against attack by Soviet ballistic missiles.
10. TNA, CAB 130/1182, Most Confidential Record to MISC 7(82) 4th Meeting, 12 November 1982; Thatcher, *Downing Street Years*, pp. 268–9. See also Robin Day, *But with Respect: Memorable Interviews with Statesmen and Parliamentarians* (London: Weidenfeld & Nicolson, 1993), pp. 221–4. The declassified text (with some redaction) of the Murphy-Dean Agreement can be found on the National Security Archive website, 'Consultation is Presidential Business' webpage: <http://www.gwu.edu/~nsarchiv/NSAEBB/NSAEBB159/usukconsult-8.pdf>, accessed 21 October 2008. A (UK) commentary on the significance of the Murphy-Dean Understanding can be found in John Baylis, 'Exchanging Nuclear Secrets', *Diplomatic History*, Vol. 25, No. 1 (Winter, 2001), p. 58.
11. Thatcher, *Downing Street Years*, pp. 171 and 259.
12. Michael Heseltine, *Life in the Jungle: My Autobiography* (London: Hodder and Stoughton, 2000), pp. 243–53.
13. Private interview with Sir Michael Quinlan, 3 August 2006.
14. Private interview with Sir Michael Quinlan, 25 November 2007.
15. Heuser, *NATO, Britain, France and the FRG*, p. 56.
16. Scott, 'Selling or Selling Out', pp. 115–37.
17. TNA, FO 973/413, NATO 'Double Track Decision: The Present Stage', April 1985.
18. Thatcher, *Downing Street Years*, p. 269.
19. FOIA, Cruise Missile Counter Force Capabilities, 19 May 1983.
20. Thatcher, *Downing Street Years*, pp. 269–70 and 328–33. See also Richard Aldous, *Reagan and Thatcher: The Difficult Relationship* (London: Hutchinson, 2012), pp. 58–9.
21. <http://www.margaretthatcher.org/archive/displaydocument.asp?docid=105592>, accessed 21 September 2013.
22. Heseltine, *Life in the Jungle*, p. 255.
23. Day, *But With Respect*, p. 248.
24. Reagan Library (NSC European & Soviet Directorate Box 90902), US Embassy London to State Department, British Reaction to Reykjavik: As the dust settles, perspective returns, 17 November 1986. Available from <http://www.margaretthatcher.org/document/110566>, accessed 21 September 2013.
25. Private interview with Sir Bryan Cartledge, January 2012.
26. Thatcher, *Downing Street Years*, p. 471.
27. Thatcher, *Downing Street Years*, p. 471.
28. Thatcher, *Downing Street Years*, p. 472.
29. Thatcher, *Downing Street Years*, p. 473. Heseltine noted that Britain signed a collaborative agreement in 1985 (followed by West Germany, Israel, Italy, and Japan) to support SDI which, by 1999, had amounted to $150m, with the project having been wound down following the end of the Cold War. Heseltine, *Life in the Jungle*, pp. 255–9.
30. Thatcher, *Downing Street Years*, pp. 477 and 481.
31. Thatcher, *Downing Street Years*, p. 482.
32. Thatcher, *Downing Street Years*, pp. 482–5.

33. In late 1986 it was revealed that the US had made sales of arms to Iran to gain the release of American hostages in Lebanon.
34. Thatcher, *Downing Street Years*, p. 771.
35. Thatcher, *Downing Street Years*, p. 772.
36. Thatcher, *Downing Street Years*, p. 773.
37. <http://www.nato.int/docu/comm/49-95/c880303a.htm>, accessed 22 September 2013.
38. Thatcher, *Downing Street Years*, pp. 775–6.
39. Thatcher, *Downing Street Years*, p. 787.
40. Douglas Hurd, *Memoirs* (London: Little, Brown, 2003), pp. 381–9.
41. Private interview with Lord Powell, January 2012.
42. John Major, *John Major: The Autobiography* (New York: HarperCollins: 1999), p. 222.
43. Major, *John Major: The Autobiography*, p. 223.
44. 'The Major Years', Blakeway productions for the BBC (1999). A transcript of the interview can be found at <http://www.johnmajor.co.uk/page4363.html>, accessed 25 September 2013.
45. Major, *John Major*, p. 232.
46. Major, *John Major*, p. 232.
47. Major, *John Major*, p. 236.
48. Major, *John Major*, p. 241.
49. Hennessy, *The Secret State*, p. xvi.
50. Hennessy, *The Secret State*, p. 320.
51. Hennessy, *The Secret State*, pp. 315–16.
52. Hennessy, *The Secret State*, p. 316.
53. Hennessy, *The Secret State*, p. 277.
54. <http://www.nti.org/analysis/articles/presidential-nuclear-initiatives/>, accessed 27 September 2013.
55. <http://www.conservativemanifesto.com/1992/1992-conservative-manifesto.shtml>, accessed 27 September 2013.
56. Michael Quinlan, 'The British Experience' in Henry Sokolski (ed.), *Getting MAD: Nuclear Mutual Assured Destruction, Its Origins and Practice* (Carlisle PA: Strategic Studies Institute US Army War College, 2004), pp. 261–74.
57. Quinlan, 'The British Experience', p. 273.
58. Peter Jones, 'Overview of the History of UK Strategic Weapons', Seminar Proceedings on *The History of the UK Strategic Deterrent*, Royal Aeronautical Society, London, March 1999. Quoted in John Simpson, 'The United Kingdom and the Nuclear Future: The Strength of Continuity and the Chance for Change', *Nonproliferation Review*, Vol. 14, No. 2 (July 2007), p. 233.
59. Defence Policy brief of April 1992, supplied to the authors following a declassification request under the Freedom of Information Act (2000).
60. Defence Policy brief of April 1992 supplied to the authors following a declassification request under the Freedom of Information Act (2000).
61. Simpson, 'The United Kingdom and the Nuclear Future', p. 233.
62. Simpson, 'The United Kingdom and the Nuclear Future', p. 233.
63. Simpson, 'The United Kingdom and the Nuclear Future', p. 233.

Endnotes

64. Aldous, *Reagan and Thatcher*, pp. 58–9.
65. Private interview with Lord Heseltine, January 2012.
66. Private interview with Lord Heseltine, January 2012. Heseltine also argues 'I never thought I'd like the idea of France being the only nuclear power in Europe. You can take whatever conclusions you like, I happen to be a quarter French, I don't think the French have got any aggressive interests against this country, but absolute power is a dangerous thing. So, I mean I have to tell you, I think I remember and have read enough about 1939–1941 to know that you can't count on anything called a special relationship or anything of that sort. I don't think public opinion could change, did change I mean, 1939, 1940, should've taught us lessons.'

Chapter 10

1. David Cameron, 'We need a nuclear deterrent more than ever', *The Telegraph*, 3 April 2013.
2. Nicholas J. Wheeler and Timothy Dunne, 'Good international citizenship: a third way for British foreign policy', *International Affairs*, Vol. 74, No. 4 (1998), pp. 847–70.
3. On the SDR, see Paul Cornish and Andrew Dorman, 'Blair's wars and Brown's budgets: from Strategic Defence Review to strategic decay in less than a decade', *International Affairs*, Vol. 85, No. 2 (2009), pp. 247–61.
4. John Ainslie, 'The Future of the British Bomb', WMD Awareness Program Web Page, p. 89, footnote 474, previously available at <http://www.comeclean.org.uk/content/future_of_the_british_bomb.pdf>, accessed October 2005. They might at times even be carrying a single warhead.
5. Ainslie, 'The Future of the British Bomb'.
6. Hubert Védrine, 'Report submitted to the President of the Republic: "The consequences of France's return to NATO's integrated military command, on the future of transatlantic relations, and the outlook for the Europe of defence" (November 14, 2012)', available from <http://www.diplomatie.gouv.fr/en/french-foreign-pol icy-1/defence-security/french-defence/france-and-nato-7177/france-and-nato/art icle/hubert-vedrine-report-submitted-to.>, accessed 14 December 2013.
7. Strategic Defence Review presented to Parliament by the Secretary of State for Defence by Command of Her Majesty, July 1998, henceforward referred to as SDR, available from MOD Website, <http://webarchive.nationalarchives.gov.uk/20121026065214/http://www.mod.uk/NR/rdonlyres/65F3D7AC-4340-4119-93A2-20825848E50E/0/sdr1998_complete.pdf >, 10 September 2007.
8. SDR, July 1998.
9. SDR, July 1998.
10. The 2006 White Paper has two references to 'our warhead design' and 'the continued availability of a lower yield from our warhead'. This appears to suggest an arrangement similar to the WE-177A, where yields of 0.5 kt and 10 kt were obtainable from the same design and weapon. John Simpson, 'The United Kingdom and the Nuclear Future: The Strength of Continuity and the Chance for Change', *Nonproliferation Review*, Vol. 14, No. 2 (July 2007), p. 236.

11. SDR, July 1998.
12. Tim Garden, 'British and NATO policy after the Prague summit', *The Guardian*, 8 January 2003.
13. Garden, 'British and NATO policy'.
14. NPT Briefing Book (2014 edition), Mountbatten Centre for International Studies and Center for Nonproliferation Studies Monterey Institute of International Studies, L-2. Available online at the Mountbatten Centre for International Studies Website, <www.kcl.ac.uk/sspp/departments/warstudies/research/groups/csss/research/nucnonprolif.aspx>, accessed 2 May 2014.
15. John Simpson, 'Options for the United Kingdom's Nuclear Weapons Programme Deterrence, Disarmament, Non-Proliferation and UK Trident', BASIC Discussion Paper 4 (March 2013).
16. BBC News Webpage, <http://news.bbc.co.uk/1/hi/programmes/newsnight/3236374.stm>, accessed 6 September 2007.
17. George Parker and Sam Jones, 'UK troops' Afghan mission "accomplished", says David Cameron', *Financial Times*, 16 December 2013. The question of whether this in fact does represent 'mission accomplished' is raised in this article.
18. John Mueller, 'Erase the Red Line', *Foreign Affairs*, 30 April 2013.
19. See also D.G. Press, S.D. Sagan, and B. Valentino, 'Atomic Aversion: Experimental Evidence on Taboos, Traditions, and the Non-Use of Nuclear Weapons', *American Political Science Review*, Vol. 107, No. 1 (February 2013), pp. 188–206.
20. David Albright, Paul Brannan, Andrea Stricker, Christina Walrond, and Houston Wood, *Preventing Iran from getting nuclear weapons: Constraining its future nuclear options*, Institute for Science and International Security, 5 March 2012.
21. 'Blair's Trident statement in full', <http://news.bbc.co.uk/1/hi/uk_politics/6207584.stm>, accessed 19 December 2013.
22. 'Blair's Trident statement'.
23. 'Blair's Trident statement'.
24. Tony Blair, *A Journey* (London: Hutchinson, 2010), pp. 635–6.
25. CMND. 6994, *The Future of the United Kingdom's Nuclear Deterrent* (London: HMSO, 2006).
26. CMND. 6994, p. 17.
27. See, for example, Dr Johnson's evidence during the Select Committee hearings. House of Commons Defence Select Committee Webpage, Uncorrected Transcript of Oral Evidence To be published as HC 986-I, The Future of the UK's Strategic Nuclear Deterrent: The Strategic Context, 14 March 2006, <www.publications.parliament.uk/pa/cm200506/cmselect/cmdfence/uc986-i/uc98602.htm>, accessed 6 September 2007.
28. Rebecca Johnson, 'The UK White Paper on Renewing Trident: the wrong decision at the wrong time', Disarmament Diplomacy, No 83 (Winter 2006), p. 5.
29. 'The United Kingdom's Nuclear Deterrent in the 21st Century', Speech by Des Browne MP, Secretary of State for Defence, 25 January 2007 at Kings College, London, <http://archive.today/0vo8U>, accessed 2 May 2014.
30. *Lords Hansard*, 24 January 2007 (part 0002), column 1107.
31. <http://online.wsj.com/news/articles/SB116787515251566636>, accessed 14 December 2013.

Endnotes

32. <www.whitehouse.gov/the_press_office/Remarks-By-President-Barack-Obama-In-Prague-As-Delivered>, accessed 19 December 2013.
33. Margaret Beckett, 'Keynote Address: A World Free of Nuclear Weapons?', <http://carnegieendowment.org/2007/06/25/keynote-address-world-free-of-nuclear-weapons/e15>, accessed 14 December 2013.
34. This included a six-hour debate followed by a vote on Trident renewal in Parliament. Ian Davis, Basic Notes: Occasional Papers On International Security Policy, 'The UK Trident Vote Explained', 15 March 2007.
35. Ian Davis, 'Basic Notes'.
36. Cm. 6994 and Michael Quinlan, 'Thinking About Nuclear Weapons', p. 128.
37. Speech by Des Browne to the Conference on Nuclear Disarmament, Laying the Foundations for Multilateral Disarmament, 5 February 2008. <www.labour.org.uk/des_browne_conference_on_nuclear_disarmament>, accessed 14 December 2013. This led to a new nuclear forensics laboratory being opened at AWE in May 2012; <www.awe.co.uk/shownews_3575a5a.html>, accessed 1 January 2014. AWE also supports the work of the CTBTO through its radionuclide laboratory: <www.awe.co.uk/set/National_Nuclear_Security.html>, accessed 1 January 2014.
38. Speech on nuclear energy and proliferation, Prime Minister Gordon Brown, 17 March 2009. Available from <www.acronym.org.uk/proliferation-challenges/nuclear-weapons-possessors/united-kingdom/uk-prime-minister-brown-speech-nuclear-energy-and-proliferati, accessed 14 December 2013.
39. Comments made by members of the Top Level Group of UK Parliamentarians for Multilateral Nuclear Disarmament & Non Proliferation at the Project on Nuclear Issues/Royal United Services Institute Seminar 'The People Behind the Policies', held at the House of Lords, 5 November 2013: <http://toplevelgroup.org/2013/11/07/the-people-behind-the-policies/>, accessed 15 December 2013.
40. John Simpson, 'Options for the United Kingdom's Nuclear Weapons Programme'. See also Nick Ritchie, 'Pathways and Purposes for P-5 Nuclear Dialogue', *European Leadership Network*, Policy Brief (September 2013).
41. *Lifting the Nuclear Shadow: Creating the Conditions for Abolishing Nuclear Weapons* (London: Foreign and Commonwealth Office, February 2009).
42. Quinlan, *Thinking About Nuclear Weapons*, p. 129.
43. CM 7675 'The Road to 2010: Addressing the nuclear question in the twenty first century', (London: Her Majesty's Stationary Office, July 2009).
44. CM 7675.
45. Julian Borger, 'Gordon Brown has put Trident on the table: Speech signals significant change in Britain's stance on nuclear proliferation', *The Guardian*, 17 March 2009.
46. Lee Willett, 'Brown's "Grand Global Bargain" and Reducing UK Nuclear Weapons Levels', RUSI Analysis, 27 March 2009.
47. 'Brown move to cut UK nuclear subs', <http://news.bbc.co.uk/1/hi/8270092.stm>, accessed 19 December 2013.
48. David Leigh, 'WikiLeaks cables: Whitehall told US to ignore Brown's Trident statement', *The Guardian*, 8 December 2010.

49. Kiran Stacey, 'MPs hit out at "rushed" defence shake-up', *Financial Times*, 3 August 2011.
50. CM 7948, Securing Britain in an Age of Uncertainty: The Strategic Defence and Security Review (October 2010). A useful breakdown of this term was provided by the late Brian Jones, formerly of the MOD's scientific staff, in 'War, Words and WMD', available from <www.sussex.ac.uk/Units/spru/hsp/documents/17-11-03%20Jones%20Paper.pdf>, accessed 15 December 2013.
51. <www.bbc.co.uk/news/uk-politics-21177620>, accessed 17 December 2013.
52. <www.bbc.co.uk/news/uk-politics-20179604>, accessed 17 December 2013.
53. Jeffrey Lewis, 'After the Reliable Replacement Warhead: What's Next for the US Nuclear Arsenal?', <www.armscontrol.org/act/2008_12/Lewis>, accessed 18 December 2013.
54. Comments made by members of the Top Level Group of UK Parliamentarians for Multilateral Nuclear Disarmament & Non Proliferation at the Project on Nuclear Issues/Royal United Services Institute Seminar 'The People Behind the Policies' held at the House of Lords, 5 November 2013; <http://toplevelgroup.org/2013/11/07/the-people-behind-the-policies/>, accessed 15 December 2013.
55. Nick Ritchie, *A Nuclear Weapons-Free World?: Britain, Trident and the Challenges Ahead* (Basingstoke: Palgrave, 2012), pp. 40–6.
56. Bruno Tertrais, 'Entente Nucleaire Options for UK-French Nuclear Cooperation', Discussion Paper 3 of the BASIC Trident Commission (June 2012).
57. Malcolm Chalmers, 'Towards the UK's Nuclear Century', *RUSI Journal*, Vol. 158, No. 6 (December 2013), p. 18.
58. CM 7948, Securing Britain in an Age of Uncertainty: The Strategic Defence and Security Review (October 2010).
59. Simpson, 'Options for the United Kingdom's Nuclear Weapons Programme', p. 24.
60. Simpson, 'Options for the United Kingdom's Nuclear Weapons Programme'.
61. Simpson, 'Options for the United Kingdom's Nuclear Weapons Programme'. See also <www.gov.uk/government/news/nuclear-weapon-states-discuss-nuclear-disarmament>, <www.gov.uk/government/world-location-news/states-meet-to-review-progress-on-non-proliferation>, and <www.gov.uk/government/publications/g8-declaration-on-non-proliferation-and-disarmament-for-2013>. All accessed 15 December 2013.
62. 'David Cameron: We need a nuclear deterrent more than ever', *The Telegraph*, 3 April 2013.
63. *The Telegraph*, 3 April 2013.
64. *The Telegraph*, 3 April 2013. 'Trident Lite' refers to the idea of replacing the current four Trident submarines with just two or three.
65. Nick Hopkins, 'Trident: no need for like-for-like replacement, says Danny Alexander', *The Guardian*, 22 January 2013.
66. <http://www.gov.uk/government/speeches/written-ministerial-statement-on-the-trident-alternatives-review>, accessed 15 December 2013.
67. *Trident Alternatives Review*, (London: Cabinet Office, 16 July 2013).
68. TNA, DEFE 68/406, Duff-Mason Part III System Options, December 1978.
69. Trident Alternatives Review, (London: Cabinet Office, 16 July 2013).

Endnotes

70. Options for CASD were examined by Malcolm Chalmers, 'Continuous-at-Sea-Deterrence Costs and Alternatives', RUSI Briefing Note (June 2010). See also Nick Ritchie and Paul Ingram, 'A Progressive Nuclear Policy: Rethinking Continuous-at-sea deterrence', *RUSI Journal*, Vol. 155, No. 2 (April 2010).
71. *Trident Alternatives Review*, (London: Cabinet Office, 16 July 2013). Even within the party, however, there has been discord on these plans. See, for example, Brian Wheeler, 'Lib Dem conference: Danny Alexander says Trident policy not a risk', <http://www.bbc.co.uk/news/uk-politics-24099425>, accessed 15 December 2013.
72. <http://www.bbc.co.uk/news/uk-politics-23117303>, accessed 1 October 2013.
73. <http://www.bbc.co.uk/news/uk-england-cumbria-25401479>, accessed 16 December 2013.
74. See <http://www.libdemvoice.org/tag/trident> for a discussion of anti-nuclear views expressed by some senior Liberal Democrats, accessed 2 May 2014.
75. There were also some signs that the Conservatives were interested in putting less emphasis on nuclear weapons in UK defence policy, in line with similar changes in US nuclear policy. See <http://glassbooth.org/expolore/index/conservative-party/>, accessed 1 May 2012.
76. 'Scottish independence: Trident removal 'not easy', *The Scotsman*, 16 December 2013. See also Defence Committee—Sixth Report. The Defence Implications of Possible Scottish Independence, 11 September 2013, <http://www.publications.parliament.uk/pa/cm201314/cmselect/cmdfence/198/19802.htm>, accessed 16 December 2013; <http://votesnp.com/campaigns/SNP_Manifesto_2011_lowRes.pdf> and <http://www.scotreferendum.com/reports/scotlands-future-your-guide-to-an-independent-scotland/>, accessed 2 May 2014; Malcolm Chalmers, 'Towards the UK's Nuclear Century', *RUSI Journal*, Vol. 158, No. 6 (December 2013), pp. 18–28, and <http://www.bbc.co.uk/news/uk-wales-politics-18509639>, accessed 16 December 2013.
77. The MDA operates alongside a parallel amendment on submarine reactor fuel. John Simpson, *The Independent Nuclear State: The United States, Britain and the Military Atom*, 2nd Edition (Basingstoke: Macmillan, 1986), pp. 191–5.
78. 'The foreign-policy implications of the Trident replacement debate', discussion meeting held at the International Institute for Strategic Studies, 13 March 2013.
79. 'The foreign-policy implications of the Trident replacement debate'.
80. Ministry of Defence Top Level Messages—November 2013, <http://www.gov.uk/government/uploads/system/uploads/attachment_data/file/255241/20131101-_MOD_Top_Level_Messages_NOV2013_updated.pdf>, accessed 17 November 2013.
81. John Simpson, 'Options for the United Kingdom's Nuclear Weapons Programme', p. 24.
82. Margaret Beckett, 'Keynote Address: A World Free of Nuclear Weapons?', <http://carnegieendowment.org/2007/06/25/keynote-address-world-free-of-nuclear-weapons/e15>, accessed 14 December 2013.
83. For a discussion of the role of trust and mistrust in International Relations, see Andrew H. Kydd, *Trust and Mistrust in International Relations* (Princeton: Princeton University Press, 2005); Deborah Welch Larson, 'Trust and Missed Opportunities in International Relations', <www.jstor.org/stable/3792108>; and Dani Nedal, 'Trust

and International Relations: A Conference Report', http://www.birmingham.ac.uk/research/activity/conflict-cooperation-security/news/2012/07, accessed May 2014.
84. Quoted in *The Times*, 21 December 2013.
85. See, for example, <http://www.bbc.co.uk/news/uk-20334974>, accessed 18 December 2013; 'Ex-military chief in cuts warning', *Daily Express*, 12 August 2012; see also Malcolm Chalmers, 'Unbalancing the Force? Prospects for UK Defence after the SDSR, Future Defence Review, Working Paper Number 9, Royal United Services Institute (November 2010).
86. Ben Farmer, 'Defence cuts "weakening effect of nuclear deterrent": Cuts to Britain's Armed Forces risk making the country's nuclear deterrent less effective, a former deputy head of the military has warned', *The Telegraph*, 12 August 2013.
87. *The Telegraph*, 12 August 2013.
88. Annual Chief of the Defence Staff Lecture 2013, <http://www.rusi.org/events/past/ref:E5284A3D06EFFD>, accessed 19 December 2013.
89. These issues are discussed in Michael Codner and Michael Clarke, *A Question of Security: The British Defence Review in an Age of Austerity* (London: I.B.Tauris in association with Royal United Services Institute for Defence and Security Studies, 2011).
90. Malcolm Chalmers, 'Towards the UK's Nuclear Century', *RUSI Journal*, Vol. 158, No. 6 (December 2013), p. 18.
91. *The Telegraph*, 16 January 2014.
92. Will Dahlgreen, 'Public Support for Nuclear Weapons', <http://yougov.co.uk/news/2013/07/16/public-support-nuclear-weapons/>, accessed 17 December 2013.
93. The Cross-Party Trident Commission, co-chaired by Sir Malcolm Rifkind, Lord Browne, and Sir Menzies Campbell concluded that: 'If there is more than a negligible chance that the possession of nuclear weapons might play a decisive role in the defence of the UK and its allies in preventing nuclear blackmail or affecting the nuclear security context within which the UK sits, then it should be retained.' See Deborah Haynes, "UK 'must maintain its nuclear deterrent'", The Times, 1 July 2014.See also <http://www.basicint.org/tridentcommission/>, accessed 19 September 2014.

Conclusion

1. K. Berry et al., *Delegitimizing Nuclear Weapons: Examining the Validity of Nuclear Deterrence* (Monterey: Monterey Institute of International Relations, 2010).
2. Walter Schilling, 'The Politics of National Defense: Fiscal 1950', in W. Schilling, P. Hammond, and G. Snyder (eds), *Strategy, Politics and Defense Budgets* (New York: Columbia University Press, 1962), p. 226.
3. Quinlan, *Thinking About Nuclear Weapons*, p. 117.
4. TNA, GEN 75/1: *The Atomic Bomb*, Memorandum by the Prime Minister, 28 August 1945.
5. Quinlan, *Thinking about Nuclear Weapons*, p. 13.
6. Quinlan, *Thinking About Nuclear Weapons*, pp. 13–14.
7. Berry, *Delegitimizing Nuclear Weapons*, and Schilling, 'The Politics of National Defense: Fiscal 1950'.

8. It can be argued that the recent history of the Second World War, including the experience of appeasement and the events of 1940 and the Blitz, played their part in the development of ideas about nuclear deterrence in the post-war period. See R. Gerald Hughes, *The Postwar Legacy of Appeasement: British Foreign Policy since 1945*, (London: Bloomsbury Academic, 2014).
9. Pierre, *Nuclear Politics*, p. 303.
10. Ritchie, *Trident and British Identity*, p. 1.
11. Zuckerman *Nuclear Illusion and Reality*, pp. 70–1.
12. Quinlan, *Thinking About Nuclear Weapons*, p. 52.
13. Defence Open Government Document 80/23, July 1980, paragraph 12.
14. Ogilvie-White, *On Nuclear Deterrence*, p. 37.
15. Quinlan, *Thinking About Nuclear Weapons*, p. 53.
16. Quinlan, *Thinking about Nuclear Weapons*, pp. 125–6.
17. Ogilvie-White, *On Nuclear Deterrence*, p. 116.
18. Quinlan, *Thinking About Nuclear Weapons*, p. 53.
19. Quinlan, *Thinking about Nuclear Weapons*, p. 54.
20. Quinlan, *Thinking about Nuclear Weapons*, p. 44.
21. TNA, DEFE 13/1039, *Note for the Record of a Meeting in the Defence Secretary's Office held on Thursday 27th May at 2.30pm*, 1 June 1976.
22. Private correspondence with Lord Owen, 29 January 2014.
23. Pierre, *Nuclear Politics*, p. 312.
24. Pierre, *Nuclear Politics*.
25. Pierre, *Nuclear Politics*.
26. Pierre, *Nuclear Politics*, p. 315.
27. Pierre, *Nuclear Politics*.
28. Defence Open Government Document 80/23, op.cit.
29. Pierre, *Nuclear Politics*, p. 316.
30. Ritchie, *Trident and British Identity*, p. 12.
31. Snyder, 'The Concept of Strategic Culture', p. 8.
32. H. Eckstein, 'A Cultural Theory of Political Change', *American Political Science Review*, Vol. 82, 1998.
33. Colin S. Gray, *Another Bloody Century: Future Warfare* (London: Weidenfeld and Nicholson, 2005), p. 88.
34. See Ritchie, *Trident and British Identity*, pp. 12–16.
35. In July 1992 Sir Ronald Oxburgh, the Chief Scientific Adviser at the Ministry of Defence, produced a report which identified nineteen accidents with British nuclear weapons between 1960 and 1991. He claimed that none of them had been particularly worrying. This was also the view of Sir Michael Quinlan. In his study, *Thinking about Nuclear Weapons*, he claims that concerns about the seriousness of nuclear accidents have been exaggerated. Eric Schlosser, however, claims that Oxburgh did not identify accidents involving US nuclear weapons on British soil and that some of these had been serious. Apart from the 1956, 1957, and 1958 incidents mentioned earlier in the study, he identifies accidents in January 1961, August 1962, and January 1987 (the latter also mentioned by Oxburgh) which were of concern. He also suggests that the Trident D-5 missile, adopted by Britain, has

been the subject of some safety concerns in the United States due to the positioning of the multiple warheads which surround the third-stage rocket engine. See Quinlan, *Thinking about Nuclear Weapons* and Eric Schlosser, *Command and Control*.
36. One contemporary commentator (in June 2014) suggested that Britain's lack of influence in the great crises of the day in Iraq, Syria, and the Ukraine reflected the way the nation was finally coming to terms with its declining power in world politics. Matthew Parris argued that '...we're coming to terms with our insignificance. Our news media, our politicians and the nation itself have acknowledged this not just in our minds, but in our hearts.' Instead of 'punching above its weight' there was now a case for 'punching below its weight'. See The Times, 28 June 2014. Whether Parris was correct in identifying an important long-term change in public attitudes towards Britain's world role which might affect its nuclear identity remained to be seen. Some would argue that events, such as those in Ukraine in 2014, are likely to reinforce the belief that in a dangerous world nuclear weapons provide reassurance and security.

Bibliography

Aldous, R., *Reagan and Thatcher: The Difficult Relationship* (London: Hutchinson, 2012).
Arnold, Lorna, *Britain and the H-Bomb* (Basingstoke: Palgrave, 2001).
Arnold, Lorna and Smith, Mark, *Britain, Australia and the Bomb: The Nuclear Tests and their Aftermath* (London: Palgrave, 2006).
Ball, S.J., *The Bomber in British Strategy: Doctrine, Strategy and Britain's World Role, 1945–1960* (Boulder: Westview Press, 1995).
Baker, R., *Dry Ginger: The Biography of Admiral of the Fleet Sir Michael Le Fanu* (London: W.H. Allen, 1977).
Baylis, John, *Ambiguity and Deterrence: British Nuclear Strategy 1945–1964* (Oxford: Oxford University Press, 1995).
Baylis, John, *Anglo-American Defence Relations 1939–1984: The Special Relationship*, (London: Macmillan, 1984).
Baylis, John, *The Diplomacy of Pragmatism: Britain and the Formation of NATO, 1942–49* (London: Macmillan, 1993).
Benn, Tony, *Against the Tide: Diaries 1973–1976* (London: Arrow 1990).
Berry, Ken; Lewis, Patricia; Pélopidas, Benoît; Sokov, Nikolai; and Wilson, Ward, *Delegitimizing Nuclear Weapons: Examining the Validity of Nuclear Deterrence* (Monterey: Monterey Institute of International Relations, 2010).
Blackett, P.M.S., *Fear, War and the Bomb: Military and Political Consequences of Atomic Energy* (New York: McGraw-Hill, 1949).
Botti, Timothy, *The Long Wait: Forging the Anglo-American Nuclear Alliance, 1945–1958* (New York: Greenwood Press, 1987).
Braithwaite, Rodric, *Across the Moscow River: The World Turned Upside Down* (New Haven Conn.: Yale University Press, 2002).
Brodie, Bernard, *The Absolute Weapon* (New York: Harcourt Brace, 1946).
Brooks, A., *V-Force: The History of Britain's Airborne Deterrent* (London: Janes, 1982).
Buzan, Barry and Hansen, Lene, *The Evolution of International Security Studies* (Cambridge: Cambridge University Press, 2009).
Cambell, Duncan, *The Unsinkable Aircraft Carrier: American Military Power in Britain* (London, 1984).
Carr, E.H., *The Twenty Years Crisis* (London: Macmillan, 1981).
Cathcart, Brian, *The Test of Greatness: Britain's Struggle for the Atom Bomb* (London: John Murray, 1994).
Ceadel, Martin, *Thinking about Peace and War* (Oxford: Oxford University Press, 1989).

Bibliography

Clark, Ian, *Nuclear Diplomacy and the Special Relationship: Britain's Deterrent and America 1957–1962* (Oxford: Clarendon Press, 1994).
Clark, Ian and Wheeler, Nicholas J., *The British Origins of Nuclear Strategy 1945–55* (Oxford: Clarendon Press, 1989).
Day, Robin, *But With Respect. Memorable Television Interviews with Statesmen and Parliamentarians* (London: Weidenfeld and Nicolson, 1993).
Diggins, John Patrick, *Ronald Reagan: Fate, Freedom, and the Making of History* (New York: W.W. Norton & Company, 2007).
Dillon, D.M., *Dependence and Deterrence Success and Civility in the Anglo-American Special Nuclear Relationship, 1962–1982* (London, 1983).
Dockrill, Saki, *Britain's Policy for West German Rearmament 1950–1955* (Cambridge: Cambridge University Press, 1991).
Dyke, R.W. and Gannon, F.X., *Chet Hollifield: Master Legislator and Nuclear Statesman* (Washington: University Press of America, 1996).
Eden, Lynn, *Whole World on Fire: Organizations, Knowledge and Nuclear Weapons Devastation* (Ithaca: Cornell University Press, 2003).
Etzold, T.H. and Gaddis, John Lewis (eds), *Containment: Documents on American Policy and Strategy, 1945–1950* (NY: Columbia University Press, 1978).
Farmilo, Graham, *Churchill's Bomb: A Hidden History of Science, War and Politics* (London: Faber, 2014).
Finlan, Alastair, *Contemporary Military Culture and Strategic Studies: US and UK armed forces in the 21st Century* (Abingdon: Routledge, 2013).
Freedman, Lawrence, *Britain and Nuclear Weapons* (London: Macmillan, 1980).
Geiger, T. and Hansen, R.D., 'The Role of Information on Decision-Making in Foreign Aid', in Bauer, R.A. and Gergen, K.J., (eds), *The Study of Policy Formation* (New York: The Free Press, 1968).
George, Alexander, 'The Causal Nexus between Cognitive Beliefs and Decision-Making: The "Operational Code" Belief System', in Falkowski, L., (ed.), *Psychological Models in International Politics* (Boulder, Col.: Westview Press, 1979).
Gowing, Margaret, *Britain and Atomic Energy, 1939–1945* (London: Macmillan, 1964).
Gowing, Margaret, *Independence and Deterrence: Britain and Atomic Energy 1945–52* (2 Vols.; London: Macmillan, 1974).
Gray, Colin S., *Another Bloody Century: Future Warfare* (London: Weidenfeld and Nicholson, 2005).
Greenstein, F., *The Hidden-Hand Presidency: Eisenhower as Leader* (New York, 1982).
Groom, A.J.R., *British Thinking about Nuclear Weapons* (London: Pinter, 1974).
Grove, Eric, *Vanguard to Trident: British Naval Policy Since World War Two* (London: Bodley Head, 1987).
Hamilton, N., *Monty: The Field Marshal 1944–1976* (London: Hamish Hamilton, 1986).
Healey, Denis, *The Time of My Life* (London: Penguin, 1990).
Hennessy, Peter, *Muddling Through: Power, Politics and the Quality of Government in Postwar Britain* (London: Indigo, 1997).
Hennessy, Peter, *The Secret State: Whitehall and the Cold War* (London: Penguin, 2002).
Heseltine, Michael, *Life in the Jungle: My Autobiography* (London: Hodder and Stoughton, 2000).

Heuser, Beatrice, *NATO, Britain, France and the FRG* (Basingstoke: Macmillan, 1997).
Heuser, Beatrice, *Nuclear Mentalities? Strategies and Belief Systems in Britain, France and the FRG* (London: Macmillan, 1998).
Hill, N., *Vertical Empire* (Coventry: Imperial College Press, 2002).
Horne, Alistair, *Harold Macmillan, Vol. 2, 1957–1986* (New York: Macmillan, 1989).
Huntington, Samuel P., *The Common Defence* (NY: Columbia University Press, 1961).
Hurd, Douglas, *Memoirs* (London: Little, Brown, 2003).
Hymans, Jacques E.C., *The Psychology of Nuclear Proliferation: Identity, Emotions and Foreign Policy* (Cambridge: Cambridge University Press, 2006).
Jackson, Bill and Bramall, Dwin, *The Chiefs: The Story of the United Kingdom Chiefs of Staff* (London: Brassey's, 1992).
Jervis, Robert, *The Illogic of American Nuclear Strategy* (Ithaca: Cornell University Press, 1984).
Jervis, Robert, 'The Symbolic Nature of Nuclear Politics', in R. Jervis *The Meaning of the Nuclear Revolution* (Ithaca, NY: Cornell University Press, 1989).
Johnson, Jeannie, Kartchner, Kerry and Larsen, Jeffrey, (eds), *Strategic Culture and Weapons of Mass Destruction: Culturally Based Insights into Comparative National Security Policymaking* (London: Palgrave, 2009).
Katzenstein, P.J., (ed.) *The Culture of National Security: Norms and Identity in World Politics* (New York: Columbia University Press, 1996).
Kengor, P., *The Crusader: Ronald Reagan and the Fall of Communism* (New York: Regan Books, 2006).
Killian, James R., *Sputnik, Scientists, and Eisenhower: A Memoir of the First Special Assistant to the President for Science and Technology* (Cambridge, Mass., 1982).
Lane, R., *Political Man* (New York: The Free Press, 1972).
Laqueur, Walter, *Europe in Our Time* (New York: Viking, 1992).
Lebow, Richard Ned, *A Cultural Theory of International Relations* (Cambridge: Cambridge University Press, 2008).
Macmillan, Harold, *At the End of the Day 1961–1963* (Basingstoke: Macmillan, 1973).
Macmillan, Harold, *Pointing the Way* (Basingstoke: Macmillan, 1972).
Macmillan, Harold, *Riding the Storm, 1956–1959* (London: Macmillan, 1971).
Major, John, *John Major: The Autobiography* (New York: HarperCollins, 1999).
Malone, Peter, *The British Nuclear Deterrent: A History* (London: Croom Helm, 1984).
McInnes, Colin, *Trident: The Only Option* (London: Brassey's, 1986).
Moore, Richard, *Nuclear Illusion, Nuclear Reality: Britain, the United States and Nuclear Weapons, 1958–64* (London: Palgrave, 2010).
Navias, Martin, *Nuclear Weapons and British Strategic Planning 1955–58* (Oxford: Clarendon Press, 1991).
Nott, John, *Here Today, Gone Tomorrow: Recollections of an Errant Politician* (London: Politico's, 2002).
Ogilvie-White, Tanya, *On Nuclear Deterrence: The Correspondence of Sir Michael Quinlan* (London: IISS, 2011).
Onuf, Nicholas, *World of our Making* (South Carolina: University of South Carolina, 1989).

Bibliography

Osgood, Richard E., *NATO: The Entangling Alliance* (Chicago and London: University of Chicago Press, 1962).

Pach Jr., C.J. and Richardson, Elmo, *The Presidency of Dwight D. Eisenhower* (Lawrence: University Press of Kansas, 1991).

Pierre, Andrew, *Nuclear Politics: The British Experience with an Independent Strategic Force 1939–1970* (London: Oxford University Press, 1972).

Prados, J., *The Soviet Estimate: US Intelligence Analysis and Russian Military Strength* (New York: Dial Press, 1982).

Quinlan, Michael, 'The British Experience', in Henry Sokolski (ed.), *Getting MAD: Nuclear Mutual Assured Destruction, Its Origins and Practice* (Carlisle Pa.: Strategic Studies Institute US Army War College, 2004).

Quinlan, Michael, *Thinking about Nuclear Weapons: Principles, Problems, Prospects* (Oxford: Oxford University Press, 2009).

Reynolds, David, *Britannia Overruled: British Policy and World Power in the 20th Century* (New York: Longman, 1991).

Rosecrance, Richard N., *Defense of the Realm: British Strategy in the Nuclear Epoch* (New York: Columbia University Press, 1968).

Schlosser, Eric, *Command and Control* (London: Allen Lane, 2013).

Simpson, John, *The Independent Nuclear State: The United States, Britain and the Military Atom* (London: Macmillan, 1983).

Slessor, Sir John, *The Great Deterrent* (London: Cassell, 1957).

Snyder, Jack, 'The Concept of Strategic Culture: Caveat Emptor', in C.G. Jacobsen (ed.), *Strategic Power: USA/USSR* (Basingstoke: Macmillan, 1990).

Snyder, Jack, *The Soviet Strategic Culture: Implications for Limited Nuclear Operations* (Santa Monica, Calif.: RAND, R-2154-AF, Sept. 1977).

Stoddart, Kristan, *Losing an Empire and Finding a Role: Britain, the USA, NATO and Nuclear Weapons, 1964–70* (Basingstoke: Palgrave, 2012).

Stoddart, Kristan, *The Sword and the Shield: Britain, America, NATO, Nuclear Weapons, 1970–1976* (Basingstoke: Palgrave, 2014).

Stoddart, Kristan, *Facing Down the Soviet Union: Britain, the USA, NATO and Nuclear Weapons, 1976–1983* (Basingstoke: Palgrave, 2014).

Thatcher, Margaret, *The Downing Street Years* (London: Harper Collins, 1993).

Trachtenberg, Marc, *A Constructed Peace: The Making of a European Settlement, 1945–1963* (Princeton: Princeton University Press, 1999).

Twigge, Stephen and Scott, Len, *Planning Armageddon: Britain, the United States and Command and Control of Western Nuclear Forces 1945–1964* (Abingdon: Routledge, 2000).

Vogler, J., 'Perspectives on the Foreign Policy System: Psychological Approaches', in M. Clarke and B. White (eds.), *Understanding Foreign Policy: The Foreign Policy Systems Approach* (London: Edward Elgar, 1989).

Walker, William, *A Perpetual Menace: Nuclear Weapons and International Order* (Abingdon: Routledge: 2011).

Wendt, Alexander, *Social Theory of International Politics* (Cambridge: Cambridge University Press, 1999).

Ziegler, Philip, *Wilson: The Authorised Life of Lord Wilson of Rievaulx* (London: Weidenfeld & Nicolson, 1993).
Zuckerman, Solly, *Monkeys, Men and Missiles* (London: Collins, 1988).

Articles

Ball, S.J., 'Military nuclear relations between the United States and Great Britain under the terms of the McMahon Act, 1946–1958', *The Historical Journal*, Vol. 38 (June 1995).

Baylis, John, 'American Bases in Britain: "The Truman-Attlee Understandings"', *The World Today*, Aug.–Sept. (1986).

Baylis, John, 'The 1958 Anglo-American Mutual Exchange Agreement: The Search for Nuclear Interdependence', *The Journal of Strategic Studies*, Vol. 31, No. 3 (2008).

Baylis, John, 'British Nuclear Doctrine: The "Moscow Criteria" and the Polaris Improvement Programme', *Contemporary British History*, Vol. 19, No. 1 (2005).

Baylis, John, 'The Development of Britain's Thermonuclear Capability: Myth or Reality?', *Contemporary Record*, 8/1 (September 1994).

Baylis, John, 'Exchanging Nuclear Secrets', *Diplomatic History*, Vol. 25, No. 1 (2001).

Baylis, John and Macmillan, Alan, 'The British Global Strategy Paper of 1952', *The Journal of Strategic Studies*, Vol. 16, No. 2 (June 1993).

Baylis, John and Stoddart, Kristan, 'The British Nuclear Experience: The Role of Ideas and Beliefs (Part One)', *Diplomacy and Statecraft*, Vol. 23, No. 2 (2012).

Baylis, John and Stoddart, Kristan, 'Chevaline: Britain's Hidden Nuclear Programme, 1967–1982', *Journal of Strategic Studies*, Vol. 26, No. 4 (December 2003).

Buchan, Alastair, 'Their Bomb and Ours', *Encounter*, 12/1 (1959).

Burr, W., 'The Nixon Administration, the "Horror Strategy" and the Search for Limited Nuclear Options, 1969–1972', *Journal of Cold War Studies*, Vol. 7, No. 3 (Summer 2005).

Checkel, J., 'The Constructivist Turn in International Relations Theory', *World Politics*, Vol. 50, No. 2 (January 1998).

Dorman, A., 'VIEWPOINT—The Nott Review: Dispelling the Myths?', *Defence Studies*, Vol. 1, No. 3 (Spring 2001).

Eckstein, H., 'A Cultural Theory of Political Change', *American Political Science Review*, Vol. 82 (1998).

Gray, Colin S., 'Strategic Culture as Context: The First Generation of Theory Strikes Back', *International Studies*, Vol. 25 (January 1999).

Haglund, D.J., 'What Good is Strategic Culture', *International Journal*, Vol. 59, No. 3 (Summer 2004).

Heuser, Beatrice, 'European Defence before and after the "turn of the tide"', *Review of International Studies*, Vol. 19, No. 3 (October 1993).

Heuser, Beatrice, 'Beliefs, Cultures and the Use of Nuclear Weapons' in Eric Herring (ed.): *Preventing the Use of Weapons of Mass Destruction*, Special Issue of *The Journal of Strategic Studies*, Vol. 23 No. 1 (March 2000).

Immermann, R.H., 'Confessions of an Eisenhower Revisionist: An Agonizing Reappraisal', *Diplomatic History*, 14 (Summer 1990).

Johnston, Alastair I., 'Thinking about Strategic Culture', *International Security*, Vol. 19, No. 4 (Spring 1995).

Jones, Peter, 'Overview of the History of UK Strategic Weapons', Seminar Proceedings on The History of the UK Strategic Deterrent, Royal Aeronautical Society, London, (March 1999).

Mccgwire, Michael, 'Comfort Blanket or Weapon of War: What is Trident for?', *International Affairs*, Vol. 82, Iss. 4 (June 2006).

Melissen, Jan, 'The Restoration of the Nuclear Alliance: Great Britain and Atomic Negotiations with the United States, 1957–58', *Contemporary Record*, 6 (Summer 1992).

Melissen, Jan, 'The Thor Saga: Anglo-American Nuclear Relations, US IRBM Development and Deployment in Britain, 1955–1959', *The Journal of Strategic Studies*, vol. 15, no. 2 (June 1992).

Moore, R., 'A JIGSAW Puzzle for Operations Researchers: British Global War Studies, 1954–1962', *Journal of Strategic Studies*, Vol. 20, No. 2 (June 1997).

Moore, Richard, 'Bad Strategy and Bomber Dreams: A New View of the Blue Streak Cancellation', *Contemporary British History*, Vol. 27, Issue 2 (2013).

Murphy, C.J.V., 'A New Strategy for NATO', *Fortune*, Vol. 47 (January 1953).

Reynolds, David, 'A "Special Relationship"? America, Britain, and International Order since the Second World War', *International Affairs*, 62 (Winter 1985-6).

Ritchie, Nick, 'Trident and British Identity: Letting Go of Nuclear Weapons' (Bradford Disarmament Research Centre Paper, 2008).

Roman, P.J., 'Strategic Bombers over the Missile Horizon, 1957–1963', *Journal of Strategic Studies*, Vol. 18, Issue 1 (January 1995).

Sabatier, P., 'An Advocacy Coalition Framework of Policy Change and the Role of Policy Oriented Learning Therein', *Policy Sciences*, 2 (1988).

Sagan, Scott, 'Why Do States Build Nuclear Weapons? Three Models in Search of a Bomb', *International Security*, Vol. 21, No. 3 (Winter 1996–7).

Simpson, John, 'The United Kingdom and the Nuclear Future: The Strength of Continuity and the Chance for Change', *Nonproliferation Review*, Vol. 14, No. 2 (July 2007).

Smith, Steve and Hollis, Martin, 'Roles and Reasons in Foreign Policy Decision Making', *British Journal of Political Science*, 16/3 (1986).

Spinardi, G., 'Aldermaston and British Nuclear Weapons Development: Testing the "Zuckerman thesis"', *Social Studies of Science*, Vol. 27, No. 4 (August 1997).

Stoddart, Kristan and Baylis, John, 'The British Nuclear Experience: The Role of Beliefs, Culture and Status (Part Two)', *Diplomacy and Statecraft*, Vol. 23, No. 3 (2012).

Thursfield, Rear Admiral H.G., 'The Lessons of the War', *Brassey's Annual* (1946).

Ullman, Richard, 'The Covert French Connection', *Foreign Policy*, 75 (Summer 1989).

Wendt, Alexander, 'Collective Identity Formation and the International State', *American Political Science Review*, Vol. 88, No. 2 (June 1994).

Index

Anti-ballistic Missile (ABM) Treaty (1972) 126, 134
Advisory Committee on Atomic Energy 17–18
Afghanistan 188
Ahmadinejad, President 189
Aldermaston Atomic Weapons Research Establishment (AWRE) 64, 90, 100, 115, 116, 132, 193, 238 n.71
Aldermaston marches 71–2
Aldous, Richard 183
Allen, K. W. 65, 68, 69, 244 n.20, 245 n.29
Amery, Julian 70–1
Anderson, Clinton P. 85–6
Anderson, Sir John 23, 34
Anderson Advisory Committee 29, 34
Anglo-American 'special nuclear relationship' 14, 74–96, 250 n.50
　Bermuda meeting (1957) 80, 81, 97, 98
　Eisenhower initiatives 77–8, 249 n.41
　Modus Vivendi agreement (1948) 76, 92, 247 n.8
　Mutual Defence Agreement (MDA), 1958 68, 69, 74, 82, 84, 86–8, 91–4, 97, 100, 119, 146, 164, 200, 214, 251–2 n.68, 254 n.89, 256 n.25
　Sputnik, impact of 81
　Suez, impact of 78–9
　technical meetings (1958–9) 88–91, 253 n.75, 253 n.81, 254 n.87
　US opposition to nuclear secret sharing 85–6
　weaponry and strategic targeting (1957) 68–9
Anglo-French nuclear cooperation, and its difficulties 14, 119–24, 153, 161, 208–9, 269 n.11
　2010 initiative 196
Armstrong, Sir Robert 159–60, 160–1, 209
Arnold, Lorna 12, 244 n.20
Ashmore, Sir Edward 127, 213
Atlantic Nuclear Force (ANF) proposal 104–5, 107
Atlas ICBM, US 84
Atomic Energy (Defence Research) Committee, 1947 36
Atomic Energy (Review of Production) Committee, 1947 36

Atomic Energy Act (1954), and 1958 amendments, US 77, 78, 86, 87
Atomic Energy Authority (AEA) 64
Atomic Energy Committee, ministerial 33–4
atomic energy programme, bureaucratic context 33–6, 41
Atomic Weapons Research Establishment *see* Aldermaston Atomic Weapons Research Establishment (AWRE)
Attlee, Clement 13, 16, 17–23, 30, 34, 37–8, 39, 153, 202
　and the Truman 'Understandings' 76, 94
Attlee government (1945–51) 16, 29, 32–3, 130, 190, 201, 207
Austria 56

B-47 bomber accidents 93–4
Baldwin, Stanley 99
Ball, George 92, 93
Beckett, Margaret 193, 202
belief systems and nuclear deterrence 2–5
　and shared values 4
　theorists 2
Benn, Tony 124
Bermuda Conference (1957) 80, 81, 97, 98
Berry, Kay 206, 207
Bevin, Ernest 13, 16, 20, 21, 22, 33, 37–8, 39
biological weapons *see* chemical and biological weapons
Blackett, P. M. S. 17, 29, 117, 214
Blackett Report (1946) 29
Blackham, Sir Jeremy 203
Blair, Tony 181, 184, 192
Blair government (1997–2007) 14, 202
　nuclear policy 185–9
　Trident renewal/replacement 189–91
Blue Danube atomic bombs 62
Blue Steel cruise missile, RAF 99
Blue Streak missile 98, 100, 18, 154, 255 n.6, 255 n.9
Booth, Ken 6
Botti, Timothy 87, 90
Braithwaite, Sir Rodric 169
Bramall, Lord Dwin 156, 169, 203

Index

Britain:
  Air Chiefs assessments (1945) 26
  Admiralty paper (1945) 25–6
  atomic capability development 60–2
  early attempts at international controls 18–24
  early atomic weapons strategy 36–9
  independence vs. interdependence 97–9, 100, 101, 213, 214–16
  and nuclear proliferation 213–14
  nuclear procedure and capabilities at the end of the Cold War 180–3
  nuclear weapons, and political credibility with the US 208
  nuclear weapons, wartime origins 11–13
  role in the nuclear disarmament debate (2007–10) 202
  as 'second centre' decision-maker for nuclear weapons 108, 139, 141, 142–3, 145, 156–7, 190, 208, 215
  soft/hard power distinctions 188–9, 200
  strategic planning (1947–50) 42–3
  veto over UK-based American nuclear aircraft 94
  see also Anglo-American nuclear cooperation; Anglo-French nuclear cooperation
British atom/thermonuclear bomb tests (1952–6) 14, 45–6, 62, 66 Tab 3.1
  Grapple tests (May–June 1957) 14, 65–8, 66 Tab 3.1, 78, 83, 248 n.29
  Grapple X, Y, and Z tests (1957–8) 66 Tab 3.1, 69–70, 83, 87, 89, 246 n.40, 246 n.41
British Peace Committee 71
Brodie, Bernard 28
Brooke, Sir Alan 36
Brown, George 109
Brown, Gordon 185–6, 190
Brown government (2007–10) 14, 202
  and *Trident* renewal/replacement 192–5
Brown, Harold 149
Browne, Des 191, 193
Brundrett, Sir Frederick 67, 69, 81
Burrow, Andrew S. 91
Bush, George H. W. 177, 178, 179, 274 n.9
Bush administration (1989–93) 178
Bush, George W. 189
Bush, Admiral Sir John 114
Butler, Sir Robin 180–1
Byrnes, James 32

Caccia, Sir Harold 78, 81
Calder Hall nuclear power station 86
Callaghan, James 124, 128, 130, 153, 268 n.78
Callaghan government (1976–9) 130
  and the *Polaris* replacement debate (1977–9) 133–50

Cameron, David 185, 195
Cameron government (2010–) 14
  and *Trident* replacement/renewal 195–201
Campaign for Nuclear Disarmament (CND) 71–2, 151–2, 167, 171, 172
  links with the Labour Party 128
  membership growth, early 1980s 162
Carrington, Peter 121, 169
Carter, Jimmy 147, 148, 149, 161, 163
Carter administration (1977–81) 159
Cartledge, Sir Bryan 140, 174
Carver, Sir Michael 125, 126–7, 169, 263 n.43
Cathcart, Brian 61
Ceadel, Martin 4–5
Chadwick, Sir James 61, 243 n.1
Chalmers, Malcolm 204–5
chemical and biological weapons 51, 170, 177, 188, 241 n.73
  and the Gulf War 179–80
Chevaline programme *see Polaris* improvement/replacement programme and Chevaline
Chiefs of Staff (COS) 42–59, 209
  atomic weapons subcommittee report (1946) 27
  adoption of deterrent policy 25
  Blackett Report (1946) response 29
  Global Strategy Paper (1950) 43, 57, 59
  Global Strategy Paper (1952) 42, 43–59, 242 n.77
  independence/interdependence debates 102–3
  and initial strategic guidance 35
  inter-service disagreements about a future war 52–3
  and international control of nuclear weapons 24
  and Middle East bases 39
  Middle East strategy (1952) 57
  and the Moscow Criterion 129–30
  and NATO conventional forces (1952) 54–5
  operational nuclear strategy, late 1960s 115, 116
  and *Polaris* system effectiveness 125, 126, 127
  role in 'nuclear advocacy coalition' 13
  Soviet Union as strategic threat 37–8, 39, 40
  and stockpiling of nuclear weapons (1946) 28
  strategic planning (1947–50) 42–3
  and thermonuclear weapons development 62–4
China 47, 48, 57, 58, 82, 217
Churchill, Randolph 60, 70–1
Churchill, Sir Winston 12, 45, 63, 65, 94
Churchill government (1951–5) 43–4, 51, 63, 77

292

Index

Clark, Ian 39, 100
Clark-Kerr, Sir Archibald 20
Cockroft, John 60, 243 n.1
Cold War, ending 178–80
  and British nuclear procedures and capabilities 180–3
Collins, Canon John 71, 72
Comprehensive Test Ban Treaty (1996) 193
Confidence Measures Towards Nuclear Disarmament, P5 Conference (2009) 194
constructivism and constructivist approaches 1, 217, 233–4 n.3
Cook, Robin 185
Cook, Sir William 64, 67, 89, 209
Cooper, Sir Frank 137, 159
Corner, I. 65
Coulport facilities, Faslane 158
Cradock, Sir Percy 179
Cromer, Lord 121
Crosland, Anthony 128, 129
cruise missiles 134, 135, 136, 137, 138, 146, 164, 175
  Blue Steel, RAF 99
  deployment in Britain 171–2, 176
  Greenham Common 159, 167, 171
  submarine-launched 135, 176
Czechoslovakia 56

de Gaulle, Charles 57, 121
Debré, Michel 121
Defence Research Policy Committee (DRPC) 35–6
Defence White Paper (1954) 242 n.77
Defence White Paper (1957) 59
Defence White Paper (1980), Open Government Document 80/23, 162
Defence White Paper (2007) 193
deterrence, nuclear 18–23, 281 n.8
  belief systems and shared values 2–5, 207, 217
  core thinking 51
  economic vitality and political values 108
  and Great Power status 70–1, 105–6, 118, 207–8
  as 'habit of mind' 200, 207
  'minimum' concept 128
  'minimum', Blair's criteria 187
  and national identity 8–10, 11, 208–9, 217
  origins of idea 24–9
  principles of discrimination and proportionality 210, 211
  and shared values 4
  and strategic culture 108
  and the wartime strategic bombing experience 17, 18–19
deterring war, distinction from conducting war 39

Dickson, Sir William 27–8, 102–3
Direct Action Committee on Nuclear Disarmament 71, 72
Dombey, Norman 68
Douglas-Home, Alex 103
Douglas-Home government (1963–4) 118
Drayson, Lord Paul Rudd 191
Duff, Sir Anthony 14, 137, 138–9
Duff-Mason Report (1979) 14, 133, 153, 154, 156, 157, 158, 168, 197, 198
  and NATO 139, 145
  Polaris replacement options 142–9, 150
Dulles, John Foster 81–2, 83, 84, 86

Eckstein, Harry 217
Eden, Anthony 37, 38, 65, 67
Eisenhower, Dwight D. 75, 76, 80, 81–2, 84, 87–8, 92, 93, 97, 249 n.41, 250 n.45
Eisenhower administration (1953–61) 57, 59, 63, 83, 85, 91
  Bermuda Conference (1957) 80, 81, 97, 98
  initiatives towards Anglo-American nuclear cooperation 77–8, 249 n.41
ethical considerations and nuclear weapons 210–13
  Cold War 210, 211–13
  and the principle of 'double effect' 211–12
European Community (EC), British accession to 124

F-35 *Lightening II* fighter 199, 204
Falklands Conflict (1982) 152
Farmelo, Graham 12
Faslane submarine base 114, 158
Fieldhouse, Richard W. 91
'Flexible Response' strategy (1967) 106, 120–1, 143–4, 156, 164, 170, 175, 176, 178
Foot, Michael 72, 166, 168
France 56, 100, 214, 217
  Defence White Paper (1972) 157, 270 n.32
  M-4 system 155
  and NATO 120, 145, 186, 276 n.6
  see also Anglo-French cooperation
Fraser, Major-General 122
Frisch, Otto 11
Fuchs affair 50, 241 n.67

Gaitskill, Hugh 103
Gallop Polls, and public support for nuclear disarmament 72
Garden, Lord Tim 188
Gates, Robert 205
Geiger, T. 5
George, Alexander 2–3
Germany *see* West Germany
Giscard d'Estaing, Valéry 147, 161
Global Strategy Paper (1950) 43, 57, 59

293

Index

Global Strategy Paper (1952) 13, 42, 242 n.77, 243 n.114
  and chemical and biological warfare 51
  and the Cold War 47–8
  and the 'complementary deterrent' of conventional forces 53–5
  and COS 42, 43–59, 242 n.77
  'deterrence in concert' 49–50
  and German rearmament and reunification 55–6
  and NATO 45, 46, 59
  nuclear weapons and deterrence 48–9
  origins 43–4
  and the over-reliance on the US 49–50
  political and economic factors 44–7, 58–9
  and tactical atomic weapons 55
  and threats to the West 47–8
Gorbachev, Mikhail 173, 174–5, 175–6, 177
Gowing, Margaret 22, 23, 29, 31, 35, 241 n.68
Grapple tests (May–June 1957) 14, 65–8, 66 Tab 3.1, 78, 83, 248 n.29
  X, Y, and Z tests (1957–8) 66 Tab 3.1, 69–70, 83, 87, 89, 246 n.40, 246 n.41
Gray, Colin 7, 217
Green Granite bomb design 69
Greenham Common, RAF base 159, 167, 171
Greenham Common peace camps and protests 162, 171–2
Greenstock, Sir Jeremy 200
Grey, Sir Edward 114
Grove, Eric 68
Groves, General Leslie 23
Guadeloupe Summit (1979) 147, 148, 149
guided missile technology 43
Gulf War (1990–1) 170, 178–9
  and chemical/biological weapons 179–80
  and *Scud* missiles 179–80

Haglund, David G. 7–8
Halifax, Lord 20
Hannay, Lord David 200
Hansen, R. D. 5
Harwell Atomic Energy Establishment 26, 30, 60
Healey, Denis 104, 112, 115, 119, 124, 126, 127, 128, 129, 130, 136, 139, 140, 149, 150, 168, 251 n.56
  on *Polaris* 108, 263 n.42
  and *Polaris* operational independence 109, 110–11
Healey-Schröder Report (1969) 111
Heath, Edward 122, 130, 153
Heath government (1970–4) 14, 119–20, 132
  and Anglo-French collaboration 208–9
Hennessy, Peter 114, 130
Heseltine, Michael 171, 172, 173, 183, 276 n.66

Hill-Norton, Peter 123–4
Hinton, Christopher 60–1
Hiroshima atom bomb attack (1945) 12, 13, 17, 18, 25
Holifield, Chet 85
Hollis, Martin 2
Holsti, Ole R. 2
Hood, Samuel 86
Hoon, Geoff 187–8
Houghton, General Sir Nicholas 203–4
Howe, Geoffrey 160
Hulme, H. R. 65
Hume, Cardinal Basil 179
Hunt, Sir John 127, 128, 137, 138, 139, 146, 147–8, 149, 150, 209
Hymans, Jacques 8–9, 12, 40, 75, 133, 169, 208

IBM 704 computer 69, 246 n.41
identity, and Britain's attitude to nuclear weapons 8–10, 11, 208–9
Indo-China and the Cold War 58
Intermediate Range Ballistic Missiles (IRBMs), US 79
Intermediate Range Nuclear Forces (INF) Treaty (US-Soviet, 1987) 176, 177, 183
international control of nuclear weapons 18–24
  immediate post-war period 32
inter-service rivalries and strategy-making 4
Iran nuclear programme 190, 194, 197
Iraq invasion and occupation (2003) 188–9
Iraq Republican Guard 179
Israel, and *Scud* missile attacks 179

Jandrey, Frederick 95
Jenkins, Roy 124
Jervis, Robert 3, 11
Johnson, Jeannie L. 7
Johnson, Lyndon B. 118
Johnson, Rebecca 191
Joint Committee on Atomic Energy (JCAE), US congressional 77, 78, 80, 85–7, 95, 245 n.37, 251 n.59
Joint Intelligence Committee (JIC) 108
  and *Polaris* system effectiveness 125, 126, 127
  targeting issues 101–2
Joint Technical Warfare Committee (JTWC) 24–5, 35
  Report (1946) 27, 29, 30
  and the stockpiling of nuclear weapons 28
Jordan 4
Jupiter missiles, US 79
just war tradition 210

Kartchner, Kerry M. 7
Kennedy, John F. 99, 100

Index

Killian, James R. 81
King, Lord Tom 196
Kinnock, Neil 168
Kissinger, Henry 122–3, 192
Kohl, Helmut 177, 178
Korean War (1950–3) 47, 48, 58

Labour Party 63, 166
  1964 election, and the British independent deterrent 103–6, 107
  1974 commitment not to replace *Polaris* 136, 137–8
  links with CND 128
  moratorium on nuclear testing, commons motion (1954) 63
  and nuclear disarmament 72, 73
  unilateral disarmament policy (1980s) 167, 168, 172–3
  and the veto of US nuclear operations in Britain 85
Lakenheath US Air Base, Suffolk 94
Lance missiles (FOTL) 176, 182
Lane, Robert 2
Larsen, Jeffrey A. 7
Lawrence Livermore National Laboratory, Sandia, Albuquerque 89, 100
Lebow, Richard Ned 8
Leitch, George 109
Libby, Dr Willard 88, 252 n. 70
'Lifting the Nuclear Shadow', government report (2009) 194
Lisbon meeting (1952, NATO) 43–4, 46, 48, 54, 55
Lloyd, Selwyn 78
Lockheed Missile and Space Company (LMSC) 101
London Disarmament Conference 80
London Foreign Ministers' meeting, 1947 38
Los Alamos National Laboratory, US 100
Luce, Sir David 108

M-4 system, French 155
Mackenzie King, William Lyon 23
Macmillan, Harold 71, 74, 75, 80, 81, 82, 83, 86, 87, 88, 89, 91, 94, 96, 97, 98, 99, 101, 122, 249 n.41, 250 n.45, 251 n.58
Macmillan government (1957–63) 57, 79, 82, 85, 118, 201
  and the proposed moratorium on nuclear testing 84–5
MacNamara, Robert 99
Major, John 170, 178–80, 183–4
  'letters of last resort' 180–1
Major government (1990–7) 170, 196
Mallaby, Sir George 36
Manhattan Project 12, 20, 61, 75, 76, 241 n.67
Mark 28 warhead, US 89, 90

Mark 47 warhead, US 89, 90
Martin, Kingsley 72
Mason, Professor Sir Ronald 14, 138–9, 149, 153
Mason, Roy 124, 125, 127, 128, 129, 133
Maud Committee reports (1940) 11–12, 209, 236 n.41
Mayne, John 127
MccGwire, Michael 9
McGrigor, Sir Rhoderick 52, 53, 63
McInnes, Colin 169
McMahon Act (1946), US 14, 30, 40, 61, 75, 77, 81, 91, 92, 121
  amendments (1948/1951/1954) 62, 98
  implications for Britain 32–3
Medium Range Ballistic Missile (MRBM) programme 98
Melissen, Jan 82
Merchant, Livingston T. 81
Middle East 38–9, 57, 243 n.114
Middle East Defence Organisation (MEDO) 57
Miller, Julian 195
Minuteman ICBM, US 84
MISC 7, government committee 153–5, 171, 209, 271 n.53
  advice of military officials 156–9
Modus Vivendi agreement, Anglo-American (1948) 76, 92, 247 n.8
Molesworth RAF base 171
Montgomery, General Bernard 36
moratorium proposals on nuclear testing 63, 83, 84–5, 87
'Moscow Criterion' 14, 101–3, 115, 116, 123, 125, 126, 127, 128, 129–30, 131, 135, 136–7, 138, 140–1, 158, 162, 212
  David Owen's critique ('thirty bangs in thirty places') 147
Mottram, Sir Richard 158–9, 200
Mulley, Fred 133, 134, 136, 139, 149
Multilateral Nuclear Force (MLF) proposal, US 104–5
Murphy, Charles 59
Mutual Defence Agreement (MDA), 1958 68, 69, 74, 82, 84, 86–8, 97, 100, 119, 146 164, 200, 214, 251–2 n.68, 256 n. 25
  significance of 91–4, 254 n.89

Nagasaki atomic bomb attack (1945) 12, 13, 17, 18, 25
Nassau Agreement (1962) 99, 100, 103–4, 108, 109, 122, 214
  and NATO 110–11
'national identity conception (NIC)' 8–9
NATO 42, 43, 48, 59, 105, 120, 141, 186, 208
  'Dual Track' decision (1979) 159, 162, 164, 167, 172–3, 178
  and the Duff-Mason study 139, 145

295

Index

NATO (*cont.*)
  'Flexible Response' strategy (1967) 106, 120–1, 143–4, 156, 164, 170, 175, 176, 178
  and the Global Strategy Paper (1952) 45, 46, 59
  Intermediate Range Nuclear Forces (INF) modernization 170–2
  Lisbon goals 43–4, 46, 48, 54, 55
  and the Nassau Agreement (1962) 110–11
  Nuclear Planning Group (NPG) 106, 111, 121
  nuclear policy, 1960s 105, 106–9, 215
  nuclear weapons as 'last resort' capability (1992) 183
  and *Polaris* operational independence 109–11, 215
  Provisional Political Guidelines 106–7, 111
  short-range nuclear forces 176–8, 183
  and the Strategic Defence Review (1997–8) 186, 187
  Supreme Allied Commander Europe (SACEUR) 110, 111, 250 n.50, 258 n.69
  and tactical nuclear weapons 108
  Theatre Nuclear Force (TNF) modernization 159
  and *Trident* 215
'neo-realist' strategic analysis 5–6
Nixon administration (1969–74) 120
non-proliferation initiatives, UK 181, 200
Non-Proliferation Treaty (NPT), 1968 193, 201
  and Britain 86, 187
  Review Conference (2010) 197
Norris, Robert S. 68, 91
North Korea, nuclear programme 190, 194, 197
Northwood firing headquarters 112, 113, 114
Nott, John 151, 161–3, 164, 166–7, 171
Nott defence review (1981) 152, 268–9 n.5
nuclear advocacy coalitions 4–5, 41, 209
  role of Chiefs of Staff (COS) 13
  'transatlantic coalition' 61
  and varying ethical stances 210, 211–13
nuclear revolution 17–18
Nunn, Sam 192

Obama, Barack 192, 197
O' Donnell, Lord Gus 200
Ogilvie-White, Tanya 40–1
Oppenheimer trial 65
Oulton, Air Vice Marshall 67
Overall Strategic Plan (1947) 42–3, 45, 59
Owen, Lord David 128, 129, 133–6, 137, 139, 140–1, 149, 150, 213
  and the Duff-Mason report 145–6
  'Moscow Criterion' critique ('thirty bangs in thirty places') 147

Palliser, Sir Michael 137
Partial Test Ban Treaty (PTBT) (1963) 120, 201

Paxman, Jeremy 13
Peierls, Rudolf 11
Penney, William 60, 61, 64, 209, 245 n.37
Perrin, Michael 61
Perry, William 192
Pershing II missiles, US 171, 175
  deployment in Britain and Europe 171, 172, 176
Pierre, Andrew 10, 11, 17, 42, 72–3, 92, 100, 208, 213–17, 254 n.93
Plowden, Sir Edwin 81, 82
Polaris 14, 26, 56, 97–118
  dependency on US technical support (1970s) 120, 121–2
  national dimension of command and control 112–14
  and NATO nuclear policy (1960s) 105, 106–9, 215
  and the 1964 election 103–6, 107
  number of submarines necessary 108
  operational independence 109–11, 215
  operational nuclear strategy, conflicting ideas and beliefs 115–17
  Sales Agreement (1963) 14, 96, 99–101, 119, 121, 146, 200
  sea trials 84
  system effectiveness 125, 126, 127
  targeting issues and the 'Moscow Criterion' 101–3
Polaris improvement/replacement programme
  and Chevaline 14, 98, 115–17, 118, 119–32, 146–7
  and Anglo-French cooperation 119–24
  Callaghan government (1977–9) 133–50
  Duff-Mason Report (1979) 138–40, 142–9, 150
  Foreign and Commonwealth Office study (1977) 134–6
  high-level politics and changes to deterrence criteria 126–30
  'Owen criteria' and the Cruise missile option 140–1, 150
  'Restricted Group' deliberations 136–8
  return of Labour government, 1974 124–6
  spiralling costs 124, 125, 126
  Soviet ABM defences and targeting strategy (1970s) 125, 126, 127–8
  successor studies and the terms of reference 138–40
Pompidou, Georges 121
Portal of Hungerford, Lord 30–1, 32, 34–5, 36, 60
Portillo, Michael 196
Poseidon missile system, US 101, 117, 123, 132
  MIRV (C-3) system 154–5
Powell, Colin 179
Powell, Sir Richard 81, 82

Index

Priestly, J. B. 71, 72
principles of discrimination and proportionality 210, 211
'Project E', Anglo-American 77
Pym, Francis 152, 160, 161, 164, 169

Quarles, Donald 84, 85–6, 87, 88
Quebec Agreement (1943) 12
Quinlan, Sir Michael 3–4, 13, 102, 106, 107, 131–2, 137, 144, 181, 206, 209, 211–12, 234 n.10, 282 n.35

Reagan, Ronald 172, 173, 177, 183
Reagan administration (1981–9)
  Camp David meetings with Thatcher (1987) 175
  'Irangate' scandal 176
  Strategic Defence Initiative (SDI, 'Star Wars'), US 14, 170, 172, 173–6, 177, 274 n.29
'realist' strategic analysis 5–6
  'maximization of power' 1
  and 'national security interests' 1
'Reflex Action' exercises (1957/58), Anglo-American 85
Renown, HMS 152
Revenge, HMS 182
Reykjavik summit (1986) 174–5, 176
Rhodes European Council meeting (1988) 177
Richardson, E. 4
Rickover, Admiral Hyman G. 84, 87, 93
Ritchie, Nick 9, 11, 96, 217
'Road to 2010', the government report (2009) 194
Roberts, Keith 64, 65
Robertson, George 185, 188
Roosevelt, Franklin D. 12
Rose, Sir Clive 137, 149, 153, 154
Runcie, Robert 179
Russell, Bertram 72
Russian Federation 181–2

Sabatier, Paul 4
Saddam Hussein 178, 179, 180
Sagan's three models 10–11
Sandys, Duncan 79–80, 98, 102
Sandys White Paper (1957) 82
Sargent, Orme 37
Schilling, W. 206, 207
Schmidt, Helmut 147
Scottish Nationalist Party, nuclear stance 200
Scud missiles, and the Gulf War 179–80
Sea Harrier, Royal Navy 182
Sellafield (formerly Windscale) nuclear power station 61, 81, 249 n.38
Shultz, George 192
Simonstown Agreement with South Africa 126
Simpson, John 182–3, 197, 201

Skybolt Air Launched Ballistic Missile (ALBM) system, US 98, 99, 118
Slessor, Sir John 17, 52, 53, 59
Smith, John 168
Smith, S. 2
Snyder, Jack 5–6, 217
Soviet Union (USSR)
  anti-ballistic missile (ABM) screen 102, 115–16, 120, 121, 126, 131–2
  atomic test (1949) 43
  British attitudes towards 36–8, 39, 40
  Communist Party at the end of the Cold War 178
  disintegration (1991–2) 181
  and early international control of nuclear weapons 19–24
  Galosh antiballistic missile (ABM) system 134
  and German reunification and rearmament 55–6
  ICBM capability 84
  Moscow ABM defences 102, 125
  Nazi invasion (1941) 158
  Reykjavik summit (1986) 174–5, 176
  SS-20 mobile missiles and deployment 171, 172, 176
  thermonuclear test (1953) 77, 247 n.11
  as threat to the west 47–8
  unilaterally ends nuclear testing 84–5
  Western contending attitudes towards 36–8, 39, 40
Sputnik 1 81, 82
SS-20 mobile missiles and deployment, Soviet 171, 172, 176
Stalin, Joseph 19, 37
Stassen, Harold 80, 249 n.32
'Stock-Taking after V-E Day' report (1945) 37
Strategic Arms Limitation Talks (SALT) 201
  SALT II 129, 134, 135, 139, 145, 159
  SALT III 135
Strategic Arms Reduction Talks (START) 176, 177, 193, 201
strategic culture 5–8
  as cognition 7–8
  as context 7–8
  and the decision to 'go nuclear' 31, 32, 33
  and 'mirror imaging' 6
  and weapons of mass destruction 7
Strategic Defence and Security Review (SDSR, 2010) 195–6
Strategic Defence Initiative (SDI, 'Star Wars'), US 14, 170, 172, 173–6, 177, 274 n.29
Strategic Defence Review and *Trident* (1997–8) 186–7
Strategic Offensive Reduction Treaty (SORT, 2003–11) 201
Strauss, Lewis 80, 82, 83

297

Index

submarines, nuclear reactors, and propulsion 84, 87, 93
Suez Crisis (1956) 10, 70, 78–9, 97, 98
Supreme Allied Commander Atlantic (SACLANT) 110
Supreme Headquarters Allied Powers Europe (SHAPE) 55

tactical atomic weapons 55
targeting nuclear attacks 26–7, 210–13
  David Owen's critique ('thirty bangs in thirty places') 147
  and the JIC 101–2
  and 'minimum deterrence' 211–13
  'Moscow Criterion' 14, 101–3, 115, 116, 123, 125, 126, 127, 128, 129–30, 131, 135, 136–7, 138, 140–1, 158, 162, 212
  policy shift early (1980s) 162
  and Soviet ABM defence (1970s) 125, 126, 127–8
Taylor, J. B. 65, 244 n.20, 245 n.32, 246 n.41
Tedder, Air Chief Marshal A. W. 36
Thatcher, Margaret 64, 149, 150, 170, 171, 172, 173, 183, 271 n.53
  Camp David meetings with Reagan (1987) 175
  fundamental belief in deterrence 174
Thatcher government (1979–90) 14, 135
  and SDI 173–6, 274 n.29
  and short-range nuclear forces 176–8, 183
  Trident adoption 151–69
  Trident D-5 163–8, 169
thermonuclear weapons development 64, 246 n.49
  Grapple tests (May–June 1957) 65–8, 66 Tab 3.1, 248 n.29
  Grapple tests X, Y, and Z (1957–8) 66 Tab 3.1, 69–70, 246 n.40, 246 n.41
  and Great Power status and political influence 70–1
  'interim' megaton weapon 68–9
  role of COS 62–4
  role of scientists and weaponeers 64–5
'third zero' disarmament option 177–8
'thirty bangs in thirty places', David Owen critique 147
Thor missiles, US deployment in Britain 79, 80, 80–1
  agreement 84, 85, 97, 98
Titan ICBMs, US 84
Tizard, Sir Henry 25, 35–6, 41, 202, 237 n. 32
  Report (1945) 25
  Defence Research Policy Committee report (1947) 29
Tomahawk cruise missiles, US 140, 147
Tornado fighter, RAF 182
Trachtenberg, Marc 93

'transatlantic advocacy coalition' 61
Treaty of Rome (1957) 82, 97
Trend, Sir Burke 112, 116, 117, 122, 123, 209
Trident I MIRV (C-4) system 14, 146, 148, 149, 153, 155, 156, 164
Trident II (D-5) system 14, 101, 138, 146, 151–69, 189, 282 n.35
  Defence Policy Staff (DPS) Report 156–9
  MISC-7, initial discussions 153–5, 271 n.53
  MISC-7 and advice of military officials 156–9
  missile storage facilities 158–9, 166–7
  and NATO 215
  post-Cold War evaluation 181–3
  purchase agreement 159–63
  and the Reagan administration (1981–8) 163–4
  revised options (1979) 154–5
  Strategic Defence Review (1997–8) 186–7
  warhead reductions 213
Trident renewal/replacement 15, 185, 199–201, 199 Fig 10.1
  Alternative Review (2013) 197–9, 199 Fig. 10
  D-5 'Life Extension Programme' 189
  'life extension' and timescales 196
  White Paper (2007) 190–1, 193
Truman, President Harry 18, 19, 21, 22, 23, 94, 202
Truman-Attlee 'Understandings' 76, 94
Truman-Churchill Agreement 94, 172

Ulam-Teller invention 64
United Nations (UN) 22, 23, 82
  Atomic Energy Commission and international controls 23
  resolutions and the Gulf War 180
United States of America
  and Britain's nuclear independence/ interdependence position 97–9, 100, 101, 213, 214–16
  British veto over UK-based nuclear aircraft 94
  Castle series of nuclear tests (1954) 63
  cooperation with European NATO allies 82–3
  early attempts at international control of nuclear weapons 19–24
  Iraq invasion 188–9
  Joint Strategic Survey Committee (JSSC) 77
  'New Look' defence policy (1953) 59
  NSC-68 document (1950) 46
  nuclear weapons testing 67
  opposition to nuclear secret sharing with the UK 85–6
  Presidential Nuclear Initiatives Programme 181
  Reykjavik summit (1986) 174–5, 176
  and the stockpiling atomic bombs 49

298

Index

Strategic Air Command (SAC) 79, 85
Strategic Defence Initiative (SDI, 'Star Wars'), US 14, 170, 172, 173–6, 177, 274 n.29
tactical atomic weapons 55
see also Anglo-American cooperation; Mutual Defence Agreement (MDA, 1958)

Valiant bombers, RAF 62
Vance, Cyrus 153
Vanguard, HMS 184
Vanguard class submarines, RN 180, 182, 196, 199
V-Bomber force, RAF 99, 103, 104, 108, 111, 113
Vengeance, HMS 184
Victorious, HMS 184
Violet Club nuclear fission weapon 68
Vigilante, HMS 184
Vladivostok Accords (1974) 134
Vulcan bombers, RAF 156

Walker, William 5
Ward, J. C. 64–5, 245 n.21
Ward, Major-General Philip 27
Washington Declaration (1945) 23
weapons of mass destruction (WMD) 188–9
and strategic culture 7
Weinberger, Casper 164
Wendt, Alexander 8
West Germany 141, 143, 145
and cruise missile deployment in Europe 172
and NATO's Flexible Response strategy 176
and NATO's short-range nuclear forces 177–8
rearmament and reunification 55–6
Wheeler, Nicholas 4, 39
Whitmore, Clive 137
Wigley, Dafydd 171
Wilson, Charles 79
Wilson, Harold 103, 109, 111, 112, 115, 119, 124, 130, 153, 262 n.32
Wilson government (1964–70, 1974–6) 104–6, 111, 114, 116
and nuclear independence 105–6, 208
and NATO nuclear deterrent strategy 106
nuclear weapons and great power status 105–6, 118
Polaris 107–8
Polaris improvement programme and Chevaline 124–6
Wilson-Sandys Agreement (1954) 79–80, 98
Wynn, Humphrey 25, 30

Yellow Sun 2 warhead 68
Yeltsin, Boris 186
York, Dr Herbert 69

'zero option' disarmament 172, 173, 175–6, 183, 192
Ziegler, Philip 124
Zinc, Colonel 85
Zuckerman, Sir Solly 115–16, 117, 123, 128, 140, 209, 261 n.117